ROTTEN

R○TTEN

NO IRISH, NO BLACKS, NO DOGS

THE AUTHORIZED AUTOBIOGRAPHY
JOHNNY ROTTEN OF THE SEX PISTOLS

JOHN LYDON
WITH KEITH AND KENT ZIMMERMAN

PLEXUS PUBLISHING LTD

All rights reserved including the right of
reproduction in whole or in part in any form
Copyright © 1994 by John Lydon
Published by Plexus Publishing Limited
25 Mallinson Road
London SW11 1BW
Tel: 020 7924 4662
Fax: 020 7924 5096
plexus@plexusuk.demon.co.uk
www.plexusbooks.com

British Library Cataloguing in Publication Data

Lydon, John
Rotten – no Irish – no blacks – no dogs
1. Rotten, Johnny 2. Sex Pistols 3. Punk Rock Musicians –
Great Britain 4. Punk rock music – Great Britain 5. Popular
culture – Great Britain
I. Title II. Zimmerman, Keith III. Zimmerman, Kent
782.4'2166

ISBN-10: 0 85965 341 2
ISBN-13: 978 0 85965 3411

Printed by arrangement with Hodder Headline Limited and St Martin's Press, USA
"Whatcha Gonna Do About It" by Samwell/Potter, published by Fanfare
Music Limited. England. Used by permission.
Cover design by Philip Gambrill
Printed in Great Britain by Bell & Bain Ltd.

TABLE OF CONTENTS

Please note: Most of the photos that appear in this book are more of a personal nature than the usual Sex Pistol pictures you have come to expect. To the best of my knowledge, very few of these have been seen. Since they were taken by my family and mates, you'll notice the deliberate lack of flash and polish. Some even take on an unintentional surreal quality. All Sex Pistols shots were taken by John Gray. Regrettably very few candid shots of Sid exist in my collection. However, I've included one of my favorites of Sid, Nancy and me, depicting life in a rotten living room. If you want posed Sid shots, consult other publications, none of which I recommend.

PAGE 15: Cocteau-esque Lydon family beach party.

PAGE 26: Despondent Lydon at early age (far left) with Mother (center), Auntie Agnes (right) with assorted Lydon brats.

PAGE 33: Pistols mafia on the town. John Gray and Rotten.

PAGE 42: Father and son sharing quality time.

PAGE 44: After meningitis, I wore glasses due to poor vision.

PAGE 52: The haircut that got me thrown out of Sir William of York.

PAGE 60: Johnny goes to college. Me during my Hawkwind phase.

PAGE 73: Early 1976, before safety pins became fashionable and a moth-eaten sweater meant poverty, not popularity. (John Gray)

PAGE 92: The Thin Faces. Come back, sixties, all is forgiven. St. Albans. (John Gray)

PAGE 95: The very first Sex Pistols rehearsal. No equipment. One guitar pick. We're ready to rock. Circa 1975. (John Gray)

PAGE 116, top: Where are my monitors? Wearing mummy's watch at the Nashville in London. (John Gray)

PAGE 116, bottom left: Johnny: Why am I in a band with him? (John Gray)

PAGE 116, bottom right: Glen: Why am I in a band with him? (John Gray)

PAGE 119: Paul & Steve: early beginnings. (John Gray)

PAGE 130: Sid the fashion victim and John the toe-rag. (Bob Gruen/Starfile)

PAGE 161: Surviving the Texas Chainsaw Massacre with the stickers to prove it. (Ian Dickson/Redferns)

PAGE 178: Malcolm, where's the beer? (John Gray)

CAST OF CONTRIBUTORS

Paul Cook, the drummer
Caroline Coon, the journalist
John Gray, the boyhood mate
Bob Gruen, the American photographer
Chrissie Hynde, the Pretender
Billy Idol, the Generation X'er
Steve Jones, the guitarist
Jeanette Lee, the King's Road shopkeeper
Don Letts, the reggae deejay
John Christopher Lydon, the father
John Lydon, Johnny Rotten, the singer
Nora, as Nora
Marco Pirroni, the Ant
Rambo, the Arsenal football hooligan
Zandra Rhodes, the fashion designer
Dave Ruffy, the Rut
Steve Severin, the Banshee
Paul Stahl, the soul boy turned punk
Julien Temple, the filmmaker
Howard Thompson, the A&R man

Much has been written about the Sex Pistols. Much of it has been either sensationalism or journalistic psychobabble. The rest has been mere spite.

This book is as close to the truth as one can get, looking back on events from the inside. All the people in this book were actually there, and this book is as much their point of view as it is mine. This means contradictions and insults have not been edited, and neither have the compliments, if any. I have no time for lies or fantasy, and neither should you.

Enjoy or die. . . .

JOHN LYDON

ROTTEN

NEVER MIND THE SITUATIONISTS; THIS WAS
SITUATION COMEDY

THE MORNING AFTER WINTERLAND, SAN FRANCISCO, JANUARY 15, 1978

Ever get the feeling you've been cheated?" My famous last words on stage. The Sex Pistols ended the way they began – in utter disaster. Everything between was equally disastrous. That last Winterland gig was a failure, and I knew it more than anyone.

The night of the gig I didn't even have a hotel room. The morning after I still didn't have a hotel room, did I? At least not with the band. Malcolm McLaren said there wasn't any room left for me and Sidney. So Sid and I slept with the road crew in a motel in San Jose, fifty miles outside San Francisco.

One of the reasons I stayed with Sid Vicious on the bus during the American tour, driving, rather than flying, from state to state, gig to gig, was to keep him away from drugs. He had already developed a keen problem back in London. The idea was to keep him clean. That's what infuriated me so much. The minute we hit San Francisco, somehow or other, Sid managed to escape and get himself a whole parcel of heroin. Funny, that. Some would call that a coincidence. That buggered him up. Totally. As a result, dear reader, the Winterland show was a disaster.

We never had a decent sound on stage. I don't even remember the sound check. Winterland held about five thousand and was almost as big a hall as we had ever played. We were touted as the new Rolling Stones. It was horrible. Once anything got to a level of importance, the Pistols were let down—not by ourselves, but by the people who should have been looking out for us. I couldn't understand why on earth Boogie, our British road manager, was behind the PA desk mixing the sound. At a major gig like this one, we should have had a professional sound engineer. It was awful, wasn't it? It was worse where I was standing, center stage. You were lucky if you were in the audience; you didn't have to put up with the feedback on stage. I couldn't hear bugger all, except Steve's guitar, which was constantly out of tune. It's very hard when you can't hear what you're doing. You can't tell. No monitors on stage were working. They were all feeding back.

That kind of distraction would normally not get in the way, but it did that night in San Francisco. People expected too much from us. Bill Graham, the promoter, moved the gear off the stage and arranged a party afterward. I was told I wasn't allowed in. At my own gig! I was told to go away after the way I had behaved.

We hated each other at that point. I hated the whole scenario. It was a farce; I realized that from our first week of rehearsals as a band back in 1975. I must have left that band so many times. We all did. It was just nonstop. In and out. I walked off stage loads of times at gigs. The only one who really did go was Glen Matlock, our original bass player whom Sid replaced. But that made us all very happy. Things improved no end the minute he exited. Bringing Sid in brought a sense of chaos that I liked. Yes, Glen was responsible for a lot of the original tunes—if you want to call them that. He had a softening effect. Glen wanted to turn the whole thing into a sort of a Bay City Rollers scene and for us to look like some Soho poofs. Can you believe that? This was *his* image of the Sex Pistols: awful white plastic shoes, tight red pants. Really, really awful. Phony gay image.

Who put the Pistols together? Not Malcolm, really. Born out of a clothes store he owned? That's the pop myth. There were several people in the band before I came along. The first connection with the store, I suppose, was that Glen worked there. Whatever they were up to before, they were nothing like what they became once I joined up! They had no image. No point. No nothing. No purpose to it other than making really lousy Small Faces and imitation Who noises. It was vile. Really, really bad, but I liked it.

They all bitched at the first rehearsals about how I couldn't sing, which was true. I still can't, and I don't really want to. The kind of records they were playing—if they call that singing—were awful. The Faces must have been the worst band on the earth to model yourself after. Acting drunk.

Teetering around the stage. That was the kind of thing Glen liked. He thought it was clever. I didn't. I thought it disgusting pub rock.

Quirky little pop songs is what they wanted. You should have seen their faces when I slapped the lyrics down to "Anarchy in the U.K." It was classic. I wish I had had a camera. "God Save the Queen" was the final reason Glen left; he couldn't handle those kinds of lyrics. He said it declared us fascists. I agreed with him. Just to get rid of him, I didn't deny it. I don't think being an anti-Royalist makes you a fascist. Quite the opposite. Silly ass. Isn't he?

There was no progress or advancement all the way through the Pistols. While we were touring America, there were large periods of not doing anything at all. However, I was constantly writing. Turns out I wrote a lot of songs for my next group, Public Image Limited, during that period. But I could not get the Pistols interested. They wanted to go back to that quirky little Who ditty thing. Songs about religion absolutely killed them. "You can't sing that! You'll get arrested!" Well, I fucking hoped so. That was the whole point.

The only violence about the Sex Pistols was the anger. Nothing else. We were not violent people. There was no death at our gigs. The one thing that used to piss me most about the Sex Pistols was our audience all turning up in identically cloned punk outfits. That really defeated the point. There was no way I was going to give them a good time for that, because it showed no sense of individuality or understanding of what we were doing. We weren't about uniformity.

Malcolm was a very destructive force on that American tour. He was totally negative, and I really couldn't see the point or purpose to it. We made our own scandal just by being ourselves. Maybe it was that he knew he was redundant, so he overcompensated. All the talk about the French Situationists being associated with punk is bollocks. It's nonsense! Now that really *is* coffee-table book stuff. The Paris riots and the Situationist movement of the sixties—it was all nonsense for arty French students. There's no master conspiracy in anything, not even in governments. Everything is just some kind of vaguely organized chaos.

Chaos was my philosophy. Oh, yeah. Have no rules. If people start to build fences around you, break out and do something else. You should never, ever be understood completely. That's like the kiss of death, isn't it? It's a full stop. I don't ever think you should put full stops on thoughts. They change.

I'm a spiteful bastard. I always have been. If I can make trouble, then that's perfect for me. My school reports show this thoroughly. Negative attitude. Well, of course.

*   *   *

The last gig in San Francisco was the ultimate, the full stop. We ended up getting paid $67 for that gig, so people had no right to moan at us.

The crew had to leave the morning after because the tour had folded. I had no hotel, no accommodations, so I went over to the Miyako Hotel, where Malcolm, Steve Jones, Jamie Reid, Bob Gruen, and Paul Cook were. I couldn't find Malcolm. I didn't know where he was, but I spoke to Paul and Steve. They were very distant and remote with me. Paul and Steve didn't seem to know what it was all about, and they didn't want to discuss it, either—other than the fact that I had ruined it for them. They wouldn't even explain what I had ruined.

I didn't know they were planning to go to Rio de Janeiro to record and shoot film footage with Ronald Biggs, the infamous great train robber from Britain. I found that out through Sophie Richmond, Malcolm's secretary. I thought it was a pretty shitty idea to support an aging tosspot robber like Ronald Biggs. It was appalling. I couldn't condone the idea of going down and celebrating someone who took part in a 1963 robbery that resulted in the bludgeoning of a train driver into brain-dead senility and the theft of what was basically working-class money. It wasn't as if they were robbing a bank. It was payroll from a mail train. Biggs never did any of the planning, he was just one of the people in on the robbery. His claim to fame was that he busted out of jail in England and escaped to Rio. I don't know how much his take was, but he couldn't have been rolling in it. I heard he was living in a shack on the beach in Brazil. That's hardly my idea of big-time success. It wasn't joyful, witty, or funny. It didn't have anything to do with what the Pistols were about before that. Instead, it seemed dour, malicious, and grim. There was no humor in it, and it just seemed like belligerence for its own sake. To this day I have never understood the ins and outs of the Rio project. Judging from the footage Malcolm shot, it was mostly just Steve, Paul, and Ronnie Biggs on the beach.

As far as I was concerned, the band had broken up. It had broken up when I had said what I said on stage. I felt cheated, and I wasn't going on with it any longer; it was a ridiculous farce. Sid was completely out of his brains—just a waste of space. The whole thing was a joke at that point. It was all very bitter and confusing at the Miyako Hotel. Sid and I weren't invited into that particular little enclave. The reason given was that we weren't booked into a room at the Miyako in the first place, and there were no rooms left. Malcolm didn't put the money up, and nobody booked the rooms. I ended up staying in an extra bed in Sophie's room. I was extremely tense, and I don't think I ever went to sleep that night.

Malcolm wouldn't come out of his room, and I didn't understand what was going on. He wouldn't speak to me, even though several people—including Boogie and Sophie—tried to get him to come down and talk. He would not discuss anything with me. But then he would turn around and tell Paul and Steve that the tension was all my fault because I wouldn't agree to anything.

I had no money to speak of. I had twenty dollars on me. I tried ringing Warner Bros., the Sex Pistols' American record label, but they didn't believe it was me because they had been told I had left the country. I was stuck in America—no plane ticket, no money, nothing.

Malcolm could never have presented that Rio trip to me because he knew what my answer would be. I don't like breaking commitments, and for a band, touring is the most viable part of the process. There was another Sex Pistols tour lined up shortly after the American tour, starting in Stockholm. We had made a commitment to play the tour. People were already buying tickets, gigs were lined up. But for Malcolm to have taken us to Rio would have made that Swedish tour logistically difficult. Even though I thought the band was over, I still felt we had to finish the Scandinavian tour. Going to Rio was Malcolm's dream—so fuck the gig and the band, fuck everything. He was only thinking of himself again and titillating himself. By going to Rio, he canceled the tour and asserted his vision. It had become a boring rock band, so going to Rio, he thought, would open new avenues of excitement. Yet the commitments to Stockholm and others were already made. You couldn't just call it a day because Malcolm wanted to go to Rio. You needed to work with other people for things to succeed. Otherwise it was just a fantasy.

My relationship with Steve around the time of breaking up was absolutely awful, especially before they all went off to Rio. I sat down with Steve and Paul in San Francisco. They thought that I didn't want to be in the same hotel. I said it wasn't true, but they wouldn't listen. Didn't believe me.

The next day Paul and Steve left with Malcolm for Rio without me. I don't think they meant to be spiteful, but I think they just went where they thought the money was. It was the easier ride of the two—go with Malcolm or side with me and find out what was really going on. Joe Stevens shared a room with Malcolm on most of the tour. He was the one who lent me the money to get a plane ticket back to London. We went to New York that very evening. I would have been truly stranded without his help because I hadn't been given my ticket home. It was nice, since he was one of Malcolm's gang. I never got that kind of respect from the rest of them.

After stopping in New York, I returned to London. I went back to my house, the one I had cleverly insisted on buying in my name just before we left for America. It was in Gunter Grove. I remember that argument very well. Malcolm wanted to sign for it. I said, "Nope. Nope. Nope. You give me the money or that's it." None of the Pistols even had bank accounts at that time. Steve and Paul lived in a flat on Bell Street that was under Malcolm's name. So they had to sort of agree with whatever he said. Poxy scum.

The Sex Pistols just fizzled. There was no final band meeting when we dissolved in San Francisco. We had no big sit-down. There was no actual mass resignation. Looking back, I understand that Steve and Paul didn't want to carry on with the band. I didn't want to, either. None of us really wanted to do a tour of Scandinavia at that point. Sid was a complete disaster. I don't remember even seeing Sid after the San Francisco gig. He was so embarrassing that I kept as far away from him as I could. He became everything I didn't want a Sex Pistol to be: another worn-out druggie rock 'n' roller. It was a complete contradiction of everything we wanted to set up within the Sex Pistols.

Steve and Paul felt that way too at the time. They were against that kind of hard-drug use. Steve got into his drug problems a long time after; I think it was him trying to sort himself out. Paul never got into anything, but sometimes I think Paul doesn't need to know, he just accepts and carries on.

When Malcolm wanted to be spiteful, he sure knew how to be. That's why I pursued the court case—*Lydon* vs. *Glitterbest*—against him for so long. I was literally dropped like excess baggage. I wouldn't have minded so much if I had been given a ticket home. This is an elephant that never forgets. He tried to run off and even claimed he owned my name, Johnny Rotten. I wasn't allowed to use the name for years after until I took him to court and got it back.

Some twelve years later, when I finally did get to Rio with PiL, Ronnie Biggs wanted to come to one of the gigs. He left a message for me at the hotel saying Malcolm owed him some money, and could he collect from me? It had something to do with royalties from the record they did together. How was Ronnie Biggs ever going to collect on it? I don't think any money was withheld deliberately. It was because of Malcolm's inefficiency. Who was going to listen to Biggs bemoan his sorry lot?

In this respect, it's funny: Malcolm even stiffed the great train robber.

CHILD OF THE ASHES

It's amazing that even with security systems, you can't keep kids out. Kids find ways in. The more elaborate the security system or the bigger the guard dogs, the more determined kids are to get in. I was no exception. We used to do an awful lot of breaking into factories. That used to be hilarious good fun. Sewing machine factories, any place that was closed at night and on weekends. It was fun to run around inside. I was young, and there would be a gang of thirty or forty of us running around inside. It was a neighborhood gang thing in Finsbury Park, North London, in the early 1960s. Organized only in the sense that if kids from other neighborhoods tried to come in, there would be brick fights. You'd pile up as many bricks as you could and throw them. They'd be doing the same across the street until one lot ran off. That was it. What good fun.

The biggest joy was living on the edge of an industrial estate. It proved to be the best playground. We'd tamper with lathes and fiddle about with tools and stuff. I never had lots of toys when I was young. We never had the money, so we had just bits and pieces—not like the other kids. Some kids at school had these expensive, bleeding sets. It drove me crazy, but I figured, they don't do the things I can do.

Benwell Road and Holloway Road in Finsbury Park had a scruffy mob of kids of all ages. We were all led by a chap called [Smoothie],* a particularly bad piece of work. He was a real problem to his family, but I used to think he was great. He was such total chaos, he wouldn't follow any rules and went in and out of Borstals. His parents sent Smoothie on all kinds of courses to try to rehabilitate him. He was English, so they had a little bit more money than us Irish, who lived across the street. His parents used to say that it was us Irish kids who made Smoothie misbehave. But I was six and Smoothie was twelve at the time. I liked the gang fights he started. Hilarious fiascoes, not at all like the knives and guns of today. The meanness wasn't there. It was more like yelling, shouting, throwing stones, and running away giggling. Maybe the reality was colored by my youth.

We have very long days in England in the summer. It gets dark very late, nine-thirty or ten o'clock. Now when I look back on the earliest part of my childhood, it reminds me of those post-World War II black-and-white English movies. You'd see dilapidated wastelands of bombed-out buildings and a distinct lack of streetlights. You saw it even in the sixties—a backdrop of desolated houses. There weren't many cars in England then. The streets were decorated with Teddy boys and slick mobster sorts walking around—Kray types with huge quiffs—the bigger and higher the better—dressed in very sharp creased suits. You know that Steve McGarrett look on "Hawaii Five-O"? Black suits always buttoned up tight. I remember all the kids running around in rags. It was quite common for most kids to have no shoes. We thought shoes were uncomfortable, particularly for my other brothers because they had to wear what I finished with. I would always be the one told off if I scuffed my shoes because "it's got to be handed down!" So it was easier to run around barefoot.

Everybody knew about the Kray Twins around where I lived. They were looked upon as heroes. There were often times you'd be given a fiver for throwing a brick through a pub window. "The Krays want you to do this!" Wow! That gangster thing was very much part of North London to the East End. It was all connected. That's where the Krays focused on. They used to thrill people. They'd show them on TV. They looked so viciously sharp, the world's best dressers at the time. So wicked and hard, without being poncey. That's how I always like suits to be worn—with a sense of vicious purpose. Ultimately the Krays weren't an influence, just a titillation—the same way kids read Superman comics. It

*Pseudonyms (bracketed the first time they appear) are designed to protect the innocent and the guilty!

was devoid of all reality by the time it filtered down to a ten-year-old. You'd see all those old gangster movies from America on the TV and think how great it was killing people all day long and never getting killed yourself. The Krays were just a craze.

We had our own gangsters living up the road. Queensland Road, near our flat on Benwell Road, was the roughest area there was in London. One day my brother Jimmy came into the house. "Look, Daddy, what I got." A policeman was shot the night before on Queensland Road, and Jimmy ran in with a gun and the copper's helmet. There was always a gang of Teds hanging around gambling on the corner, and we would hear shooting at night. Some of the characters on the street were complete killers. They used to have guns and vicious dogs.

I was actually very shy as a kid. Very retiring. I wouldn't speak to anyone, and I was nervous as all hell. I was apparently born in London. I'm not so sure. There's some vagueness about the date on my birth certificate since it was issued two years after I was born. Apparently it was lost. It was really difficult to get a passport because it wasn't in the records office. Great mysteries of all time. I'm probably a bastard since I am by nature. For all intents and purposes, I was brought up a Londoner. That's the place that educated me, but every year we'd go to Ireland, where my father and mother were born, for six- or eight-week holidays. That would be it. Ireland is not my kind of place to be. It's all right when you want to get drunk. You wake up, and there's nothing to do. That's not very purposeful. I could never be willful on a farm. The only things you can antagonize are the cows. My Irish half provided my sense of devilry. Like Oscar Wilde, my philosophy became, Just do it, see what you can cause.

It's no accident that the Irish invented stream-of-consciousness literature. It was out of absolute necessity. Poverty and the deprivation of their own language made this very important. Hence long-term memory, which is a Celtic thing. The American Indians live by this concept, too. Time flows. The Celts believe if you must resort to writing down your history, you lack the intelligence and conviction to recall.

There was also this tradition of the Irish before they had gas fires and central heating. It's called "Child of the Ashes"—I remember reading about it. Being the oldest son, this is more or less what I am. I didn't get to my ashes in Ireland, I got to them in England. You put your children in front of a real coal fire and let them work it out. They either touch the flame or the ashes. If they're stupid enough to touch the flame, then they're not a real Gael. If you're going to put your hand into it, you're a moron. But if you go for the ashes, that's it. "Child of the Ashes." Dirty fingers. Isn't it romantic?

I used to love to play with the ashes, particularly by using the hot poker. This is my earliest childhood recollection. Every weekend when I was really young, my father would give me the poker and sit me down in front of the fire, and I'd poke it in, get it real red hot, and then plunge it into a mug of Guinness. It would fizzle and be nice and warm. I think the heat kills off most of the alcohol. Then you would sip it. I must have been about three or four. That's as far back as I can remember. It was an Irish family ritual, one of the very few Irish traditions my family passed on to me. Unfortunately, I can't pass it on to anyone else. Gaelic times in London are gone.

I was raised in a tenement, working-class slummy. I was brought up to about the age of eleven in a two-room flat. No bathroom. Outside toilet. It would be a slum in anyone's language. There was an air raid shelter outside next to the toilet. It was infested with rats, and that used to thrill me. It was totally open, and you could go in and play in it.

The building was a Victorian dwelling that held forty or fifty families. I've got three brothers. I'm the eldest, and we were all born relatively close together. I don't know how old they are, to be quite frank. Don't know when their birthdays are, and they don't know mine. We're not that kind of family. We don't celebrate that kind of thing. Never had any interest in it. Until recently, I wasn't close to my father at all. I don't think I ever seriously spoke to him until the day he kicked me out of the house.

"It's time to get out and work for yourself, you bastard!"

Then things changed. Afterward it was "Hello, son! How are you? Now you're fending for yourself." It was right that he did that because I would have been a couch potato or a vegetable, just poncing off them on the dole.

My family background is very, very poor. My father was christened John Christopher Lydon. I'm John Joseph Lydon. His father was an absolute nightmare. The lot of them all had to come to England from Ireland for jobs. He was a right cunt, womanizer. "The old fella" is what they used to call him. I think my dad hated him. Very odd family, I suppose, but colorful, I'll tell you that. Extremely. A very violent family, too—all the cousins' side of it. There used to be fights on the weekends. They'd come over, and they'd be punching shit out of each other in the backyard. My father's from Galway. He was a crane driver. It's true, the Irish laborers all had hands like shovels. They practically used them as such, too. It's the Irish way to go into laboring.

The Lydon family leaning on our Finsbury Park limousine. I'm the shy retard on the right. Little Bobby in front. Jimmy is on the left. Mum in the middle. Age? Timeless.

Building sites. Shit shovelers. John Lydon, son of a shit shoveler. That would be no disgrace. Practically everyone I was brought up with was the same way. It used to be a nightmare when he would drag us to work with him. He probably hoped we would follow in his footsteps—as shit shovelers extraordinaire. I hated sitting in the crane with him. It was a noisy, huge, metal stinky thing. Other kids might have liked sitting in the crane, but this kid didn't. I saw myself as being way above all of that.

My mother's side is very quiet. Thinkers. My mother's from Cork. Eileen Barry before she married John Lydon. Her father was famous for being in the Irish independent army. I just knew him as Granddad. Excellent gun collection, I remember. He hated the English and probably hated me and my brother Jimmy. We spoke with thick cockney accents that he could not stand. My mother's accent was totally Irish.

Londoners had no choice but to accept the Irish because there were so many of us, and we do blend in better than the Jamaicans. When I was very young and going to school, I remember bricks thrown at me by English parents. To get to the Catholic school you had to go through a predominantly Protestant area. That was most unpleasant. It would always be done on a quick run. "Those dirty Irish bastards!" That kind of shit. Now they transfer it onto the blacks or whomever. There will always be hate in the English because they're a hateful nation. That's the trouble with working-class people throughout the world. They always try to spur their hatred onto what they see as being lower down the scale, rather than going for the fucking jugular of the upper- and middle-class bastards who are keeping them down in the first place. We were the Irish scum. But it's fun being scum, too.

Picture this. Dead-end ladies leaning out the windows with their hair up in curlers. Beans on toast with fried eggs. The works. The Victorian slum dwelling on Benwell Road, off Holloway Road, isn't there anymore. They pulled it down. It's now illegal in Britain to rent out buildings like that. It wasn't a house, just two rooms on the ground floor. The whole family shared the same bedroom and a kitchen. That's all it was. A tramp lived in the front room, which used to be a shop front. The smell of his room was awful. There was just a door connecting us, so you could always hear him farting and smell him stinking away.

We had a tin bath that my mother used to pull out. Zinc-alloy baths were so uncomfortable on your fingernails and your toenails, and you could never get it hot enough because nobody had big enough pots to heat up the water. We only had a kettle and a soup pot at the time, and when it was ready for you to get in, the water would be freezing cold. I used to get scrubbed with Dettol, a toilet cleaner solvent we also used for the sinks, to kill off the bugs. The stiff toilet brush was severe. Dettol and brush—once a month, if you were unlucky. In the winter you could stretch it out to six weeks if you were clever. You'd lie and say, "Oh, no, we went swimming today at school, Mum." I was perfecting my rotten, filthy ways even way back then.

I was always very confused about my family, how I felt about them, and where I came from. Was I happy with them? I remember wanting different parents. I was very impressed with people who had nice big houses. My God, why couldn't I have been born there? Why don't they sell me to them? It was a natural thought, but unnatural in the way that I would take it to the end extreme. I'd sit and analyze it for a long time as a child. People in decent houses or flats used to amaze me. Their places didn't stink of food all the time, whereas our place had an awful smell of brussels sprouts to it.

There used to be enormous rats that would come up from underneath the sink. Apparently the sewer line broke underneath, and they ate their way up. Great big sewer rats. I remember because I watched them kill a cat. They tore it to pieces.

My main chores as the eldest—when my mother was ill, which she frequently was—consisted of looking after my brothers. I would get them ready for school. I made the breakfast because often when the money was tight in the early days my old man used to have to work far away from home. That's what Irish houses are like. We had no sisters to pin it on, and I couldn't say no. I don't understand why girls should be roped into taking all that kind of responsibility. It should be taken by whoever is the oldest, regardless of sex. It's your family, you're related to them.

I learned that from my mum and dad. They always had aunts and uncles involved in raising us. When I was very young and Mum was in the hospital, I would be looked after by Auntie Pauline for weeks on end. Auntie Agnes helped out, too. It was that Irish way of spreading families about. It isn't a bad thing, either. It doesn't spoil your attachment to your real parents. On the contrary, it makes you appreciate them in a more accurate way. It gives you a sense of individuality and independence. Living apart from the family with relatives during the summer was more like an outing or an adventure for me—it was much better than being sent off to some silly summer camp. That was just like school extended.

My mum was ill with miscarriages throughout most of my early childhood. Lots of failed pregnancies. My parents must have been going at it like rabbits. Every year was another miscarriage. I'd sigh and say, "Oh, no! I'm going to have to pull out the bucket and catch the blood again." I was about six years old, but it didn't scare me or bother me as a young child because I took it as normal. Sometimes kids can be more resilient than adults. They don't realize that kind of blood loss can result in death. It's just, "Ooooh, what a mess, and doesn't it smell!" But somebody's got to do it. Even as a youngster, I liked having things to do and enjoyed my strong sense of responsibility. The more I had, the more I enjoyed it. The bigger the problems, the more I got into it. Easy work loads never appealed to me at all. I've always preferred everyday life bordering on the edge of disaster. That's what it's like trying to get your three younger brothers to school—especially when they're constantly trying to not get there. Very often I was the only one who showed up. The headmaster would ask, "Where are Jimmy and Bobby?" I had sent them out an hour earlier and had no idea. My brothers were never interested in studying. School was a place where we went to be tormented for a few hours. English Catholic schools were boring and severe. Freedom at four o'clock was the only relief.

Not having a father around early on to discipline us when we were younger presented all kinds of possibilities for Jimmy and me—we tried all of them. From up until age seven, I don't ever remember going to bed before eleven or twelve o'clock at night. I was up well past when the dot went out on the TV. I would go outside and play. It was different times then. There wasn't so much violence on the street, no gaggles of psychopathic rapists and pedophile killers. Young kids could get away with a lot more. By the time my youngest brother, Martin, was born, my father began working closer to home.

Heinz catered dinnertime every night at the Lydon house. Fifty-seven varieties, and I've had them all. Open up a can of something. Nobody was into healthy food back then—only whatever was cheap and available. Heinz fed Britain for decades. They must be furious today with this salad generation. But if Heinz could find a way to cram salad into a can, they certainly would. We ate all the soups, baked beans, and the beef stews. At the end of the week we might have a treat with boiled cabbage and bacon, which, done the Irish way, calls for a slow boil all day long until the house absolutely reeks. Eight hours later, it tastes like dirty laundry.

We drove the car yearly to Ireland. Once on the way back through Wales we were attacked on the motorway. These two big Welsh rugby players, as big as two houses, came after my father. He got out of the car and noticed there were two more guys in the other car sitting in the backseat. As my father walked back to our car, Jimmy, Bobby, and I bravely

Cocteau-esque Lydon family beach party.

ran out with our lemonade bottles. We yelled, "C'mon, dad. You're not scared of them! We're behind you."

We were well behind him!

Some of my worst memories as a child were of being taken to the cinema to see dreary movies: *The Bible. Mary Poppins. Chitty Chitty Bang Bang.* I have particularly bad memories of cinema because those were my early experiences. The movie house was a place of torture. Films would go on forever and were deeply childish. I was never childish, never into kids', things. I didn't understand how kids could be all sentimental and woozy over rubbish like *Mary Poppins.*

I hated starting school. I was frightened of it and didn't like it at all. It made me very nervous. I had several embarrassing incidents at school. I would shit my pants and be too scared to ask the teacher to leave the class. I'd sit there in a pants load of poo all day long. Irish Catholic schools had very wicked teachers. A lot of them were nuns, and they were particularly vicious and very cruel. They used to love to whack you on the hand with the sharp edge of a ruler. That used to hurt like fuck. I wasn't into arithmetic as a little kid. I was artistic. I'd draw anything. I loved geometry, but not the math side of it. I liked the penciling. I loved history because I don't believe any of it. I have a good memory for it, but since I've seen my own musical history buggered up so professionally, I really can't believe anything about anyone else. In twelve years the media changed me into God knows what for their own benefit. So what on earth have they done with Napoleon and the rest? Any kind of history you read is basically the winning side telling you the others were bad.

Then came the first step that put me on the road to Rotten.

My mother and father couldn't wake me up for school one morning. I kept passing out, limp in my mother's arms. So it was off to the hospital. At first the doctors denied there was anything wrong with me. Such is the National Health. I remember my thoughts all being very weird—drifting, kind of like daydreaming. It was almost like watching a movie. You're detached from everything, a very strange feeling. There was no drug substitute for the hallucinations I experienced because, heaven knows, over the years I've tried. Fucking hell, some of the things I'd see. Astounding. I still can remember them very clearly. Green dragons burning breath of fire—I can still feel the heat burning me. I must have had quite a detailed imagination to allow that to happen in my head. I suppose all kids are frightened of dragons. Lousy TV does that to you.

You can catch spinal meningitis from rats pissing in the water. I'm not sure how I caught it. It's a brain disease—which explains a lot—but

I was in hospital for a year from age seven to eight. I almost died of meningitis, a condition where the fluid in the spinal column affects the brain. The hallucinations kept occurring, and I couldn't focus on objects around me. Terrible, terrible headaches. Very hot, swollen. Unable to eat. I was vomiting all the time. Then I would just doze off into a deep sleep. I slipped into a coma. They put me on penicillin, and I was kept in hospital for the year. I was in and out of a coma for six or seven months, with a few more months of rehabilitation.

My mother would visit, but that would be for one hour a day or whatever. One hour in a child's life is nothing. St. Ann's Hospital in Highgate was right next to a Catholic church and was lousy with visiting priests. You thought you could get away from all of that.

"I'm ill, for God's sake. Keep those vampires away." Even at such an early age, I never trusted those religious maniacs.

The hospital ward had about forty beds in it. Very old-fashioned. You see them in the old World War II movies. The metal framed beds. It was all kids of all ages. Nurses would bother you, and every six hours I had to have penicillin injections all over. They were particularly painful. Kids like me were scared of needles, and nurses did fuck all to alleviate that fear.

They would draw fluid out of my spine, which was bloody painful. I'll always remember that because it's curved my spine. I've developed a bit of a hunchback. There're all these idiosyncrasies about me in the Pistols that come from fucking up in a hospital. The stare is because I developed bad eyesight, also as a result of the meningitis. I have to look hard at things to focus in and see what they are, yet I can read very well in the dark. I just can't stand the brightness. That's part of the "Lydon stare." If I could caricature myself, the closest I've seen to it would be Laurence Olivier's *Richard III*. That's so funny. I can see bits of me in there. Fucking excellent. What an absolute bastard he was! Beneath his hunched deformity, Shakespeare's Richard was wicked and psychotic, mixed with a fatally cruel sense of humor.

When I caught meningitis, the last thing I remember eating was a pork chop the night before I passed out. I've stayed away from pork ever since. I heartily recommend meningitis if you want to get something out of your diet—a liberal sprinkling on the top of whatever you shouldn't be eating. I swear, you'll never go back.

When my parents came to the hospital to take me home, I did not recognize them. I was terrified. I couldn't remember where home was until I walked in the door. Oh, was this one unhappy child. It's back to the slums. I suppose you start to get devious and invent illness, anything just to get out. Mind you, it was so squalid you didn't have to invent anything at all. Just being in a place like that would contaminate you.

There're still a few pictures of me about when I was small, but I don't like looking at them. I hated me when I was small. It's something I want nothing to do with. You look at yourself when you're young, and you think, Why couldn't you have been a bloody bit smarter? Of course you can't. I'm despondent about the early years of my youth. I was terrified by everything, such a little pussy really. I didn't want to do anything. I always felt ill. I still get permanent headaches and God knows what from the meningitis. I can cope with it a lot better now. Maybe it's not right to expect that at eight years old you're not ruling the world.

When you miss a year in school, you've really fucked up, you feel ashamed. Kids are very age conscious. They try very hard to be adultlike, and you have to work double time to catch up. After my illness I went right back into the same age group, but I was very behind because I didn't understand what they were doing. I had to catch up on my own. I didn't get much help from the teachers. Not then. It might have changed since, although I've yet to see it. The results of what pours out of English schools at the moment is piss and shit.

After I came out of hospital after the meningitis thing, I never managed to fit back in with the other kids in school. From there on in, I always felt a bit detached. Once I came back to school after twelve months, I didn't recognize anyone. A year in a comatose state at that age tends to take some of the memory away. My perspective shifted, and I saw myself as apart. Before, I felt very much in it, although I hated it because I was so bloody shy. Slowly but surely I thought about what being shy meant. I thought, For God's sake, so what if I'm the ugliest thing that walks the planet. Does it matter? Who to? So I gave that notion up, and from there on in things got better.

It was back to dreary school again and the same old, tired regime. I never had a good time at school ever. I absolutely hated the physical sports. To me that was the hell of it. It was more fun being ill and not taking part in football, rugby, and tennis—all those fucking boring sports. Again it was back to money. Catholic schools made you buy your own supplies, and if you didn't have the right colors, they wouldn't let you take part. I didn't want to take part anyway. I wasn't athletic. Muscles are something you hire.

RAMBO: I was an original skinhead when I was twelve in 1969. If you lived in Finsbury Park at that time, everybody at that age in school was a skinhead. We had to wear size six Dr. Martens boots because if you wore your proper size, like a size four, that was Junior Dr. Martens and those looked like kids' boots. So I had to wear boots two sizes too big. Ben Sherman shirts would start at size fourteen, so I had this fourteen-inch shirt on even though I only had a twelve-inch neck. We used to go Paki bashing, but mostly out of town. We called it "rolling" and used to rob 'em because they didn't fight back. I didn't do an awful lot of it, but sometimes they would fight back and then you would have a good little row on your hands.

In England public school is really private. They call it "public" because it's open to the public to buy their education. You should see some of the people who come out of those institutions. English public schools tend to turn out little snobs. They're taught a sense of superiority, which is the kiss of death. They have the privilege of social status, but that doesn't mean shit in the real world—except in England, where they don't live in the real world. They're absolutely screwed up for life, but with this awful sense of superiority based on nothing. Actually, it's based on torture. They have their own little cliques. The country's run by them.

I remember going to mass with my parents when I was young. The smell of the church used to annoy me, and I would always sneeze through the services. Church was a place where women wore hideous hats, and all the Irish laborers in the back rows smelled of sweat. That's my view of religion. I've never had any godlike epiphanies or thought that God had anything to do with this dismal occurrence called life.

My parents dragged me and my brothers to mass. Our Lady of the Sacred Heart. It was the church connected to the primary school in Eden Grove that I went to from the age of five to eleven. When we moved from Holloway Road to Finsbury Park, my parents didn't like the new church. The new cathedral in Finsbury Park was one of those modern structures, stripped bare. No gaudy statues. No musty smell. That alienated my parents, so church was out. I guess you could call it an architectural decision.

When my mum and dad lost interest, it was easy for me and my brothers to express our disinterest, too. I'd vanish on Sunday morning, and that was all there was to it. All my brothers would stay away from the house until we knew there was no more mass. My parents were not religious people. The house was never full of crucifixes and holy water. If anyone liked the gaudiness of the icons and religious symbols, it was me. There's something vaguely vampirelike, Gothic, and creepy about it—willing yourself to be haunted.

One priest we knew locally got busted for gun smuggling. He was a pretty boy who fancied himself a gigolo and was always milling around with the soppy housewives. "Hello there, Mrs. [O'Brien]. Can I do anything for you?" Dirty little snob! I was pleased when he got it. I think it happens a lot with Irish priests. They'll do things like smuggle guns to get in with the boys. This is not a myth, it's the truth—they are very seriously inclined to that kind of criminal behavior, not so much for political reasoning, but more for appeasing the community and wanting to be one of the lads. "I may be a priest, but I can shoot a gun as good as anyone!" They're like Jimmy Swaggarts. They preach one thing and live another. They'll outdrink anybody in a pub, but I've never seen a priest pay for a pint of beer. The paddies like getting their priests well pissed and hearing them swear and talk about [Mrs. Brodie's] knickers.

Things like gun running usually occur with Irish priests who are going back and forth between England and Ireland. You'd see them running around the Irish centers, collecting for "our friends up North." My old man would yell back, "I've got no friends up North." You can't allow yourself to get involved in that crap. Whatever those people are doing up there is not for the reasons they're pretending. It's like two mafia gangs punching each other out—UDA/IRA, IRA/UDA. They both run their extortion rackets and plague people to no end. When the British army patrols are gone, they run around houses, put guns to people's heads, and say, "Donate kindly to our charity—or else!" It's Al Capone-ville. I have relatives on both sides of the fence. The Northern Ireland problem is a terrible thing, and it's only the ignorance of the people living outside of it that keeps it going. There's a vested interest and a political gain involved: keep the Irish squabbling, and things run fantastically for Britain. The British government doesn't do anything without a reason. They're stopping the Irish from being industrialized. How's that for a fantastic theory? As long as the Irish are killing each other, they're certainly denied their opportunity. Most of the Protestants have Scottish ancestry, which makes them Celts anyway. We're all part of the same bloody race. You should not take sides. You cannot justify murdering people and parking bombs in pubs and shops. I've never seen anything solved by violence. History usually comes back to where it all began; you either learn to assimilate or exterminate, and not just your enemy, but yourself.

Culture is a hokey fraud. We're near the twenty-first century—who needs it anymore? Culture was something humans held on to because they were afraid of demons and gods. People used it as protection from metaphysics. It's sad that all culture seems to be about old pots and corny old folk songs. Those things are so removed from real life. Modern man hasn't accepted that culture moves on. Who needs the trappings? Culture is merely rules, and it goes hand in toe with soppy religious stupidity.

I was fairly anonymous as a schoolchild. I didn't start making trouble until much later when I was twelve or thirteen in secondary school. I had had enough of being bullied around. It was absurd. I'm not a fighter, you see. I don't like violence, so I was an easy target. I enjoyed reading and learning things, but I thought the way they were trying to teach us was stupid and ridiculous. If anything, school was hindering me, and I resented that. I didn't like the way we were taught English literature, for instance. The teacher would tell us what this or that author meant. I'd be thinking, No. He doesn't mean that at all. It seemed wrong, and if I dared mention that, I would be labeled a troublemaker. It just escalated from that. If asking questions makes you a troublemaker, then that's what I became. If anything, the schoolmasters maneuvered me in that direction. Then I could be quite violent about my questioning. I would disrupt lessons as much as possible. I would question everything, particularly in the religious classes. I found them really offensive. They weren't teaching religion, they were indoctrinating and brainwashing us.

Ages eleven to thirteen meant changing from primary school to secondary school. Starting secondary school was hell, as the older boys would obviously pick on the new lot. It was a period of victimization for two solid years, until you could find a way of maneuvering around it. I found humor the best way. I certainly couldn't fight my way out of it. Toward the end of primary school, I got fed up being bullied all the time. That's when I became a bit of a loner. I found it hard fitting back in. People didn't remember me. Things changed. Hard, my gosh, I had it hard, but don't all kids go through that? You're gangly. You're insecure. You're naive, and the older kids know because they've been there. So they really give it to you, they really know what hurts. It's not so much a bash on the nose, it's much more vindictive than that. It's what's said, that peer pressure thing, that tells you, "You don't fit in."

Kids are very conservative at that age. It's all about being the same, anti-anyone-who-doesn't-quite-fit-in-the-mold. I'm sure the teachers instigated a great deal of that. Fortunately secondary school wasn't a formidable time for me. Up until then I was a bit of a church mouse. Fuming inside. An explosion waiting to happen.

I broke out of the mold at around fourteen, fifteen. That's when I exploded. I'd had enough. That's when I'd seen through it all. The teachers were absolutely furious because I'd fight them in such a clever way. It was all about manipulating their anger, annoying them by staring without blinking throughout an entire lesson. That used to drive them crazy. Excellent fun. The other kids in the class—the ones I was playing up to—were very impressed. Suddenly you're in and you're on top of it all. From there on in it's just a giggle.

Sports and I never saw eye to eye. I would do anything not to attend a single sports class. I'd be ill. I'd be absent. I wouldn't have the proper uniform, which was a valid excuse since they insisted you have the correct football kit, tennis outfit, or cricket gear. Poverty made that a no-no. It was the perfect excuse.

"We can't afford it."

"Well, you'll just have to sit on the bench."

"Yippee!"

Then they got wise to that, so that's when we organized demonstrations of nonparticipation. I remember the sporting trips. They'd take all the classes to Hackney Marshes, set us up in teams. Three-quarters of us just said no. I was blamed for being the inspiration behind that, which was vaguely true. There I was with the rest of the lazies, all of us having the time of our lives while the rest were running up and down in the sweltering heat. Who's winning here? It was marvelous when they threatened to cane the lot of us. Fine. We stood up. *Thwack-thwack-thwack*, the first twenty kids—which included me—and that was it. Even they got bored. The next week they didn't bother. By the next week the sports department of our school was just a shambles.

I hated rugby, and there was no way they'd ever get me to participate in a game so foolish. Badminton was goddamn awful. Why did you have to wear those ridiculous white outfits? White plimsoles, white socks, white shorts, and a nice little white Fred Perry shirt with your little badminton bat. It was all so rinky-dinky. No way, I'd decided; I wouldn't do it, so I dug my heels in. I suppose it was also a test of power. They really couldn't have a go at me because on the education side I was up there, well smart. I wouldn't listen to the rubbish the English teacher would be spouting about Shakespeare. I knew he was talking rubbish, and I proved it a few years later when I finally did get to take my exams. They'd thrown me out before I had the chance to originally. I never really failed any exam I'd sat for, except woodworking. That was so boring. I was clever enough never to take chemistry and physics, two subjects that made no sense to me whatsoever.

Mathematics was all well and fine until they started introducing logarithms. They wouldn't explain what they were for, hence it seemed absolutely stupid to me. Things like the binary system. They should have told us it was the computer language of the future! They didn't tell you anything that would make such things relevant. It's too much bother. Bad teachers inspire negative attitudes in their pupils when they don't keep their interest.

Outside of the Catholic schools, there are state schools. Catholic parents sent their children to Catholic schools because they thought that was the right thing to do. My parents learned their lesson with me and Jimmy. My other two younger brothers, Bobby and Martin, went to state schools after that. They weren't buggered up by the Catholics. You assimilate better in the state schools, and you don't feel cut off from the world, which is what these Catholic institutions do. You're landlocked in there with priests and nuns.

I've never been a thief, and I don't like people who are, but one day after school Jimmy and I broke into one of the garages near where we lived. We weren't stealing. We were just funning. We were seeing how things worked and rooting through the toolsheds, just being nosy. No real thievery. The police caught us and brought Jimmy and me to the front step. My father answered the door.

They asked him, "Are these your sons?"

"Never seen them before in me life."

He slammed the door in the policeman's face. There was nothing they could do with us. We were underage, so they had to let us go. At first I was horrified, but later I realized that was the smartest thing I'd ever seen my old man do. He impressed me no end, because he never mentioned it again, either. I thought I'd get the hiding of my life. No. Never mentioned it. So the lesson was: Don't get caught.

My father had a much harder life than most people I know. His early childhood was hell on earth in Ireland. He had a stepmother, and his father was an alcoholic. There were a lot of children, so Dad did the best he could. He came to London at fourteen and drove a truck. Fucking big bollocks. That's why he could call me a fucking sissy when I would sit around the house with my long hair.

Looking at my parents' wedding photos from way back in the fifties, I notice my father had this enormous quiff—quite a radical statement for those days. John Lydon, Sr., has always been a rebel. What he's done all my life, which I never understood until the day I left home, was to deliberately make sure that I would always be my own man and not be led or fooled by anyone. He never gave me an easy time about anything. No matter what I did, he called it crap. I hated it at the time, but it made me question. He would never compliment any of us—Jimmy, Bobby, Martin, and me—when we would do something good because we were supposed to know. Unfortunately, sometimes we didn't. After Mum died we all sat down together, brothers and daddy, and worked this out. He has said more to me in the last few years than in our entire life together before.

In later life, everything my old man taught me has held true, and I love him very much for it. He's as hard today with me as he was way back then. But his eyes are a little softer, and I know he's proud that I'm my own man. His worst nightmare would have been if I had grown up to be a moron and joined the army.

Looking back, I cannot disagree with any of my father's decisions on how he raised me and my brothers. I wanted to at times because I felt hurt and betrayed when there wasn't that camaraderie that dads were supposed to have for you, but lo and behold, he did everything a father should do. No one will ever get one over on me. They might at some point, but eventually vengeance is mine—and I don't mean in violent ways. My old man calls it patience.

Once he made me take over the controls of the crane when we worked together on a job site. I had to manipulate these pedals and an armful of levers all at one time. I broke my ankle, and he had to take me to the hospital. I went home and would not tell my mum how it happened because that was something between the two of us. It wasn't the first time he broke my ankle. He broke it when I was five years old. We were watching "The Rifleman" on the telly, and he was playing about. He came in and yelled, "Get to bed, you kids!" Bang went his shovel on the bed, and my foot was there. He shattered my ankle, the same one, twice.

Saturdays and Sundays were a nightmare for me because my father would have me outside underneath his car, trying to show me how an engine worked. He used to drive me nuts. He would drop heavy things on me. "Feel the weight of that!" The old man didn't have the powers of communication back then, but he meant well. He thought I would be perceptive enough to pick up. But I just wasn't . . . until I left home.

Mum was a whole different kettle of piranha. Mum loved the music I used to buy. Just before leaving home, she would always come upstairs to my room and ask in her heavy Irish brogue, "What have you bought lately, son? I heard some noise earlier on that I rather liked."

"No, Mum, I'm sure you won't like this. It's Hawkwind's first album." She would sit and listen and absorb the music. She was genuinely thrilled. She loved "Funhouse" by the Stooges. It was hard trying to be the rebellious one here in your room when your mum's sitting there listening to "Funhouse." Oh, no! Get me out of this crazy family quickly.

Then back would come the old dreams. Why wasn't I born into a wealthy family that would leave me alone? It would be ever so much easier. Kids are romantic like that. All children love to believe that their parents don't love them. It's a wonderful dream that the teenage years require. But it's not the reality at all. You think, God, did I really need to talk to them that badly? Then you realize, Yeah, because I know when they were young they did the same thing.

I once had a job as a minicab dispatcher when I was ten. I did it for a year because there was no money in the house. Bad times. It was an easy enough job to tell the drivers where to go, since I knew the area. I had fantastic fun even at such an early age, because I was always good at responsibility. But I got bored with it only because the boss was a miserable old Irish git. He was one of those old Teddy boy sorts. He wore a huge quiff and a draped jacket, another monster from the past. He used to hate the clothes I'd buy as soon as I got my pay packet.

"You fucking look like a girl, you cunt!"

"But the passengers don't have to see me. I'm sitting in a room out back." Maybe I wasn't aware, and I was giving him problems with his libido. That's probably what that anti-long hair thing was all about back then.

My old man was working for a spell on the oil rigs in Norfolk at a place called Bacton On Sea. I remember the family staying in Eastbourne, Hastings, Norfolk—all very far from London. We lived in a holiday camp one winter. It was bitter cold, and we were the only people in this empty camp. It was off season, and they were closed down. It was a frighteningly desolate existence much like in *The Shining*. Very strange. I remember this silly, desolate holiday camp facing the North Sea, with the gales blowing in and the winds whistling. Yet I loved the bizarreness of this empty camp. I would wander around for hours thinking about what it would be like in the summer when there were thousands of people crammed together. I remember a drained swimming pool. Exhilarating.

My mum and dad would always play these mind games. My dad liked things screwy or off center. He wouldn't ever say anything, but you knew he was enjoying it. "Jeez, we're having a lot of fun here!" It was so preposterous, it was fantastic. Mum would look over: "Mmm. Boiled potatoes again for dinner." There was a lot of black humor in my family. My dad would tell us ghost stories and really wind us up. He'd get us terrified and then make up a silly way out at the end. "By the way, I lied." You knew you were fooled. It would be humiliating.

Despondent Lydon at early age (far left) with Mother (centre),
Auntie Agnes (right) with assorted Lydon brats.

I loved my mother's family in Ireland. They were such strange and freaky people. They used to love telling ghost stories, and I loved listening. I suppose they were very primitive. They had the feel of, say, Yugoslavian peasants, yet they were so warm in the weirdest way. They would never talk to me directly, they would just sit next to me and stare. That stare would tell you everything, and you knew you belonged and everything was all right. They insisted on babbling to me in Gaelic when I was young. I could not get a word around it.

Would my mum teach me Gaelic? No. Both my parents had decided when they left Ireland that they would never speak Gaelic again. It was some modernistic urge they felt; they might have been ashamed of their roots. I suppose they cut it off so I wouldn't inherit the grief that they went through when they came to London. But it left me isolated and shallow inside. I wanted to go out of my way and find out about my own Irishness, but when I did get there, it was never as romantic as books make it out to be. The truth is always mediocre. How on earth would I have been able to use Gaelic, being raised in London? It would have been absolutely useless. My parents were right. It just took a long time for me to suss it out.

My father's Irish side was always a little strange because he never had a respectable family life. Every time we'd go back to Galway, it would always be very difficult. We would see only his sister after my grandfather died. My father's father was a grizzly old sod. He'd smoke all the time and drink whiskey, port, and Guinness day and night. He lived with a working woman of many occupations called Moll and fathered seventeen kids. It must have been tough on my father. They used to live in a pub called the Donkey, which is kind of aptly named. I remember my mum saying something once when I was really young. "Oh, that donkey's at it again." Lo and behold, I'd find out. Another kid from my grandad on my father's side.

He finally died shagging a prostitute on a doorstep. He fell backward, cracked his skull, and that was the end of him. Age seventy. He died with a hard-on. I had to take my aunt, my father's sister, to the hospital morgue. They pulled him out, and they had just severed his skull and put it back on really badly. It was kind of lopsided, and Grandad's nose was twisted. Bits were missing out of the back. But I remember seeing this huge penis. It literally was the biggest penis I think I've ever seen in my life. In all the porno flicks I've ever seen since, there was nothing to compete with it.

My aunt looked down at her dead father and screamed. She couldn't believe what she was looking at. Have you ever seen a rotting dick? It was an unbelievable boner of contention. Then when we got back to the Donkey that night, she was in the bedroom opposite me, screaming all night because she had nightmares. What went on when they were young? At the time, I thought, You silly cow. That was your own father.

Beer had always been there for me as long as I can remember. I was eleven when my old man's father died. During the wake, I could easily hold my own in the pub with the rest of them. It caused a big fight among my old man's cousins. They thought it was an absolute disgrace for an eleven-year-old kid like me to be sitting there, downing pints of Guinness. These people around me would get drunk, and there I would sit, still sober. They say alcohol destroys the brain cells. Apparently it hasn't done its damage to me. Whatever there was worth destroying must have been already buggered up by my illness. What's left is well hearty.

The Irish like their country and western music played badly on accordions and violins. They're time warped. My uncle's farm in Cork doesn't even have electricity yet—it's still candles and a gas cooker. It's as if there's no reason to change, even if they're freezing to death. The Catholic church still runs the Irish government, which is why everything is so suppressed. That's what scares the Protestants in Northern Ireland the most, and I don't blame them. There's no creativity in the Catholic regime—including procreativeness or divorce. It's all bicycles with no brakes going downhill. If you think the anti-abortion lot in America are wicked in their tactics, you ought to see the anti-divorce lot in Ireland. It's nuns with pickax handles on the street, in gangs roaming towns and villages. Wicked bitches!

BILLY IDOL: My mother came from Cork, just like John's mum. When I was a little boy we'd go up to Ireland at least once a year to see her family. They used to call me the British kid because I had such an English accent. It seemed like everywhere I went, I was the outcast. When my mother used to watch something about Ireland on TV she'd say, "I hate the British."

You can see why my mum and dad could never live in Ireland. We'd go back there in the summer for about six weeks, then it was back to Britain where things "don't work" better. If I went back to my uncle's farm in Ireland today, the boat with the holes would be in exactly the same place, and the stupid horse would still be chewing on the same stupid tree. It's all like a postcard scene. It never moves. It's a void. How can you have a sense of belonging to something that never changes? No future, literally.

JOHN GRAY
SCHOOL DAYS, NORTH LONDON

As a matter of style, the Lydons took the piss out of one another; it was natural for them. When John and I first met, we went to the same Catholic school, Sir William of York, which has since amalgamated with Aloysius College. It was on Gifford Street off York Way in Islington, very near Pentonville Prison, now a big industrial area. Funny enough, John's been back there to rehearse PiL in the studio on Brewery Road. It's ironic how the school site that John hated so much is now a big band center where everyone rehearses before they go on tour.

I lived in Kentish Town/Camden Town, which was half an hour's walk or an even shorter bus ride away. When you're eleven, you get invited round to each other's houses. The first time I went round to John's house off Holloway Road, they lived in a storefront with a big shop window facing Benwell Road. The whole front room consisted of this shop window with a net curtain over it. Eileen Lydon, John's mum, was very hospitable and served us Spam-and-tomato sandwiches on white bread—the traditional Irish greeting at the time. What she didn't realize was that even then I was a vegetarian. I must have looked horrified when she put the food in front of me. I didn't want to offend her so I picked off the bread and left the Spam. I came from the same background as the Lydons, and I loathed all the Irish-type cooking and food. But when you go to an Irish household, it's an offense to turn down their offerings.

The Lydon tea was watery, weak, and milky. To this day John drinks it like that. When sipping this liquid I thought, God, I have to be polite. Afterward John and I walked up to the Arsenal football grounds, which was round the corner from Highbury football grounds. I'm not sure if we saw a match or not. I wasn't much interested in football or sport. At that age you're pressured into following a team. I went along with it, thinking Arsenal would do. To this day John is a loyal Arsenal fan. I remember going to a match with him in Nottingham Forest, standing in the terraces for an hour and a half, freezing cold, bored out of my mind.

RAMBO: I used to go to football in the seventies with Jimmy Lydon, John's brother. John used to go out to football with us, but I became a friend of Jimmy's first before I knew John. When me and Jimmy used to go to football all the time, Jimmy had a Dave Bowie haircut. I used to like David Bowie, but you used to always wonder what your other mates thought of him. He was queer, but he was accepted among the football teams. They were all thugs, but they had Ziggy Stardust haircuts.

JOHN LYDON: Professional team sports was a local thing. All the schools nearby wanted to play for their team. They'd send coaches and scouts down to the social clubs. Everybody wanted to be a football hero, a fine thing to want to be when you're young. It gave you a point and meaning.

I'd have rows with people, but I have to be honest. I'm not a physical person. Never have been. I don't like fighting. I don't understand it. It hurts, and quite frankly I don't want to hurt other people, no matter how much they annoy me. My weapons are my words. While I tried to stay away from any football violence, at the same time I'd still be part of that "home game, no one's gonna take our end" stuff. I loved the shambolic nightmare of it all. True anarchy was happening with football. The police couldn't stop it. The gangs didn't want to stop it. Yet nobody really seemed to have gotten too hurt. It was all about fisticuffs. The razor blades, stabbings, and guns came in much later. Gangs that ran with knives were always looked down on as being wankers. If they needed weapons, it meant that they couldn't hold their own.

The football clubs pretended that the violence wasn't happening. I'm sure they appreciated the away support when they played road games, but the clubs have never done anything to stop football violence other than fill the terraces with police, which is not the answer. You've got to involve the fans more with the game. You have to make them a part of it. In England now, wearing team colors has nothing to do with violence at all. It's quite the opposite. It's the ones who don't wear the colors that you have to look out for. Those are the knife-in-the-back merchants.

RAMBO: I started hangin' around with the people who were all from Finsbury Park. We had this whole group. A lot of black people—mostly West Indian—along with white people. In them days you were breaking the barriers. We were Finsbury Park, but you'd have Islington and the other part of Islington called Highbury. You still had a little bit of the racist thing going on up in Highbury. They were Arsenal as well, but we never got on with them. We used to have battles with them. We were a mixed mob—blacks, white, and that. But Highbury was a white gang. Sometimes we'd hang around together, but there was always a little bit of division. In Finsbury Park we had a head start, and that's why we ended up miles ahead of other areas because we were automatically hanging around with black people, Greek people, a lot of Irish, and Scottish. You had to get on with each other. We used to fight at the Tottenham Royal against Tottenham blacks—with blacks in our mob against their black gangs. By 1973 Arsenal had quite a few black people in the mob.

We both drifted into music and began buying music from a very early age. By about age nine, we got jobs. I got a Saturday job in a supermarket and would spend all my wages on one LP. During that period I bought early Lennon solo albums and stuff like that. John lurched off into a different area—he got into Captain Beefheart and Can. While we started getting into the exciting groups, we liked the mainstream as well. We were big T. Rex and Gary Glitter fans, and we also went for the NME rock types. Then we started going to gigs. I was first; I saw Marc Bolan at the Roundhouse just before "Ride a White Swan" was a hit.

The Roundhouse was quite easy to get to from where John and I lived, so we'd go every Sunday. There would be these amazing all-day bills with about six groups. We saw everyone from Arthur Brown to Can. The deejay used to play all our favorite records full volume through the PA systems. It was brilliant.

BILLY IDOL: Once I saw the MC5 at this place called Phun City. They had these two guitarists dressed in spangled jackets who twirled around and jumped in the air! Here was this one blastoid rock 'n' roll band in among all this hippie shit!

During our early teens, John and I got into going to the bar, drinking Newcastle Brown. I'm sure it's called underage drinking now, but in those days we got away with it. We had long hair, and our main cultural activities consisted of gigs, listening to records, and drinking beer, the usual teenage stuff.

Meanwhile we were still in school, and the schoolmasters wanted us to conform. It was a Catholic all-boys school, and they were heavily into uniforms, religion, and discipline. I remember getting into a vociferous argument with a trainee priest and getting ejected for being too questioning. John would take the piss out of it more.

Once we had to wear a tie, but John didn't wear one.

"You can't come back tomorrow unless you're wearing a tie," the priest told him.

So John would turn up the next day wearing a tie and nothing else. Just a jacket, pants, a tie, and no shirt. The teacher would ask him, "Why aren't you wearing a shirt?"

"You asked us to wear a tie. Make up your mind."

I came from a family of five kids, John from a family of four kids. Irish people didn't have loads of money to throw around, so we wore these cheap baseball boots. The teachers would then tell us to get black leather shoes. You could go home and pester your parents all you like, but it wouldn't matter. In fact, John's parents were much more forthcoming with their money for their kids than my parents were.

Anyway, I remember being told off at school for having these baseball boots on. We'd get hassled by the teachers every day.

"Why aren't you wearing the statutory uniform?"

When John was about fifteen, just about the time we were approaching the exam periods for O levels, John pushed the patience of one English master, Mr. Prentiss. It was a crisis point for John. There were only about six of us in the sixth form at that point, and we were this lit-

Pistols mafia on the town. John Gray and Rotten.

tle alternative gang within the school. There was Dave Crowe, Tony Purcell, John, myself, and a couple of other kids. We were all quite intelligent, even though we didn't play the game. Yet the teachers had to cling to us because we were the only students who were game for the exams.

"You aren't going to be entered for the exams unless you get your act together," one of the teachers threatened, so some of us knuckled down and started studying.

John had really long hair at this point and was testing things to the very limit. Eventually he was expelled, and his parents were invited to the school. I remember his mom having a big to-do; it was a big explosion. I think that if John had backed down, he might have gotten away with it. As it was, his parents backed him to the hilt; they were horrified at the way he was being treated. I think there was a negotiation period where he was told he could come back if he apologized and promised to be a good boy, but by this time both his mum and his dad were so pissed off at the school, that they just said, "Stick it." So John didn't come back

From there he went on to another college, which is where he met Wobble and Sid. We still hung out occasionally. I was at school with Dave Crowe doing A levels. John was at college, starting at Hackney, then off to King's Cross, where he worked. We carried on our social life outside of school. In fact, the social life must have taken over. I didn't finish any of my A levels. O levels are what sixteen-year-olds take. A levels are more for seventeen-, eighteen-year-olds. John went ahead and got a few of his O levels a little late because he'd been expelled early in the spring term, so he had to wait until the following September to enroll into a college. During an academic year, you just couldn't walk in the middle of a year.

John was disillusioned before the time he was expelled. In those days, we had to choose certain subjects, and that interfered with John's talent for art and English. The combinations of subjects were arranged in such a way that the artist types couldn't just take art. John and I were artistic, but the school only let the less intelligent children take it because they saw art as a kind of cop-out subject. We were pressured to take math and science. That immediately disillusioned John. John's strength was in painting and drawing and talking about books. Ironically it was in those classes he had the most confrontations with the teachers.

John Sr. and Eileen must have realized they'd made a mistake sending John to Catholic school at that age. Before, he went to Eden Grove primary school, which worked okay for primary age. John, being the oldest boy, was stuck with Catholic school. When disillusionment set in, the parents sent the younger siblings to non-Catholic schools. The parents finally saw that there was an overfocus on religion while the rest of the curriculum was being ignored.

As youngsters, John and I never got into trouble or in any gang situation. We had individual skirmishes. We were too clever to be caught as a gang subverting authority. We did it on a one-to-one level. I was always punished for answering the teachers back. John was usually in trouble for individual acts of disobedience, although we did back each other up sometimes.

One incident was when we all threw chalk at the blackboard when the teacher went out of the room. Chalk all over the classroom, wrecked. The teacher came in and said, "I'm going to cane the lot of you."

I stood up indignantly and said, "I never touched any chalk, and I refuse to be caned."

The teacher then fumbled around and let me off. Naturally John's hand shot up, and he said, "Sir, I didn't throw any chalk, either."

Before long there were twenty-nine children refusing punishment. The teacher lost it. He caned only a few of the children. They never really birched our bums at school. It was very much the hands at that point. I got caned once, when I was chased around the corridor for insulting somebody. I don't remember John ever getting caned; he was always too clever.

John and I had this math teacher named Mr. Harnett who was particularly lethal. If you couldn't get your sums right, he'd belt you round the head and then knock it against the blackboard. We used to attend his lessons shaking with fear. It was the biggest adrenaline rush I'd ever had in my life. It was really naff, and the experience was probably what made me become a teacher because he made me determined not to teach kids like that. Anyway, in this class we started off in the math B grade, there being A, B, C, and D. In those days, students were streamed by ability. The D's were considered hopeless. The C's had some chance. The B's were average—getting their act together. The A's were the high flyers. Our first year, we were put in the B's stream, but after a couple of months it became obvious we were in the wrong class. So they put us into the A stream. We were bright! We could write, we could string sentences together. We weren't particularly hardworking, though. We got by on natural brains.

There were no girls in the school. Now, you get the boys hanging outside the girls' school or the girls going to the boys' school. There wasn't a girls' school for miles around. All we got were boys from other schools coming to beat us up. There were violent clashes between local schools when the whole school would be under siege. Gangs would descend on the school at lunchtime and throw bricks and wood over the playground gate as some of the D streams and C streams from our school would rush off and retaliate.

RAMBO: Finsbury Park was one of the biggest mobs in the early seventies. We were a gang, and in the early days we used to be called Holloway, which is a stretch from Finsbury Park all the way down to Holloway. Jimmy used to come with me. Johnny was there every now and again. He was game for it. There was [an Indian] geezer called [Serious], a skinny little bloke. He used to be a lunatic. Now he's one of the top veterinarians. He used to go around with these surgical knives and scalpels. He was game and would jump out at the geezers and just cut 'em. Now he's one of the most quiet blokes going and still there in Finsbury Park. We had another two buds called the [Beasts]. They had a big reputation name on them. They were twin black blokes who used to hang about with us. There was another geezer called [Dock] and also [Caesar] and his brother, called [Romulus]. John's friend [Julius] used to go to school with me. These were the characters who hung around Finsbury Park.

We loved the excitement. John's always been interested in hooliganism, violence, and football, more like an academic interest, I would say. He wasn't interested in participating. As for girls, we never saw them. It wasn't until John was in the Pistols that girls started figuring in on the scene.

As for music, we used to have choir practice and singing sessions during our music lessons. We had this modern music teacher who brought the Who's "Tommy" in one day and tried to teach us music through "Tommy." John and I certainly weren't Who fans, nor did we like "Tommy," but he forced us to sing.

When John sang, he deliberately took the piss out of the whole thing. He went up and down like a yodeling cat being strangled. That was the first time I'd ever heard John sing. The teacher shouted, "Stop stop stop! I've heard enough."

Rather than coping with teenage rebellion, the Catholic schools used it as an excuse to get rid of you. If you're used to dealing with teenagers, however, you should be used to rebellion, because most teenagers are difficult. But they held up religion and uniforms as a barrier that, if you were half-intelligent, you'd want to break down. I must have conformed a bit more than John, although I do remember going to a physics lesson with purple hair. Later when we were at college, John had green hair.

I don't know where we got that from; maybe we were influenced by David Bowie. We bought Crazy Color—I distinctly remember the name, it came in tubs—down on Denmark Street or somewhere near the Marquee or near Piccadilly Circus. We used to travel there specially to buy it. I put my color on top, and it went purple. John, who is naturally blond, wanted his blue on top. Of course blue and yellow makes green, so he ended up with this bizarre chemical green color.

My dad was horrified; he didn't know what to say. I think John's dad was horrified as well. He might have thought it was funny because he had more of a sense of humor, but it's possible he was quite shocked.

Eileen Lydon, however, was a friend. She wasn't like a mother. She was totally different from my mother—we could talk openly. She seemed much younger than she actually was and didn't seem like a grown-up half the time. She was extremely broad-minded. For a woman of her age and upbringing, I was amazed at how very close I was to her. We would while away endless hours talking away in the kitchen.

Eileen Lydon wore glasses and was quite short. She had typical Irish-styled, mousey hair. She was very gentle but extremely hardworking. I remember thinking, What a liberal household! It was much more liberal than mine, so I spent ages there. I could never have friends crashing round. Normally you'd have a kind of rigid respect for your friend's parents, and maybe you could even relate to them. She was extremely loyal and was very supportive when the band started happening for John. You couldn't wish for a more supportive mother. John used to tell me stories about her gynecological problems. One time he was alone in the house with her and she had a very bad bleed. He had to call a doctor. He might find this too painful to talk about.

I remember the digging jobs his father had. John was working with his dad at some kind of building site. I've seen pictures of John up on the crane, killing rats. He used to go on and on about the rats; he loved talking about killing them. He had the special job as the rat basher—keeping the rats from crawling up the wires of the crane. We also worked summer holidays with kids in the play center, day care center.

The attitude, especially in our Irish households, was that if you weren't going to school, you had to go to work. You weren't going to lounge around at home being lazy; you had to do something useful until you went to college.

John's job paid for lots of things. He always had lots of money for someone his age; he made hundreds of pounds at one point. He used to buy loads of records with it. None of this saving for a rainy day. I know I never thought like that.

When we left school we didn't go on the dole, as many of the myths suggest. John may have, briefly, but I don't think so. John wouldn't have been able to get dole very easily anyway because he was doing part-time play center work and he was living with his parents. There was this big cliché about punk bands being on the dole and how horrible it was for them. To get dole you had to be on your own, homeless, and with no income. John could always work at the odd play center or work with his dad, and he had a very supportive family who helped him out with pocket money, even during the beginning of the Pistols. He had everything he wanted living at home.

JOHN LYDON: I've always had different groups of friends who very rarely mixed and matched due to the diversity of my interests and tastes in people. For instance, the Gang of Johns never knew the Finsbury lot until a much later date when the Pistols brought all sorts of unlikely elements together. It was quite some time before Sid met Wobble, before either of them met John Gray or any of them met Rambo. When they did meet, the timing had to be right because mixing and matching is a dangerous game best played in no-man's-land.

I stayed in school until I was quite old—eighteen and a half; but my heart had already gone out of studying. I was going into youth work fulltime; John was at college. When he was at Hackney and Kingsway Princeton College, we met up with Wobble and Sid. By then we had an even bigger core of friends. We were distancing ourselves from certain crowds at schools because they were boring. Once we got together with our new friends, we'd go to gigs, hang out, and became interested in fashion.

We were only available to work during the evenings and holiday periods. Every July and August we'd work in a different place—we weren't secure. I was working at Hampstead, Kilburn at a youth center that was halfway between my house and John's. Eventually I worked up a good relationship with the boss of the play center, which put me in the position to recommend John, who needed work. So they took him on for the summer holidays, all six weeks.

There were quite good provisions offered to the children. They had coach trip outings, there were playgrounds and art rooms, and they provided lunch. Every area of London had a special center staffed with experts in pottery, woodworking, sewing, and art. It was quite difficult for us because we'd get kids from five different schools who were timetabled to visit different centers at different times. John was the woodworking teacher Monday through Friday.

We had a high turnover of different children, so we couldn't build up relationships, which made it all the harder to work with them. If we'd had five days a week with the same kids, we wouldn't have had any problems, but with busloads coming in—a morning crowd from one school, an afternoon crowd from another—it was rough. But John thought of some really interesting things to keep the kids busy. Even in those days John was into American Indian artwork, totem poles. He made the kids design back scratchers that were carved with forks at the bottom—something you'd get in a tourist shop now. He taught them how to make airplanes. For every class you'd need an endless stream of ideas to keep the kids occupied.

The head of the system came to visit one day—Mr. Cutbush. He's since died. He wasn't so bad, but John didn't want to conform or bow down, so he got his back up and answered back when the headmaster came around, and he got kicked out.

Even in those days John had the green hair and wore a baseball cap from back to front. He wore baggy army trousers and a T-shirt with holes. Nowadays you could be a teacher and look like that. You'd be considered creative, wacky, and artistic. In those days you were considered a lunatic. It wasn't really fair. If they had judged John on how he was producing with the kids, he would have kept the job. He became very bitter about it because he didn't like being judged by his appearance.

John is incredibly artistic and practical, but he's left-handed, which makes it difficult. I don't think he ever had the chance to became a sculptor, but I've seen some of the things he's carved. He's interested in three-dimensional stuff, but mainly he's interested in painting. He could put his hand to it if he had to.

JOHN CHRISTOPHER LYDON
FINSBURY PARK, NORTH LONDON

I was born John Christopher Lydon in Tuam, Ireland, a little town near Galway. While it's a very musical town, we didn't have much to do there outside of joining the brass band. My father used to play the violin, and just like me, Johnny's the image of him. My mom died when I was five years. I had an Irish driver's license at the age of twelve and first drove a truck loaded with sugar beets. Then I went to Scotland and drove a truck in Dundee County. I was only fourteen when I arrived in London.

I have a stepbrother named P. J. Lydon who was in the Irish army for twenty-two years as a band instructor. He's still there. He's never seen a gun in his life. You know how the army bands are. He plays marches and football matches, big shows. He was musical, a lot of the Lydons were. My sister married into a family from Castlebar, Ireland, which is in Mayo. Her husband is a professional musician; he played saxophone with show bands. All *his* brothers played in show bands. One of the brothers' wives was a professional singer with a show band. Funny, isn't it? Music is in the Irish blood—or at least in our family blood. Me, I've done a bit of everything. I read music. I speak Gaelic. I'm a car mechanic, lorry driver, cabdriver, crane driver, sea diver.

When John and his brothers were wee kids, we used to put the television on. John and his brother Jimmy danced crazy all day long. Once the music was on, they got carried away—as if they were in another world completely. When they were small, I used to think they were crazy, always dancing, singing, and imitating things.

My wife, Eileen, was musical as well. My brother introduced me to her in an Irish pub. I was working nearby when the sea wall was flooded. Eileen liked her music. Her family were country people who lived in a little village called Carrigrohane, near Cork, in Southern Ireland. Eileen loved the traditional Irish music.

We married when I was seventeen, so I more or less grew up with the children. For years I was a crane driver on the North Sea oil rigs. Then I took up diving with the Americans. During a twelve-year period I worked on the rigs while my family was living here in London. I did that right up until the time my wife died in 1979. In fact, I packed up not six months before she died. I was still working then. When the children were young, on the weekends I was home. I'd put them all in a caravanette and drive to the seaside. The kids would be asleep or looking out the window. We'd have a day at the seaside and come back again. Often times the family would stay in London while I was working on the rigs. I had three weeks on and ten days off. They used to fly us there and home by helicopter. For years I worked with the Americans on the pipelines—when they first came to this country. I used to be up on the front end with the welders—I drove the machines. I used to drive the big American Caterpillars. The company often brought the American stovepipe welders over here because English welders were scared of the work. I worked for William Press & Company for twenty-seven years. I also worked for Press International. I've worked on a lot of the oil refineries in this country and most of the gasworks. Sometimes I was the crane driver. I put up fuel tanks for the planes. Sometimes when I was out on the rigs, I brought the family to stay nearby. For a year I had a job to the south on the coast in Eastbourne, where we rented a house in a holiday camp that was next to a graveyard. It was empty and strange. During the wintertime, when there was nobody living in there, we rented a chalet in the camp. So my family learned to travel with me.

Once we were all driving along the motorway, coming back from Ireland. Jimmy, Johnny, my wife, and I were in the car. There was a

Father and son sharing quality time.

set of headlights behind us on the motorway that kept flashing. I let this carry on for a while, when all of a sudden I completely lost emotional control. I pulled up in the middle of the moor, jumped out of our car and into theirs. There were four Welsh blokes in the car. Johnny and Jimmy came out with their lemonade bottles, and we attacked them right there on the motorway. Johnny was about eight. I never dreamed there would be four of them in the car, but they were no match for our Irish tempers.

Confrontation runs in the Lydon family. I remember my Bobby; I came home from work one day, and my wife was at the door with a kid. The poor lad had squares with naughts and crosses all over his face. I said to my wife, "What's the matter with that kid? He looks silly."

"Never mind," she said. "You go indoors."

After a while I asked her again. She told me that Bobby jammed the kid in the lift because he called Bobby an Irish bastard or something like that. Bobby grabbed him and drew all these naughts and crosses on his face.

Benwell Mansions on Benwell Road is where Johnny was born. It's down at the bottom of Holloway Road near the Arsenal football grounds. John was football crazy—still is. We didn't have a lot of money. We had enough to survive and buy the odd t'ings, that was all. So Johnny's mum used to knit the gloves, hat, and scarves in the Arsenal colors for the boys. They'd go off to the football grounds to see their team play, their scarves streaming. Even today John jumps to see Arsenal; he loves them. Back then the kids would have the odd punch-up. Somebody'd nick John's scarf and he'd nick somebody else's. He's got plenty of guts in him, Johnny, I'll tell you that. He won't back down, either. If he's pushed to a corner, he'll punch his way out. He's not a chicken, he's hard.

When Johnny was eight he got quite ill with meningitis. He was very bad. It started off with a pain in the back of his head, and then he lost his memory. He was in the Whittington Hospital. They gave him injections in his back, and then they'd draw fluid to ease the pressure from his spine that had settled on his brain. I'd go into the hospital during the evenings because they couldn't give him injections during the day. So we'd strap him down in the bed and give him the spinal injections. I was the only one who could hold him.

To this day Johnny can't stand injections. He'd probably jump through the window at the sight of a needle. I don't know how he gets vaccinated or injected now if he needs it. That's why I can't see Johnny doing drugs. He'd be gone; he'd faint.

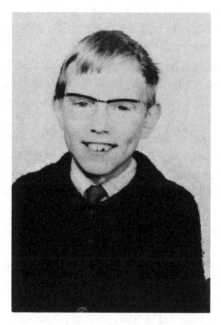

*After meningitis, I wore glasses due to
poor vision.*

Losing his memory completely due to the meningitis probably caused half the aggravation he suffered at school. When you have fluid on the brain, you see double. The pain is on the back of your head, not in your forehead. When Johnny came out of the hospital, he didn't recognize anybody—not even his parents. He couldn't spell c-a-t. So his mum sat down with him every night. I didn't have the patience—I'll be honest about that. But my wife would sit there every night and put things back into his brain. So his mom taught him everything that she knew. Johnny lost everything. As far as education is concerned everything Johnny knows came from his mum. She was just an Irish girl gifted in math. After a few years, Johnny became very intelligent and witty. With it. Together. I suppose he had to learn everything twice. But before his recovery he was like a dummy, so he learned the hard way how to get on. The kids would tease him, "Dummy! Dummy! Dummy!"

As a youngster Johnny was very, very shy. For years he was so shy it was unbelievable. If somebody come to the house, he would go upstairs. He would never mix. As Johnny got older, when his mum and I went out for a drink, he'd look after the children. I have a picture of his baby brother, Martin, sitting on Johnny's knee. Johnny was just like a dad to him. He could control his brothers and look after them. He changed Martin's nappies. Johnny also used to work with me on the weekends. We'd do car repairs on the side. I'd do anything I can. I'm handy with my hands. Johnny used to be, but since he went into the music, he's never bothered with any of it. He just loves music; he's crazy about it. Even when you're talking to him, he's playing or listening to music.

Sometimes I used to work locally driving a big mobile crane in London. I'd go to all the gas companies and all the oil refineries. I'd be on call at night, and if they'd ring me up, I'd do a job in the evenings on standby. Around the time Johnny first started listening to music—in this very flat here—I came home one evening and he had long hair. Right down to his shoulders. I said to him, "When I come back this evening, I want to see that hair cut."

Next day he had it dyed red.

I went away to work and for a few days thought no more about it. One evening I came in. Johnny used to listen to his record player upstairs. He'd sit up there almost twenty-four hours a day. Eventually he came down. He walked into the room and said, "Well, Dad, how do I look now?"

And his hair was dyed green! It's a funny thing. We had a little budgie, and it was same color green. I couldn't look at him. I had to turn around. I almost died. What can you say? I never thought anyone would take to dressing up like that. Johnny used to do outrageous things.

English people are very sensitive. In fact, Johnny was very quiet and sensitive when he was growing up. But as he got into the music, he changed completely. First we had a bit of a problem with his schoolteacher. I think the teacher was very aggressive, and Johnny gave him a bit of lip. Whatever happened, Johnny got expelled. He couldn't have been more than thirteen. One Sunday morning, the doorbell rang and there he was, the cardinal or somebody—from the Catholic church. You have a priest, an archbishop, and then a cardinal, then a pope. This little guy had a red hat. At first I thought he was a Jew boy. He was at the door. I said, "Good morning."

"Good morning, Mr. Lydon?"

"Yeah, come in. So who are you?"

"I'm the cardinal."

He sat down, I made him a cup of coffee, and then he said, "By the way, I'm trying to get your son back into college."

"What do you mean?"

"He was expelled."

"I never heard anything about it," I said honestly.

Sending Jimmy and Johnny to Catholic school didn't work. Johnny was expelled, didn't go to school for nine months, and I didn't know it. After the cardinal came by and told me, I said, "Thank you very much."

I looked at his mother, then I looked at Johnny, and he said, "I didn't like that damned school anyway."

Johnny wouldn't take abuse from anybody. Never. I noticed that as he grew up. He was quiet up until he was fourteen or fifteen. That's why he got expelled. He was a bit rough, and he wouldn't swallow crap from no one. He'd always speak his mind: "If you don't accept me as I am, then don't accept me at all."

That was Johnny's attitude and still is.

If you've ever seen the big construction engineering gear, big cranes, I used to drive them. When he was in college, Johnny worked as my banksman. He'd guide me when I was driving so I didn't hit anything. He was pretty good at it. Once we had this job on a big sewage farm. Johnny's job was to kill the rats, to keep them out of the cab. We drove a dragline with a bucket; it's like a great big crane, only you use your feet to work the pedals. The cab is bigger than a house. As I'd swing it around and throw the bucket out, Johnny used to guide me and we'd lower these huge draglines together. I have a photo of Johnny on top of the drag. He could drive those things as well as I did.

Anyway, once we were digging out a sludge ravine. It looked like an ordinary field, but as we were digging it out, we found it was all live sewage. Rats came out in the hundreds. As banksman it was Johnny's job to keep them at bay. So there he was with this great big slash hook, chopping at them. When we'd throw down the bucket, the rats would cling to the ropes that connected the bucket to the top of the crane. As the bucket went down when I was digging the earth, the rats would run up along the ropes. Johnny would slash them up, keeping them away from me, because if they came through the windows and jumped on me, with my hands and feet engaged, I couldn't do anything. It was hard work, but the point was that when he was on his school holidays, he had no cash, except what we'd give him as pocket money. But Johnny was never satisfied with just pocket money because he wanted to buy records. So I got him an extra job once he was off college.

When I was on the big machine and Johnny was my banksman, I'd say to him, "I'm going to the bog. Drive the thing. Load the lorry."

He'd say, "I can't drive that thing!"

You see, your feet are on the pedals and you're holding up the bucket with them. You have six levers in front, and you're using your elbows and everything. I'd put the loader in gear, jump out, and leave him with it. He'd be screaming, "Dad, Dad, Dad, I'll be killed!"

What happens when you work those machines for a while is that the muscles on your legs build up. The backs of your legs get as strong as a horse's. Johnny was only fourteen.

"Look, Dad, my muscles are killing me."

I'd give him a boot in the back of the legs. Go on, drive it, I said, and kept booting him until he did. That's how he learned. Once there was a guy who had a heart attack while he was driving another machine. He thought he had indigestion, but I knew he was having a heart attack. We sat him down in the canteen. Johnny was with me, and I told him to go drive the other machine.

"I've never been—"

I locked the door and switched it on. That's how Johnny had to approach music, and that's how he approached life.

He's very well educated, Johnny is. He went to Kingsway College. So did Sid Vicious, but Sid was a suffering idiot. He was like a gimmick. If he was sitting here and nobody was taking any notice of him, he'd cut his hand or something to attract attention. You'd have to take your mind off everything else and look at him. That was all Sid ever did. He could never sing or play anything. He used to come here to the house with Johnny when they went to school together. Stupid, he was—really stupid.

CAROLINE COON: Sid seemed open but very vulnerable. Having come from a sadomasochist childhood myself and being suicidal for a great deal of my adolescence, it moved me. Having been involved with young people who were self-destructive because of their bravery and inability to confront the adults who were manipulating them, I could see something in Sid. If you're not allowed to express what's really paining you, if you're left hanging in limbo with your vulnerability and pain, you're going to be self-destructive.

Clothes were always important, even if Johnny wore them differently. For instance, he had long hair, even when the schoolteachers were strictly against it. They were like typical sergeant majors, they thought you should do everything they told you to. When Johnny was young, he wore a uniform—a blazer—to Catholic school. That didn't go down too well with him. So years later, when he'd become famous, me and the wife went out and bought him a lovely dress suit, including a shirt with lace. He said, "Mom and Dad, that's beautiful."

He went upstairs to put it on. An hour later he came down and he'd cut it to bits and pinned it together. We spent a fortune on this dress suit and he'd cut the sleeves right off! The shirt was all torn to rags. Johnny looked like a scarecrow. He asked, "How does it look, Dad? Do I look nice?"

If there was a hole in the floor, I'd have jumped in.

ZANDRA RHODES: The punk movement—with all its tears and safety pins—was a creative movement that started from the street, in the sense that actual youth were being creative with something that was within their price structure. The people who were so-called punk obviously weren't going into elegance; they went into a totally different direction.

John was always making something different out of his clothes. If he had a pullover sweater, he'd cut one sleeve off. A brand-new dress suit with lace on the shirt, torn to bits! If the dog had been chewing it for a week, it wouldn't have looked as bad!

I consider myself working class. We're lazy, good-for-nothing bastards, absolute cop-outs. We never accept responsibility for our own lives, and that's why we'll always be downtrodden. We seem to enjoy it in a perverse kind of way. As working class, we like to be told what to do, led like sheep to the slaughter. I loathe the British public school system with a passion. How dare anybody have the right to a better education than me just because their parents have money! I find that vile. They talk this sense of superiority, and they do have it. The upper classes have all the right connections once they leave school, and they parasite off the population as their friends help them along. You never see that with the working class. If you have any kind of success being working class, your next-door neighbors or your best friends will turn around and hate you instantly. "You're not working class anymore." Being successful or good at anything demotes or promotes you out of that class bracket.

That used to worry me when I was a young boy. "Oh, my God, I'll be classless. I'm doomed." I couldn't give a toss now. I regard myself as working class, but I know damn well working class doesn't regard me that way. That's just the way it is. It was always that way in school. If you managed to read a book and knew what it meant, then you were a snob, a poof, or a sissy. Fine, I accept all those labels. A bit of intelligence was a lot more useful than just being a beer monster and manipulated all your life.

Music was a big thing at age fourteen. I started buying records. That would be my most fun, not actually going out anywhere, but just sitting indoors playing my records to myself. I really got off on that. I'd never had any inclination to become a musician. I still don't. I'm glad I'm not. I'm a noise structuralist. If I can remember how to make the same noise twice, then that is my music. I don't think you need the rest of the fiddly nonsense unless you're in a classical orchestra. Instant pop with access to cheap emotions. The basics. I eventually began listening to classical music much later when I was in a better frame of mind. But never as a child.

It would be terrible times when the school would take us to Fairfield Hall. We'd have to listen to these dismal orchestras hour after hour. There would be loads of other schools there, so there would invariably be school warfare and rivalry, absolute murder to control. Hilarious. Five hundred kids battling the hell out of each other to the tune of an orchestra playing away on the "William Tell Overture."

Dud-dud-dunt. Dud-dud-dunt. Dud-dud-dunt-dunt-dunt.

Bang! Crash! Boom!

I certainly didn't acquire my love of music from school days. The music lessons in Catholic school were farcical. It was so soppy. We'd play *Swan Lake* or something cruddy like that. Then they would give us these little triangles. We were thirteen years old and made to feel thoroughly ridiculous! This is how backward Catholic schools are. Of course, there wouldn't be enough triangles. There would only be six in a class of forty kids, so six triangles would do the rounds. We had plastic flutes, but there were only two flutes. You were expected to buy your own, but no one could afford them. The whole thing ended up nowhere. Then they would try to get us into the choirs. The plan was to sing as badly as possible so that you would never be put in one of those girl dresses and made to sing in church. That's all they were doing, it seemed, recruiting for the priesthood. You had to be real clever to keep out of that.

Maybe schools are a little different now. They never used to encourage discussion. It was absolutely rigorous—just read and form your own opinion, and they couldn't give a damn what that opinion was. They gave kids no guidelines, so the old-fashioned way of teaching proved quite aimless—too much belligerence and animosity from the teaching establishment. They're there to humiliate you and browbeat you. Believe it or not, there's people who are trying to bring that back into the schools again, to restore law and order to future societies!

Catholic schools in Britain were very ghetto-like. They had to be because they are not state run, which means they're independently financed, apparently. With forty in a class it was near impossible to keep any kind of organization or discipline. But it's not so much the discipline that's necessary—it's to make the education process interesting, and they didn't do that. Catholic schools resorted to authoritative measures, which is "Shut up! Be seen, not heard." That's where things went wrong. That's when little tykes like me become quite nasty. We can see the weaknesses in that system and know how to use them when authority shows weakness; anything that is rigid and doesn't bend with the breeze will snap sooner or later.

Back when I was away from school in hospital for a year with meningitis, I felt like a complete stranger when I returned. I had to work hard to catch up with the schoolwork. Once I did catch up, I took another path. It wasn't a matter of being better than anyone else or any of that, I just went my own way. All of my friends were people who went their own way. I don't have many friends, but the few I still have are well worth keeping because of just that. Highly individualistic. Unable to fit cozily into systems.

I like crazy people, especially those who don't see the risk.

School was just like prison. They try to use the bullies to keep the masses down. All you have to do is find a way to bribe the bully into a better way of life. That's what we did. Just roped them in with us. You tell them what you're doing and why you're doing it. That's very appealing to a bully. They don't like the system any more than anyone else. If you show them by the efforts of your work that you're cracking it at the seams, they like the deviousness of it. Maybe I was lucky. We had good bullies. I wasn't tough. I was an absolute weed. I got away from getting picked on by just being clever.

The whole idea of my having to say "sir" or "Your Majesty" to someone self-appointed offended me. I've always hated the word *sir*. It got to me when I had to call the teachers "sir" or "miss." Sir implies subservience, and I disagreed with that notion. I don't understand why education should imply subservience. Sure, you can respect a teacher for having more knowledge than you. The idea is to drain them of that and improve yourself, not that you're a lesser human being. That's what the word *teacher* implies. At the time my friends thought I was being stupid. "So what, everybody does it." Nonsense.

The haircut that got me thrown out of Sir William of York.

I never thought I would ever become a performer when I was a kid—except at school, when we had drama class once for a year. They used to have a drama class at William of York I liked only because the teacher was stunningly gorgeous. Things like that didn't happen at our secondary school. Our teacher was Sally. Long black luxurious hair, long blond thighs in a miniskirt. Hmmm. I could get into this acting lark. The idea you could put on a persona and be completely different seemed really good fun. She wanted us to go to late night drama classes at the universities and attend meetings, but that's when I lost interest. That was no place for working-class people like me. Acting and drama seemed confined by four tight walls, judged more by who you know and not what talent you had. The idea of passing exams to be an actor struck me as absurd.

Looking back, I guess I had a progressive family. But it certainly didn't feel like it at the time. They had not done any harm with excess parental baggage. A lot of it was my mother. "Leave 'im alone. He'll work it out." It was commonsense Irish. I've seen some "noncommonsense" Irish people who were absolutely vile to their children. You know, the Holy Joes. They open the religious cupboard every time they think you're doing wrong and make you light a candle and kiss all those statues.

I got caught jerking off as a kid at home. Actually, my younger brother Martin told my mum. I forgot to lock the toilet door. He yelled, "Mom! Dad! John's sitting the wrong way on the toilet and doing something funny." It was horrible! God, the embarrassment! They never said anything about it. They just let it go and told Martin to shut up. He was very young at the time. You can imagine me and the "Father Knows Best" approach, an American TV sitcom of the late fifties. Robert Young sits you down as Mother with the apron stands behind the sofa. In that respect, I must admit I never had a tortured childhood. It wasn't a middle-class guilt thing that happened with families where they try to make their children feel humiliated over what are really perfectly normal functions.

I didn't get birched that much when I misbehaved—not so much as my younger brother Jimmy. He was a real piece of work. I was much more quiet, very subdued. I didn't do much that could be conceived as wrong or right. At Christmas parties I would always be sitting in the darkest corner in the room. My brother Jimmy would get up and do his soldier dance for all the relatives and their applause. It's funny that I ended up being the one doing the soldier dance on stage later on.

And yet I was thrown out of Catholic school at fifteen for having a disruptive attitude. I was a constant, total pain-antagonist. I would stare.

They hated me. No thought went into it, just pure fun on my part. They translated it into my being a future psychotic mass murderer or whatever. If they'd sent me to a psychologist, I would have failed dismally. I would have been found out as a fake, and that wouldn't have appealed to me at all. My schoolwork was faultless, but it came with all this other stuff that they could not handle. That was the most annoying thing for them. One day I turned up late to class, walked in, sat down, and proceeded to read whatever I wanted. That was it for the teacher. He saw me as some anti-Catholic git and kicked me out of class. Mr. Prentiss. I called him Piss Stains because he used to wear this awful dogtooth suit. There was this piss stain on the crotch, deep yellow and ironed in. Pissy Prentiss. I found out a year later he'd died, and I went and pissed on his grave.

After Piss Stains threw me out, I walked out, went home, and told my parents—eventually. "School's out forever." Alice Cooper reference.

They went to see the headmaster, and he said they couldn't have me back in school under any circumstances. "John causes too much trouble. We don't like the way he dresses. Look at his long hair, shabby clothes." I did not wear the Catholic school uniform, which was absolutely sinful for them. It had nothing to do with fashion. Fashion was just as bad as the school uniform in that respect. I didn't have the money to buy a uniform, thank you very much. These are poor people you're dealing with, Mr. Headmaster.

RAMBO: John had long hair, and he used to wear a bovver hat. Then the next day I'd see him and he had blue hair. He started changing his image, and back in those days that was really different, really weird. To have blue hair, you would have had to have a lot of front, especially in Finsbury Park. I was in a chip shop one day and I saw John walking past. There were three other geezers coating him off and taking the piss out of him. He stood his ground. John hit one of them, so I ran out of the chip shop. We both steamed into them. We both done 'em. We done two of them bad, and one ran off. John was little and slim. He had a row, and he might have looked a bit weird, but he stood his ground.

In England, if you are still underage, you have to carry on schooling until you're sixteen. I had to do another year. The Catholics didn't want me anymore, and that put me in the hands of the state. The Catholics couldn't throw me out for being stupid, because I wasn't. I had to go to what they called special schools. Hackney and Stoke Newington College of Further Education.

The school, William of York, took us on a geographical expedition to Box Hill. Two weeks out in the wilderness of Guildford. We were supposed to be learning how to use compasses and become jolly good at geography. I'll tell you what I learned with John Gray and Dave Crowe—we learned how to find the pubs. They foolishly left them on the maps as landmarks. Splendid, and they served us, too. It was the color of our money that the barmen were interested in. Besides, they're mostly country bumpkins out there. They start early with the booze.

There would be terrible times, too, especially with some of the physical education teachers. They'd lurk around while you were taking a shower or insist on handing you your towel only if you raised your arms to make sure you washed underneath your armpits. Stuff like that I found extremely suspect. It's funny, the macho boys didn't seem to mind, while I found it thoroughly offensive. The bully boys, the leaders, what they call jocks in America. It was no doubt shyness on my part, but there was more to it than that. I've never trusted that macho, muscle-bound thing anyway. I've always seen that lifestyle as suspect. Some of the teachers were definitely into fondling kids. But they weren't going to fondle me.

I was practically unlovable most of my early life. I wouldn't even let my parents go near me. From a very early age I've always felt, "Get off, don't touch me, leave me alone—I fondle myself."

I never screamed as a youngster. That shocked my mother when she first heard the Sex Pistols. She'd never seen that side of me. I was a stone-quiet child. She probably thought that she'd raised a lunatic, and I proved her right. I've always maintained a certain isolation. I feel safer when people aren't trying to grab me. It's different with my wife Nora, but even that took a long time. Basic sex I could handle, two minutes and fifty seconds of something is not quite the same as people, loved ones, trying to get inside your head. While it's gotten better in recent years, I feel that isolation is a cover-up of feelings of inadequacy inside my own self. I never thought highly of myself right from day one. Had I not had my family, I probably would have turned into something psychopathic and asocial. But I've learned along the way, as indeed you must.

The good side of me is that I do learn from other people. I watch people all the time. When they're doing something right, I want to know why, why aren't I doing that?

About the time I worked at the play centers looking after the kids we were into vampire hunting. Dave Crowe was deadly curious about all the reports on TV and books about vampires in Highgate Cemetery. John Gray didn't believe it. Of course there was me, I'd read too much, so I was well spooked. The fascination was there. To this day I enjoy a really good horror movie. I love being frightened.

During that summer period, when we were about sixteen or seventeen and I was going to school in Hackney, we'd break into the crypts where the bodies were on shelves, open up the coffins, and have a look. We'd see which bodies hadn't deteriorated. Was this vampire thing real? So many people were doing it, it was almost like a social club down there. You'd meet so many people, loonies mostly, running around with wooden stakes, crucifixes, and cloves of garlic. We'd get bored with that; there'd be a pub at the top of the road, and we'd drink a bit, then go back into the crypts later that night. I had money because I worked for my father. I was well stacked, so we could do these crazy, stupid things. At the time, it was highly unusual for kids to leave their districts and go off into the far reaches of London and dance at nightclubs or vampire hunt. People were still village oriented and rarely traveled to other regions because you could tell they were outsiders by the way they walked, talked, or dressed, and that usually led to confrontation. We were quite lucky in light of how weird we would dress. Maybe it was because we weren't a gang who dressed alike. Each one of us looked and acted completely different. People considered us nutters and left us alone.

I was pleased to go to the state school. What an adventure at last! The sheer freedom of it! You wear what you want, you could be what you are. There was no pressure to conform all the time. I liked the sheer variety of people, including the huge Jamaican contingent in the school. It was marvelous because I really loved reggae, and the dances were fucking brilliant. Me and my bloody long hair reggae-ing out, mon! There were social activities that made me want to hang around. It got my brain working without using stupid, childish ways of antagonizing teachers. I enjoyed that part of school. That's where I took up all my exams. It was around the time of the 0 levels. I passed everything I sat down to take halfway through the year at state school. It was easy.

STEVE JONES: I knew Paul Cook when we both went to Christopher Wren School on Blue Fontaine Avenue in White City Estate, Shepherd's Bush. Before that he used to go to a different school, but we used to pass each other all the time. Then we became skinheads when that movement first started. It was great—soccer matches, dressing up, and looking better than the other guy. I stole all my clothes, so I always had a good wardrobe. I was a good thief, and I had a knack for going into the shops and taking stuff. After the soccer matches you could loot stores. That's what I enjoyed—total chaos and anarchy. Football hooliganism was a great outlet if you're a frustrated kid. I wouldn't call myself a tough guy, but I was definitely a street person. I wouldn't stay home, so at fifteen I was left to fendfor myself. We would hang around at the Shepherd's Bush market. We supported Queen's Park Rangers, Chelsea, Fulham, but it wasn't as much the game as it was the whole scene. We didn't really watch the matches. We just walked around the grounds trying to look good.

At state school, my mates and I were starting our prepunk look, which is really what Malcolm McLaren and the others picked up on later. They couldn't relate it to anything. I think that's what got them interested.

State school is where I met Sid.

Sid was an absolute wanker. We became friends a couple of weeks after I entered state school. I called him Sid, after my pet, the softest, furriest, weediest thing on earth, this soppy white hamster that used to live in a cage on the corner table in my parents' living room. One day Sid the hamster was going around on this wheel inside his cage, and my mother took him out and cuddled him up to her. My father walked into the room and thought it was a rat at first. As she put Sid into his hand, the hamster took a bite out of my father's hand. He flung it across the floor. We dubbed Sid the hamster "Vicious" after that.

Sid's real name was Simon Ritchie or John Beverly; even he wasn't sure which. It all depended on his mother's whim at the time. She was just a hippie mother. Sid was an absolutely goofy kid with a Dave Bowie hairdo, dyed red at the top. His father apparently was a grenadier guard or some sort. How funny. If the queen only knew who her soldier's offspring were. Sid was brought up for a few years at Ibiza, off the coast of Spain. That fascinated me because I had no concept of exotic foreign islands. They lived near the state school in Hackney. They were poor and would be moved by the council from place to place practically on a weekly basis. Sid and I took the same classes.

He would always find a way to laugh at things—except at himself, of course. Everything else was a joke to him. That amused me because I was quite somber at times. I picked up on that.

"This is useful humor. I can use this."

Sid was an absolute fashion victim—the worst I'd ever known. It was appalling. Everything about him was wrong. He'd buy these ridiculous *Vogue* magazines to study them and copy people. It was just terrible. He'd get it wrong so badly. He couldn't quite grasp that the idea wasn't to follow, it was to lead. I found that very funny. He used to annoy people so much because he'd take it all so seriously. He'd

wear nail gloss and think of himself as being very dainty. He was a gangly, awkward git. Trying to dress effeminate was wrong, wrong, wrong.
He'd wear sandals in the snow with no socks when he wanted to show
off his toenail varnish. It was a Dave Bowie thing. After I ribbed him
too much about that, he went out and got a Marc Bolan perm. That
made him look like an old woman. He was very pimply and ugly—yet
thought of himself as being stunningly beautiful. He wanted to be a
model. Yes, Sid did some modeling at St. Martin's College in London.
The art class needed someone to stand in the corner. It was perfect. It
gave him an excuse to go home, hang upside down in the oven to get
his hair to stand up like Bowie's, and pose in the latest clobber he'd
bought. Complete fashion victim. Nothing he wore ever really suited
him. It was as if the clothes wore him.

JOHN GRAY: We spent a lot of time round Sid's flat, sometimes crashing
out. We'd listen to music. Sid was also a mad Bowie fan, obsessed with
David Bowie beyond all reason. In those days Sid wasn't particularly
interested in drinking. Not the way we were. That came later on.

Once Sid was boiling an old-fashioned metal syringe in a saucepan
of water. He was sterilizing it and then injecting speed and amphetamine sulfate. I was quite horrified. I asked him where he got it from,
and he said, "It's me mum's."

Sid would often stay over at our house. My mum thought he was a bit
retarded. He would strike you that way. It would be midwinter and bitter cold outside. He wouldn't wear a jacket because he would buy this
new shirt or something. He had to be seen in this shirt. He would be
frozen stiff at the door, shivering. "Is-s-s-s J-J-J-John in?" I got my first
nasty hangover after Sid and I mixed up a punch bowl of Southern
Comfort, Cinzano Bianco, and Martini Rosso and drank it in a rush. I've
never touched any of those drinks since.

My mum never met Sid's mother. She was always cooking something
weird like deviled kidneys. My family was the baked beans and boiled
bacon brigade. Her kind of cooking struck me as really bizarre. I was
horrified that someone would cook something so vile, plunk a plate of
it in front of me, and then eat it. Oh, please! Sid's mum was an oddball
hippie. "Oh, hello, Sid," she said when we came by their flat. "I've just
cooked a quiche." I didn't know what a quiche was. It sounded like
she'd just tie-dyed a T-shirt.

Musically I was into Alice Cooper and Hawkwind at the time. T. Rex
gets in there, too. Bits of Bowie, but not too much. I didn't find his stuff

very interesting. Never Yes or any of that stuff. That was too arty, distant and remote, all about 6/4 masturbation.

When we were sixteen there were a few girls. Our look would attract girls, but not to any great extent. I was the moonstruck one. I used to follow one girl around and carry her books like a real toe-rag. Her name was Sylvia Hartland. When I think about her, it's absolutely humiliating. I was so totally subservient, and she was upper class. That's what really struck me as being odd about it. I really hated people with that accent. "Oooh, yaww." But I found her absolutely enthralling, much like a Barbara Cartland novel. Now that I look back on it, it brings tears to my eyes, it's so corny and sappy.

I never really had much of an interest in girls until I went to the state school because we were mixed. Then things blossomed. I thought it was brilliant. I don't understand to this day why they have same-sex schools. It doesn't make sense. It's a much better environment with girls in the class. You learn a lot more, as diversity makes things more interesting. There's much more to look at, it's not just mindless. And if there were naughty girls there, it was worth turning up on time.

It's around seventeen that I believe you begin to form a definite attitude on sex. It was that way with me, except then I really hadn't worked it all out until about twenty-one. And I thought, Right! Now I know. Done this, I'd done that. Didn't like this. Didn't like that. Now I know what I want.

When you're sixteen, you think you know it all. Now you know you didn't. Anybody who looks back on their earlier years will blush. You can become so arrogant at that time that it's the necessary part of growing up. Being in the Pistols didn't fuel that arrogance for me. The circumstances were a bit different because there was so much stop and start and squabbling. It wasn't easy to be an arrogant rock 'n' roller when we were struggling and things were so unstable. The Pistols were the exact opposite of arrogant. We weren't arrogant, nihilistic, asexual—none of those things that people associate with us.

For a kid, sex can be messy, horrible, embarrassing, and third-rate. "See you later," as you run off into the bushes with a smirk on your face. Then you wake up the next morning—Oh, my God, I hope I didn't catch anything. Why is life like that? Why is there always that guilt or fear thing at the end of sex with strangers? I could never give you a catalog of who I shagged. It really wouldn't amount to very much. Before the Pistols it didn't happen that much. Sex didn't interest me when I was young. You can call me a retard or a late developer, but that's the truth. Sex is something you can't or don't want to avoid. You always want it to be the ulti-

Johnny goes to college. Me during my Hawkwind phase.

mate conclusion to something, but it never gives you quite what you want—ever, no matter what you do. It's not the end-all. It's not the teenage dream all these pop songs make it out to be.

My father was appalled with some of the girls I would bring home. I suppose that kind of pride is in every father. But there were never any restrictions on me and my brothers in our house. We could bring in girls and stay the night anytime when I was seventeen or eighteen. There was never any pressure about that. We were typically open about it. I know very few who had that kind of openness with their parents. I think it's healthy because you tend not to go out with any old trollop anywhere you can. You can be selective, and you have a good place to go to. You're not going to bugger up a good thing. I used to bring over a lot of my outrageous friends. There was a hairy Irish chap who was a bit of a drag queen. I liked him because he was really funny. He had a thick Irish accent. I took him over to the house one day and introduced him as my mate. I thought it was hilarious that my old man didn't explode. He didn't seem to care. They just talked about Ireland. It was so funny. My father's much more open than he lets on. The bark is worse than the bite.

RAMBO: In the seventies, the football violence wasn't so organized. It was mass violence. Thousands against thousands. Two or three thousand against two or three thousand kids fighting. We very rarely got mentioned in the newspapers. Football in the seventies was like mass brawls.

In 1971 Arsenal won the league championship on Tottenham Hotspurs' ground. We tore the place apart. Arsenal took over the whole ground and outside as well. There were as many outside as there were inside. Some started wearing white butchers coats with the name of the team written down the side. We'd meet at the George Robey. There were three or four thousand kids walking four or five miles to the match. We rode up to the match on the back of a lorry from Finsbury Park to Tottenham. Jimmy and Johnny Lydon came along with me. We were all singing:

> Hi-Ho, Hi-Ho,
> We are the Arsenal Boys,
> Hi-Ho, Hi-Ho,
> We are the Arsenal Boys,
> And if you are a Tottenham fan,
> Surrender or you'll die,
> We will follow the Arsenal!

After I passed my O levels, I got into a row with my father and was thrown out of my house because of my long hair, which came way down to the middle of my back. It was the most annoying thing I could do at the time. The old man insisted I go get it cut, so I thought long and hard and did exactly that. I had it cropped and dyed bright green, a very savage thing to do in those days. It was green dye that wasn't used for hair, I think it was clothes dye. Lo and behold, I looked like a cabbage. I walked in and that was it.

"Get the fuck out of my house, and take that fucking cabbage on your head with ya!"

I went to Sid's place. He had a squat at that time.

Sid and I even went on to college to study A levels up at the north part of King's Cross in High Holborn. There we met Wobble, who later formed PiL with me. However, we never went to any of the lessons. Didn't have to. There was no such thing as report cards. It wasn't about that. It was there if you wanted to improve your life. If you didn't, they couldn't give a shit about you. It was sort of a progressive school. The foreign exchange students paid to get in, but I got in because I was brought up in England. I studied English literature and art, I liked poetry and the writings of Ted Hughes. We were supposed to study Keats, but I found him too tweedy for my liking. That's when I got into Oscar Wilde. I thought his stuff was fucking brilliant. What an attitude to life! I preferred his letters to his actual works. *The Importance of Being Earnest* was good stuff, but his comments were what impressed me. Here was a man ruined by his mother, so his whole life was a kind of vengeance against her. He turned out to be the biggest poof on earth at a time when that was *completely* unacceptable. What a genius. No Rimbaud or Baudelaire for me. It read like poncey shit, and it didn't fool me for one second. But Oscar Wilde, there was a writer.

During the A level days at King's Cross, we practically never went to class. Sid never turned up at all. I hung around mostly with Wobble at the time. We spent most of our days at the pub nearby. I made a lot of money working on the building sites with my father and didn't mind having a drinking partner. I learned most of my studies with the teachers in the pub. I would sit with the them in the pub during lunch break. Sometimes they wouldn't go to class, either.

It was the first total looseness I had ever seen in school. When the teachers got a bit inebriated in the pub, they tipped me off on the ins and outs of the subjects and topics. We talked about Shakespeare. Reading Shakespeare, I found his characters vivid. They thought very differently back then—far more emotional and less on the logical, thinking side. I loved *Macbeth*—a gorgeous piece of nastiness. The characters did what they felt, not exclusively because they were evil, but because they didn't have the inclination to behave any other way. They just fitted in with the times. Plus it was much easier to use murder as a solution then.

As a teenager, I found the language of Shakespeare a little difficult until it was properly explained. I actually got an inkling of it at William of York with Mr. Prentiss. He explained that, although slightly buttered up, that was the way people talked then. Once I got into the poetic beat of it, I began to understand the gist of Shakespeare. At Kingsway College, they explained to me that it would lose its point and purpose to modernize the prose. It's the same logic as to why you can't live out a seventies punk rock environment today in the nineties. It's not valid now, and it doesn't connect with anything around it. You had to get into the dream of it—a vision complete unto itself.

I much preferred barroom discourse with teachers to sitting in the class having to work it all out for myself. The teachers' opinions gave me something to grasp. That's why I like to talk so much. That's how I learn. You can get other people to open up. You learn far more through discussion than any other way.

At about age sixteen, I was out squatting with Sid, and he started selling speed. We'd live off of that. It was a very cheap life-style. There was nowhere we wanted to go, we just wanted to be up all the time, that's all. After leaving home—me with green hair—Sid and I started squatting in more abandoned buildings. We never bothered to go back to college in King's Cross, either. Once I'd moved in with Sid—fuck it—school was too far to travel. It became too boring to get up in the morning. Why bother? There were a lot of Teddy boys in our building because at that time there was a rock 'n' roll revivalist movement going on that I found loathsome. Here were sixteen-year-old kids into Buddy Holly and Elvis Presley. I thought it was an absolute disgrace. You shouldn't be propping up somebody's grandad as a hero. They weren't making any life of their own. They were living in somebody else's fucking nightmare.

The law clearly stated back then that if the premises were unoccupied and you could gain access, then you had rights to stay there. Considering my background in burglary as a boy, it was easy access. I'm in! Here's Johnny! Now it's fashionable to squat in old buildings again and not pay rent. It had definite tinges of hippiedom. Unfortunately, lack of money forced me into such a position. In England, squatting has now turned into a profession again. It's an absolute way of life rather than a way of getting from A to B.

We ended up sharing this squat in, of all places, Hampstead, which is an upwardly middle-class posh area surrounded by millionaires. Sid found the building. He knew someone from the college who got him in. It was funny, some of the people who lived there. They were insane, totally screwed out of their brains on drugs from the hippie days, which is where my contempt of hippies comes from. These people were caricatures with their silly scarves thrown over milk crates to make things look ever so nice. The smell of joss sticks. They all sat on cushions on the floor.

JOHN GRAY: I wasn't into living rough in some squat, and I certainly wouldn't have lived with Wobble, Sid, and Mad Jane. She was one of Sid's early girlfriends, and I was quite friendly with her as well. Sid would strangle cats and slash himself with an old Heinz baked beans tin lid.

Ironically the building was very much like what I'd been brought up in during the early days, a Victorian slum dwelling. They'd become illegal for people to live in officially. So in went the squatters because the council didn't bother to pull the place down. No electricity. There was plumbing, but no hot water. By this time my school days had petered out. What was the point? It cost money to travel. Actually, that's not strictly true. Few of us in those days ever paid anything to travel on the subways. It was easy to jump over the fences and turnstiles. I don't know how the tube system in London ever managed to keep running. I never knew anyone who ever paid or bought a ticket—outside of American tourists.

I did have some money left at the time. Before the winter we became squatters, I worked on building sites during the summer. My dad got me the job at twenty-five pounds a day-a lot of money, so I was rolling in it. I had a lot of money building a sewage farm in Guildford. I hope the people in Guildford are thankful. Johnny built your sewer!

I worked with the site engineers and learned a lot taking measurements and surveying. I loved that. Fascinating stuff. There I was, green hair and all. Laborers don't give a damn, particularly the Irish. It's your fucking life, that was their attitude. If you can wield a shovel as good as anybody else, that's fine.

I wouldn't have minded being a teacher. After dropping out of college, I landed a job working at the play centers near where I lived in Finsbury Park. I had friends working there, and they recommended me. It was definitely a heady, fantasy job. You knew you were doing it for all the right reasons. Easy sainthood, but they paid so badly. I worked at the play center, looking after five-year-olds during the spring break and the summer holidays in England. Just prior to joining the Sex Pistols, I worked there for a couple of months, looking after the kids of people who work all day during the summer. In America they call it day care. The first job they assigned me was with the three-, four-, and five-year-olds. I wasn't very happy in bah-bah-goo-goo land, so they moved me to the woodwork center. I was very good at teaching nine-year-old kids how to build airplanes. I would show them how to cut out wings out of balsa wood. The children were real problem kids from the neighborhood, so I was told not to give them knives because they might start hurting each other. I would have none of that. No kid was going to hurt themselves in my class. I wasn't into bullying the kids, and they hadn't started one fight among each other, which certainly wasn't the norm up until then. The headmaster was Mr. Cutbush. God, how I would have loved to cut his bush off. He was such a nasty fucking git! He walked into the woodwork center, took one look at the kids, and waved me to come over. "This is not on," he whispered emphatically. "These children all have knives."

I explained, "Yes, but nobody is getting hurt. Don't you understand?"

He said there were knife fights in the class before—but not when I was teaching it.

Then came the sack. Actually, it was worse than the sack. They wanted to send me off to an education center where I could learn rounders and go to session groups to be taught what the rules were and how teachers were supposed to conduct themselves. I found it so offensive. Surely if you're dealing with kids, you should be intuitive; otherwise you're not catering to them as individuals. It's just block booking again. I still feel I could have become a teacher if I'd followed through on it. Basically I already was a teacher doing reading, writing, a bit of maps, and a bit of woodwork. I suppose having green hair didn't help, either. Parents were complaining. "He's weird. He might try to fiddle with the kids." They didn't realize; they just didn't get it. That was the very thing the kids focused on. "He's weird, we like him." I wasn't a cane-wielding maniac, into discipline. I found children disciplined themselves if their interests were kept high. Like crime, mischief springs from boredom. When you're overly repressive with kids, then you're breeding perverts of the future.

Back inside our building were the squatters. All around the neighborhood were these wonderful Georgian terraced houses where the upperclass twits lived. The neighbors fucking hated us. The other squatters hated us as well because of the way we looked—short cropped hair and old suits. That's when Sid started to come around to my way of fashion. I gave him his first decent haircut, which was the punk style as it soon became. You'd literally cut chunks of hair out of your head. The idea was to not have any shape to your hairdo—just have it fucked up. That was the beginning of it all.

Sid and I used to mess around with cigarette burns. It was mostly me. I don't know what prompted it. Insecurity. I got it from a Michael Caine movie. They were torturing him with cigarettes. I thought, That doesn't look too painful. I can handle that. It isn't really, except it's a bit bad when you burst a vein because it does spout. There's scars all up and down my arm. I stopped when I got up to the tops of my arms by my shoulder. Forget it, there's a lot of muscle tissue around there. Really stupid stuff. I think it was a badge of self-pity more than anything. I wasn't looking for attention. There were much better ways than that to get attention.

I used to jam in the subway stations with Sid on acoustic guitar and me on violin singing Alice Cooper's "I Love the Dead." We would sing the same song over and over, hour after hour. Sid couldn't play guitar and I couldn't play violin, but we had the most fun. We used to do loads of things like that together. Busking was a big thing at the time, but it was always these naff hippies with their acoustic guitars singing Donovan songs. People would throw us the occasional two shillings just to make us shut up. "Yes, yes, we've heard enough. Do you have another song? The train is late and you've played this for a half an hour upward! I think I'm going to kill you." The other song we sang was "I Don't Love the Dead." Another favorite of ours was "I Left My Heart in San Francisco," sung as "I Left My Heart in Some Crummy Disco." Those were the only words in the whole song.

It's funny. I read recently about some disco git in England who theorized that punk actually began in the discotheques. There was, he wrote, a club called the Lacey Lady in Ilford, and he recalled seeing punks there who danced to all the disco records. He remembers it well. Johnny Rotten stole it all from them! Ha! Those punks happened to be me and my mates. Sid, Wobble, John Gray, Dave Crowe, and Tony Purcell—a right motley crew. We used to go down to the Lacey Lady every weekend because we knew someone who lived nearby.

JOHN GRAY: We'd go to the Lacey Lady and dance like lunatics. Although we were into all of this rock stuff, we were also into the Black Byrds with Donald Byrd, the Ohio Players, and other soul/dance groups. Most of the patrons would shuffle around the bar, drinking vodka and orange juice, but we'd go wild, dancing in the middle of the floor. We'd have spiky hair, dressed in ordinary jeans, with ties around our legs, baseball boots, and silly T-shirts. We must have looked bizarre. The deejay still talks about us, he remembers John and me. We thought it was strange that people formed a circle around us and watched us dance. Sometimes we'd stay all night at Tony's, though it was uncomfortable sleeping on the floor. Usually we'd catch the all-night train. Once we'd done that club and explored it, we started going to reggae sound systems and black clubs.

We enjoyed going to gay clubs because you could be yourself, nobody bothered you, and nobody hit on you, unless that's what you wanted. There were always loads of girls in those places. Always. They were there for the same reason we were, to avoid the boot boy harassment. Besides, pubs were no places for girls because they would be seen as tarts. In pubs, men always outnumbered the girls ten to one, so they'd become victims very quickly.

The gay clubs always had the best records. The House thing and the Rave thing comes from that scene. Extreme twelve-inch mixes that weren't available in the shops. It was an underground club thing. You'd find the addresses of these record stores that didn't sell to everybody. Same thing with reggae in Finsbury Park. I went out of my way to make sure I always had the best records because I put a lot of interest into it. Most kids were probably buying Tamla/Motown, which was something I never liked. I took immaculate care of all my records.

If Bowie was important, he was important to Sid. I didn't quite get it. Sid thought he was God. What was odd was that all the football hooligans would be deeply into Bowie. Bowie did bring all different sorts together. A Bowie concert would be quite an event. All walks of life were there. You'd have to go because the social aspect of it all was phenomenal. In London, I don't think people took David Bowie's gay thing seriously. It didn't mean anything at all. He was very clever at it. But of course he had many years to practice his art. That's what's so unfair about the way punk was judged. We were judged in the same light as those who had been learning their craft for ten years. We weren't given any breaks for being young.

As I recall my old mates, it reminds me how much people change, as they should do. John Gray is a teacher now. Dave Crowe's a teacher as well. Wobble has since become a serious bass player and bandleader.

Tony Purcell became an accountant. There were a few others in our mob. I don't know where they ended up. Some are in jail, I suppose, because a few of them were quite violent. We used to terrify a lot of the regular boot boys when they'd see a mob like us. We looked like nothing anyone had ever seen. They couldn't relate us to anything. They seemed miffed that we'd quite easily defend ourselves and more. That left impressions. When you stand up for yourself, you get some kind of respect. If punks hadn't stood up for themselves initially, they wouldn't have gone very far. Punk would have been just another prissy affectation.

Those ten, twenty guys—that's definitely where the whole punk thing germinated. We had nothing to do with Malcolm McLaren or the other Pistols then. We were quite well formed and organized on our own long before they came onto the scene—and a long time before I joined the band. This is what the Sex Pistols bought when they got me, the whole image. It came lock, stock, and both barrels.

"I WANT YOU TO KNOW THAT I HATE YOU, BABY"

Destiny. Do you really believe in destiny? Things happen because you make them happen. There's no such thing as destiny or fate or any of that. Everything seemed impossible to the Sex Pistols—even gaining an audience. During our heyday, it was the arty-farty lot—the socialites and trendies—who would come to the gigs. I especially liked the working-class bit creeping in. That didn't appeal much to Malcolm McLaren and his friends because they were pushed to the back of the hall very quickly. Those were chaotic days. The only real violence we would get would never be from our audiences, it would be from outsiders—usually the men wearing blue uniforms. The regular boot boys—football hooligans—never needed victims. They were vicious gangs of drunkards that roamed the streets looking for anything to prey on, as long as there were fifteen of them and one of you. The skinheads were fizzling out in 1976. Skinhead gangs were fighting too much among themselves to be much bothered by anything else. There were rightist skinhead gangs and very left-wing extremist skinheads. The whole thing became more of a fashion thing as the real skinhead movement had come and gone a long time before—between 1966 and 1969. They evolved out of the mod thing with their very sharp, neat style of dress. When it was rejuvenated in the seventies, it was completely different. It was no different from the punk imitators who grabbed on to the idea of one steady uniform being rigidly adored. I've always hated the idea of a uniform. If you have any kind of a movement at all, you should reject things like that. You're not moving, plus it's sterile.

Malcolm owned a shop that sold rubber wear and bondage gear, which, of course, was highly appealing to any teenager who wanted to be decadent. Lovely stuff, skintight rubber T-shirts. Malcolm's shop sold it all. I got a great one there; it was a skintight, turtleneck, long-sleeved rubber sweater. I hacked up the neck with a razor so it was torn and shredded. Then I cut out the nipples. That was excellent, definitely offensive.

Malcolm seized the moment. He watched it all unfold because he ran the shop and was already selling this stuff, if only to perverts on King's Road. The shop was called Sex at the time. Later he found a way of manipulating it with Sex Pistol T-shirts, which took off rather well for him. T-shirts with two cowboys with their pants down, their knobs almost touching. Others of young boys totally nude. Cambridge rapist T-shirts. Vile imagery, but it worked. I could understand what he was doing. Most of that had a lot to do with Vivienne Westwood. Malcolm took a lot of the praise, but I think she did most of the designs.

BOB GRUEN: When I went to the Sex store, Malcolm was selling pants with belts on the middle of the legs. He said it was so you could tie your legs together. Who the hell would want to do that? Six months later kids all over England were walking around knock-kneed, with their legs tied together. I thought, Oh, my God, he sold it.

During the pre-Sex days, Malcolm and Vivienne sold sex aids to dull people as well as Teddy Boy gear and the Bowie-esque puffed shoulder blouse tops. They also had fifties' rip-offs like pegged pants and smooth slip-on shoes. It would be the same old cut from the fifties, but their angle would be to make the pants pink instead of black or the shoes gold instead of brown or blue. I would buy from the shop occasionally, but that would only be part of my mix and match. I'd buy clothes everywhere, and it would always deeply annoy Malcolm and Vivienne.

CHRISSIE HYNDE: All the bondage gear wasn't supposed to stimulate you in the sexual sense. It was more of a statement; two fingers up at the Establishment. They would have T-shirts with pictures of rapists wearing rubber masks as if they were reflecting something from the culture back at us. They were extremely anti-Establishment. When the punk kids walked around wearing swastikas and bondage gear, it was their two fingers up at the Establishment. They weren't buying into or in any way associating themselves with nazism or the National Front or sadomasochism. These were teenagers who were just trying to say, "Fuck you!"

When I was seventeen I used to slash up suits and safety-pin them back together. I also used to get the shit beat out of me wearing that kind of stuff on the street. It's difficult to explain, but I always sensed a certain flair of how bums dressed in London. Street urchins, bums, tramps—whatever you want to call them—had a much better way of wearing their clothes. Forgetting the dirt, they looked so stylish to me. They always wore suits or had a peculiar angle to the hats on their heads. I sensed an indescribable jauntiness to it, almost cavalier and reflecting pride in what they were. It's not *Aqua-lung*—more like Aquascutum. Wearing bin liners came from watching the transients in London. I used to love the way they wore bin liners. I thought it was so shiny and neat, much better than leather. Just sew some sleeves on that and you're happening. So I did.

"John, you look like a fucking tramp!" "Yes, Dad! I've got style."

At the time, what we had wasn't a gang as much as a collection of extremely bored people. I suppose we'd come together out of desperation. There was no hope as far as any of us were concerned. That was the common bond. There was no point in looking for a normal job because that would be just too awful. There was no way out. We had no inspiration, musical or nonmusical, until the band started. Before the Pistols, me and the boys used to like to walk up and down King's Road, where people would be buying all of this ridiculous fashion gear. There we would be, these ugly monsters right in the middle of it. That was the place to be, the fashion center of London.

JOHN GRAY: When John and I first stalked the King's Road, we wore jumble sale clothes, not leather jackets or straight-legged trousers. Either they weren't being made or we couldn't afford them. We were coming out of the flared trousers scene, which we felt looked quite ridiculous. So I'd have big loons on; pants that John gave me.

I had no money for clothes, so I'd wear his old gear—black platform boots four inches thick, completely cropped hair, and a
Vivienne Westwood top! We must have looked completely bizarre
and incongruous, but that was right for us because we just made
the best of what we had: something wacky here, something ludicrous there.

Then there was our hair, a mixture of spikes and Ziggy Stardust,
all jelled up and spiked in different colors. We used to buy lots of
Vaseline. Sid used tons of it. You wouldn't dare have him sleep on
your pillow because he'd leave a big grease stain. My hair might
have a pink rinse that turned into a lilac color. It was Crazy Color,
so it never turned out as deep a color as was on the lid.

At first it was just the boys; no girls would go along with this! You
know what girls are like; they want to look pretty—particularly the
English because they want to keep their secretarial jobs or whatever.
Slowly but surely it all came together. The first girls to join in was the
Bromley contingent, Siouxsie and the Banshees and people like that.
They joined in for a more fashionable reason. They were into the Roxy
Music look of sophisticated elegance. Eventually they got bored with
that, so they started to rip their fishnets and wear plastic bin liners.
They got their name because they came from Bromley, a suburb of
south London. After a Pistols concert, they'd invited all of us over to
their house for a party. For me, the party ended up like a discussion
while the rest danced to their silly Bowie records. We discussed how
this whole thing should be approached, and what we should be thinking about. You might call that plotting, I don't agree. We were definitely pointing the direction. A few years later, of course, antifashion
became a fashion unto itself. Then it was time to move on.

CAROLINE COON: The punk movement was the first time that women
    played an equal role as partners in a subcultural group. Up until
    then there were no female equivalents to skinheads or Teddy boys.
    It was even more interesting seeing women standing side by side
    with men in the context of patriarchy. It was a huge step forward.
    For me, one of the most liberating things was the death of the hor-
    rible archetype of this hippie chick sitting at home embroidering.
    Johnny Rotten had his safety pins holding his clothes together! No
    more women's work! Johnny Rotten had ripped clothes, so he was-
    n't going to go home and ask his lover to
    sew up the seams of his clothes.

Early 1976, before safety pins became fashionable and a moth-eaten sweater meant poverty, not popularity. (John Gray)

The punk thing started pretty much nonmusically. Bernie Rhodes spotted me wearing my "I Hate Pink Floyd" T-shirt on King's Road and asked me to come back that night to meet Malcolm, Steve Jones, and Paul Cook in the Roebuck pub on the King's Road. I wasn't going to go alone. I could have gone with Wobble, but I brought John Gray. Fuck this, it sounded like a setup to me. Malcolm asked me if I wanted to be in a band. I thought they must be joking. It seemed very cynical, and that really pissed off Steve. He was a bit thick, and he couldn't make out what I was talking about. He didn't seem to understand me. Paul just sat there grinning all the time, trying to be reasonable. When the pub closed, it was Bernie Rhodes who finally broke in and said, "Well, let's go back to the shop and see if you can mime or sing to a few songs." I could mime fine, but of course I couldn't sing a note. I knew all the words to Alice Cooper's songs, whereas I knew practically none of the records inside Malcolm's jukebox because it was all that awful sixties mod music that I couldn't stand. The only song I could cope with was Alice Cooper's "Eighteen." I just gyrated like a belly dancer. Malcolm thought, Yes, he's the one. Paul thought it was a joke and couldn't have cared less. Steve was really annoyed because he instantly hated me. "I can't work with that fucking cunt! All he does is take the piss and moan!"

STEVE JONES: I first met John in McLaren's shop. He came in with green hair. I thought he had a really interesting face. I liked his look. He had his "I Hate Pink Floyd" T-shirt on, and it was held together with safety pins. John had something special, but when he started talking he was a real asshole—but smart.

I admit I was an asshole when I first met Steve and Paul because I was nervous. They had this situation set up, and I didn't know what they wanted from me. They explained very little. When we sat in the Roebuck, they just stared at me. It was awfully hard to come to grips with.

I understand why Steve thought I was so deeply peculiar. I can be extremely unpleasant with people if I think they're not playing the game fairly with me—and the other Pistols definitely weren't playing fair that night. They were arrogant, smug, and content with their own cozy little group, and they didn't want anything that threatened that. My attitude was, "Fine. I don't need this, either. Fuck off." Steve was antagonistic and annoyed because he and Paul had already formed in their minds what they thought a good band would be. Rod Stewart and the Faces, good-time rock 'n' roll band. I told them that was going nowhere. Too many imitators had already been out there doing that. Anyway, it was dull and it wasn't the music or the attitude I was interested in. "No, I will not mime to 'Maggie May.'" But Steve wouldn't give it up. He was intrigued, even though he couldn't quite work out why I had got to him.

In that respect I was the dumb one because I didn't realize I was getting to him quite that way. I'd love to be able to say, "Oh, yes, this is the way I planned it." But it wasn't that at all. I was deeply confused when I left them that night. It was one of the most bizarre meetings I ever had, and I never wanted to go through that kind of nonsense ever again.

All my friends were extremely different characters. One could be a complete yob, the other could be prissy, but they're all obsessive and committed to their beliefs. That's always been the people I hang around with. You'll always find me where there's lunacy. Most of my friends tended to be named John—Gray, Wardle AKA Wobble, and Ritchie. Glen Matlock couldn't understand why everyone I knew was called John. It just seemed to be a name that was tagged on kids who were destined to become obsessive and individual.

RAMBO: Before Ziggy Stardust, you had *Clockwork Orange*. Everybody used to dress like the *Clockwork Orange* film as well. When *Clockwork Orange* came out, we used to wear white boiler suits. Some wore bowler hats. Practically everybody who supported Arsenal had a white boiler suit. We were already into rows and that, but then the film came out and that became another fashion to follow. When we played Tottenham, everyone supporting Arsenal was *Clockwork Orange*. You'd write things like "Arsenal" or the manager of the team on the side of the boiler suits. We'd wear red scarves in those days. You would carry canes, as far as you could get away with it. But umbrellas were the thing. We had the Arsenal lot from Bethnal Green, who also dressed in the boiler suits. All the Boreham Wood Arsenal had tattoos. Newcastle fans used to come down all dressed up like Alice Cooper with all the black makeup and the Alice Cooper gear on. Man United fans dressed like Dave Bowie.

ZANDRA RHODES: Punk was an antidesign movement. Isn't the movement from punk just an extension of the *Clockwork Orange* film by Stanley Kubrick that came around a bit before that period? It's anti-commercialism, and depending on which side of the chasm you're on, it's either an antidesign movement or a design movement.

RAMBO: Every Sunday night we used to meet up and bunk into the pictures in the West End. Caesar was a specialist in bunking with a coat hanger. He'd get the coat hanger, bend it round, lift the bar up, and get in. Julius saw *Clockwork Orange* around twenty times. I saw it eight or nine times myself. Everybody saw it a couple of times.

Sex Pistols influenced by the characters in the film version of *Clockwork Orange?* Definitely not! Stanley Kubrick's film centered around a gang mentality, not individuality. It was about everyone looking and being the same. The four Johns weren't interested in that. We were more like Pinkie and his gang from Graham Greene's *Brighton Rock*. That's what made that book so riveting for me. His gang was deeply peculiar, extremely different from each other. They weren't a bunch of clones, nor was it ever explained how Pinkie, being as young as he was, could be leading around this bizarre collection of strange, older people. I hung around with people who challenged me continually about everything I stood for. Constant challenge. The *Clockwork Orange* connection to the early punks is too easy. It's an arty analogy and ready-made, but not reality.

STEVE JONES: Everyone claims they had a say in the music. Malcolm didn't have any say in the music. Everyone claims they did. John claims he did everything. But we all played our part, and that's what made the Sex Pistols. Everyone and anyone can say they did everything, but it takes a team to make it happen. I also think it worked because we were all so diverse.

Eventually a rehearsal was set up. I arranged to meet Steve, Paul, and Glen, and none of them turned up—not even a phone call or anything. The next day I rang Malcolm and told him to fuck off. Then they rang me back and begged me for about a week to go back to another rehearsal. Two weeks later I had moved out of Finsbury Park again while they tried to get in contact with me through my father. Next time we met, it was accidentally in a pub, and they apologized. It was actually Malcolm who made all the efforts, while Steve and Paul were still remote. That made the early rehearsals very hard. Finally, out of sheer morbid curiosity, I suppose, I went. At that point I was intrigued, plus it was good for my ego to be asked so persistently. I took the subway in. At the studio it was even more awkward than the first encounter. Steve loathed me. We got together upstairs in a little pub in Chiswick. The barmen were constantly complaining about the noise. There was no soundproofing, just thin cardboardy walls and a stink of stale beer. That first day was hell, it was so embarrassing. There was no proper sound system, and to make a bad job worse, my voice was coming out of a guitar amp. I could not hold a note with my dreary, deadpan voice. I had no concept of a melody, tune, or anything. Even when I played records at home, I never sang along with them. I could never relate to Elvis Presley or the Beatles. Ever. The thought of being a singer had never occurred to me. I had few musical heroes at all, yet the idea of jumping in the deep end and leaving it up to sink or swim in this band intrigued me. So I was really pushing for it. We started to rehearse on a daily basis to see how we would progress after a week. Glen Matlock wanted to give up. Paul did give up and quit; he could see no hope in it at all. But Steve was coming around because I had written lyrics by then. By week's end he said, "C'mon, give him longer than that!" None of them wrote any words, so they thought that was good.

The difficulties arose when they tried to change me into a Bay City Roller sort—being nice and singing these daft old songs, which of course I would not do. But I stuck with it because when I get my teeth into something, I won't let go. Even though it was a struggle, there seemed some point to it. I suppose spite was my major motivation. I decided not to let these fucks do this to me. I could prove I was better than them. I knew they couldn't write songs, because when I asked to see what they had, they had nothing at all. Not even three lyrics strung together. It was sad when they told me they had been rehearsing for two years. So I started handing in my own lyrics. I mean, why not anarchy? It was probably something to do with what I was reading at the time, no other reason. The destructive element fit in quite well. A lot of people feel the Sex Pistols were just negative. I agree, and what the fuck is wrong with that? Sometimes the absolute most positive thing you can be in a boring society is completely negative. It helps. If you're not, you show weakness, and you must never do that! You must always be totally committed.

JULIEN TEMPLE: I was initially attracted by their ferocity and the originality of the Pistols. Not as musicians, but as a band, an attitude. You can't just take one side in terms of the Sex Pistols' importance. It was more than a band, it was a theatrical presence onstage. Shock theater that was beautifully designed. It had incredible anger and power that seemed rooted in things older than rock 'n' roll.

CAROLINE COON: What Johnny was doing with the Pistols was
dramatizing rage. That was always misunderstood. I've always
pegged the Pistols as the Theater of Rage, a very good place to
put your violent feelings. What resulted was the mistaken notion
that punk was violent. But the reason there was violence in the
punk movement is another issue. It had nothing to do with the
core of what punk was about. What Johnny may have liked to
have seen was more the performance of rage as an articulation
inside a rock 'n' roll format.

Apparently Nick Kent, the British journalist, used to jam with the
band from time to time. That's what Steve told me. They never
made him a band member, although he considered himself as such.
He's never written a good word about me ever since. When I came
along, I took one look at him and said, "No. That has to go." They
told me, "He's not in the band anyway." They had never written
any songs together.

I know a lot has been said about Glen being the melodious one, and
that without him we would never have had hit singles. For God's sake,
who gave a damn about a hit single? Irrelevant and, apart from that, a
lie. For all of Glen's melodiousness, he didn't exactly do very much
when he left us, did he? I don't think people realized that it takes all
members to fit that together.

STEVE JONES: Matlock could definitely play. Musically it was easier
to have Matlock in the band, but I didn't like his personality. He
was such a good boy; he was so clean and had that look, like he had
never gone without a meal. He was always fed and looked after,
which is all right. Each to his own, but when you're in a band with
someone like that, it gets annoying. He had this pompous face you
wanted to slap. Glen was always trying to show me these complicat-
ed chords, which aggravated me even more. I wasn't interested in
his Beatle-type chords. I couldn't play the chords he tried to show
me. If we had played those chords, we would have sounded like Dr.
Feelgood or one of those pub rock bands.

The first song I wrote with the band was nothing that ever got used.
It was a song about a girl called Mandy who wanted to kill her parents.
It was such a boring name, it was irresistible. I can hardly remember
the lyrics. It went something like "There's blood on the carpet, blood
on the stairs, And dear old Mandy's got blood in her hair."

It was so silly. Glen couldn't cope with it. "Why does it have to be so negative?" So then we started doing other people's songs—things like "Whatcha Gonna Do About It?" I would change—more like mutilate—the lyrics.

I was absolutely embarrassed as all hell. Once I had heard my voice come out of that speaker, it was the kiss of death to me. I thought I was doomed. I had to really work. Yet I was actually pleased that they considered carrying on. Maybe I didn't realize they were so desperate. They must have been, to put up with me. It was like trying to teach a deaf man to talk.

Steve was playing badly because he was only learning himself. He was constantly out of time and out of tune. But I didn't mind that at all. I thought it was great fun. I loved it. I had never been that close to an electric guitar before. The sheer power coming out of the amps filled me. The more awful the noise, the better it sounded to me.

STEVE JONES: I didn't know how to play, but once we got John in the band I had to learn guitar seriously. I'd wake up in the morning at our studio on Denmark Street, take a black beauty, and play along with an Iggy Pop record and the New York Dolls' first album. I would listen to them over and over again and play guitar to them. I would learn those bits along with what we were rehearsing the previous night. I barely got my barre chords together to play songs. I threw a little bit of Chuck Berry in the lead and that was it.

"Funhouse" by Iggy and the Stooges was my kind of music. Our sound was pretty damn close to that. Behind all that we had Glen's soppy bass line, playing something rinky-dink. Really twee. Paul has played the same way from the first day I heard him, right up until now. He has not changed. It's complete Charlie Watts—boom, tat, boom, tat. He never varies, and that's not a complaint. He was so solid that we could rely on that. So the chaos can fall very neatly into place. I don't think it would have ever happened if Paul wasn't there. In the early days, I decided right from the start that if Paul and Steve weren't there, there wouldn't be much point to it. I wouldn't have wanted to do it with any other people. As I said, it was sink or swim. I didn't feel like a front man. Actually, I felt more like the back man. I was still working myself out on stage. When you don't know who you are, it takes a lot to get to the point where you throw yourself into the fire in front of other people. I had gotten over my shyness. The next step was failure. The idea of failing utterly appalls me. I don't give people an easy time. I don't make liking me very easy at all.

Why should I? I test people. I find out what they're up to and where they come from. I don't like people who readily accept things. If it was easy joining the Sex Pistols, then I wouldn't have been too interested. But it wasn't. It was very difficult. I made them dislike me all the more. Then it was worth fighting to get into.

Malcolm convinced them that I looked the part, although they were still somewhat doubtful.

CHRISSIE HYNDE: Malcolm recognized the poet in John Rotten. What Malcolm would do was put people in motion. He tried to do it with me with a couple of different bands. His idea, and what he tried to put together, would never be the obvious, and it wouldn't be what anyone else would try.

I was emaciated—very thin with spiky hair. I was wearing what later became full punk garb—ripped shirts and safety pins. The band didn't know where such a look came from since it didn't come from anything that they'd recognized. It was me rehashing all those awful pop star images, taking bits and putting it together. Bits like taking a Pink Floyd T-shirt. Once you add the words *I hate,* you've made it something completely different. Everyone was wearing flares at the time. There was no way you'd get me into a pair of flares. I wore my trousers preferably baggy, tight at the bottom. Remember all those World War II old men's suits that they had at the secondhand clothes stores? I loved all that. The baggier and bigger, the better. But when you buy these old tatty things, they do tend to fall apart. So the safety pins were not decoration, but necessity. It was either that or the sleeve falls off.

BOB GRUEN: Coming from New York, I first noticed differences directly related to fashion. The New York scene was very severe. Richard Hell had started wearing ripped-up T-shirts. From what I understand, some ex-girlfriend . . . to whom Richard owed money got pissed off and ripped up his clothes. Out of desperation for something to wear, Richard. put them back together with safety pins, and that became the style. But the funniest thing Richard Hell ever wore—that I saw, anyway—was something he had on while walking on the Lower East Side. It was a T-shirt with a target painted in the middle that read "Please Kill Me."

At the time I was rehearsing with the Pistols I moved about a hell of a lot. I moved back to the old man's house for a short period of time—on and off for as long as my old man and I could bear each other. He asked me back because he'd seen the Hampstead squat.

"No son of mine will live like that!"

I had run into him on the street, so he and my mother wanted to see what I was living in. So I invited them over. This was long after I had dropped out of school. I showed them all right. They were none too impressed. They came over one night and nearly died. The place was a real tip with a collection of very dirty people sitting around with candles bemoaning their lot.

"We're doomed. Life's dismal."

Sid lived there, and they knew him from before. He used to come around their house during college practically every day. My old man said he was as daft as a brush. He'd be dolled up in some new fashion victim outfit, making himself look bloody ridiculous. They didn't like the girlies we were keeping company with, either, some real fucking freaks. I showed them everything.

"This is my room."

"Where's the bed?"

"There isn't one. I sleep on the floor."

That was a lie of course. I had moved the mattress next door. I love sympathy. My father gave in and had me back until I could sort myself out. I had no qualms about going back. That's where my record player was, the only thing I owned at the time. I had precious little to play on it, though. "Tago Mago" by Can. It's stunning, my fave. "Bitches Brew" by Miles Davis. I loved that album. Captain Beefheart. When I had the money, I would go to the record store and pick out something and see what I thought. I liked the luck of the draw. Now it's all so predictable, the way they file everything. Because of the soppy pictures of the bands on the front, you already knew what the music was like.

I couldn't stand living at home. It didn't go too well. I wrote "God Save the Queen" at the kitchen table that's still there to this day. I wrote it one morning waiting for my baked beans to cook. I wrote the lyrics in one sitting and went straight to the rehearsal studio. I handed them over to the other guys. The tune was already worked out, and I just put those lyrics over it. It did not amuse Glen at all. He could not cope. He thought it was evil.

"You can't do that! We'll get killed."

It was worth the risk. Nobody had openly declared any anti-opinions of the royal family in ever such a long time in our ridiculous feudal Great Britain. I thought it was about time somebody stood up and said something—and I was more than pleased that it be me. I'd been thinking about it for a long time. This is how I write most of my songs. There is no set format, I tend to think a long time before I put pen to paper. When I'm ready, I'll sit down and write it out in one long piece, more like an open letter than a song. It becomes valid confrontation. There's an element of glory to it. The record, of course, took off. It was bound to because so many people felt the same way. It was utterly pointless trying to convince Glen that "God Save the Queen" was not fascism, that it actually was against fascism. Maybe he thought I really meant to save the queen and her fascist regime. Well, for shit sure, the queen didn't appreciate it none.

I couldn't have enjoyed myself much more if I had sat down and thought, How can I annoy them today? What a pain in the ass I must have been. I wish I had done it deliberately, but it wasn't quite like that. Looking back on it now, I'd like to think that was what I was doing, but it isn't true.

I got the name Rotten because I had green teeth. It was Steve's nickname for me: "You're fucking Rotten!" That's what he used to say. It was, and it wasn't an affectionate nickname, pushing it on both ends. I never had any violent confrontations with Steve, ever. I'd like to think there was some kind of respect because I definitely baffled him.

STEVE JONES: I didn't like knowing I was going to have to work with this guy. At that time I was into Rod Stewart and the Faces, and John was totally not that way at all. He made me uncomfortable, and I thought his attitude was fucked.

We were rehearsing in Chiswick. After that we used a place called Tin Pan Alley on Tottenham Court Road. There was a group who split up called Badfinger, and they had a two-room rehearsal studio. Malcolm rented and eventually bought it. I know he got it dirt cheap. There was no toilet, so he wasn't exactly breaking the bank.

BOB GRUEN: When I first met Johnny Rotten he'd been nursing a sore throat for a couple of days. Still, Malcolm wanted me to do a photo session of the band rehearsing. They seemed to respect me, which was odd given that they seemed to have no respect for anybody. But they liked the fact that I worked for *Creem* and *Rock Scene*, the only music magazines that seemed to have a sense of humor. Both tended to be irreverent, and they poked fun at everybody.

I don't think anything about the Pistols was nihilistic. We certainly weren't on a death trip. Maybe it was wreck-and-destroy stupidity, but I would hardly think that's nihilistic. Quite the opposite. It's very constructive because we were offering an alternative. Not just anarchy for the sake of it. This was a very antistar band.

There was a thing about the band and a glamour about Malcolm and Vivienne's Sex shop that made me stick it out. It was the most radical place in London, a wacky shop. It didn't do much business because it appealed to perverts, freaks, oddballs, and people with disturbed personalities. I fit in somehow. There was nothing else going on in my life. I was chucked out of college, home, jobs, everywhere. What else? You can only hate Pink Floyd for so long.

RAMBO: We used to wear Pringles, and all of a sudden Paul Young turned into a punk. He still looked smart as a punk. He and Anthony English wore bondage trousers. Sometimes John would look like a Ted. He would wear his hair like a Ted, but it wasn't really. It was more of a piss take of a Ted.

Early on, Vivienne Westwood was someone I wanted to like but could never come to grips with. She never liked me and always made it completely clear because I was too smart. I could not be manipulated. I would not wear what she wanted me to wear. Her vision of a rock 'n' roll star was not mine. I wouldn't be what she wanted me to be. She resented me for not going along, and that made life with her an impasse. I didn't like her friends or her attitude.

I remember very odd things about Vivienne. We once went to a pizza restaurant together. I lied and told Vivienne that I never had pizza before, and she absolutely took it as a fact. Fine, I thought. I'll go with this. She ordered the weirdest pizza on the menu—capers, green olives, and anchovies.

"Gosh, what's that?" I let on. "How do you eat it?"

She proceeded to cut the segments and handed me a piece and said, "By the way, these are olives, an acquired taste. You might not like them at first." For such a put-on it was great, telling me everything I wanted to know about why I should dislike her. Vivienne carried it on and never got it. When I watch her doing interviews on TV, I get that same feeling I had in the pizza parlor; she doesn't get it, she doesn't realize that people are laughing at her. She's deeply silly. Wacky shit. Ingenious, but not bright—much like a dotty college professor. In fact, that's how Malcolm met her. She was a teacher.

When I bought a rubber polo-neck sweater from her, just because we were Sex Pistols did not mean we didn't have to pay full price. We certainly did, and this rubber sweater cost forty pounds, quite a lot of money then. When I hacked up the polo neck, Vivienne became furious. "You don't get it, do you? It's not worn that way!" I paid full whack for the sweater, so I did what I wanted with it. I eventually wore it on stage at one gig, supporting Ian Dury and the Blockheads. I passed out from dehydration after our third number because it was so hot. I couldn't manage it. How foolish and easily worth it. Ian Dury was more than impressed. Worst thing he'd ever seen, oozing style without affectation.

Chrissie Hynde and I became friends. One reason I hung around with her was because Malcolm and Vivienne didn't like her, and that was a good enough reason for me to be intrigued. Chrissie was a hard girl. She played guitar and bounced around between Akron, Ohio, and London, a woman without a country. She lived in Paris before she came to London and hung around the Sex shop with her friend, Judy Nylon. Chrissie fell out with Vivienne Westwood because Vivienne apparently had a fight with Judy over nothing in particular. Vivienne suddenly ostracized the both of them because, well, that's her thing. Banned from the shop!

"You go with the flow," as Vivienne would say, pointing towards the door, "and it goes that way."

CHRISSIE HYNDE: One day I walked into the shop and Vivienne asked, "Chrissie, what are you doing here? I thought you'd gone to France."

"I did, but I'm back," I said.

"I want you to get out of my shop," Vivienne yelled. "You're a despicable little piece of shit."

I never knew why they were mad at me. I never saw her again until ten years later when she spoke to me and we'd become friendly again. I always admired and looked up to Malcolm and Vivienne—to the point where I thought, Why should they like me? Maybe I am a despicable little piece of shit. Look at my clothes. I've got no style. On the other hand, I was the girl who was musical. Vivienne was shocked when she saw me play a guitar.

"You really can squeeze some chords out of that thing, can't you, Chrissie?" They were all surprised that a low-life like me actually could do something.

I couldn't get Glen or Steve to teach me, so Chrissie offered to give me guitar lessons. We'd sit and play acoustic guitars on the grass together at Clapham Common. I knew it intensely annoyed Vivienne, who insisted at every opportunity that Malcolm sack me from the group. She felt I must be no good because I was hanging around with Chrissie Hynde, that bitch from hell, which started the Vivienne vendetta against me.

CHRISSIE HYNDE: Malcolm got pissed off when he found out I was trying to show John how to play some chords on the guitar. Pissed off! According to Malcolm, John was not to be the guitar player, he was to be the poet, and Malcolm didn't need someone like me interfering. Even so, I would meet John on Clapham Common, where we would sit down together and I would try to show him how to play. Unfortunately he was left-handed and all fucked up, but I was determined and he wanted to learn. However, he lost interest early on, even though he desperately wanted to become a little more musical. Maybe John thought playing guitar would help him write songs. I'd also showed him the Bhagavad Gita and I tried to get him interested in my little spiritual trips. John was into beautiful, colorful pictures. He loved colors. That period of minimalism never seemed to appeal to him—he liked opulence. Of course, that didn't go down a storm with Malcolm and Vivienne, either. They were very protective and didn't like people entering their inner circle. Malcolm was possibly afraid I'd influence the guys musically.

When I started bringing Sid out to the gigs, that was Vivienne's opening. "Get rid of John! Sid will do because he doesn't hang around with Chrissie Hynde." That's the kind of childishness that used to go on with Malcolm and Vivienne. There was that kind of subterfuge going on. Here I am at seventeen and eighteen thinking, My God, these are old people in their thirty-pluses. They should know better, such an unrealistic outlook on life.

After I left the play-center job, and just around the time the Pistols started rehearsing, Chrissie got us house-cleaning jobs. Sid got the job first after working at Heals, the health food restaurant. I didn't like cleaning office buildings. Too much stuff would go missing, and they would point the finger at me while Sid would stand there, sheepishly innocent. Then Chrissie found this other cleaning agency that specialized in doing residences. We only worked together once, then it was on to solo jobs. That was hell on earth. I usually worked for old rich bitches, gray-haired, overdressed, with Harrods bags everywhere, the kind of domineering old biddies that England seems to have an overabundance of, usually unmarried.

The agency would give me an address, and I would show up at these women's doors.

"Hello!"

"Arrgghh!"

I was well and truly odd looking at that point, just after my green hair phase. Invariably these old battle-axes in purple rinses would follow me around their house, convinced I would steal something, pointing angrily at the dusty spots.

"Look at that there! You didn't do that properly!"

I was desperately earning money to live. I would make their beds, do the laundry, clean up the kitchen, and scrub the house down. It was a full day's job that they usually wanted done in an hour and a half because they always had someone coming around for tea, and could I put the kettle on while I was about?

The money wasn't brilliant. But the sheer nausea used to thrill me in a perverse way. They were such cows, especially to young boys they didn't find attractive. Barbara Cartland with a battle-ax.

I didn't stick with it very long, sorry to say. Chrissie got the best job of all—Keith Richards's place. I could have definitely had a fun time doing nothing there. You can't tell me he knows the dust is piled up in the corners.

CHRISSIE HYNDE: I got John a job at one point cleaning houses, but I don't think he lasted very long. I got Sid a job modeling at St. Martin's art college. We were all low-lifes, so we'd do what we could for each other. I was the only one who didn't live at home with my parents. Sid lived in a tower block with his mum. I remember all of us would be looking for something to do and Sid would say, "We can always go to me mum's and smoke hippie drugs."

Before the Sex Pistols, music was so bloody serious, all run by university graduates. It was all head music devoid of any real intellectualism. There was no deep thought in it, merely images pertaining to something mystical, too stupid and absolutely devoid of reality. How on earth were we supposed to relate to that music when we lived in council flats? We had no money, no job, no nothing. So the Pistols projected that anger, that rock-bottom working-class hate. I don't think that had ever been dealt with in music outside of a "show bizzy" way. Rap had that initial anger when it started, that rock-bottom gut feeling. Now rap's become show biz as well, all about making money. The Rolling Stones did live in a hovel, but wasn't Mick Jagger from a nice wealthy family?

Before the Pistols, most of these dropout people and their hovels were self-inflicted. Being an economics graduate is not quite the same thing.

CAROLINE COON: During the sixties, it was rock 'n' roll that saw the class system breaking down. It was rock 'n' roll that served as counterculture class politics and therefore instrumental in breaking things down. Mick Jagger faked his accent to sound more working class. His view of what it was to be working class was that you should be thick and stupid, yet another conceit about the English class system.

I was pushed out into the world. I'm sure there was a lot more to do with it than just hair, although the hair broke the camel's back. My mother, when we'd meet, was always supportive. She agreed that it was right that I go out and make my own way. While I tried to agree, I felt horribly neglected. Looking back, I think it was a very sensible thing to do. You can't have intelligent children hanging around the house. They've got to go out and live in the real world. Now I appreciate it. It was very good for me. I have no regrets.

As for not going out and becoming a drug addict, all you have to do is look at them. Look at them! Where's the enjoyment, the pleasure, the point, the purpose? There isn't one.

In the beginning, I hated the music the Sex Pistols were playing. Musically they were a nightmare. They tried so hard to play in a boxed-in, pedestrian, nicey-nice way. I wanted a bit more shambolic chaos. The better gigs were when things were so fucking out of tune. It was excellent fun to confront an audience and watch them just stare. The best gigs we'd ever done was when the audience didn't even bother to clap. Those gigs were usually at the universities. Outside of the universities, you'd find that people were a bit more understanding. Isn't that odd? Our worst enemies were university students. They thought they knew it all with their Emerson, Lake and Palmer albums. Places like St. Martin's College—which was literally across the road from where we rehearsed. It was funny, walking across the street with amps and guitars to our first gig. St. Martin's was an art college that Glen Matlock went to. We got the gig there supporting Bazooka Joe, with which Adam Ant was a member. I was nervous as hell.

BOB GRUEN: Johnny Rotten was standoffish at first, everyone else was quite friendly, having drinks, chatting, pretty loose. Steve and Paul chatted up the girls, trying to score for the night. Johnny was more aloof, with his wild, angry eyes. I remember my first response being, "What's his problem? Who's he pissed off at? I don't even know the guy. Why is he looking around like everything sucks?" He had this angry attitude about everything.

I really do think the crown and glory of the Sex Pistols is that we've always managed to disappoint on big occasions. When the chips were down, we never came through. We were so bad, it was gloriously awful, as it should have been. You can never change anything by playing nice melodies and singing lovey-dovey lyrics to people, that is, unless they don't want it. Details were never ever worked out properly. Things such as road crews, equipment, PAs, monitors. That would be the screw-up right there. A lot of our gear was stolen, though not by me. They had most of it—their guitars and things—before I joined up. A singer doesn't need anything, does he? A bloody microphone, which most of the time we'd borrow from the main band and proceed to destroy. I did that a lot. I would stick the mike into the monitors until it fed back and blew itself up. It was wonderful.

STEVE JONES: As a juvenile I had a criminal record—fourteen convictions. I went away to a proovy school for a year and a half, but I never actually went to prison. Most of the stuff I did up until the age of seventeen was as a juvenile. I got popped for stolen equipment. After eighteen you go to prison, and the Sex Pistols kept me out. After the band happened, I didn't steal that much afterward. It saved me.

Steve stayed in the rehearsal studio that Malcolm had rented. Paul lived with his mum and daddy. I squatted with Sid at Hampstead. Finally I'd decided I'd had enough of that, so Malcolm got me a flat in King's Cross. I proceeded to move in something like forty people.

I'm not much of a loner. I love company. Love it. It was around that time that the yobs and boot boys around Finsbury Park where I had grown up began to like me and my friends. They never used to. They always thought us weird, but they started hanging around, poncing free drinks. But who cared?

So I kept to myself and my own set of pals, away from the other Pistols. But what did they want of me? All during the Sex Pistols—Malcolm, Steve, Paul—would go to parties all the time. The socialite Andrew Logan affairs, whatever. I wouldn't be invited, so what was I supposed to do? Stay at home and watch TV? Bollocks to that. I'd be out on the town with my mates. If they resented that, well, that's too fucking bad. Soon it became a matter of indifference to me what they thought.

STEVE JONES: I was a real pussy hound. It was an ongoing thing for me—I was constantly looking for anything to fuck. I was molested [as a child], so that had a lot to do with it. I kept thinking if I could get laid, then I must be all right. Some people have to be validated constantly. John gets that feeling in other ways—like having people tell him how wonderful he is. I'm sure he won't like to hear that, but that's what I think. He was an outsider like I was an outsider in the band—by choice. I didn't see myself as a social person; I used to leave on my own after the gigs, too.

There was rarely a time when the four of us were friends. Right from the start at rehearsals, I'd go out to the toilet—or tell them that—and listen at the door. I would hear them say, "That cunt. Fucking hell!" Then they'd go off, pack into someone's car, and leave me standing behind. I'd go home by myself on the train. That would be it, night after night after night. It was always like that, me being the outsider.

As for why I was ostracized, Malcolm told me that he wanted me to be the "mystery man" of the band, which of course I didn't want. That meant I didn't go anywhere. It was unfair because people complained that they never saw John. Nobody ever got to know me. On top of that, Steve, Paul, and Malcolm had known each other a lot longer. I was the new boy. They'd already formed their little thing and they weren't going to make room for another, particularly someone as bad as me who wouldn't take the shit.

In Glen's book, he claimed all I ever said to him was "Drop dead." That's right, Glen. Drop dead. Unfortunately for him, he doesn't seem to think I meant it. I fucking well did. Continuously. But, out of the lot of them, I must say this about Glen: he was the only one who attempted to kindle any kind of friendship with me, which is odd because I despised him so. Everything he stood for was wimpy, poncey, just dull. He didn't like to offend. He wanted everyone to like him and to have a good time. So boring.

I had nothing to do with the Sex Pistols' music at all. I couldn't play. I didn't understand what they were doing. Tuning up, to me, was a waste of time, something very annoying. As the years went by with the Pistols, all two of them, I got more interested in the music. I bought the book and got addicted to music, which I never was into before. Up until then, making music meant little to me, although somebody must have realized I was on to something good. It couldn't have been Paul or Steve. It must have been Malcolm. I knew very little what the band felt about me apart from the times I'd listen from behind the door. But somebody must have realized that I had a different angle about me. If the Pistols had taken any other route, you wouldn't know them today. That's not me praising myself. They were just so different from me that the extremes put together worked exceedingly well. It's nothing you can plan; it just happens. Out of all shambolic glory, something lent itself to chaos.

I always wrote the lyrics and insisted on that right from the start, which infuriated the band no end. They all had these daft covers, silly love songs they wanted me to sing. But I just wouldn't, couldn't. I don't believe in that kind of love. Very few songs that sing about love are real. It's not love, it's something else—a false emotion, opium for the masses, not accurate, a deceit.

Early on, the band wanted to do a song by the Small Faces. The lyrics went something like "I want you to know that I love you, baby/I want you to know that I care." Well, I couldn't have any of that, so I changed it to "I want you to know that I hate you, baby! I want you to know I don't care/So happy when you're not around me/I'm so glad when you're not there." The exact opposite seemed to work much better.

PAUL COOK: Glen Matlock attended St. Martin's College, and he set up our first gig there in November of 1975. We rehearsed across the road and wheeled all the equipment down Charing Cross Road about six in the afternoon. We set up and played for twenty minutes. Total chaos. None of us knew what we were doing. We were very nervous and all over the place. We played cover versions like "No Lip," "Substitute," "Whatcha Gonna Do About It?," plus "Satellite" and "Seventeen." We were still learning our trade.

JOHN LYDON: There was not one single hand clap.

COOK: People yelled at us to get off because they wanted their Bazooka Joe. We nearly had a fight with them. They thought we were an oddity because of our attitudes.

LYDON: The college audience had never seen anything like it. They couldn't connect with where we were coming from because our stance was so anti-pop, so anti-everything that had gone on before. Adam may look back on it all rather sweetly by saying he split up his band after seeing us play, but the reality was that he was very bitter and annoyed with us—as indeed most bands were that played with

The thin faces. Come back, sixties, all is forgiven. St Albans. (John Gray)

us. Adam Ant's band was furiously jealous because they spent so much time sewing up those silly silver jackets.

COOK: We weren't being nice. That was the main difference between us and them.

LYDON: I didn't care. We didn't do it to be loved.

COOK: That was outrageous for 1975. You have to understand what it was like at the time. Everything was so conventional—

LYDON: So English. Nobody wanted to offend anybody, and everybody was bemoaning their sorry lot, but never doing anything about it. If you stood up to express an opinion, that would be offending someone, and therefore that wouldn't be British, a terrible thing to have to fight against. Quite frankly, looking at Britain right now, that's what it's all reverted to. Everybody wants to be nice again.

COOK: We used to turn up at college gigs opening up for hippie bands. We weren't booked at a lot of those gigs because they wouldn't have us on. We would play unannounced at places like Holborn and the Central School of Art and Design. Holborn was arranged by Glen's friend, Al MacDonald. Then there was Finchley, Queen Elizabeth College, Chelsea School of Art, Chislehurst Raven, St. Albans, Aldgate, and Kensington. These were just learning gigs around Christmastime of 1975. The strange thing was that people latched on to us straight away. We got a reaction wherever we went; a lot of it was positive.

JOHN GRAY: There were always two types of fans in the audience. There were the ones who took it at face value—the yobs, pretty vacant thickos. Then there were the ones who could see it for what it was—very powerful rock music. The early gigs with Glen Matlock were tight as hell. There was no mucking about. Glen was a workman musician; a bit boring, but he made the group start on time, end on time, and keep the melody intact. John could then go wild when he knew the background was stable. As long as he had an anchor, he could go wild at any point. If everyone was wild, it truly was chaos.

Also consider that Steve and Glen weren't coming from an improvisational school. Chaos is okay in a jazz sensibility. But with three thickos bashing away trying to be chaotic, that would have been ridiculous.

LYDON: We were terrified doing these gigs because of the fear of it all being totally new. It worked a lot better this way than if we would have spent six months to a year learning our craft in a studio, then coming out and just being musos. We had to learn our skills from a live perspective. It wouldn't have worked any other way. That's what was wrong with most of those bands then—and still is. They were too much into the perfection of it all.

COOK: There were a lot of gigs where once we started playing, they just wanted to get us off.

LYDON: Usually for an opening act, the worse they are, the better it was for the headliner. In our case, as bad as we were, it was too fucking good by far. We had something none of these people had—energy and sheer, brazen honesty. We couldn't give a fuck what people thought because we felt what we were saying was much more relevant. And that sometimes became a threat. We showed up at a couple of Andrew Logan's parties. We had done a gig there some months before. The second time I turned up was to a party I wasn't invited to. Malcolm rang me up at my old man's to invite me while I was in the pub across the street. When I got to the party, Malcolm had since decided it was a bad idea inviting me because Vivienne decided she didn't want me there. I didn't know what it was all about, but they wouldn't let me in. I was considered too uncouth, so I kicked up a huge stink. Something was going on between Malcolm and Vivienne. They thought my image should be one of mystery. That was fucking shit: Malcolm rang me up, got me there, and then I was told that I wouldn't be let in. He wouldn't even come to the door.

COOK: The Marquee Club gig in February of 1976 with Eddie and the Hot Rods was a lot of nervous energy. They thought it would be a good idea to put the Pistols on the bill because they thought we had something in common.

LYDON: From what I could gather, Eddie and the Hot Rods were showcasing for a record company that night. They knew we had a reputation, and they wanted us there. "Sure you can use our monitors." Since we never had our own stage monitors, we had to rely on others for their equipment, and if they bugger you about, that's the end for you. If you can't hear what you're doing, you're fucked. But when it came to the actual gig, somehow the monitors were turned off. I call that industrial sabotage or a major mistake and didn't take kindly to it. That's when things started to go sadly wrong for Eddie and the Hot Rods. I put a mike stand through one of their monitors.

The very first Sex Pistols rehearsal. No equipment. One guitar pick. We're ready to rock. Circa 1975. (John Gray).

COOK: Bands like Eddie and the Hot Rods thought there was going to be some great movement, so they wanted everyone to huddle together into this cozy little alliance. Being totally selfish, we weren't into that at all. It was all the other bands that had this idea of a great big movement together.

LYDON: Eddie and the Hot Rods to me was everything that was wrong with live music. Instead of fighting all this big stadium nonsense, they would narrow themselves into this tiny clique by playing in pubs. It was all about denim and plaid shirts, tatty jeans and long droopy hair. Looking awful and like nothing . . . looking like Nirvana! That was the look then. It really annoys me now fifteen or so years later when these bands say they were influenced by the Sex Pistols. They clearly can't be. They missed the point somewhere. You don't wear the tattered uniform of blandness—not if you're interested in the Pistols at all. It's all about being yourself! Be a fucking individual. As a band, the Sex Pistols were all completely different as people—the way we dressed, everything. We didn't give up our individuality just to be a Sex Pistol. That's what made the Pistols, that difference.

HOWARD THOMPSON: What occurred was a significant power shift that exists today, explaining such bands as Fugazi, the Riot Grrrl movement, Bikini Kill, Bratmobile . . . a strong political awareness now going on with bands to the point where they're sometimes able to do it all themselves, creating their own labels, charging only five dollars entry to every gig they play, keeping the costs down so their audience can follow them on their own terms. That part of the Pistols revolution stuck.

COOK: In April of 1976 we supported the 101ers, who eventually turned into the Clash. They were another pub rock band like Eddie and the Hot Rods, Ducks Deluxe, and Roogalator. That's what was going on at the time. We didn't want anything to do with them. We wanted to break out and be better and bigger. We didn't like that "please like us and have a good time" attitude. We also didn't want to play in pubs for the rest of our lives. People used to climb on stage, jump up and down, and fuck with us—

LYDON: Usually because they thought they could do it better. Our fan base did start early, though it started quite small. The first tours, particularly in northern England, were a real nightmare for us. Up north they really couldn't take us; they tended to be backward and primitive. We're talking way up north, places like Barnsley, Scunthorpe. All these gigs ended in fights. Any kind of response from an audience, even if it's hateful and resentful against you, is better than mild applause. Some of the best gigs the Pistols ever did was in front of stone-cold silence. We would headline shows in northern England discos where some Billy Choogleys were use ta' their "blooody pop songggs." Then out we'd come, and they wouldn't connect it at all. It was an amazing feeling—hearing complete silence after kicking up a filthy racket on stage. It can be the loudest sound on God's earth. Nothing. Not even chitchat at the bar. Stone-cold dead silence.

HOWARD THOMPSON: The Pistols fans wanted to bring down the walls and change the face of music. So here I was, watching all this stuff going down. There were constant fights. I'd never seen any band jump off a stage and join in on fights before. That was novel. On stage, the Sex Pistols were pretty damn good! John was fairly nasty—ranting, spitting up phlegm between songs and being cynical. He would try to cajole the audience into reacting to him. He was like a red rag to a bull. The fabulous thing about it was there were only seventy-five to a hundred people in the audience.

COOK: They wouldn't come up and tell us what they thought after the gig. We would come out to the coach after the show, tired, and find our van's tires slashed

LYDON: They had a "cockney bastards" approach to us. We certainly didn't encourage it. I wasn't aware of that nonsense. That wasn't why I was in this band. The Sex Pistols were never into divisionism in England. You must bear in mind that it reflects on the moods of Britain at that time, very provincial in its attitudes. One town would absolutely hate everyone from the next town and so on. It was as if they were warring states. We were seen as filthy, uppity Londoners rolling in money. "You must be fucking rich, you must!" Why? "You come from London."

Nobody was turning up at the northern gigs because we were new outside of London. You'd see thirty of the local yobs behaving badly and throwing things at the stage. I remember Scarborough because we were told that the local casuals were going to come and duff us up. They threw a few glasses, and of course there was no security. I remember standing on stage and challenging them, but they wouldn't come up to the stage.

COOK: Malcolm would just set us up with a van and send us up north—just us and Nils Stevenson, the tour manager, driving. We set up our own gear. Looking back, I realize it was a bad move to do those gigs. We took nothing but grief from the local people, plus the van and the equipment would always break down.

LYDON: What was the alternative? We played in an awful club in Manchester where there was a bunch of City and United football supporters. The Lesser Free Trade Hall was quite well attended. The Buzzcocks were fine, if not just a bit laughable. They were just starting themselves. But they weren't punk imitators; they had their own thing going, which was perfectly fine. I loved them because they did an old Captain Beefheart song. I thought Ha! That will do nicely. The bad joke before the gig was giving a banana and two apples to Pete Shelley!

COOK: Ian Curtis and Morrissey turned up. The Buzzcocks played support. Howard Devoto phoned up Malcolm and got us the gig. It showed us that there were some people outside London who had seen us and hooked on to what we were doing. We always did all right for equipment. That was never a problem. Steve was very good at procuring. Before John was in the band we used to steal a lot of our equipment. We were so poor, we couldn't afford to buy. There was no other way we could have been in a band or learned to play. Steve was a kleptomaniac at the time, and money was always too scarce to spend on things like equipment. He actually made a living out of being a burglar. We were sorted out quite well. Even drum sets. We did get caught once or twice.

LYDON: That impressed me right from the start. I thought this was really tough and hard, bleeding criminals rehearsing above a pub. I'd run through it. Hmm. This mike came from . . . I could catalog things like cymbals. It thrilled me. I thought it was hilarious. There was nobody else doing stuff like that. Nobody had that kind of gall and energy. Anything that wasn't nailed down would be in the back of our van. A week after the Hot Rods show, we did a High Wycombe gig opening for Screaming Lord Stitch. That was one of the funniest gigs ever, seeing that fool come out of his coffin. We were all at the back of the hall in fits. They got upset because they said we'd broken some of their equipment. They wouldn't give us a sound check or any space on stage to put up a drum kit. It's still that way now; you can usually expect a bad attitude from the bands that had to put up with it before you came along.

COOK: John would stand at the edge of the stage and mess up the people's hair in the audience. It's lucky he didn't get killed because he wouldn't back down. It would get frightening. There were fights at all of the gigs. John used to instigate them. He'd get that attitude from the crowd, an aggressive attitude that worked both ways. They would ask, "Why have you got short hair?" They couldn't understand, and they would get jealous, then violent.

LYDON: When you're on stage, no matter how much you don't like violence and all that, it is your stage. No one is going to tell you to get off—it's as simple as that. If you give up and back away, then give up completely. My role was purely defensive. If you don't like what I'm screaming and yelling about or the way I'm doing it, then go to the bar.

COOK: The thing that came out of the High Wycombe gig was that some guy named Ron Watts saw us and we got the residency at the 100 Club. He promoted the Lord Sutch gig and also promoted the 100 Club on Oxford Street. He liked the chaos of it all, and he thought the madness would be great. Ron Watts was an old mod. We reminded him of that scene, but much more severe. We ended up getting banned at the 100 Club because they stopped doing punk gigs altogether. There was too much violence that wasn't actually involved with us. Sid shattered a glass off a pillar, and a girl got cut in the eye. The press made a big thing out of it.

LYDON: I never, ever found out the truth about that incident. You know how they run the press in the U.K.—the hearsay aspect and that's it. What is said first is what counts. No girl was ever shown anywhere. The whole thing could have been complete nonsense. Chuck a couple of names in and see if the shit hits the fan. There was the legend about those two Shanes and how he bit her ear off. It was total rubbish. It was a lie. Shane MacGowan used to come and see us play all the time. He'd be down in the front totally pissed out of his head in his Union Jack T-shirt. When he joined the Pogues, he traded it in for a tricolor. So funny. Just like that—instant nationality swap. Drink was an important part of the Pistols because a large part of the audience would get so pissed.

Booze was cheap; so was amphetamine sulfate. There was always a lot of speed and booze about. It was a nice marriage at the time. You would be up and down—in a deep state of confusion about everything. I suppose that was the best way to enjoy a punk festival. But that's when the imitation bands would start to throw glasses, overdo it, and try to out—Pistol the Pistols. Fans let you down. They don't get it. Sid really let us down, too. He didn't get it, either. He was constantly trying to out-Rotten Rotten or out-Cook Cook or out-Jones Jones in every aspect. It was ludicrous.

COOK: Malcolm figured Sid had the right image. In the early days, when he did rehearse, Sid was all right. He learned the songs quickly and could play. I think some of the best Pistols gigs were when Sid first joined the band. He was keen to learn the bass.

LYDON: Sid used to have a very good image, where he would stand still in the corner, just play and look moody. It worked. Later on he ended up walking into the middle of things on stage, standing in front and forgetting the tunes. I think the only reason Sid really stayed in the group was Malcolm. Steve and Paul didn't want it to continue. I know I didn't. I felt deeply ludicrous because here was my mate, I was the one who put him forward. I didn't know what a useless monster he would turn into.

COOK: The March 1976 gigs at the 100 Club were good because they were regular gigs. All these other bands would start up because it was a place for punk bands. We relied on it each week as a regular place. I suppose that's what actually started the punk movement going. We were shocked when we used to turn up for the gigs and there would be a queue right around the corner with these wild, crazy-looking people. We didn't know where they came from. The gig would be sold out. We must have been doing something right. We used to play every Tuesday. So many people wanted to have a go at punk by this time. Everybody was just getting anything together just to play down there.

BILLY IDOL: Johnny wore a red jumper with slits up the sides and lit-tle sunglasses. Steve Jones was really skinny and had the tits T-shirt on. I was always impressed with Glen Matlock because he was a great bass player. Despite all the things they said about him, I thought the way he brought out the rhythm was fantastic.

HOWARD THOMPSON: I happened to be in the bar one night talking with some friends having a small discussion about punk music, which at the time was just about ready to break. My point was that in all kinds of music, there has to be certain amount of discipline. Upon hearing the word *discipline,* this person who was standing a yard or two behind me swung round and said, "Discipline? You don't need discipline, you fucking wanker!"

It was Johnny Rotten, to whom I said, "Well, *you* might not need discipline, but for this to go any farther, somebody's going to have to organize things and bring together all this excitement in a proper and appropriate fashion so that everybody can enjoy it."

We bantered for a couple of minutes, then Johnny went away while I felt sheepish thinking that I sounded a bit like my old man. So I shut up and carried on drinking. That was our first meeting.

LYDON: On Wednesday they'd have the Lord's Prayer, which was Marco Pirroni, Sid, and Siouxsie. I named them the Flowers of Romance. They were followers, copyists. But we were very happy with that 100 Club crowd because at that time there was no punk cliché uniform. It wasn't wall-to-wall studded leather jackets and Mohawks. That came a long time later.

COOK: They were mainly a crowd that had been going to gay clubs-ex-soul boys and girls, ex-Roxy Music fans, ex-Dave Bowie and Glam rock types, anyone who wasn't a college student. It's hard to explain this, but college students at the time were so fucking snobby. They were like the royal family in their attitude. They became the upwardly mobile yuppies of later generations. That's the way these college kids used to behave during the Sex Pistols era. They were so damned self-righteous at their hippie festivals, never connecting with the general population. They knew how to save the world, and we had better learn to appreciate it! It's funny because Malcolm, being an ex-student, was the source of a lot of antagonism. He and his Jamie Reids. This was my argument with them. They would try to run the Pistols in a student union way. Again, they would form a decision and attempt to tell us what they thought we should be doing. Then we wouldn't do it, we would do what we normally did, but they took the credit at the end of the day. We could have gone on without them from the word go. That's what really pisses me off about those people who were involved. They have such a conceited opinion of themselves involving the Sex Pistols. They really think it wouldn't have happened if they weren't there. Jamie Reid, Boogie Tiberi, Malcolm, Dave Goodman—all one of them. If they were so important, why weren't they out there on the stage—or, for that matter, on the streets—taking all the shit? Yes, there was always tension in the band because none of us ever expected to be in a band together when we left school. Trying to make a go of a band was the last thing on our minds. It was all a bit strange for us. Plus there was the most animosity between John and Glen.

LYDON: By the end of April of 1976 I had a huge row with Glen at the Nashville. I could never bear Glen's simplistic attitude about everything. He just wanted to be nice and not offend anyone. That's not the way around solving problems. If you're going to play that kind of a game, you're never going to get anywhere. Nothing is concluded, and you look wishy-washy. This is the man who would ring up his mother on tour after a gig to tell her it all went nice. It used to deeply annoy me. It was just not on. I wouldn't call my old man. He'd find out what he wanted to.

COOK: He soon found out all about us when he saw "The Bill Grundy Show."

LYDON: Both Nashville gigs were horrid. During the first one there was an argument with Glen and a squabble in the audience. There was supposedly a fight, this big symbol of early punk rock violence. It was just a load of people falling all over the place. Vivienne smacked some girl. It was nonsense—fisticuffs and handbags, really. The pictures of that fight make it look a lot worse than it was. It was a bunch of silly bitches squabbling. There was an argument between Paul and me at the second gig. I don't know what we were arguing about, but we were really yelling and screaming at each other. Then the curtain went up, and we stopped fighting and went on with it. That second gig was particularly bad. When the curtain went down, I went over to Malcolm and said, "I quit. I've had enough." I had no money. I had nowhere to live. I was fucked off with it. The money from gigs did go for expenses. There just wasn't enough of it. It's hardly worth being a bitch about since we're talking twenty to fifty quid here at most. But sometimes these clubs would be full and the bars would do very well. We would just go in, play, then leave. I had to go home on the fucking subway with half the audience—not the big star trip I had in mind. Seriously, it was damned fucking dangerous to be doing shit like that with our reputations. I would have thought a cab or a lift home would not have been an impossibility. There were plenty enough people who had cars.

HOWARD THOMPSON: When I first saw the Sex Pistols at the Nashville Rooms, I remember coming away from the show with a million questions in my head. I'd just seen something unlike anything I'd ever seen before.

COOK: I quite liked the Nashville gigs, particularly the second one. We played the second night under the pretext of hiring the club for a private party. That was a good gig because we had our own sound system. It was so much better when we had control of the situation. We could set the gig up and use it for our own end. We would have monitors that worked. We were relaxed and playing well by this stage, and the crowd really liked us. The gigs we could organize ourselves—100 Club, the Nashville, or Screen on the Green—always turned out to be the best shows.

LYDON: Glen would say stuff to me like "The lyrics to 'God Save the Queen' have to be changed." Because his mum didn't like it! When somebody talks to me like that, I just don't listen any longer. I won't even debate the issue. Also in April of 1976, we played the El Paradise, a really dingy little place on Brewer Street in Soho. We had about ten people inside watching us gig. I burned myself really bad. I stumbled and fell on the lights that were normally anchored above but were on the ground. I couldn't see what I was doing, and I stumbled and hit them on my side. I still have a huge welt from it.

STEVE JONES: The El Paradise strip club in Soho was a shady scene—fat, ugly chicks stripping. Malcolm put that together. There were strippers actually working before we went on, and then after we finished, they started stripping again.

COOK: It was a terrible place to play because it was so small and so loud. We ended up breaking up a few things. These Maltese blokes who ran the club turned up. It was such a shithole, they were worried we were going to wreck it.

LYDON: They were standing there at the front of the stage, looking at us, shouting, "Get that filth off!" And this place was basically a wanking shop. The funniest thing about the El Paradise was upstairs on the roof. They didn't want us up there during the day. I managed to go up one day with Steve. We broke into a room they had way up in the back. It was bare brick with a thick wooden chair, like a throne, in the center. It had hand bands and straps attached to it. They had all these weird implements of torture hanging on the walls—whips, spikes, objects of cruelty—things that were designed to go places that weren't designed to receive them. Odd things must have gone on up there. I grabbed some whips and stuff. That was the major reason for the moaning from those Maltese geezers. "Where's our whips, you bastards?"

COOK: Before we'd go on stage, we would always have to go looking for Steve and find him in a cupboard with some disgusting girl. Steve was completely obsessed with sex, more so than any of the other band members.

LYDON: There would be no problems with support bands at those shows, either. The Screen on the Green gigs were excellent and very funny. The chap who promoted those gigs used to chuck on these mad Kenneth Anger movies before we got on. The whole night would be extremely hilarious. These films were originally supposed to be perverse, but in that environment they became laughable—deeply funny. I loved the aspect of taking all this decadence and laughing at it. We had this impression that in New York people wallowed in it and took it seriously. They would put it in an arty context. Any kind of porno flick or any of that stuff amused me greatly. I can't see how people can find that kind of entertainment to be anything other than comedy.

COOK: Screen on the Green was this small cinema in North London we used to rent. Malcolm knew the manager who ran it, and they showed late night picture shows there. They agreed to put on our little get togethers and all the chaos that went with it. The Slits played there with us at the second gig.

LYDON: I remember when Viv Albertine of the Slits lent me a wedding dress she had. I came out after to see what was going on—in a green wig and a wedding dress. "Oh, hello, John." Everyone was so nonchalant. What the fuck! That gives you a fair idea of how liberal the attitudes were. There wasn't any sense of posing at all. The only places I could ever go and relax were at other people's houses. I couldn't go out during the day. The only real club to go to was the Roxy or Louise's before it became fashionable. Louise's used to be a lesbian bar, and they wouldn't give you any hassle. There were no other clubs we could go to at the time. That would be it for my social life—a few lunatics, prostitutes, and dykes. I moved around an awful lot, and I would live anywhere I could stay. Steve and Paul lived on Denmark Street at the time. I moved in for a short time with Linda Ashby later at the St. James. We loved the Houses of Parliament, and the parties she'd get us into were always good fun. I generally found the Tory MPs the worst. I remember a famous politician named John Stonehouse who gave a lot of parties. He threw a party one Friday night, and on a Monday morning he disappeared. I last saw him, or a body double, standing in the corner of a room in a suit, smoking a joint and asking where the coke was.

Our interest in politics at the time was zero. I've changed since. I follow politics closely now because I find it all very thrilling. But during the Pistols, I was too young. I couldn't even vote. I just knew they were all corrupt—like the people who would run off with the money and fake their own deaths.

COOK: Then there were the gigs in France and the Scandinavian tours.

LYDON: Siouxsie Sioux was a nightmare when we went down to Paris. Silly girl, she wore practically nothing except swastikas and a see-through titless-bra—in a former Nazi-occupied country. The stage at the club we played at was brand new, and we were the first band in there. I almost broke my neck because the stage was lit from underneath, and as you trotted out you couldn't see anything. When you're lit like that, it really affects your eyes. It was visually painful, and they had this ridiculous gay disco flashing thing happening where the lights would run through a fast circuit pattern. Now I'm prone to epileptic fits in that kind of situation, especially if the flashing lights are on a certain frequency. That kind of stuff fucks me up. The Club de Chalet du Lac in Paris was awful for me, and the French audience weren't too happening, either. They've always had an attitude there, although it has been changing over the last eight years. Before that, it was always, "Entertain me. I dare you!"—worse than any London crowd because they were so into being French. So Billy Idol and Siouxsie drove down. Billy told me years later that they would come visit us with some girls. They'd be left behind, and the girls would disappear, only to come back an hour later looking shagged out. Wonder why? I always had good memories of playing in Scandinavia. We used to have a mad, crazy crowd around there. We'd get followed around by these biker chaps. Really wild audiences who understood right from the start. Even though they were a little older, they were into the music. They had a good time and never posed. There was no problem of a glass being thrown into someone's face from across a room. They knew what real violence was. It's always the pretenders who do that kind of stuff. Real yobs don't. They don't need to prove themselves. It's funny, but most of the trouble created at the punk festival at the 100 Club was on nights we weren't playing. It was the other incidents blown out of proportion, practically none of it turned out to be true. The Sid and Nick Kent incident was a personal battle and had nothing to do with the audience.

COOK: Nick Kent came down for a rehearsal where we had our equipment set up. He just came down and played a few songs. Frustrated
musician.

LYDON: I remember when Sid and Wobble got into a row with Nick
Kent at the 100 Club. They were probably being very protective
because Nick Kent had a snobby attitude at the time. Nick Kent has
never had anything to do with me. He apparently rehearsed with the
band sometime before and told people I shouldn't be up there. Then
Nick Kent would constantly slag me off in the press, so when he
turned up at our gigs, I would have something to say to him along
those lines. Maybe the discussion continued and was pursued by
Wobble and Sid. You know you were doing well when you get the
likes of Mick Jagger slagging you off in the press—the so-called rock
star untouchables. They would see us once on the telly, then they
would say, "They can't play." It was deeply ridiculous for Mick
Jagger to say the Sex Pistols couldn't play. Now the Rolling Stones
are hardly cultivated, are they? In fact, they made a career out of
being the exact opposite. We were banned from the Marquee. We
banned ourselves from the Nashville by sheer choice. That was a
back-to-the-pubs thing. You could get a lot of people in, but it was
still a stinky pub with a damned beer-sodden carpet. The Nashville
and the Marquee stunk of the old rock 'n' roll cliché. We spent a lot
of the money we made from gigs mostly on demos. We once did a
July 4 gig with the future Clash supporting us. Strummer and the
rest of them had a horrible attitude at that gig. Keith Levene was in
the band, and he was the only one who could actually hold a decent
conversation with us. Bernie Rhodes, Malcolm's ex-partner, was
managing them and it was their first public gig. Malcolm and Bernie
were competing, so Bernie was revving this band to take a very
anti-Pistols stance—as if they were the real kings of punk. I've never
liked the Clash. They weren't good songwriters. They would run out
of steam halfway through their gigs because they would go so mad
at the beginning. The Sex Pistols learned dynamics on stage. I
would credit Paul for that. He could break the tempo down.
Strummer would start everything off and from there on in, it was
just full-on speed. That's not good enough because you're not saying anything just by being fast. You can't dance to it, and you can
hardly listen to it. It's unpleasant after half an hour. To me the
Clash looked and sounded like they were yelling at themselves about
nothing in particular—a few trendy slogans stolen here and there
from Karl Marx. The Clash introduced the competitive element that

dragged everything down a little. It was never about that for us. We were just the Pistols. We never saw ourselves as being in a punk movement. We saw ourselves as just the Pistols, and what the rest of them were up to was neither here nor there. Quite frankly, they weren't there in the beginning. They laid none of the groundwork. They just came in and sat on our coattails. Rat Scabies and the Damned, he used to say, "My band is better than yours!" Yes, Rat. He used to roadie for us. There you go. It was made very clear that we weren't distant superstars you saw on a huge stage four hundred miles away from your seat. Yet a lot of bands that came after jumped on the superstar, ego shitwagon.

HOWARD THOMPSON: After the first four or five months of the Sex Pistols' short history, suddenly all these bands started cropping up—Siouxsie and the Banshees, the Clash, the Damned, and the Adverts. The Pistols had changed the whole musical scene. Everybody started doing it the way the Pistols did it.

LYDON: Audiences fell for it and walked straight back into the same old traps. I think there's something basically wrong with the general public that they do need their icons. I'm an icon breaker, therefore that makes me unbearable. They want you to become godlike, and if you won't, you're a problem. They want you to carry their ideological load for them. That's nonsense. I always hoped I made it completely clear that I was as deeply confused as the next person. That's why I'm doing this. In fact, more so. I wouldn't be up there on a stage night after night unless I was deeply confused, too. If I had all the answers, I wouldn't be involved in something like this at all.

COOK: I think the press fueled these rivalries among the bands. The press was jealous of the Pistols, too. "Wow! Here's the Clash. They're much better than the Sex Pistols, blah, blah." They took to the Clash a lot easier than they did to us because the Clash were more accessible. That's what started the rivalry, though it really wasn't much of one after all. We only socialized or saw each other now and again. A band like the Damned was just jumping on the bandwagon. The other punk bands would play three minutes of thrash with no break in it at all. You could say that about the Clash as well. Although they were a bit better than your usual mainstream punk bands, the Clash went on like that, and that's why they always seemed knackered halfway through their set.

CAROLINE COON: Three bands represent the three different prongs of the punk movement. There was the personal politics of the Sex Pistols, the serious politics of the Clash, and the theater, camp, and good fun of the Damned.

LYDON: I think the audiences gobbing on stage came from me. Because of my sinuses, I do gob a lot on stage, but never out toward the crowd. Maybe off to the side. But the press will jump on that, and the next week you get an audience thinking that's part of the fashion and everybody has to be in on it. There's not much you can do to stop it after that.

STEVE SEVERIN: Siouxsie got gobbed in the eye one night, and she had to wear an eye patch at the next gig because she got conjunctivitis. I don't know who started it, but it was probably that arsehole Rat Scabies from the Damned. Maybe it was a nightmare. We'd be covered in it; it was so disgusting! The funny thing was that nobody'd say anything about it. That's what we couldn't understand. Siouxsie would always say after the first song, "If you don't stop gobbing at me, I'm gonna come down there and black you one."

COOK: I was always at the back, so I could try to get out of the way of it. Some of the spit would come past me and, bang, take the paint off the wall. It's disgusting when you think about it. John still gets it when he plays live.

BOB GRUEN: It seemed disgusting to have to stand on stage while people spit on you, and to take it or you didn't get paid. The bands told me their fans were communicating with them by sharing the experience; that the only way they could reach them or touch them was by spitting.

LYDON: Only in Britain, and it's usually one asshole who will walk to the front and thinks he knows it all. It's some New Age traveler Mohawk—some Johnny-come-lately who has read a few things but hasn't read enough to know better.

What I remember most about the Lyceum gig—our biggest gig—was a famous groupie turned up from America. She came into the dressing room and announced, "I must add you to my collection. I must have you." I said, "Oh, really? Fuck right off." That was my impression of Americans at the time. They were like vultures.

COOK: We didn't go on until about three o'clock. I wasn't able to wake up. It was dead late. It was ridiculous idea to do a gig at three in the morning.

LYDON: Malcolm once bussed up some Americans for a gig we did at the Circus in Manchester. Seymour Stein and Lisa Robinson were there. It was a bit more organized and together than the previous Lesser Free Trade Hall gig. It was a lovely hall, and we liked playing in Manchester. We liked the crowds—way back then they were very good. They were obviously on to it because there were all these bands coming out at the time. Slaughter and the Dogs supported us. They had a very young guitarist who was astounding. He looked like he could have been a star, but egos got in the way. They didn't have the prejudices in Manchester, and they liked us for what we were. They hooked on to the energy instead of the *NME, Sounds*, and *Melody Maker* gossip angle. Those papers weren't really treated with any kind of respect at all up north, were they? Somebody once wrote that we debuted "Anarchy in the U.K." at that gig. We never debuted anything! It wasn't seen as that. If there was another song ready, it would be chucked in at any particular order, rather than "And now we're going to feature our latest, greatest hit!"—then into a three-minute introduction. We also taped a guest spot on a show there called "So It Goes" with Tony Wilson—our first television appearance. Clive James worked on the show as the sidekick who warms up the crowd during the show. He would stand in the middle of the place and try to be funny. He threw a few insults our way, and I threw a few back.

COOK: It wasn't anything outrageous. John said something back, and things went all right after. Peter Cook was on the show with us. He had a new Derek and Clive album out. It had some abusive language on it that coincided with our appearance on "The Bill Grundy Show."

LYDON: Clive James is a funny man, but he was out of his depth. Between Peter Cook and me, he was stoned fucking dead. Again, we had no monitors on stage, but we did our best. There was very poor sound, and we couldn't hear what we were doing. It was almost like guesswork, but because we had done so many gigs, we somehow stumbled through the song. It was like the early "Top of the Pops," when bands would mime, which is as bad as playing live and not hearing yourself properly. All I could hear on the show was the drums behind me. The guitar and bass were so low, they seemed nonexistent. Everything relied on counting. We were tough and did what we had to do. We looked great—with no Vivienne Westwood gear on any of us.

COOK: The Vivienne gear at the time was lots of parachute tops, lots of straps and bondage trousers, Karl Marx shirts. John would come in and make up his own clothes. Three weeks later Vivienne would have them in her shop. That's what Vivienne and Malcolm did. They got ideas from anywhere they could. It wasn't as if we were decked out in their clothes all the time.

LYDON: A lot of the northern press would say we were just clothes horses and models for Malcolm's shop. Of course, Malcolm would not deny anything—even though Malcolm's shop was run by Vivienne and everything in it was done by her, the same way Malcolm thought he wrote Pistols songs. There was a lot of Viv selling stuff that she took from everything and everyone, particularly me. I was angry about that. I would put things together, and she'd have it in the fucking shop a couple of weeks later—mass produced. There wouldn't be the slightest blinking or guilt about it. While a lot of her clothes were brilliant, Vivienne's designs struck me as sexless. She would create these little blouses for men. I remember these small round-collared shirts, but the patterns were great. I liked clothes that annoyed people, but not just silly for the sake of it. Unfortunately, I think Vivienne is now just silly for the sake of it. She has no inspiration, apart from royalty. She makes clothes for the disco crowd and the terminally fashionable and rich.

COOK: Ultimately we needed a record deal, so we proceeded to record a series of demos.

LYDON: Dave Goodman got into recording demos with us because we used his PA and monitor board with his mate, Kim, around July of 1976. They were two chaps from North London who had hand-built his gear, and it was in their front room. That's how they got involved. Making demos became a bargain-basement opportunity with the people we went on tour with. We had previously cut three tracks, including "Problems" and "Pretty Vacant" with Chris Spedding. By then it was very important we eventually get signed. Abso-fucking-lutely. You cannot exist without that guarantee of cash. We had to have records on the market. Remember, a lot of these imitator punk bands had already been signed while we weren't. The Damned and a couple of outfits claiming themselves as punks were already banging out records. It was very important for the Pistols to get a record out there to combat that stuff because we could have just fallen by the wayside in the same way the Pretty Things did way back in the sixties with the Rolling Stones. Everybody remembers that the Pretty Things were better than the Stones, but they didn't get the records out there. That's the point. You have to make your next move and be very decisive.

COOK: Malcolm was in a terrible fix, and he knew we needed a deal. We wanted a proper record company to compete with all the bands we were slagging off. We also had to get a good producer.

HOWARD THOMPSON: Many people were generally frightened of getting involved with the Sex Pistols. While they were without a deal, they were creating headlines in the papers just by the way they acted—whether they were insulting figures of authority or throwing up in an airport. They weren't the kind of band you could take home to mother.

LYDON: The fix for Malcolm was to get a record company interested, period. He would receive absolute insults. CBS threw him out of the building while we waited across the street. It was quite clear from the start that the last thing we ever wanted was to sign with one of those small indie labels. Then we would be back down into pub rock land again and we'd never get out. What finally sold us to the labels was through all the put-downs, they would come to the gigs and see these audiences they could not recognize from any place else. That eventually became the selling point, and that always will be. If you're playing the same old songs in front of the same old crowds, you'll get nowhere. You can't manipulate crowds and fill it up with a bunch of haberdashery specials. It has to happen naturally. No Situationist scheme will do. You can't buy a public until after you've made a record. Look what EMI did with us—potentially the biggest band in the universe. They froze. They were used to bands in a Rick Wakeman and Steve Harley manner. It was safe, all about units. Adverse publicity was a new thing to them. They had never known anything like us. You'd think they would since they claimed to have marketed Elvis Presley records. EMI dug their own grave with the money they threw at us.

COOK: The old boys couldn't handle the outrage that came with the Bill Grundy TV episode. People like John Reid and "The Old Grey Whistle Test" would get pressure from somebody else on top. That was it, and we were off. The A&R department at EMI didn't want us off. It was all the bourgeoisie businessmen. I didn't know fuck-all about them and their multicorporate organization. But they couldn't handle us, and it wasn't us who wanted to leave.

LYDON: One thing we absolutely understood: if we signed on a small label, we were going to be promoted and pressed in a small way. Not enough records to not enough stores. If you're going to make change in this world, you have to attack from the inside out, and not be on the outside pinpricking your way in. We all turned down Virgin early on because of their smallness. They wanted us right from the start, but they didn't have any money. At the time, all they had were a few stores. It would have been a stupid move to have signed with Virgin early on. It wouldn't have worked. They needed to sell a few more Mike Oldfield records to be able to afford what we had in mind.

COOK: "Anarchy" got good reviews and was generally well received. It was withdrawn by EMI straight away, so it was all over in five minutes. It entered the charts at about twenty-eight, then out. The Grundy incident happened immediately after the record's release. EMI had us on there to promote the single. We were getting ready to go on tour at the time.

LYDON: We were supposed to go on and be nice boys. Grundy must have had a drinking problem. Steve was goaded into swearing after something I mumbled. Grundy turned to me and asked, "What were you saying?" and Steve just jumped on it. Bill Grundy was a fat, sexist beer monster who knew nothing about us and shouldn't have been interviewing us in the first place. All we did was point that out. All he was interested in was the tits. A few of the Bromley contingent came with us and were in the background. It was the Banshees' first TV appearance. A Renta-Crowd for the Pistols. I remember we all danced around during the closing theme song.

COOK: Grundy had a problem—us. It was an exciting time.

LYDON: Except when finances were never resolved. We were young and asked to sign a contract without being furnished with separate legal representation, not good business by anyone's standards. Malcolm was practicing a fifties kind of managerial policy. But there we were in the seventies. Then there I was in the eighties finally catching up with him. It's almost poetry. That whole court thing was a nightmare. I remember one time jokingly saying, "Well, if push comes to shove and we all have to go to jail, I know I can survive it. But I know Malcolm can't." It eats you up. I was trying to keep PiL together as a band. Because of the lack of money—a situation I was well used to—it went on and on and on.

COOK: It's surprising there was any money left at the end for anyone to get—with all the receivers and lawyers.

Some visualize the Pistols era in shades of black and white. It wasn't. Actually, the colors I envision are neon or army dirt green with fluorescent pink—anything that would annoy. Maybe I'm an intellectual after all, but I've always thought that colors, like words, like intonations, affect people.

BOB GRUEN: They did things in pink, green, and yellow Day-Glo. I found that childlike, bright, and happy—they were the colors little kids liked. Contrary to popular belief, the Pistols didn't use a lot of blacks and dark blues. The graphics were well organized, and in America we hadn't seen designs like that outside of an occasional band logo. In England, much more so than here, the record companies picked up on the wild and loud artwork.

There's no such thing as a completely original thought. It's not possible. You regurgitate one way or another. We took everything from the sixties we could and abused it. It was a free-for-all, and it still is to this day. Some of us dressed down, which was seen as dressing up—but never flared Levi's or tie-dyed shirts. It was a youthful film noir look, but colourized. We were sixteen or seventeen, trying to dress smart and making it up as we went along, absolutely pretentious. Whatever you thought Cary Grant would have worn, that would be nice. If you looked appalling in it and matched it with plastic sandals, you didn't know any better. I've always had this aversion to wearing denim. I had one pair of jeans that I borrowed from Paul Cook when my pants fell apart at the arse. I was forced to wear jeans for a week, and it was awful. The only other pair I had were straight legs, which caused howls of derision in the council flats. You see, flares were the order of the day.

HOWARD THOMPSON: People walking about in garbage bags, safety pins and syringes hanging off their epaulets, images of naked cowboys, photos of women's breasts on their T-shirts. This was all very new! It was also inflammatory and immediately demanded a reaction. Either jail me or fuck off. Music and fashion had became a direct challenge.

When you see film footage of the Pistols live, visually we were quite stunning. It wasn't drab. That was the shock of it all. Bondage outfits. Slashed-up suits. Torn up mohair jumpers. Every other band was a dowdy T-shirt, blue denims, and the acoustic guitar. The Sex Pistols were gaudiness incarnate. Musical vaudeville. Evil burlesque.

CAROLINE COON: I was able to watch objectively because I'm not from the Tom Wolfe school of journalism that puts yourself into the center of an article. For a while I was able to silently watch John as a young artist at work. The interesting part was sheer talent versus lack of training. The nerve it took to get out on stage and perform without any of the training that, say, a dancer would have. Without any technique, your talent struggles across your nerves. I thought John's performances—which, of course, he would trivialize—were heroic. Here was the courage of a young performer without technique who had something really interesting to say. I don't mean to belittle him in saying that he was a natural, charismatic figure, because I think that everything John was doing was very well thought out. I admired the way he was styling himself, the thought that went into how he presented his persona and the wonderful layers at work. I loved his talent for writing, which was a combination of nerves and ambition. Here was somebody, nineteen, writing poems. That's what makes someone an artist. It's what moves you.

When you see that kind of performance, and the dynamic that's going on—the electricity between the courage it takes to go on stage and to express yourself, and to learn your technique—it's riveting to watch. It's emotional. It moves you. The Pistols had a mythical kind of macho diffidence that said you don't need technique, all you need is to strum a few chords. I think John had a precise idea of what kind of poet he wanted to be.

The sinister, kidnap letter graphics of our gig flyers and singles sleeves really threatened people. We used what was around. There were a lot of ransom letters and terrorist kidnappings on the news at the time. Malcolm, Julien Temple, and Jamie Reid would love to take all of the credit. Steve, Paul, and Glen showed no interest whatsoever in the Pistols' graphic designs. I'd like to take all the credit for it, but to be honest it was a combination of everyone. None of these people had final and total say. To me the presentation was as important as the content. I would always insist on being in on where the direction of the graphic look was going. This used to drive Malcolm spare. Not so Jamie Reid or Bernie Rhodes.

BOB GRUEN: I found the Sex Pistols' graphic presentation interesting, striking, and quite different. There was fear in those kidnapping/ransom note logos. At the time, it was almost frightening seeing the band's name written as it would be in a threatening letter with everything safety-pinned. Having grown up in a Jewish community, I was a bit sensitive about the swastikas. They were verboten and scary, so it took me a while to realize the Pistols were using it to create fear as opposed to starting a Nazi movement. Or maybe they were poking fun at fear since they probably hated the Nazis as much as they hated everything else. Maybe they were merely trying to get a rise out of their fans.

Jamie and Bernie were quite talented in the arts, and if anybody got me into that aspect of it from the start, it was Bernie Rhodes. He was important to me in so many ways. When I first joined the Pistols, Bernie would often take me aside and tell me, "Go with it. Honest, it will be good. You'll get there." He would indicate to me where the problems with the Pistols would be in the future. He would sow a seed and then wait to see if I would pick up on it. After the first couple of rehearsals, he'd say, "Now you have to start thinking about how you're going to be presented to the world. Who's going to take your photographs? What about album

Top: Where are my monitors? Wearing mummy's watch at the Nashville in London. (John Gray) Bottom left: Johnny: Why am I in a band with him? (John Gray) Bottom right: Glen: Why am I in a band with him? (John Gray)

covers?" That was the way before we were anywhere near that stage with the Pistols. Through Bernie, I learned to get involved early on.

CHRISSIE HYNDE: I didn't think Bernie had any ideas. I know a lot of people credit him for the punk thing, but not me. Obviously he was in competition with Malcolm, and he wanted to get in there and do something.

Bernie Rhodes got on quite well with Glen Matlock, but Glen was an art school student with average talent. Matlock couldn't paint very well. He didn't like oppositions. His paintings would tend to look murky gray, and the colors wouldn't stand out from each other.

It was laughable when Glen was in the band. When Steve Jones would masturbate, he'd pour hot water down a hollowed French loaf, chuck some raw liver down it, and then fuck it. The hot water would cook the liver, and I supposed his dick cooked it, too. Then he'd come in it and set it aside. I would turn up and Steve would say, "I'm sorry, I've done it again. Should we make Glen Matlock a sandwich?" I particularly remember how he used to love how soft the bread was.

I asked Malcolm about the Beatles when we first started. He told me what amazed him about the Beatles was that they could actually play and keep a sense of rhythm and order. You could hear them clearly.

JOHN GRAY: Malcolm hadn't a clue about music. He's totally tone deaf. Malcolm may have been a good "thrower together" of ideas, but his jukebox at the Sex shop was indicative of what he was really into—either kitsch, camp, or nostalgia. Phil Spector. He had a mess of musical tastes. I'll never forget when I was deejaying at Screen on the Green for the Pistols gig, he tried to get me to play old fifties ballads and sixties crap. We were playing Yoko Ono, dub, and Irish jigs; over-the-top stuff. He would come up with his pile of scratched forty-fives—Johnny Ray or stuff like that.

People in London were used to more chaotic-sounding bands like the Pretty Things. That was something no London band at that time had. When you think about it, the Rolling Stones could never have taken off if the Beatles hadn't written some songs for them. There's a lot to be said for that; people are quite boring, and they do like good tunes. That will always confound me. I've always preferred the raw edge, the racket. A good tune is just a good tune, it's neither here nor there. I'm not interested anymore once I understand it.

I never felt Malcolm and I were ever in synch with the Sex Pistols. I never, ever liked Malcolm as a friend. I always thought he was a bit of an operator. There was never a feeling of camaraderie or teamship. You could never sit at a bar with Malcolm, because he wouldn't buy his rounds. He wouldn't buy sod all. He would never put his hand in his pocket—not ever! He's as tight as skin on God's earth.

There was always this controversy about the Sex Pistols and New York's Ramones. Who came from whom? Yes, there was a Ramones album out at the time, but they were all long-haired and were of no interest to me. I didn't like their image, what they stood for, or anything about them. They had absolutely nothing to do with life in Britain. Sid liked them. But then Sid liked anything that he thought was stylish. The Ramones fitted in well with Sid's visions of New York night-clubs—you could go and get fucked up on drugs while maintaining a healthy existence.

CHRISSIE HYNDE: The Ramones were the only American band that the English punks recognized. Sid learned how to play guitar playing with the Ramones albums for two or three days. He fucking loved the Ramones! Few punks recognized the rest of the American bands while the Clash element, the more art school types, liked Patti Smith. I don't think Rotten and those guys had too much interest in her. They probably saw Patti as an old hippie.

I only found out about Richard Hell when he came over to England after the Pistols' failed "Anarchy in the U.K." tour. I saw him play at the Camden Palace, and the audience was giving him a terrible time. They were throwing stuff, and I walked on and said, "Let him play!" Then they stopped, listened, and didn't like him anyway. We were being bombarded with this nonsense that we were imitating New York. It was not true at all. There was a connection with Malcolm, because he had something to do with the New York Dolls. I didn't know that when the Pistols were forming. I couldn't give a second toss about it.

It's funny when people do things for the wrong reasons—for instance, when the gobbing craze started after I used to spit off stage. Nobody realized they were imitating a physical illness, not a political stance. I've spat like that all my life because of very bad sinuses and a phlegm problem. It also comes quite natural, particularly when you're on stage and you're ripping your tonsils apart through every song. So you just gob it on the stage. But the sheep out there who love to bleat do likewise. Maybe if I'm feeling particularly spiteful and

Paul & Steve: early beginnings. (John Gray)

depressed, I'll slash my fake plastic wrists and see how many followers I could take with me.

It was very unlike working-class kids to be doing the things we were
doing just before the Pistols. Why are the working class so angry, lazy,
and scared of education? Why are they so scared of learning and stepping outside of their clearly defined class barriers?

CHRISSIE HYNDE: The class system is what punk was all about. I
    never quite understood that because I'm basically a classless being.

The Brits love wallowing in their misery, I have to say it. They love
their phone system not working. They love British Rail being as goddamned awful as it is. It's the joke of Europe, the scandal of the world.
Inefficiency helps them moan their way through life.

"How was your day, dear?"

"Oh, it was awful!"

"Must have had a good time then."

Have you ever noticed that there's always too much weather in
England? It's either too hot or too cold. It rains, or it doesn't rain.
They're never happy. There's no such fucking thing. They love to see
their idols and stars take a good kicking from the press. Everybody gets
their turn. They build you up to tear you down, then throw you away
like used tissue paper.

It still pisses me off and pissed off all the people I hung around with
as a kid. I still know all these people, and they're all out there doing
good work, changing things and not going along with the norm. They
still don't fit into little brackets. Some of them are artists and teachers.
Wobble has gone on to do his own music and is doing quite well.
Wobble never went for the money, either. He's much more interested
in the head work. Important.

Wobble and I rented a four-bedroom house in Tottenham in 1977
for six quid a week. Wow! What a deal! We decided not to pay the rent,
so the landlord came around with two bouncers. When they turned up
we told them to come in. They wouldn't. We told them we wouldn't
pay the rent unless they came in. The rent money was in the kitchen.
They still wouldn't come in. I tend not to believe these kinds of stories,
either, but the doors in this house used to open and close in the middle of the night. I'd be sitting in the room and I'd see some old woman
in the corridor. The door between the corridor and the front room was
glass and you'd just see the shadow of someone walking by. You'd open
the door, look around, and there would be no one there. It was very

annoying when you would hear someone on the staircase and you knew no one was upstairs. The neighbors wouldn't go near the place. Wobble wouldn't go in on his own. We used to ring each other up and wait outside. Out of four bedrooms, we'd all sleep in this one room.

We moved out after two months into a house on Burton Street in King's Cross. It was owned by a bunch of Muslim Indians. They couldn't take the massive crates of lager arriving nightly. We had a deal with the local off-license to buy six or seven crates a day. They would deliver them, and the Muslims would go mad. "No alcohol in our house!" Our friend Paul Young (not the singer) threw our television set out the front window. The walls were so thin, Wobble's foot went straight through and into the next flat.

The Pistols played a concert inside Chelmsford Maximum Security Prison. We insisted Malcolm do something and book a gig. That was all he could come up with, so we drove up and played to these long-term to life jailbirds. It wasn't quite as severe as American prisons, but the inmates looked pretty damned psychopathic. It turned out great. The warders just said, "Get on with it!" The guards left and literally locked the doors behind them and waited outside while we played to these crazies. We got the vibe that the warders wanted them to do us over. There was no security and no barbed-wire fences to play behind. I was five feet away from the first row—five or six hundred inmates were sitting there, gritting their teeth. We had really good fun—another receptive audience whose tastes weren't ruined by the press.

"Ouch! I'm going to die! But I might as well die . . . fashionably!"

We just went for it and did our best. What else could we have done? Huddled in the corner? We earned a lot of respect that day. Some of the prisoners came up to us after the gig.

"Thanks for coming," they said as they filed back to their cells.

"Great!" I answered back, strangely moved. No one had ever thanked us for anything before, much less for playing.

Malcolm opened an office off Oxford Street. It was in a slum dwelling with scabby peeling paint on the walls. The windows were painted closed. He didn't like us showing up, which I found strange, so I would show up as often as I could. You would walk in and there would be a bunch of bored people hanging out, not doing anything, people like Simon Barker, Jamie Reid, Berlin, and Sophie Richmond. There would be oddball people milling from one office to another. Inside the same building was the offices for *Sniffin' Glue* magazine. It seemed totally inept. There was only one godforsaken band that was being managed, the Sex Pistols. Malcolm wouldn't even tell Sophie, the secretary—who ran the office—what he was doing. Nobody would answer the phones when I was there. There were empty filing cabinets, and the only filing I saw was nailfiling.

Before we had this office, Malcolm took the Pistols over to Chris Spedding's place. We did a demo with Spedding, who was a respected guitarist. He was the first "musician" who publicly said he didn't understand why we were put down all the time. He thought we were damn fine.

There were virtually no independent labels when the Pistols started. All that came after as an outgrowth of the so-called punk movement. One of the only independent labels was Chiswick—and that was someone's front room in Chiswick. It's really not what you want for a band. You set yourself bigger than that; you want to be heard by as many people as possible. Unless you have distribution, there's no point. When you sign with these independents—as they call themselves—they go and lease the contract to the big labels. Again you've defeated the point, you're now twice removed. Some independents think they've broken the backs of the monopoly. Bollocks! They still need to go through the major labels to get the bloody records pressed, distributed, and paid for. If the major stores don't recognize your label and won't take your record, you're doomed.

I knew very little about the intricacies of the record contracts we signed. I kept way out of it. To be honest, the only interest the band and I had was, how much do we each get? Like true humanitarians. Quite frankly, you can't tell an eighteen-year-old to think any other way. It's impossible at that age, you don't want to be bogged down reading fine print that you will not understand. It's taken me a long time to decipher the words in record contracts, and that's because I've had to. I surround myself with the people who know and the books that tell me otherwise. You'll find that the two can differ. Advisers can be a nuisance. We would have signed anything that was shoved under our faces. In that respect, I was as dumb as everybody else. I was nowhere near capable of understanding what was going on. I realize now that the contracts were shockingly bad. Malcolm hadn't the slightest idea what he was doing, either.

A lot of musicians in the United States don't even enter the wonderful world of music until they are twenty to twenty-five. In England you start at about sixteen or seventeen, even earlier—a major tragedy because you're absolutely open to the hawks. They'll tear you apart, and there's not a lot you can do. Your parents are as dumb as you are. The American record contract with Warner Bros. was signed in perpetuity, forever and ever.

I would have liked to have had more band meetings in the first few months. We'd have a monthly sit-down to say what we're doing or ask Malcolm what was happening. "Where's the money?" That soon fizzled out. Early signs of trouble.

Malcolm went to CBS, and he was physically thrown out of the building. We sat on the bench opposite a little park outside. We sat there and he said, "I'm going to get you a deal now." Everyone was very naive. I thought it was hilarious. Go on, impress me. I said, "I've got an appointment. I'll be back shortly." They wouldn't let us in at first. That was the reason we waited outside. Malcolm went in and was quite literally, physically thrown out. CBS wasn't interested at all, but Malcolm barged his way in. I suppose they found him and the whole idea offensive. That scummy, awful band. How dare you? God, he was so humiliated! It absolutely tore him apart. "Oh! I don't know what happened!" He got so extremely pompous. "How dare they! I'll call the police!" One of the secretaries shouted out, "No need. They're on their way." So then it was a quick runner. We would have all ended up in jail for riotous assembly, nothing more vicious than wanting a record deal. That happened more than a few times. Particularly with booking agents as well. It was hysterical, exactly what I wanted to see happen. When you get that kind of behavior, then you know you're doing something right. You're offending all the right people.

HOWARD THOMPSON: I would think about the ramifications of getting involved, which meant befriending this pack of unruly and completely reckless characters. They were doing things totally against the way music and business was normally done. How would I articulate this to the record company or, worse yet, to my social circles? They were in the papers, vilified daily in the national press. Plus there was something else that I'd never really told anyone before.

My father was a heavy and important figure in the music department at the Arts Council of Great Britain. One of his main responsibilities was to subsidize through government grants most of the big orchestras in England. He would also find soloists and give them grants. He had a huge influence in the classical world. So I had to come to terms with whether or not me and my old man would ever be able to speak to one another again. We'd already had a difficult few years at that time, and I was trying to patch things up with him. The Sex Pistols would have killed any chance of that happening. He would have been absolutely horrified if I had signed this band to a record contract.

We visited Mickie Most, the famous record producer of the sixties, when we were label hunting. He was quite pleasant, but, looking at me, he didn't think we had the right cutie boy image. He wasn't nasty or horrible toward us, and not many people at that time knew much about us. Mickie Most-type production was all that was really happening in pop rock apart from supergroup, dinosaur shit or the disco nonsense. It's absolutely beyond me why we went there. We knew what the answer would be before we got there. At least I did. We were plumbing the depths.

HOWARD THOMPSON: I didn't feel with their modus operandi that they could last. I wasn't about to invest a lot of Island's money in something that was going to self-destruct. Now my only regret in eighteen-plus years of doing A&R is that I *didn't* sign the Sex Pistols.

It was an achievment rather than a detriment when EMI signed and——three months later—dropped us. I honestly didn't care. The check landed. EMI struck me as a lame label. Guys in suits; that's all I remember about EMI. They had one A&R chap with vaguely longish hair, and he'd be allowed to wear jeans and a nice shirt. He was the token jester to make out how jolly rock 'n' roll they all were. But when you visited the EMI offices, there was nothing but guys in suits at every table and secretaries all dolled up from nine to five. They seemed bourgeois for me, a lack of looseness. EMI at first mentioned transferring us to Harvest Records, but that never came about. Malcolm didn't even know what Harvest was. I did and promptly told EMI what to do with themselves. That was not for me. I suppose EMI thought they could push us off to one side. We wanted it to say EMI on the record.

EMI didn't like us, either. Other artists sent in complaints and didn't wish to continue with EMI if they had the likes of us on board—or on bored. There goes the old school tie, from the likes of public school boys and upwardly mobile sorts like Rick Wakeman, Steve Harley, and various others. It was the same old shit again, the class system coming down on us.

BOB GRUEN: I went over to EMI with them. We'd all been drinking beer, so we were feeling pretty good. I remember it was late in the day, six or seven o'clock. Most of the EMI offices were empty, except for one guy who was waiting for the Sex Pistols. Eventually a few more people, mostly lawyers and A&R men, trickled in. The band signed the papers as we took photos. Then the EMI guys broke out the champagne to celebrate. Now we'd been drinking good English beer all day, so after a cup or two of champagne everybody was pretty sick. I remember Steve throwing up in the parking lot. The next day it was in all the papers that the Sex Pistols had thrown up at their record company.

The punk explosion had all the record companies quaking in their boots. That's why they ran out and signed up anything that remotely looked like punk. They wanted to absorb it into the system and make it mainstream. They weren't going to initiate punk, merely jump on it once it's happening. The record companies say, "Go away and make yourself incredibly famous. Then come back and we'll sign you." I don't give a damn about the name *punk*. I never did. It's a label that was assigned to us by the journalist Caroline Coon. It's an American word for a male prostitute in prison. I don't want to be no king of that! You can shove that one. There was something about the Pistols the record companies could not grasp. They didn't know what the threat was. They wanted the poncey little tarts that most groups are made up of. They were disturbed with the real McCoy.

"Oh, God, they're not acting."

The Sex Pistols were always disastrous. Every bloody day, something would go completely wrong, backfire, and put us in the shit. I never knew life to be any different, so it was perfectly fine. Lo and behold, here I am many years later and nothing's changed really.

It would have been easy to turn the Sex Pistols into the new Rolling Stones, but that was something I never wanted. To his credit, Malcolm never wanted it that way, either. He needed the band to conform to his vision, rather than sharing. In the days before the Pistols, new bands had to become part of the industry machine. But the Sex Pistols proved that it need not be the case. It's a shame few have learned that lesson, because music has since gone back to the old ways.

HOWARD THOMPSON: All of a sudden bands weren't being told what to do by record companies. Record companies weren't in the position to demand that bands do this or that. Artistic control went back to the creators themselves. Musicians found vehicles, whether it was through a small independent label or a deal with a larger label who understood what it was they were trying to do. Bands were putting their own artistry through in an uncompromisable and radical fashion. In fact, the bands began to dictate the terms as record companies began to scramble to sign anything new that moved.

The Pistols were never in with all those musical insiders, writers, any of them. We did "Top of the Pops" once and some of those chart shows, but usually we'd be thrown off for bad behavior. That became repetitive in itself. Oh, dear, banned from another show—and for the most inoffensive things. People believed the myths, therefore the slightest infringement of the rule would be magnified. It was good fun to know you were annoying the powers that be to the point where they got hysterical and lost control.

Take, for instance, Bill Grundy.

The whole Bill Grundy incident was lovely. It was heaven. He ruined his own career. It wasn't me. At the time we were asked to appear, we were rehearsing on Craven Park Road in Harlesden for our upcoming Anarchy Tour. EMI arranged an interview on the "Today" program. "Today" was a show with idle banter and chat that was programmed throughout the nation. We did not even know we were going to be on live TV that very day. ITV sent a limo over to pick us up. Yippee. There were drinks available in the car, then more drinks available in the hospitality area. The TV station had a reception room, which was just an excuse to get shit-faced. That's where we met Bill Grundy.

Grundy was filthy dead, pissed drunk when we got there. We also had Siouxsie and the Bromley contingent with us. We were there for at least an hour before the show. Grundy started coming on to the girlies, particularly Sioux. He behaved like a filthy, dirty old man, and that's what came out in the interview. He more or less told us we were all filthy scum. The only decent thing there were the tarts—and they were just about worth fucking and that was it. That attitude came out in the interview, and we were not amused by him. When he was behaving antagonistically from sentence one, it was just let rip. I started that by saying something under my breath. He asked, "What was that?" Steve jumped in with whatever he said. Then Grundy just went off. They had no idea what they were letting themselves in for. Or maybe they did. Bill Grundy was a professional alcoholic. His behavior was bad before the interview in this so-called hospitality room. We were made to feel like dirt. The producer and director must have known. They must have watched and wanted it, but they weren't quite prepared for what they got. They thought we would crumble. They got every single obscenity known to mankind. "You fucking rotter. You dirty fucking bastard." That kind of stuff. That's all very well and good for broadcast at six-thirty, right after the news. It was so wonderful to read in the newspaper the next morning that a man in Liverpool kicked in his TV in disgust and was suing the TV station! The press loved it. I think they were meaning to fire Bill

Grundy anyway, which they did not long after. Before he died, Grundy did these walkabout TV shows in places like Yorkshire and Lancashire called pub routes. He walked through the moors in search of pubs.

STEVE JONES: I definitely started the fracas on the Grundy show. We were down in Camden rehearsing for the "Anarchy in the U.K." tour with the Clash and the Heartbreakers. We were fucking about on this big stage when the people from EMI came down with a big limo and said, "You better come down to the TV station now because Queen was going to do it, but they couldn't make it. We have to fit you in." The BBC put us in this little hospitality room that had a fridge filled with booze. I was nervous and downed three bottles of Blue Nun. The next thing I knew we were walking out onto the set and I was drunk and pissed off. I thought Grundy was going to talk about our upcoming album tour, but I could see straight away he just wanted to make us look stupid. Siouxsie told Grundy she had always wanted to meet him, and I think she was sincere. He said to her, "We'll meet after the show." He was being an old sleazy bastard, so I started swearing at him. Actually John said "shit" and nobody heard it. Then I started saying "fuck this" and "fuck that." I thought they bleeped stuff on TV. It's common practice, and I can't work out why they didn't that day. Maybe somebody deliberately let it go out. It was amazing. But I had no qualms about telling this guy where to go. Straight afterward we rushed into the limo and zoomed off. I remember someone saying, "The phones are going crazy! Everyone is calling up and going crazy!" It felt really exciting.

HOWARD THOMPSON: When the Pistols did that to EMI and A&M, I'm sure it was devastating to the labels involved, but for all of us, it was a gas. It was hysterically funny and completely expected. I think it was Rick Wakeman who went public after the Sex Pistols signed with A&M for one week. He didn't like being on the same label as these scruffy Herberts who couldn't play their instruments, so he talked to Derek Greene, the managing director. So they were off the label. It was like, bang bang, who's next?

As for our relationship with EMI, it ended soon after we sold fifty-five thousand copies of our first single, "Anarchy in the U.K." We parted company after Malcolm collected about fifty thousand pounds total in record and publishing advances. EMI—Every Mistake Imaginable, and they're still making them.

HAND ON EYES

Hey, you! You look suspicious. Empty out your pockets," they yelled.

And that was it.

On January 12, 1977, I was busted for nothing more serious than crushed slimming pills, illegal at the time. In America they call them diet pills. I only had a tiny amount, 138 milligrams—you could only see the particles under a microscope. I was arrested during rehearsals in Soho when I took a break and went out for something to eat. I got done in between the studio and the sandwich shop. There was a wagonload of policemen with little python emblems on their helmets. They were the killer squad—the serious boys. I don't know if they were a special drug squad, but they were certainly hooligans. I can't recall which station I was taken to. I was too bloody terrified.

At the station, I was strip-searched in front of a female police officer. They went through everything—my shoelaces, my belts, even the safety pins I had holding my shirt together. They went through my shirt seams. Everything. Then I was locked in a cell, and I didn't get out until later that evening. That was the first time bail was arranged for me. It was minimal, and Malcolm actually fronted it. The judge ordered me to stay with my parents until I appeared in court, which put me in Daddy's custody. Another nightmare, huh? The time they gave me to go back into court for my hearing was not the same time they had on their records. Theirs showed my appearance scheduled for a week earlier, so I was watching television at about six-thirty one evening when the police came to the door. Bang bang bang.

"It's the police! God, what have I done now?" I ran upstairs and was going to jump out the second-floor window, but that's where the officers were waiting. My old man was at the door, trying to hold them back, but they came in with their dogs. They brought me down to Hornsey Road station, the local one in Finsbury Park. This time Malcolm wouldn't come and sort out the bail, so my old man had to come up with it by midnight. My parents were ringing Malcolm's office all the way through the evening, but he couldn't be fucking bothered.

There were two holding cells in the station near Finsbury Park. On the wall of my cell was a list of the Lydons who had done time in it. Jimmy and Bobby had written their names there. We had all been through that same cell. I wrote my name underneath and joined the list—a good club. In London, people used to get pulled up all the time. They had a law called suspicion that allowed the police to hold you as long as they liked. Usually they would keep you for a couple of hours and then throw you out. It was designed to annoy you more than anything else.

I was alone in my small eight-by-ten-foot cell. It had big steel bars, white tiles, and an overflowing toilet—a bit like a mental hospital. It absolutely stank. My parents bailed me out that night, and another court appearance was set for a couple of days later, when they sentenced me to pay a forty-pound fine. Malcolm, the man holding our purse strings, showed up and said, "Oh, I don't have any money on me." The judge, in his infinite wisdom, sent me back to the slammer. The police marched me downstairs and told my parents that if the fine wasn't paid by three-thirty that afternoon—before the court sessions closed—they would upgrade the conviction. Malcolm probably went off and had lunch somewhere. He came back with ten minutes to spare and paid the fine. My father wanted to kill Malcolm for his scandalous behavior; I could have murdered him on the spot. By that time we all knew that he was never going to change; he was always going to be a skinflint. That was the constant problem. Malcolm was hardly showing much interest in his budding young stars.

The only way you could get money out of Malcolm was to threaten to quit. Suddenly the money would be there. It went on like that all the

Sid the fashion victim and John the toe-rag. (Bob Gruen/Starfile)

time. I don't think Paul and Steve had that problem. Their attitude was, "Malcolm never did us any wrong." And he probably didn't. He knew them a lot longer, and they were more easygoing. It was so easy for them to just go with it all. "Malcolm wouldn't lie. John's just a moaner."

For fun, sometimes we would go to transvestite clubs. I've always found them and the gay clubs to be a hoot, much looser than other places. Without gays, there wouldn't be much of a nightclub scene anywhere, giving a city like London a lot of its vibe. If you leave it to the regulars, it merely becomes a beer hall for the locals. There were loads of transvestite clubs in London. I met Linda in one club off Oxford Street. The red lights there used to drive me crazy, but it was free drinks and something to do. I put up with it. That was my sunglasses period. Again people thought I was posing because I was wearing a blind man's pair of glasses. I was shielding myself from bloody red light! My aversion to red light is probably psychological. Most of my problems are. I have weak eyes that relates to the meningitis.

CHRISSIE HYNDE: I'd seen Sid pull a long link of chain out of his jacket and spin it around to clear an entire dance floor. If anyone got caught in the chain, it was tough shit. He definitely could be violent.

Sid never fought. He was worse than I was. But he used to love carrying weapons—like chains and things. He thought it made him look tough. We had a particularly bad night once when we got pulled up on Tottenham Court Road. Sid was waving his chain, and the cops come over. "Right. You're nicked. Possession of a dangerous weapon." We invented this awful, elaborate lie. Knowing how racist the British police were, they were so easy to manipulate. Here's the story: "Yes, Officer, we stole it off this black man. He's in a huge gang, and there's at least twenty of them. They chased us for miles, and they're just around the corner. One of them has got a gun." The police loved it. "Really?" They spun off up the road to get them. They took the chain. Maybe now, looking back, they thought, What a pair of tossers, man. Don't you just feel sorry for them?

All these incidents were more laughable than anything else. When the press gets hold of things, they can escalate them into some kind of frenzy. We let the press have a free hand. They could say whatever they liked. Malcolm said it right from the start: The press will just make it up anyway, so just go with it. I could see that would be true. And, lo and behold, it was. Deny nothing.

CAROLINE COON: The whole stance of journalists, white macho journalists, was anti-intellectual. Their conceit was that working-class rock 'n' roll had to be stupid.

HOWARD THOMPSON: As exciting as it was, it was also immensely frustrating and aggravating and fantastic and completely new! Who knew? It was one of those situations where you saw something going on and there were a few people in the audience who got it as well as a handful of journalists writing about it. I remember Caroline Coon, Jonh Ingham, and Giovanni Dadomo, all part of the early scene writing about this music in a very enthusiastic and sensationalistic fashion.

I was rushed to hospital after a gig in Walthamstow supporting Kilburn and the High Roads because I foolishly walked on stage in a rubber T-shirt. Three songs in, I collapsed, and then it was oxygen tent time. I ended up selling what was left of that same shirt to Sid, and precisely the same thing happened to him. Midsummer madness. The fool walked outside, and it was eighty-five degrees. Fashion-first Sid. He collapsed.

Nobody really looked like us at all. A whole punk audience imitating us slavishly came a long time later. We changed our looks frequently. For instance, one week I looked like a complete Teddy boy. I used to enjoy quiffing my hair up. Teddy boys were the enemy. Therefore, they interested me. So I'd go to the Teddy boy gigs. They'd know who I was, but they would think it was funny that this horrible king of the punks was sitting there among them with a better quiff.

We used to cross the line all the time. That's what it was all about when we'd go to that soul boy club, the Lacey Lady. The boot boys there never gave us any trouble. They thought if we had the guts to look like that and stand in the middle of the floor bouncing around like yo-yos, good luck.

It's amazing what you can get away with if you push hard enough. There was a lot of violence in the streets between punks and Teddy boys during the late seventies. But if you went smack into the middle of the enemy's camp, they'd back off because they couldn't believe you'd have the cheek to do it. If you act like you feel out of place, somebody will suggest you leave. If you're comfortable in your new surroundings, then there is not a lot people can say. So what. If they're going to beat me up, they'll beat me up anyway. Meanwhile, it gives them a mental block and they can't figure it out. By having that devil-may-care attitude, I made some friends in the Teddy boy movement. One of them was a Millwall football hooligan. He was at the

Speakeasy, and he absolutely pummeled Joe Strummer one night. A big fat motherfucker he was, real hard. He didn't like Joe, and he thought what the Clash stood for was all lies—working-class fakes. Soon after, Joe was going on about being beaten up by gangs of Teds. It was only one in the toilet at the Speakeasy. Later when I went to America, this guy moved in and squatted my place to look after it while I was away.

The Teds were different from the punks in that there were many ages—there was the older lot, all the dads, along with the younger kids. The punk thing was very young. It was like going out and fighting old men, kind of ridiculous, really.

I like Steve Jones very, very much. He's honestly dishonest. He'll steal anything. He'll steal your fucking shoelaces, but if you confront him, he'll admit it. He'll tell you yes straight out. He doesn't deny it, and I like that. Is that childlike? I think it's an admirable quality in itself. Not the stealing, the admitting it. He's compulsive, and a lot of that has to do with his upbringing. He had a terrible fucking childhood. He felt his mother hated him. I remember walking the streets with him. We were really broke, and he needed something at his mother's house. We walked to Battersea from the King's Road, a fucking long walk. We got there and Steve's mum wouldn't let him in. So he pushed his way in. We waited until she went out, and in went Steve. I never forgot her malevolence toward him—it was astounding. I never saw her while I waited downstairs, I heard her scream, "You fucking bastard!" Maybe Steve was a bad son, but c'mon, Mummy, lighten up.

Steve Jones used to despise going home for as long as I knew him. He's always had extreme communication problems. If you sat him down and tried to discuss a situation, he couldn't deal with issues and would rather get up and run away. It's only been the last few years that he and I see eye to eye, instead of being sarcastic with each other. We can have real conversations now. I think if Steve ever lost his childishness, I probably would stop liking him. That's the very thing that makes him such a good chap to know. The stealing was all part of seeking attention. Although he used to be very aggressive with his sexual drives, it was a ridiculing thing because Steve never had any time for women at all other than wham-bam-thank-you and that's it.

Steve never saw much of me outside of rehearsals. He knew little about my background and where I came from. Paul used to hang around with me much more than Steve. The only time Steve and I spent time together was when I literally had nowhere to live. Then I'd stay with him on Denmark Street. Even then we didn't really speak, we'd just sit there across the room. There wasn't any animosity between us. It was just much better when we didn't talk than when we did. Steve always had this thing that I was too arty. He assumed I came from that background until I took him to my family's house. In fact, I brought Malcolm and the whole band up to the old man's in Finsbury Park. We had picked up the very first test pressing of "Anarchy in the U.K." and brought it to the house to listen to. Nobody else had a record player at the time. My old man freaked when he saw Malcolm in a black lace outfit.

Steve was shocked to see my extreme working-class family environment. He was angry because there was both a mother and a father. Even though my parents kicked me out, they still showed love, something Steve never had. I know that upset him.

STEVE JONES: I had a fucked-up childhood. I came from west London—Hammersmith or Shepherd's Bush, same thing. The first thing I remember is being in Hammersmith with my nan, my grandad, and my mum. We lived there until I was about twelve, and then we moved to Benbow Road in Shepherd's Bush. I lived in a basement with my mom and stepfather. It was a one-bedroom flat, and my bed was at the end of my parents'. We had a tin bath you had to fill up with hot water. We were very poor, and my mum was very young. My stepfather was an asshole, and I was just extra baggage—you know what I mean? I had a distant youth, one outside of the family. I never had any meaningful conversations about anything with my parents when I was young. I didn't have any plans for work, but I always had an interest in music. My subconscious was telling me music was a way to get out of the shit hole I was in.

For a time, I lived at Linda's. Linda was a good friend who had lots of cash. I was not living with her—rather, living off her. I had no money, and she was such a laugh. A lot of her attentions worked in the Houses of Parliament, so there was major, lovely filth going on. I'd be sitting there, having to answer the door when they came to our flat at the St. James Park Hotel, which overlooks Buckingham Palace. Many an MP I've shaken hands with. What goes on in the Houses of Parliament, particularly in that late night bar—they have a twenty-four-hour bar in the Parliament—is shameful. You could bring down a government on what we knew about those people. We're not just talking dirty old conservative MPs either, we're talking about a lot of them. It was Linda and a couple of other girlies in action, and I'd open the door and let the boys in.

Nancy Spungen came over to England with Johnny Thunders & the Heartbreakers, who were remnants of the New York Dolls. We knew what the Heartbreakers were into.

BOB GRUEN: The one thing Johnny Thunders and Jerry Nolan liked about England was that it was easier to be a junkie there. In America it was a hustle, whereas in England you could get certified and receive a prescription supply. You could buy fresh needles, all kinds of codeine and cough syrups with opium in them—all over the counter.

CAROLINE COON: Up until then I hadn't seen heroin around. Of course, the English bands are very vulnerable, being as noticed as they were, and they needed the biggest painkiller of all.

Nancy stayed with Linda because she'd been thrown out of the Heartbreak Hotel. She turned up at the door, dumping Nancy onto Linda and her girlfriend. Nancy was a real pain in the arse, all over me.

BOB GRUEN: When Johnny and the Heartbreakers went over to England, Nancy lost her playmates, so naturally she followed them over.

Sid got thrown out of his place and came over one night. So I fobbed Nancy off on Sid. Initially I thought of her as a filthy cunt, which of course appealed to Sid. To be hated, loathed, and despised so much by me, he naturally went for her. She, being a woman of loose inclinations, reciprocated. That was it. From that moment on that was the end of both of them. So, yes, I fobbed Nancy off on Sid, which got her off my back. I thought he'd do the same. I thought he'd see through her. Everybody else did. I'm not very good at handling stupid people, I must admit. I think that's what it was. Sidney was basically stupid, so easily led into anything. You could tell him anything and he'd suck it up like a sponge and believe it.

Sid was drinking at the time, so at least you could control him. He was very easy to maneuver. You just pointed him in a direction, and he'd go for it. Impressionable. Did I manipulate him? Yes, but not in a bad way. I got him in a band—not a bad thing for me to do—if that's manipulation. And I got him a girlfriend. Nancy. Very bad.

As far as I know, that was his first girlfriend. Sid never had girlfriends. He loved himself too much. I think he was a virgin. In fact, I know so. What a way to be introduced into the wonderful world of sex. Linda and I left them in a room together, and that was it. We did what we wanted with him off my back for a night. I don't feel guilty about it. Linda's girlfriend was a reason she and I fell apart because Linda found me with her one night. They tried to set Nancy up with an escort agency because, in Nancy's words, she wanted to "do some tricks, man." The chap who hired her was so offended, she got sacked after one night because of her behavior.

BOB GRUEN: One day David Johansen was at my place and Nancy was telling us about this brothel she was working in. She would tie guys up and beat them with whips. David and I were fascinated. Guys pay you to tie them up and hit them with whips? We couldn't believe it. "Who does that?" we asked. According to Nancy, mostly bankers, lawyers, and German guys. I remember her offering, "You guys can come up anytime and we'll show you what it's like—on the house."

Years later, David and I used to joke about it. We'd be driving around at three or four in the morning. "You wanna go to Max's?" we'd say. "The Mud Club? What do you wanna do?"

"We can always go over to Nancy's and get beat up for free."

We never took her up on it.

People make their own decisions. Introducing Sid around was good for him. He made serious efforts to learn to play da-da-da on the bass, but the minute Nancy got her hooks on him—and I should have seen it—he bought the whole New York decadence trip. And that was it. It was all over. Can you imagine them living at Sid's mother's place? The three of them? Can you imagine what on earth they were up to? Sid's mother had a council flat by then. Very strange scenes, I'm afraid.

BOB GRUEN: The first time I'd met Sid he was badgering Malcolm for money. He wanted another seventy pounds. He was screaming and stomping around the place. Sid finally left. A year later, while riding on the bus, we talked about it and Sid admitted that he was putting on a little show. He thought I was some big-shot journalist from America, so he decided to lay it on a little heavier than usual.

Another someone I knew whom I tried to pass on to Sid was Chrissie Hynde. She needed the English equivalent of an American green card in order to stay in England. I agreed to marry her, only I didn't have the courage to turn up at the Town Hall. So I sent Sid. And he went. She wouldn't have him. He was so filthy, Sidney did not believe in washing at the time. This was his antifashion period. He'd gone the

other way from the prissy nail varnish to total hound-dog of the first
degree. Really bad but with a punk hairdo. Chrissie took one look at
that and wouldn't have it!

CHRISSIE HYNDE: There was a time when I was supposed to marry
John, so I could stay in the country. I was stuck and I had to leave.
I never could tell if John was fond of me or if we were friends or
what, but he hung around with me a bit. He was so painfully shy of
women that when he would come and stay the night in my squat,
you wouldn't dare get too close to him because you would not want
to freak him out. You would immediately recognize his space and
keep a wide berth around him. John didn't exude any sort of active
sexuality. He was shy, and you would respect that. To tell the
truth, I was pretty shy myself. At the time, I was squatting and
shoplifting, I didn't own anything except a little amp that Chris
Spedding had lent me. I had nothing and didn't want anything. I
was an infinitely better shoplifter than John. I had a little tiny lock
on the door to my squat that I gave to Sid, and he put it on his
chain.

A few weeks later I couldn't get hold of John, and my time was
running out. I had only a few days to stay in the country, and I was
really losing it.

One day, just after the Bill Grundy show, it became obvious that
he was about to be famous. John and I took a long walk, and he was
very depressed. He was afraid his friends would change and that
things would change drastically for the worst. You see, he was very
close to his mother. He was just a little Irish boy from Finsbury Park.
He had really taken on a lot with all of this, and I think it freaked
him out. He was still very close to his working-class Irish family.

I still needed to marry someone to stay in the country. Finally I
found John drinking with Sid down at Roebuck's pub. I walked up
to him and said, "John, what's happening about our arrangement,
you know, remember?"

"Ohhhh, Gawd!" he said and he put his head down on the bar.

Sid asked, "What's going on? What's going on?"

Someone mumbled something about my visa running out. Sid
stood up and said, "I know! You want to marry John because he's
going to be a famous rock star! And then you'll get pregnant, and
then you'll . . ."

He went on and on, describing this absurd scenario—something
like a seventies groupie girl might think. Everyone was horrified

that Sid would have such a straitlaced idea. Suddenly he realized what he was saying and then volunteered, "Well, I'll do it, but there has to be something in it for me."

"Two pounds," I offered.

"Okay, done," he said.

Then I had to find Sid somewhere to stay. I dropped him off at my place in Clapham, went up to Hackney to get his birth certificate because he was underage, and then went back to Clapham to spend the night while he had a squelching session with this other girl in my bed. Sex wasn't anything you got too sentimental about back then. I remember their knees and elbows in my back all night.

Next morning I had to hang on to Sid by the wrist all day so he wouldn't get away. I took him down to the registrar's office, but it was closed for an extended holiday. Then Sid had to go to court the next day for putting somebody's eye out with a glass or something, so we never got married. I was never Mrs. Vicious, but I almost was. I was also almost Mrs. Rotten, but I suspect that John's background and his relationship with his mother—his close family ties—would have prevented him from marrying me. It would have hurt his parents if they found out.

When I shared a flat with Sid on Sutherland Avenue—with Nancy, of course—there were a couple of bedrooms. I had all of my mates at one end of the house and Sid had Nancy at the other end. I hated their heroin thing so much that when they went out one night, Wobble, John Gray, and I found their needles. I cleaned my fingernails with their hypodermic needles, putting them back. Seems dangerous now, but the idea was to put dirty fingernail filth into the needle so that she'd kill herself or whatever. Maybe that's premeditated murder. I think I did it more out of spite. I couldn't stand her any longer. She was that bad. You cannot believe how bad this woman was. Nonstop. "Ooooh, Sid," with the most annoying voice. She was so dumb, like those awful gangster molls you see in the movies. Where was she from? "Neeew Yooork." Why was she here? "Drruuugs."

BOB GRUEN: Nancy Spungen was originally a friend of Johnny Thunders' and Jerry's. Not a girlfriend particularly, because she wasn't attractive. In fact, she was quite unattractive, not to mention the fact that she whined all the time. Nancy could be a real pain in the ass, but she had a heart of gold. I have nothing against her. She was nice to me and to a lot of the other guys.

CHRISSIE HYNDE: The New York people came and brought their heroin, end of story. They also brought Nancy Spungen, who turned Sid into a sex slave. It was a simple equation; everyone disliked Nancy and told Sid to dump her. But remember—why was Sid called Sid? Because he hated the name. So if anyone said Nancy was horrible, get rid of her, there was no way Sid was going to. He was a very contrary boy. Just the fact that it got on everybody's wick that he was with her made him want to keep Nancy around. Plus, we couldn't use reverse psychology and show approval because no one liked her enough to even try to work that much out.

The so-called Anarchy Tour of December 1976 with Johnny Thunders was a hilarious affair. Malcolm did most of the details for it. An agency booked the whole tour, and it was great fun having all the bands on the same bus. We got along like a house afire—the Damned, the Heartbreakers, and the Clash. There was a falling-out with the Clash because they wanted better billing or some bullshit. They decided to travel separately. Then the Damned decided they were the greatest thing since sliced bread. Egos made it fall apart. The only reason the Heartbreakers stuck it out was because they were utterly without egos. Thunders was so out of it on drugs, nothing mattered. Sid was around all that time. It can be awful sleeping in buses, but not so bad if you're with a bunch of people prepared to enjoy themselves. You're less prone to hate each other instead of seeing just the same four faces. As a manager, Malcolm could have tried a little harder. What was the point in setting all this up, calling it a tour, and then sending us up north, drive from town to town, spend two nights in a hotel, do one gig, then drive around for a week with nothing to do? I think we have a concert at-no canceled, next town. There were no escape hatches or alternatives and again, no money. It's difficult when two hundred journalists with cameras are following you around.

CAROLINE COON: When they [the Heartbreakers] were brought in, it was as if Malcolm had the big success of the Pistols and he wanted to prove that success to the bands in America. So he brought them over, but they were old men who had nothing to do with the optimism and creativity of the Clash, the Pistols, and the Damned.

We were huge, but we couldn't play anywhere, so we couldn't earn any money. Nobody wanted to release our records. We were quite literally paupers—well, some of us! You tried telling anyone that and they would not believe it. They thought we were all millionaires. To be a millionaire you have to work and earn something.

We had an idea to hire a circus tent with a carnival and tour Britain. It would have had rides and the whole circus, fanfare thing. I thought it was an amazing idea. We were having trouble booking normal gigs. It fell apart because insurances and councils didn't want that kind of thing in their town. What a pity! It would have been marvelous. That's the way to do it. If you hate the band, you could still have as much fun as you like on the bumper cars.

Paul, Steve, and I were always skeptical about all these so-called canceled gigs we had during the Anarchy Tour. Malcolm knew by that time it was spinning out of his control. But we trundled on.

Not gigging turned the Sex Pistols internally against each other. We became frustrated and began looking at each other suspiciously. We were bored and at each other's backs. Today the animosity has transformed into a sense of loss.

It proved quite outrageous for modern Britain in the mid-seventies, so much so that you could get the local church to organize a choir to sing hymns because of "the Anti-Christ" coming to their village. The Welsh village of Caerphilly held such a demonstration and tried desperately to stop all of the local kids from getting into one of our concerts. The campaign worked effectively because there was practically the entire parenthood of Caerphilly at the doorsteps of the concert hall. Sure, it was deeply silly, but I did think it was excellently silly. They set up the choir in front of the concert hall. There they all were with their hymn books. The local vicar held his conductor's stick. The TV camera crews filmed us giggling as we went into the hall as the police cordoned the area off to keep the bystanders from rioting.

We only had about thirty people in the building when we played our concert that night and about two hundred outside. I don't know what they thought we would be doing to their kids. Turning them into sex fiends? The promoter lost a fortune, but it was well worth doing because what on earth did these people think they were banning? I gave them a wonderful week's buildup of entertainment and then a sweeping culmination when they got to sing those dreadful hymns outside the concert, that's where the promoter should have been. They were so chuffed with themselves, it was brilliant! You can't be upset or angry with people like that. They amused me greatly. To this day that incident still gives me pleasure, with their silly hymns. They even did "My Sweet Lord" at one point! It wasn't even ten years before when they probably branded George Harrison as some drug fiend monster from hell!

I wrote "God Save the Queen" all in one piece. I remember being really precious about the words. I still am to this day. I keep the lyrics so close to me, the only chance the band gets to hear them is once I start singing them. If you show them the lyrics first, they won't get it. It's the way you deliver that counts. Then you don't get that "Ooooo. They don't rhyme," because that's the kind of comment you will invariably get. I say cut all that crap out and go straight into the deep end.

I did some writing with Glen. We worked very well together, and there was a period where we really did get on, but ultimately I just didn't like him, so there was no point continuing. Malcolm told Glen to make an effort and stop thinking of me as this awkward person who always stood in the dark side of the rehearsal room, moaning, "It's dismal. I hate it." Which is, of course, what I did. But Glen didn't see it as humor at work or veiled shyness—both the same thing, really. I was going for their response. It got rough for me, too. I was definitely reciprocated in a like manner by the other Pistols. We would wind each other up so bad, sometimes they wouldn't talk to me for long periods. I used to have certain phrases that I would practically rehearse for maximum effect: "I hate you!" or "Dismal." "I'm bored."

CHRISSIE HYNDE: John hated Glen so much that he'd occasionally pick up the microphone stand and with his back to Glen, he'd chuck it over his shoulder and try to hit him.

Glen couldn't handle the teasing. I used to love saying to him, "I hate you." He wouldn't know whether I meant it or not.

"I can't believe he hates me! Oh, Paul! Steve!"

I just wanted to see his look. He was such a mummy's boy. He wouldn't perform "God Save the Queen" because his mum didn't like it. That was the excuse given to us. I found it unbearable because he wouldn't say it forthright, but it would come out after an hour or two of badgering him.

"What's wrong with it, Glen?"

"I'll show it to a few people."

"Who, Glen?"

"Well, my mum. Well . . . well . . . but she liked the other songs!"

I instigated Glen's leaving the band. I definitely maneuvered that. It was down to, quite frankly, either he goes or I go. I couldn't put up with him any longer. This is the man who wouldn't have anything to do with "God Save the Queen." He wouldn't play it live, so we used to do it without him. He'd stand in the corner, off stage. Same with

"Anarchy in the U.K." If he was to remain, I had to change some of the lyrics because he'd found them offensive. He'd say, "What do you mean? Do you want to hurt people?" Glen, you're missing the point. But never mind, yes.

STEVE JONES: John wasn't getting along with Glen, and McLaren didn't want him in the band, so one day McLaren told Glen to walk. I was relieved. I didn't mind Glen leaving at all. It was after the Grundy thing, so at this point it didn't fucking matter; nobody gave a fuck about the music anyway. But then, I thought, Who were we going to get? Sid had been coming to our gigs.

I wanted Sid in the band because then I'd have an ally in all of this. It wouldn't just be me out there. Sid couldn't play? So what. Anyone can learn. I learned to sing, didn't I? That was my argument. He took lessons and learned quick, actually. He wasn't too bad at all for three chord songs. It's a bass guitar, for God's sake. Who listens to the bass guitar in a rock 'n' roll band? It's just some kind of boom noise in the background.

STEVE JONES: John said, "Let's get this guy Sid." Sid looked great, but he couldn't play. I thought, Oh, no! This is going to be a headache. It became a circus. Sid was up John's alley—he was the same type of guy—that cocky art student with a smart-ass atti-tude. When he first came around I thought, Oh, no! Here we go again. Not another one! I could deal with John, and now there were two of him.

Sid wasn't very good at recording. On a record, it's quite different. A live gig is one thing, bass on plastic is another. Sid was too fucking drunk, quite frankly. It was desperation time, so in came Glen. We literally hired Glen Matlock. What a nice touch! Shame on him, he actually did it. Isn't that awful? That, more than anything tenfold, explains my contempt for him. I think I'd rather die than do some-thing like that, wouldn't you? It's so cheesy and such a state of des-peration. Malcolm hired him back as a session player. He did all of the dirty work—well, some of it, anyway. Steve played some bass parts as well. The rest of the dirt was ours.

There were a few songs Sidney worked on, one of them was "Submission." I worked quite well with Sid on that. We had lots of good ideas. Only they never used our mix. Apparently there was a fight.

Up to that time, Sid was absolutely childlike. Everything was fun and giggly. Suddenly he was a big pop star. He could do whatever he wanted. Hence vodka, beer, anything. Pop star status meant press, a good chance to be spotted in all the right places, adoration. That's what it all meant to Sid. I never dreamed that he would perceive it that way. I thought he was far smarter. Looking back on it, I must have had an inclination. He took it all too far, and boy, he couldn't play guitar. Dave Bowie reference. In the end, particularly when Nancy started influencing him, heroin started to creep in.

The first rehearsals on Denmark Street in March of 1977 with Sid were hellish. Everyone agreed he had the look, and I was really pleased because Sid was my mate. Great! Another one out of the slums. Success here. It could have been Wobble, but Wobble frightened Steve and Paul too much because he looked dangerous. Sid really tried hard and rehearsed a lot. It was Sid's turn to be the outsider, because we would all go out afterward and he would have to stay at home and practice his bass lines. Sid would have much rather been out partying.

Poor old Sid. I even got him the girlfriend who ruined him. It's terrible. Nancy was the only girl I had ever seen him with up to that point. He was so vain before they met. Girls could never get into his picture because they would probably cast a shadow. There are lots of people like Sid in this business, and I don't mean they're gay or asexual. They're just so self-obsessed with their own looks. Nothing could get in the way of that for Sid. Suddenly when he joined the Pistols, he was transfigured. Now he could do anything. He didn't need to shave, not that he needed to shave anyway. But the idea was that he could wake up anytime in the afternoon. He read too many bad books and bought the New York attitude. Spotty old Beverly. When someone, even yourself, keeps telling you how handsome and good-looking you are, chances are you're not. He was so self-obsessed, it was deeply humorous.

Sid and I moved to a place in Chelsea called the Cloisters. We were in the Pistols, but we had no money and nowhere to live. We were sick of trying to ponce off people, and people were sick of us. We sat in Malcolm's office practically the whole day and insisted he get us somewhere to stay. Eventually he got us into the Chelsea Cloisters, which is exactly what the name implies—a cloying, old, jaded, perverted place. The hallways smelled of old women's fannies. It was like a nunnery, small rooms ten feet square with a sink and a toilet. It was off the King's Road, and there was nothing to do in that area at night. We had no money and could never go out.

One night I met a debutante. She spotted me on the street as I was going for some shoplifting. She said to me from her car, "Oh, yaww, aren't you Johnny?"

"Yes, I am, dahling! How can I help you?"

"Oh, we have a splendiferous party. You simply must come. Bring all your friends, it will be a jolly good wheeze."

She was a spoiled rich girl, and she was celebrating her coming-out party, where they all wear their ballroom gowns and are introduced to all the available young men in their class structure. She invited me, Sid, and Nancy to her debutante's ball. It was fan-fucking-tastic! This was the only time I actually enjoyed Nancy's company because she was so repulsive that night. They took us into a posh nightclub called Wedgies, where they only let in the ultrarich. There were a few royals there. Prince Andrew and David Frost were there, along with loads of fat ugly old women in tiaras who spoke in highfalutin voices.

There we were, like the street urchins we were. I was dressed in tatters, old secondhand torn-up clothing. Sid wore something aproaching a leather jacket, but there was a sleeve missing. Nancy had piss stains all down her tights. She could never be bothered to clean herself, and her legs were so dirty that you could see the white marks where the piss dribbled.

You had to wear a tie to get in. I had no T-shirt, just a tie on with a torn suit. Sid didn't have a tie, so he used his boot lace—a nice touch, very classy. Rules are meant to be broken, or at least bent. They had to let us in because of the people we were with. The party took place in a large ballroom with all the food upstairs.

I planned it like a general leading his troops into battle. First we ran straight toward this glorious banquet of food because we were hungry. There was no question of knives and forks. We were just munching in and being as piggish as we wanted. Then we went for the bar and did some dancing, followed by more food and back to the bar. There was so much free booze. They were playing some effete Euro-disco music, the Giorgio Moroder stuff without those nasty black people singing over the top. I asked David Frost for a dance, and that didn't go down too well with him. Here was the same pontificating bastard you see on TV crossing his legs and being so smarmy all the time. We loved it and offended so many of the upper crust in one night. You can see why we weren't invited to many of those affairs. Apparently we were making lewd suggestions to the young boys and girls. But that was the thrill for this young deb—to have Johnny Rotten turn up at her affair. I never knew her. She was one of those spoiled girls who just wanted to give it back to Mumsy and Dadsy. This girl wanted us to be vile. She followed us around at a safe distance, giggling hysterically: "I wonder who let them in?" Her mother, a duchess, was actually good fun—a horrendous old boiler in another tiara.

The security men followed us around wherever we went. There were cameramen there, but I saw the security people stopping them from taking any photos of us in their company. They didn't want it to get out that we were among these people. That was such a subtle gesture. The manipulation that goes on in the upper reaches is fantastic. That's part of the show they put on, but they don't like to be caught out being as filthy and horrible as they really are. The way those people go on, they put any punk gig to shame. It was debauchery. It's amazing how much booze those people can put away, shockingly more so than your average working stiff. But these are professionals, and they can afford the hangover cures in the morning. I saw a lot of drugs at that place—people in their dickie bows and cocktail outfits, sniffing away in the corners. We were at the party for over four hours. It was such a rare delight and was the only good thing that ever happened at the Cloisters.

We managed to stay at the Cloisters for two weeks when the office forgot to pay the bill. They gave us no money for food, and the flat was cockroach infested, and the rent wasn't paid. So we were thrown out. I spoke with my father through my brothers. I needed a car to get our stuff out because the bill wasn't paid. I didn't want him to know, but later I was glad he found out. As bad as it was, it was better than nothing. I had to call because we had nowhere else to go. It was me eating humble pie. He drove over to pick us up, and my old man really held back because he wanted to beat the shit out of Nancy. She sat in the car and moaned nonstop until we dropped them off at Sid's mother's place.

"We're stars. We deserve a bigger car than this!"

It was my father's car, bitch! Did she expect him to rent a limo for her?

"If we were in New York . . . She went on and on and on. . . .

I explained to my father that we didn't have to live with Nancy. Sid did. Let's face it, it was what he deserved at the time. Yet I was very uptight about having to call my father in the first place. It was a bad, bad situation, and I was really pissed with Sid and Nancy. It was unforgivable and so ungrateful. There were lots of incidents like that. We used to share loads of apartments, but when Nancy turned up on the scene, it would always amount to the same thing. Her whining would be unbearable. She made life so utterly, completely painful—and for no good reason. If you've seen the movie *What Ever Happened to Baby Jane?*, with Bette Davis, that's what Nancy looked like all the time.

Screwed out of her tree, vile, worn, and shagged out. Sid settled for second best immediately. He disliked himself so much that he did the worst possible thing he could have ever done—hook up with that beast, Nancy Spungen. There's nothing vindictive when I say she was a beast. She was a very self-destructive human being who was determined to take as many people down with her as possible. Nancy Spungen was the complete Titanic looking for the iceberg, and she wanted a full load. She was a real spoiled cow, and that left a vivid impression on me about what Americans must be like.

CHRISSIE HYNDE: Nancy was an opportunist. I'm not even going to say whether I liked her or not, but she had a negative effect on Sid and he didn't need that.

Sid and I picked up a flat on Sutherland Avenue, but that soon fell apart because, as I then learned, you can't live in the same house as a member of your band. We used to hold what we called Beer Keller contests to shut her up. Money was starting to come in then, so I could go out and spend three or four hundred quid on just beer. Everybody else would chip in, and we would sit down and decide to drink the lot to see if we could do it in one stretch. That would stun Nancy because there was no way she could come on with that usual rhetoric with a houseload of serious drunks. There were complaints from the dustbin men about the garbage. They refused to take that many beer bottles.

Sid's idea of fun at the time was taking drugs with Nancy. My idea of fun was taking drugs with anyone but her, and the two didn't tarry well. Sid's drugs were the hard-core stuff, and I was just speeding, boozing and having late night parties. Nancy and her withdrawals proved unbearable. Sutherland Avenue was rented through the office, so that wasn't good for me. A little bit of money eventually came my way, but not a great deal. Twelve thousand pounds. I put it directly into a house in my name on Gunter Grove, which apparently Steve Winwood and Island Records used to own. It was one large room like a single office space with two bedrooms above. It suited me fine. That's when Johnny started to think wisely about himself.

I remember Sid telling me a story. He thought this was great. Ha ha ha for decadence. They were so broke, they were looking out their window, which overlooked a garage. There was a black mechanic working down there, and Nancy went down and gave him a blow job for fifteen quid. Sid thought that was marvelous because he got to watch. What a couple.

They would tell these, well, not stories, because I have no reason to doubt them because these people seemed incapable of lying. It was so far gone, so outrageous, they could absolutely appall people, particularly Malcolm. He couldn't cope with it. It freaked him beyond belief.

NORA: Sid totally believed in her. He beat her up so badly sometimes. He was dependent on her. "Look, you work now. You go hooking. I need some money." God, the way he would talk to her in the clubs. Such a demeaning demeanor. If John talked to me in public like that, I would have hit him.

We did everything to get rid of Nancy. Malcolm, Steve, Paul, and I put together this little plan where we bought her a plane ticket and a cab ride when Sid went somewhere. We literally shoved her into the cab and sent her to the airport with a ticket. Go. Here's money. Just go. Get rid of yourself. We went that far because she was so bad for Sid. She had to go. She was killing him. I was absolutely convinced this girl was on a slow suicide mission, as indeed I believe most heroin addicts are. Only she didn't want to go alone. She wanted to take Sid with her. That was her whole point and purpose.

She was so utterly fucked up and evil. I don't believe that people are naturally evil. You make your own decisions, but parents can definitely put you in the wrong direction.

We banned her from being on tour with us, but she would manage to find out what hotel we were in. When we banned her, Sid had to put up with it. When he wasn't on drugs, he was fine and he agreed. The minute she'd turn up and the gear was there, then it would start all over again. He needed her, but he also fought it. Soon he craved the drugs more than her.

BOB GRUEN: She was whiny and not very good-looking, and that made her easy to dislike.

God, I don't know how many nights I spent with Sid trying to get him off those drugs. It was ludicrous. I'd literally lock him up at Sid's own request. I'd spend weekends, a week, whatever it took, not letting him out of the house. That's what we would do, my friends and I— these so-called bad influences on me. We'd lock him in a room and let him go through it. I know it's an awful thing. He'd come out of it hating me. I sat there with him through it all. I had done that several times with Sid. I've done it with other people, too. You grin and bear, because it's a serious thing. Heroin addicts go nuts. They want to kill you, but you just have to do it. They yell abuse at you because they can't sleep. It can go on thirty-six, forty-eight, however many hours it takes. Then it starts all over again for another period of time before gradually they come down. Of course you have to give them something. Usually methadone, gradually lowering that. Not easy, let me tell you. Vile. Awful. Then of course the old bitch would turn up and that would be the end of it. Down the drain. So I gave up. Eventually I didn't want anything more to do with either one of them.

When we went to America, I decided I would try to help him again because there were other people on the bus, the crew. That was slightly easier, but then it all fucked up in San Francisco, so it was utterly pointless after that.

I cannot understand why anyone would want to put out a movie like *Sid and Nancy* and not bother to speak to me; Alex Cox, the director, didn't. He used as his point of reference—of all the people on this earth—Joe Strummer! That guttural singer from the Clash? What the fuck did he know about Sid and Nancy? That's probably all he could find, which was really scraping the bottom of the barrel. The only time Alex Cox made any approach toward me was when he sent the chap who was playing me in the film over to New York where I was. This actor told me he wanted to talk about the script. During the two days he was there, he told me that the film had already been completed. The whole thing was a sham. It was a ploy to get my name used in connection with the film, in order to support it.

To me this movie is the lowest form of life. I honestly believe that it celebrates heroin addiction. It definitely glorifies it in the end when that stupid taxi drives off into the sky. That's such nonsense. The squalid New York hotel scenes were fine, except they needed to be even more squalid. All of the scenes in London with the Pistols were nonsense. None bore any sense of reality. The chap who played Sid, Gary Oldman, I thought was quite good. But even he only played the stage persona as opposed to the real person. I don't consider that Gary Oldman's fault because he's a bloody good actor. If only he had the opportunity to speak to someone who knew the man. I don't think they ever had the intent to research properly in order to make a seriously accurate movie. It was just all for money, wasn't it? To humiliate somebody's life like that—and very successfully—was very annoying to me. The final irony is that I still constantly get asked questions about it. I have to explain that it's all wrong. It was all someone else's fucking fantasy, some Oxford graduate who missed the punk era. The bastard.

When I got back to London, they invited me to a screening. So I went to see it and was utterly appalled. I told Alex Cox, which was the first time I met him, that he should be shot, and he was quite lucky I didn't shoot him. I still hold him in the lowest light. Will the real Sid please stand up?

As for how I was portrayed, well, there's no offense in that. It was so off and ridiculous. It was absurd. Champagne and baked beans for breakfast? Sorry. I don't drink champagne. He didn't even speak like me. He had a Scouse accent. Worse, there's a slur implied in this movie that I was jealous of Nancy, which I find particularly loathsome. There is that implication that I feel was definitely put there. I guess that's Alex Cox showing his middle-class twittery. It's all too glib, it's all too easy.

Sid wanted to be hurt, that's what he wanted. That and attention. He'd get himself into all kinds of fights, and he'd always lose. He was always covered in scars and black eyes. The sadomasochistic behavior was something I'd never seen in him before Nancy. He bought that image and lifestyle. There were so many incidents, it's not worth bothering to even remember them. It was continual.

CAROLINE COON: Sid didn't want to be self-destructive. The adults around him didn't give him the opportunity to go any other way. When I first met Sid as part of the young fans around the Pistols, absolutely loving what they were doing, Sid didn't want to destroy himself. Consider how fluid your sexuality is around that age. Then came the adult men, a decade older, around him. They got their thrills from the huge element of hatred in their own psyches. Evil is easy to explain; evil, the enjoyment of destruction. Young people inside that circle didn't stand a chance. I'm not talking so much about the dark side as much as the hidden side. When I was a nineteen-year-old, I was damn lucky because of the people who took care of me. That was important. That was part of what was missing for them. I guess what I'm challenging is the behavior of the adults. I'm saying that Malcolm, Bernie, and company were of the age of consent and were dealing with men who were very young.

Malcolm, leave those kids alone. Pink Floyd reference.

We signed our second record contract with A&M outside of Buckingham Palace. We didn't last long there, either—one week in March of 1977. We had a huge fight in the limo on the way. It started out when Sid was taking the piss out of Paul. Sid used to always be on Paul's case. He called him an albino gorilla in the limo. One remark led to another, then fists flew. We all got hurt, and when we fell out, it was black eyes, I'm afraid. These were not bad things. Every band does it. But it doesn't help when there's a load of press waiting at the other end and we're all fighting out in the street outside Buckingham Palace. The police weren't amused, either. Then it was on to a press conference, which was another farce. We weren't briefed, and we had no idea what we were going to be asked or what was going to take place. Again, it was tabloid press goading in their particular offensive way. They try to trick you into saying stupid things. We all just clammed up. Sid threw a custard tart at someone. It was as stupid as that. The press got what they wanted—foul-mouthed yobs. They were happy.

A&M invited us over to their offices and plied us with champagne and booze. Malcolm had hoped to try to control us. Sid got violently drunk in the toilet and broke a urinal with his boot. Boys will be boys, as they say. Somebody was sick in a rubber plant in some executive's office. I have a drunken vague memory, and I don't like to incriminate myself, but I think it was me. Steve was aggressive to some of the secretaries. One woman ran out screaming. Was Steve offensive? He may have touched some things on her, but I didn't see it. Paul was quiet and reserved. He's laid back, but he follows what Steve does to see if there's something in it for him. He'll pick up the tail end, so to speak.

We were totally uninterested in A&M. They were just another load of men in suits. Somebody high up in the company thought that we were utterly loathsome. It's funny how people point fingers and stand up for the Moral Majority. Always be suspicious of he who shouts loudest.

I've seen that collector's copy of "God Save the Queen" on A&M in that record store in Greenwich Village in New York. Even I don't have one—and I fucking made the thing. A&M never got around to giving us copies. They pulled it right off the market the second it was pressed. They didn't press many, and what they did press, they instantly set about destroying. We were on A&M for one week. We were ecstatic! They gave us seventy-five thousand pounds to leave. That was brilliant.

You'd think one of these labels would have had the sense to stand back and say, "Hold on, we're being scammed here!" But no. They all fell down like dominoes. Maybe they didn't see a financial future in it. They all thought it would be an overnight flirt and that would be the end of it. The way record companies are such a tightly knit little circuit, they only sign up bands that fit into molds. That's why the music industry is as boring as it is. It's not for lack of ideas and artists out there, it's for lack of signings. The bands can't get signed up, so they fade away. Sometimes labels sign bands to kill them off. If they have a catalog of one type of music and they sense something that might be changing the emphasis and would threaten the rest of the catalog, they sign it up and just bury it. They're seeing something that threatens their already well-established treadmill.

Virgin, our third and final label, was very "public school boy." But they were far more open about it and more into having mad fun. I like Richard Branson because he is chaotic and he takes chances. He doesn't fit very well in that old established business network. He's made his own rules. Virgin was always there when we signed with the other labels. They wanted us. I think Malcolm didn't bother with Virgin because he thought they were just too hippie. At the time, all they had was Mike Oldfield and avant garde bands like Faust, Henry Cow, and Gong. Ugh. We decided to make the best of it, then ironically fit in quite nicely.

When we first met, Richard Branson was kind of buck-toothed and giggling all the time. He was a very nervous, fidgety man. Virgin's offices were brand new at the time the Pistols signed with them. At least it was new. We tried and failed with all the others. Who else was there? RCA? No hope in hell. But we were never desperate-more curious, I think. I was intrigued just how few record labels there were. It never occurred to me before what a small world the music business is. There's five or six companies and that's it. Britain is such an isolated, class-oriented, pop-cultured country. The whole scene is magnified, with music being one of Britain's biggest exports. What else do they export? Crappy cars! It's a real fool who buys an English car, condemned to a life of garage misery! Can I have a sponsorship?

Apart from Sid, the Pistols weren't self-destructive, nor were they on the road to hell—quite the opposite. We were out to wreck the system, but certainly not wreck ourselves. Branson was wacky enough to enjoy it all. He perceived the Pistols as a jolly good fun ride, mostly because he was up and coming and his company was new and not firmly established into any set format. He turned out to be the best person for us to be with. He was always interested right from the start, even with us sneering at his beard. That kept us apart. He looked like one of those Greenpeace followers—the sensible sweater, the casual beard, and the corduroy flares. The old duck collector that he is, he has a huge house in Oxford with a pond full of exotic ducks with their wings clipped so they don't fly away. Give me a bastard in a three-piece suit any day, because at least I know where that's coming from and it's something I can deal with. A let's-be-kind-to-everyone hippie is something I can't have.

I've been proved right about Rich-ass Branson. Actually I like him a lot—a public school boy to the nth degree. But he doesn't use it against you. He plays one on one, and with him everything is a game. He loves to get one over on you, any which way he can.

Today Vivienne Westwood and Richard Branson have been sucked into the system. They pretend to themselves that they're really changing everything, but they're not. They're part of the same problem ad infinitum. Virgin could have single-handedly changed the whole record company perspective, but they didn't do it because a while after signing the Sex Pistols, Branson lost interest in record companies and had very little to do with the daily running of the record company. He barely knew who was on or off that label at any particular time. He just collected the money, the ego, and the reputation of it all. Virgin used to see themselves as a family company who would look out for their artists. Very few acts on Virgin made big money. The few that did made an awful lot. Many bands have since been unceremoniously ditched. I recently dropped Virgin myself just in time before the EMI acquisition.

BILLY IDOL: We used to go to clubs like Louise's and hang out together. We wanted to do things together so we could feel it growing. But later on it got bitchy. Everyone started getting their own bands, and it was wild how we started to slag each other off. At the time, the scene had no name. Then Caroline Coon came up with the name *punk*.

By 1977 the tabloids absolutely reveled in "how to be a punk" articles. They'd have a centerfold of these boring kids that they would pick off the street and dress them up as they thought punks were. It was really bad—ironed leather trousers, cardboard-stiff jackets. There were a lot of people who did mutilate themselves with safety pins. I used to stick a safety pin through my earhole. Is that mutilation? It looked much better than a normal earring. A lot of girls used to do it through their lip and nose. It would go all swollen, bruised, and filled with pus. You can't drill holes through your lips or cheek. Your lips swell up, now a fashionable Hollywood actress look.

CHRISSIE HYNDE: The beauty of the punk thing was that from January to June of 1977, nondiscrimination was what it was all about. There was little or no sexism or racism. For a start, everyone loved reggae music. It was uncool to be judgmental of somebody's sexuality. If Sid Vicious saw a girl with big boobs, he may have said, "Whoa, you got really big tits," but it wasn't really a macho come-on. There was a kind of innocence, and when I say innocence, I mean innocent!

NORA: The sixties was organized peace and love, and I was never for that. The Pistols was not about organizing for other people. I hated all those hippie concepts of cuddling up and all that stupid painting on the body. You did it because everyone else did it. In the punk days, you didn't do something because others did it, you did it because you wanted to do it. The hippie period was totally organized. You go to an open-air concert and they preach love and peace, leave garbage behind, and not mean a word of it. Because a few women showed their tits and a few men ran around naked on the boulevard, it was not liberation. It was merely a fashion. Big business and society told us it was the "in" thing. But society was totally against punk. We were told it was bad.

Malcolm and Vivienne Westwood were jumping on all of this gloriously. They were sewing together bits of old Marks and Spencer's shirts and dyeing them different colors, calling them "anarchy jackets"—with an outrageous price tag to go with it. It was utterly funny. When I saw people go into that shop and pay forty pounds for a dyed shirt—the picture of Karl Marx and an upside-down Nazi symbol—I thought, Fools! Make your own. For God's sake, I did. Again, people like their statements sold to them rather than making their own. That's why a shop like Vivienne's worked.

I used to love all the sex gear she used to sell, but I'm still angry over some of my designs. I designed some of my stuff and had to pay full whack for her to make it. I'd see copies soon after in the shop. That used to piss me. The tartan kilt. The bondage gear. I did a series of photos in a straitjacket. I really liked being in that straitjacket, so I wanted gear on stage that wouldn't be quite so restrictive but would look like it. That's how the bondage gear came about.

I never found Vivienne attractive. From the first minute I saw her, I always used to think turkey neck. I know she never liked me.

I used to go to the movies a lot when I was in the Pistols. I remember when *Texas Chainsaw Massacre* first came out. We all went with Malcolm and Vivienne. I liked it so much I went back. It was the funniest movie I had ever seen. It was so vile to be cut up by a such an ugly thing as a chainsaw. You couldn't fight it off! "Oh, stop it! Go away! It's not happening!" Hand on eyes. You can enjoy

the gristle of it all. Outcast characters in film always attracted me. I
enjoyed Jose Ferrer in *Cyrano de Bergerac*.

Best of all, I loved the way Laurence Olivier played Richard III. He
portrayed the character as so utterly vile, it was great. As I said before,
Johnny Rotten definitely has tinges of Richard III in him. I saw it a long
time before I conceived Rotten. No redeeming qualities. Hunchback,
nasty, evil, conniving, selfish. The worst of everything to excess. Olivier
made Richard III riveting in his excessive disgust. Having seen it aeons
ago, I took influences from Olivier's performance. I had never seen a
pop singer present himself quite that way. It wasn't the norm. You're
supposed to be a nice pretty boy, sing lovely songs, and coo at the girlies.
Richard III would have none of that. He got the girls in other ways.

Occasionally I think of Richard III when I do interviews with journalists I don't like. I'm very sharp and give one-word answers. I bounce
off people's characters. I do that a lot. If someone is all right, then I'm
all right. If I think they're an ass, then I hand it back to them. I'll merely mirror their images for the sheer fun of it.

CAROLINE COON: John thought himself ugly and unattractive, and he
played that part with a hell of a lot of style. He was ethereal, with a
face like a Giotto painting.

Vivienne Westwood always made me laugh, and it annoyed her no
end. She's like Malcolm; she likes to manipulate people, but if they
don't agree with her, then she doesn't want them around. Silly bitch.
She went nowhere fast after punk and found herself stuck for lack of
ideas. She went to Italy to work in one of the fashion houses there and
claims it disciplined her. Methinks not. She just joined the bleeding
brigade. She went with the flow. To be weird just for the sake of it is
incredibly uninteresting, and that's what Vivienne's into now.

Vivienne Westwood's clothes are completely sexless—totally alien to
sex. They incorporated all the trappings of sex, but they were presented in such a way that they were more like items of fun. You certainly
could never wear anything of hers and go out and expect to be picked
up. There's no sex appeal in anything she's done; she never designed
with that in mind. But Vivienne thinks her clothes are romantic, sexy,
and erotic. I'm sure she's convinced of that. She misses the point. Years
later on the "South Bank" television show, Malcolm intimated he created designs for her. I think they both got it wrong. It's neither romantic, sexy, nor erotic. They were always blabbing on about sex and freedom, but that's exactly what they denied the very people who worked

for them. They didn't share their ideas. It was all dictated; this is the way you must wear it. It must never be mixed with anything else; it's a uniform. It's just a neat little box and so blinkered in its vision. But that's the way Vivienne thinks; she's completely indoctrinating.

It was nice that "God Save the Queen" came out two weeks before the Silver Jubilee. Originally it should have come out on A&M a long time before. There we go. Lucky timing. But not deliberate. Renting the boat was wonderful. Well played by Malcolm here. I loved that because we were quite lethargic at the time. We weren't allowed to play anywhere for all kinds of weird reasons. There were Sid's bloody problems and all of that. So we chartered this boat—the ones the tourists go up and down in to see the Tower of London from the Thames. We invited a lot of friends, fashion bloody designers, and whoever was doing something new and different in London at the time. Painters, for instance. Rabble-rousers. Filth. And loads of tarts. It was not at all the way Alex Cox projected it in that film. According to his movie, everyone had mohawks and leather jackets. Well, that image didn't come along until much, much after. On the boat you would have a John Travolta type next to a beatnik next to anything. The sheer mixture was what made it offensive to the British public and the police. But I liked that. I loved the diversity of it. That's when I knew there was something really important happening. It's very important when you combine different elements getting on very well with each other. According to the normal rules of society, we should all be at odds. Yes, again the Alex Cox movie fucked up big time. It missed the major point. There's no point preaching to the converted or the clones.

The whole idea of the Jubilee was that you could do anything you liked for twenty-four hours. It was supposed total freedom. All the pubs were open all night. Everything was open. People were supposed to celebrate, so that's what we did. We rented a boat, went out on the river, turned up the volume, and played our favorite new song. No doubt countless complained because the amount of police who turned up to stop us was out-fucking-rageous. Motor launches. They waited on every bridge in case any of us jumped off and got away. Fabulous. I wasn't arrested. I managed to escape. I suppose the good old days of burglary—get in and out of tight situations—helped. My brother Jimmy got nicked. It was pathetic. The charges were so stupid and trumped up. It was an amnesty of volume declared to celebrate the Jubilee! The fact that we were slagging off the queen was our own business. But that's what they arrested us for. Breaking the peace. What peace? Can't you see the streets are full of people? In the papers the next morning was a photograph of my brother in the *Daily Mirror*. He had the typical boot boy look at the time. Hair squarely cropped, suede jacket affair, and flares. There was this caption: PUNKS IN MAYHEM ON THAMES or whatever they said. They nicked Malcolm, but he got out of it. That was the shit.

Steve, Paul, Malcolm, Glen, Boogie, and Sophie rarely mingled with music or the possibilities. They would slag off bands and not know who or what they were talking about. Sid would slag off bands as aging hippies but didn't really go to many concerts. He didn't know what he was talking about most of the time, either. Malcolm guided Steve and Paul into this regressive sixties mod band vibe. Paul Cook was really into the Raspberries and the soft California rock sound. Suddenly that went by the by. Malcolm helped make their musical decisions in that respect.

That's why I was such a cunt to them. I knew more of what I was talking about. When the band would say, "Let's do a Kinks-style song" I'd ask, "Which album? I've got fifteen. Would you like to pick out a track?" They might have had one album from the sixties where the band was sitting in a Mini-Cooper on the cover. They didn't know the range of Ray Davies's music. Glen had a couple of friends who would pass records his way. Then he'd think he knew it all. But I would know more. One evening I got fed up with Glen accusing me of knowing it all. We sat around with his friends and played library, and I won hands down. Glen hated me even more. There's no joy in that, but why should people treat knowledge as something disgraceful?

"How dare you know, and why can't you be like the rest of us? Vague. Muddled. Indifferent."

JOHN GRAY: John has always maintained that if he had more control over the band, they would have been unlistenable. But that's partly what made the Pistols a brilliant group, the fusion of the members. Steve's power chords; Paul's plodding Ringo Starr drums; Glen's Beatle melody mentality; John's anarchy and free-form expression. It was those ingredients put together that made the Pistols such an exciting band.

I'm writing this book because so much rubbish has been written about us that it might be interesting for someone to get the correct perspective on it and see it for what it really was, rather than what the fantasists of this world would have you believe. There's so much exaggeration and intellectualizing going on about what was basically real human beings trying to come to grips with each other and somehow or another actually writing songs that mean something. It's such an intense process being in a band, but some of the books out there never understood that. These writers have never been in bands, and they have never really committed themselves to other people in such close quarters. They're more like solo performers, and there ain't no such thing as that in any band. You should never leave any single member in a band up to their own devices. I don't care how big-headed the lead singer is, it all comes down to the fact that he must eat shit in a rehearsal room. The histrionics of the lead guitar, the excesses of the drummer, and the stupidity of the bass player have to mix on equal footing.

We were teenagers making teenage music. It was never meant for subtlety, was it? The mechanics on my part of getting Sid into the Pistols was that he looked the part, but he was becoming a Johnny Rotten clone. There was no one else. At the time we were just about the only band in Britain with short hair. The rest were still in flares. We stuck out like sore thumbs, and Sid was there. I even helped get Sid a day job at the Sex shop, and he used to come to all the gigs. The Pistols ruined him. He just didn't understand it. He was much better as a member of the audience than being in the band. He didn't have the grasp of what it was all about. I thought he would fit and adapt. I didn't realize he was that stupid. Once Sid joined the Pistols, he became jealous of me. He wanted to be center of attention in the band. I should have seen it. This goes back to his fashion victim days when we were in school together. He always had to be noticed. The nail varnish and such. He had to be loved and adored by millions. He tried his very best to out-Rotten Rotten, but he didn't understand Rotten was my alter ego. He would think that would make me a fake. That's the primitive way his logic ran. He got it all wrong, and he was egged on by Nancy.

"You're the star, Sid."

"I am. I must be. Nancy told me."

At the start Sid was actually getting into learning how to play. Then he would come out with these ridiculous Ramones stances—with the legs spread as wide apart as they possibly could. He was imitating the Ramones' bass player. We had to sit him down one day and say, "No! You can't do that!" Make up your own style, don't slavishly adhere to something else. But then again, that's the fashion bit of Sid. "Ooo. That's what everyone does." God's sake! Then he'd go home and huff and be back the next day and try to imitate me.

"Oh, I can sing that better."

"Okay, do. Now write something equivalent."

"Duuhhh!" Pause. About turn.

He got it pretty close toward the end. When I hear Sid's version of "My Way," it sounds like me. There's a line he added: "What is a prat who wears silly hats?" That's about me. Silly boy. He hated my hat collection—comprised of all the most unfashionable things the world has ever known. Top hats or whatever, things I would buy at jumble sales.

JULIEN TEMPLE: Sid would make fun of John for wearing Rasta hats, but at the same time Sid would be there shaking and sipping methadone from a straw.

I didn't want to be forced into this ridiculous rock 'n' roll theory. I think the music you make should reflect your real personality, your real self. Unfortunately, before the Pistols came along, that generally wasn't the case, was it? It was a lot of people living up to what they thought they had to do. That ultimately destroys musicians, which is why a lot of them end up heroin addicts. They can't cope with the lie of it all.

What impressed me about Sid when we were both younger was that he knew the pitfalls and didn't want to end up like that, but somehow once he joined the band, he got into that groupie thing with that awful Nancy Spungen. She convinced him that heroin was the way it should be. To be a true star, you must mess about with dangerous drugs. So he eventually bought the whole rock 'n' roll lifestyle. He absolutely, thoroughly believed the Velvet Underground, Lou Reed thing, that whole approach to life, that drug commitment. It never occurred to Sid that it was just an image, that they were not necessarily living it themselves. Sid got into being a heroin addict as an observer. "Gee whiz, there must be something good about it. All these great, decadent New Yorkers." Sid, they're not great! They're fucked up!

As a kid, when I knew him, he wouldn't go near any hard drugs. Wouldn't touch them. Some took speed. But then we never viewed speed, amphetamines, as a drug at all. It was so easy to get, you could buy them anywhere. If you wanted to stay up and not miss anything, that's what speed was for. It was a mod drug. I got it by spending my dole money, all of it. You could get a gram for ten quid and that would last you a whole weekend, easily. Speed had no high, no hallucinogenic effect. It kept you awake so that you could do other things. That was fine. I liked that. That meant I could drink more. I could go see all those bloody films all night long if I wanted to. I could go to any club. I could do all of it in the same twenty-four hours. Very nice. Unfortunately, speed absolutely tears you apart. That's why I stopped doing it.

As much as there was animosity between us, when you see footage of the Sex Pistols live, we were so damned tight that the aggression and lack of communication somehow worked on stage. Steve, Paul, and I could have been a fucking awesome threesome. We could have done without that bass nonsense. This will annoy a lot of people because of the Sid mythology, but the Sex Pistols never really needed a bass guitarist! Sid was just there because that was the thing that bands had. Now I can say this years later. Why? At the time it never occurred to any of us because it seemed to be so deeply essential. I had seen Iggy Pop and Ron Asheton play as a duo at King's Cross. It didn't strike me as particularly radical.

Paul just needed something to flop his bass drum with. We sure put Paul through it all with Sid on stage. What a torture for a drummer having to constantly slow up and speed down so you could accommodate a drug-crazed idiot twanging away. How do you go "boioioioiinnngg" on a bass drum?

When the Pistols sold thousands of copies of "God Save the Queen," I felt more detached than anything. It felt unreal. The chaos and nastiness against us and the political intrigues inside the organization of what you'd jokingly call the Pistols made it somehow not seem like an achievement at all. Quite the opposite. Success just seemed to make it worse. I felt as if management had no grasp on what was happening. I didn't know what to do or when things would happen. Malcolm would never discuss what was going on because he didn't like people to contradict his ideas, no matter how few he had. He would announce a plan or a weekly schedule, and that was the end. It made the Pistols' success grim.

THE SKATERS OF STREATHAM / NORA, MY WIFE

NORA

I wasn't interested in John when we first met. I came to notice John because Ariana, my daughter, was such a fan of John's that she formed a punk group called the Slits. She was only fourteen, and all the Slits were in ecstasy over John. In 1977 Ariana jumped up on stage at a Pistols concert in Soho, ran up to John, and said, "You are the greatest," and kissed him.

I first saw the Pistols at the 100 Club. I thought they were awful. Steve played guitar like the Who and John's awful screaming voice was so unusual. You had to listen to its piercing sound. It was so bang-bang, rock 'n' roll.

In the early seventies I promoted big concerts in Germany with bands like Wishbone Ash and Rory Gallagher's Taste. I was always into promoting, but I didn't come over to England to promote concerts. It was too much hassle. I came over to England from Germany in the midseventies. I took Ariana out of boarding school when she was thirteen and brought her with me to England.

I was living with a m
All the Sex Pistols
saw John. I was
thought we'd
that time

JOH

Surviving the Texas Chainsaw Massacre*m with stickers to prove it. (Ian Dickson/Redferns)*

...an who later made demos with the Sex Pistols. ...ame over to meet him, and that was the first time I ...very aloof at the time. I just went upstairs. I never ...ever see each other again. I was very narrow-minded at ...didn't want to deal with someone who didn't look classy.

...N LYDON: We met again a couple of months after we recorded the demos, and Nora was even more aloof, positively rude. The nose went ten feet up in the air in her forties film star outfit. Long blonde hair. Padded shoulders. That forties femme fatale look—which I was a complete ham for. Women were still wearing those crushed-velvet tops, denim flares, and bell-bottoms. Nora wouldn't have anything to do with it, which was absolutely fine by me. So few people wanted to break that boring mold. I was the filthiest thing on earth to her.

John and I knew each other for that six months before we got together. There was no dating at all.

JOHN LYDON: I had never been on a date in my entire life. Ever. The concept was bizarre to me. It's ridiculous! Real people don't do things like that. That only happens in TV-land. You meet, you meet, and you meet. That's it.

John asked me for a lift to the Speakeasy. He had no money, and he kept asking me for a drink inside. I just passed him by because I was with other people. I was embarrassed by him and his bad reputation.

JOHN LYDON: Nora was meeting someone. She just drove to the Speakeasy and said, "I'm going now." She wouldn't even let me walk into the club with her. I had no money. She said in her thick German accent, "I'm not payings." Nora was so cruel, and I love cruel women. She did not want this embarrassing lump near her.

We had a horrible argument in front of the Speakeasy when John wanted a lift home. He screamed blue murder: "You bitch! You dropped me here, so you drop me back." I told him I wasn't going to give him a lift home. He climbed into the car. I said no. "Get your stuff out." So he walked all the way home.

JOHN LYDON: It took hours to get home. She left a lasting impression on my feet.

There was no physical attraction at first. I didn't even think to be nice to him. I was brought up differently as a teenager in the fifties. I was totally old-fashioned the first time I was married. Oh, God. My sense of chaos comes because I was repressed all my life. When you are not interested in a man, you pay no attention. I felt embarrassed with John in the very beginning. After that horrible incident, I was at another gig with someone else and John passed by my table and said, "Drop dead!"

I never heard expressions like that before. I expected people to be polite. Even when people used words like "f-u-c-k," I never heard it that much. Then he says, "Drop dead." So we don't speak again for a long time.

Then one day he came up to me and said, "You never invited me to your house. I know people told you—"

"People told me," I said, "you would destroy everything in the house."

He was drinking and being more open. I was more open as well. By then we had all the same friends, so I thought that we should talk rather than harbor the hostility. We started to talk, and I saw he was quite a pleasant person. I told him to come around. We talked about our forced religion and found a kindred spirit there.

When people found out he came around to the place I rented in Shepherd's Bush, they were jealous. A lot of men, including Steve and Paul, warned me that he was terrible and mad. They didn't say he would steal, but they told me John would spray-paint the house and the furniture. John sprayed the word *Arsenal* all over the garden and alongside the pavement.

Later on he came over to my house with a lot of people. I hardly knew all the punk boys and punk girls except Debbie and Paul Young. This was still before John and I had any close relationship. He used to come around the house with Wobble, Sid, and others. It was so wild; things went missing in the house. Someone had classical records and some really rare classical music on tapes up in the loft. John used the tapes and recorded reggae over them. But I didn't mind because it was rented. Some of the girls started to cut up the curtains. The kitchen was black and burnt out. It looked horrible.

We had terrible scenes there. A neighbor complained about noise because John was banging up and down on the piano with his bum for a couple of hours. The neighbor didn't ring police or anything, he just came over. Somebody dumped water over his head. He was a nutter, and he came back with a knife and wanted to stab Ariana. He attacked me, and the knife went into my arm. John came out with fists raging, so he rushed off. We rang up the police and told them to look for the man.

The police recognized John immediately and told us that we probably asked for it. It was around the time John was being attacked on the street by royalist fans. They wrote our names down and told John, "We're going to get you, Cocky. One more word from you and you're off."

There was a law in England that you could stay in a flat at least three months without paying the rent while they evict you. I knew I wouldn't get my deposit back, so I just had to move out by the moonlight. It's a miracle they never chased me after I left.

After John found out that I was attracted to him, that's when he turned around. We were together on and off during that first six months. When I fell in love with John, it was his turn to be nasty. He was really terrible then.

JOHN LYDON: Revenge was sweet. Nora was a spoiled schoolgirl and I was a spoiled brat, so we just annoyed each other. When Nora started following me, I was going through a bad time in the Pistols with Sid and all of his problems.

I fell in love with John because he surprised me. He was pictured really bad, but he had a really sweet attitude. We both had a Catholic upbringing; he had to go to church all the time, I went to the convent school. He was more innocent and not like the rest of the group. He was more interested in having fun with the boys than taking groupies into bed.

John was into getting drunk, using speed, and he started smoking marijuana. I never touched any drugs in my life except when John gave me some heavy marijuana once. The earth moved when I was on a mattress on the floor. My heart went fast. I didn't have the strength to go to bed. John yelled, "People pay a fortune to feel that way, and you are complaining."

JOHN LYDON: The speed made me very paranoid. I used to love sitting there thinking, They're out to get me. When you're that watched, you become very insular and cold. You build walls around yourself, and you can't trust anyone. So I used to have a huge entourage of circus freak types around me.

As we got close John realized I wasn't so arrogant. He changed his attitude as well. He didn't do all the wrecking. John was too shy because he was so scrutinized. I started to like him, so I seduced him. It was difficult for him. The first time he was at my house it seemed the whole of London must have known about it. Our friends tried to make him look like a monster. Finally he came to my house alone. The morning after, Ariana almost came in. I saw John secretly at first because I didn't want Ariana to know. She loved John as a teenager. He was her hero. But she didn't like any of my lovers after I split up with my ex-husband. Then she said to me, "Finally you have someone decent."

There was a time when Ariana started getting nasty with me when I started to see John. Ariana took the whole punk thing too seriously. That's when she started to get really nasty. I was alone with John at Gunter Grove, when his mother came around. She was very ill, but she brought John a nice set of plates over for the house. Ariana turned up soaking wet, yelling, "Let me in! Let me in!" It was embarrassing. I could have died. She was wearing stiletto heels and a short miniskirt. Then she swore. We couldn't get rid of Ariana. I didn't know John's mother very well at that time. There was conflict between my daughter and me. I told Ariana quietly not to use bad words, but she wanted to listen to records. John told her to leave.

John and I became close when Sid first joined the band. Sid locked me in a toilet once at a gig near Birmingham. I had lost my driving license and some money and went back to look for it in the toilet after the show. Sid locked the main toilet door. He was jealous when John suddenly was open about him and me. It was already very late, and nobody heard my screams. Everyone was sitting in the dressing room. Sid would do everything to antagonize me. John was either shy or angry, but Sid was such an attention seeker. In that sense Sid and Nancy were brilliant together. They were both like that.

Before John and I were close I used to see him with Linda. She was a very nice girl, but I didn't know who or what she was. I was a bit intimidated by that. I was so naive in that aspect. John wouldn't tell me, but Ariana used to come around her place at the St. James Hotel. John used to tell her not to come around. I didn't know that Ariana was over there with Linda and Nancy.

I knew Nancy very well. She came around my house immediately after she turned up in England. Ariana liked her because Nancy had that open New York attitude. Ariana was too naive to figure out that she was a whore and brought her around to Shepherd's Bush. I'll never forget first meeting Nancy with her big mouth. She looked and talked very cheap. I asked her what she was doing in London.

"Wanking men off for twenty dollars."

That was the very first thing Nancy said to me.

"Oh, very nice. Would you please leave?" But she would take no notice of me. You couldn't believe how offensive Nancy was. She didn't say it for a joke. She kept coming around because she thought Ariana had money.

Nancy kept coming around the house because Ariana liked her and insisted she stay. Ariana liked Sid a lot, too. When Sid was in the hospital with hepatitis, Ariana insisted on bringing our television there when she visited him. When Sid came around in the early days with John he had that show-off attitude and would do anything to get attention. He was acting, but I didn't like him.

Sid and Nancy would be constantly arguing. The only time they were quiet together was when there were drugs. That's why I didn't want her coming over to my house. I was so worried that Ariana might be at the age to be attracted by all that. Nancy had an influence, I knew that from Sid.

When John was having problems with the Pistols, he would never tell me much. I didn't know it was so bad internally with the Pistols. I did not go to many Sex Pistols concerts anyway. I might have been to two or three the entire time. The violence against him was over the top. Bricks would come through the windows. After John was stabbed, whenever we would go to a club he had ten bouncers around him—Wobble, the English brothers, John Stevens. I thought it was ridiculous, but necessary. If anyone would come close to John in public, his friends would go crazy.

John's other friends from Finsbury Park were bad news, even though he wasn't violent himself.

RAMBO: I ran with a smaller Arsenal group in Finsbury Park called the Herd. I've been stabbed in the kidneys. I got a brick on my head at Luton. I bent down to pick it up and got another on the back of my head. Two full-grown house bricks. I got cut with a Stanley knife on my shoulder and one down my back. I got a screwdriver stuck in my leg. Most football mobs either know me or respect me. It was the way I was. Basically, I'm a small bloke, and wouldn't run.

I would stay outside the eye of the storm. I couldn't go out with them, and John would go nowhere without them. It must have been like Elvis Presley's friends. They were constantly around. They would stay in the front room at my house drunk, and John and I would go to our room.

A traumatic thing happened between me and John after we first met in 1977. I became pregnant from John. I was with no one else by that time. We weren't together very often because of the Pistols, yet I panicked thinking at the time that he was so young: Why tell him when I can look after it?

The next time we saw each other, I told John. We didn't live together at the time, and some of the other women he knew were sluts and some whores. John was much more shocked than I was. "Oh, no. Are you sure it's mine?"

Funnily enough, Ariana said the same thing as John. I told her I loved John and wasn't with anyone else. She was in ecstasy about getting a sister or brother.

Nobody believed we lost the child naturally. I screwed in some light bulbs and lost my balance, falling badly right on my belly. Ariana saw blood all over the living room in our house on Waterford Road. Pains shot up to my neck. I just knew. I booked into a clinic. It was the second month, so it was very early.

John had gone off to tour in Sweden, and he didn't even know I lost the baby. He was on the road a lot, but I'm sure he was worried that I was going to hit him for money. At that time, lots of girls came to John. You wouldn't believe how many girls claimed to have had a baby with him.

Nobody thought about abortion then. When I had Ariana, I had to marry because my father told me to have Ariana at a Swiss hospital and have her adopted. That's how good parents were with the shame. The Pistols definitely helped change the whole social concept about sex.

John and I didn't even talk about the miscarriage until years later. John probably thought I reacted too quickly about not having my period. But I always knew. John was only nineteen then, so he must have felt the whole thing was my decision.

JOHN LYDON: I felt responsibility, but that would have been the next step. There are areas where you shouldn't interfere and it's a woman's choice. Even if she would have had an abortion, it wouldn't have been my decision. If Nora would have had the child, we would have done something about it. I would deal with it one step at a time. You know what runs through your mind: Oh, my God. Nappies, feeding, school, commitment. Tied down. It was an ongoing thing for women to approach me. Just recently my father got a phone call from someone who was thirty-two years old and reckons he was my son. Talk about starting early. I mean, four years old?

John lived in King's Cross and just got back from Sweden. We didn't see each other because he was touring on and off for five months. Then after that John and I started being serious. I had never had someone with so much age difference. It was also the first time John had met someone older, too. People didn't think anything about my being fifteen years older than John. My friends didn't use terms like "baby snatcher." I think John's father was shocked because he knew I was much older. It never bothered John, and he didn't care what people thought.

John remembers seeing me go into the Sex Boutique when it was called Too Fast To Live. John was behind the counter. This was 1975, a long time before the Pistols. John thought I was a loud woman with no shame, but wonderful. I never knew he'd seen me.

JOHN LYDON: Nora would buy women's clothes for strange men, particularly this unknown person. She'd drag him in and he'd be all shy and trying things on behind the screens. She made him squeeze into a rubber skirt. Nora would pull the screen out with a shop full of people, shouting, "No, that rubber one's too tight." The geezer was dying of embarrassment. If he wanted this stuff and just went in and put it on, no one in that place would have noticed. But he was trying to be all coy and shy behind the screen, and Nora being Nora was yelling, "It's too damns tight! She's ripping you off. I'm not standing for this!"

The punks didn't even know what the swastika meant. In Germany we couldn't even talk about it. Punks used it innocently just to show off. They were told that the swastika was forbidden and should not be brought up, Siouxsie wasn't particularly educated about it at that time. To them it meant that it was taboo and antisocial. They never questioned what it stood for because they were too naive. Do you think Sid knew what the swastika stood for? Sid's idea was that it was naughty, and that was as deep as he went for it. It didn't mean anti-Semitism to Siouxsie or Sid.

John's attitude with the Sex Pistols was letting everyone be what they wanted to be, not making too much difference between boys and girls. Girls didn't need to worry about being frowned upon when they came out with their own opinions. Before punk, women kept it inside. After the Sex Pistols there was no age gap or sex gap. It all melded into each other. Suddenly women like Caroline Coon did talk about sex. I don't remember her being so open before then. She was for the underdog, and because she came from an upper-class culture and was educated, she wanted to help the ones who were unjustifiably put down. Caroline had other boyfriends who were very uneducated; Paul Simonon of the Clash was a good example. She was kind of a converter, because then everything became so free.

I was shocked when I saw Siouxsie at the Screen on the Green. This was still before John and I were close. She was walking around wearing some suspenders and a bra with her whole tits out. I was stunned. How could she have the nerve? I think she contributed a lot to the women's free movement. Madonna got it all from Siouxsie, who was totally on her own then. That night I couldn't listen to the Sex Pistols at all because Siouxsie was sitting one row behind me. I was so uncool because I couldn't stop looking at her tits. Siouxsie and her friends looked like what Russ Meyer would have liked to see a Wagner opera look like.

JOHN LYDON: Siouxsie came from the Roxy Music, Dave Bowie dress-up world and got fed up with that. When the Pistols started they jumped straight in on it. Instead of all that dressing up, they just dressed down—or out. There were lots of gays with them in their crowd—a real mixture of people.

I was the first woman of my age to roller-skate through the whole London town. The newspapers even wrote about it. JOHNNY ROTTEN'S LOVED ONE IS ROLLER-SKATING THROUGH TOWN. The *Evening Standard* made up this headline called THE LONG-SUFFERING NORA, and about how I had to put up with John and his bad manners.

I was the very first older person who went to Battersea Park to roller-skate. Back in 1977 there were no roller-skaters, and this was pre-roller disco. John and Keith Levene had a pair of roller skates, and there was this big terrace. I tried it out there, and I could do it instantly. I bought myself a new pair and taught everyone around Streatham how to skate. After two years they were spinning around on one leg. They all learned so quickly because they were young. Some of the gay discos turned into roller discos, and I would give them lessons. John would come home from the studio and there would be all these gay guys in the front room on roller skates.

John used to get very weird sometimes. I knew Leslie McKeown, the lead singer from the Bay City Rollers. He was a fan and wanted to come over to meet John and maybe play some music with him. I arranged a meeting, and John said it was okay to bring him around. The moment Les came up the staircase, John disappears. It looked as if I didn't even know John. John was into his antifood thing, and he locked himself inside his room. After two days I would ask him what he wanted to eat. I left an Indian meal outside the door, and John kicked it down the stairs.

One time we met Peter Townshend, and he was in awe in front of John. He gave a harangue about how much John was his hero, how he changed the world, and how elevated he felt standing next to John. Townshend was very open-minded.

JOHN LYDON: The McCartneys would send me their calendars and invited me to their place. They got my address through a PR person. But I wasn't capable of sitting down with Paul and Linda McCartney and having a regular conversation. The McCartneys wanted to make records with me. I could see that if I fell into that, then I would become Johnny Showbiz. The whole thing would be unreal and fake, and I couldn't cope with it. One day Nora and I were driving past Harrods in a cab. McCartney and his family came out, saw us, then ran after the car. I locked the door so they couldn't jump in. The driver turned around and said, "Jesus, I've seen it all now. I remember when people used to chase him. Now he's chasing you."

I sensed when John was unhappy in the band and it was falling apart. John never wanted to discuss the problems and be a whiner. I could see it from his attitude that something was wrong. John was very moody when there was tense confrontations with the Pistols. There was no way I could even talk to John. Even when we had good trysts together, it was just for the time being.

I looked after John's house in Gunter Grove when he was off on tour in America. He was excited about getting a passport to leave, but he didn't seem so excited to go to America. He wasn't scared but felt apprehensive about what would happen next. The fear of the unknown was there. Sid was becoming so difficult and more and more addicted.

John rang me from America. We talked all the time. I gave up my flat in Shepherd's Bush to stay in the house in Gunter Grove. It was a nightmare for me to be alone. The house was on a corner, and one day the door was smashed down by squatters. I got them out, and another night someone came in through a little window in the kitchen. I almost had a heart attack. I had to hide the big speakers and cover up all the heavy amplifiers. Somebody pitched a tent in front of the house, and the police would do nothing. They couldn't care less.

John had a fit one day and destroyed the whole bedroom. It was macabre. He didn't like the fitted cupboards, so he just ripped them out with an axe. He left me with a bedroom like that. I had never seen a room in such a state. He ripped the wallpaper down. He had a tombstone that somebody stole and gave to him. He used it as a headstand for the bed.

The whole place was flying around with moths. There were many moths in the carpets, in the living room and the bedrooms. The end result was I gave away all of his moth-ridden clothes from the Pistols. I just kept on throwing them out the window. I never thought that one day they could become memorabilia. One person started to rummage around outside, and soon they came all the way down from the King's Road as the word spread. The queue was around the block. They didn't know John was in America, but they knew where John lived and that those were his clothes. It was like a social event, but I didn't dare go out of the house. They could have ripped my clothes off thinking they were John's clothes.

We didn't have a lot of time alone during the Sex Pistols. That came later. After America we got really close together. It was the end of the band.

My father read something in a magazine in Berlin that his daughter lived with the murderer of his girlfriend. They said I was going out with someone from the Sex Pistols who killed his girlfriend. They didn't mention Sid or any name. They got John mixed up with Sid, and they mentioned my name as well. My father was outraged and shocked. He said, "The company you're keeping, I can't agree." My father didn't even ask me if it was true. He believed what was written. Maybe that gave him a heart attack. He died very soon after that.

STEVE SEVERIN
BATTERSEA, LONDON

Bromley is in the south of London—the last stop before you hit real countryside. Bromley was its own breeding grounds, a mismatch of people who came from all parts of London. That included me at age eleven when my family moved from the Irish parts of North London. My father was a librarian for the *Daily Express* newspaper, and most of the time my mother was a dressmaker. I was also raised by my grandmother, who was fantastic.

Moving to Bromley was supposed to be a move up in the world in the sense that you could go from a terraced house to a semidetached abode. Bromley was greenery abound, where the schools and the facilities were supposed to be better. High Street was the center of town. Central London was only fifteen minutes away by train, far enough away from the hustle and bustle of London, though not quite enough for us to be considered isolated. Bromley isn't just one town, it's a cluster of them, so our "Bromley contingent" was just a rare collection of people from several different outlying towns in and around the south of London. And 1966 was a strange time for the area. What changed things for

Bromley was that just down the road was a place called Catford, and it became one of the main arrival points for drugs coming into England. So Bromley was quite drug-infested. Nobody knew where the stuff came from, just that our part of south London was always awash in them. Maybe there were lots of small drug factories around there—who knew? Amphetamines, marijuana, and, of course, LSD were rather rampant. Perhaps that set the tone for the youth culture of this little town, which was otherwise perceived as a normal suburb.

BILLY IDOL: In 1970 we moved up to Bromley in Kent, a district on the farthest edge of the suburbs of London. Twelve and a half miles or a fast twenty-minute train ride and you were in the den of iniquity.

Something in the atmosphere of the time and the place made a lot of people want to break out and do something different. The catalyst ended up being the Sex Pistols and a clothes shop called Sex. By the time we'd hit our mid- to late teens, we were mainly going around as a group. This was even before the Sex Pistols came along. By definition, and out of need, we were into making our own fun. Because of the way we looked and the kind of music we liked, there weren't that many places we could go in and around Bromley—even London, for that matter. Now there's a club or a part of town for every different music cult or gang that you can imagine. Then it was either the Bee Gees or gay discos, so we gravitated toward the gay discos because they were much more tolerant of young people like us being different; they left us alone.

Everything sprang from that gay scene.

CAROLINE COON: Where did you find the most interesting aspects of sexual politics? In the discos. The gay scene. It was pop culture.

I can see how the role of the Bromley contingent has been miscast and misunderstood, as there was such a short transition between the time we were a bunch of people on our own and seen as acolytes to the Pistols. When our path crossed the group's, it was more a meeting of the minds. It was never so much that we were fans as much as they just happened to be guys who played in a group. At that time, nobody knew what was going to happen with the band. The circuslike notoriety hadn't yet set in.

I remember the moment we met the Pistols. It was me and Simon Barker. Simon was actually the first person to notice them. I was in the bar drinking, and we weren't even aware they were playing. This was at

Ravensbourne Art College, not too far from Bromley. Simon saw their last couple of songs and came running back, saying anxiously, "This band—they're kind of like the Stooges."

We'd met Malcolm before through the shop, Sex. So after the Ravensbourne gig, we got to talking to him and the band. I can't remember if Vivienne was there or not. Malcolm invited us to the Marquee the very next week, so we shuffled along. That was the gig where they played with Eddie and the Hot Rods. The Pistols were fantastic! That was it. While we purposely didn't go to every show, we went to what we felt were the important ones, particularly those at the El Paradise and the 100 Club. There was me, Simon, Siouxsie, a girl called Sharon, Tracy, Debbie, and a guy named Berlin. Lots of other people—in and out—were attracted to this new sound, particularly guys who were known then as soul boys. It was a rather strange grouping, but the thing that brought us all together was probably the music of David Bowie.

Bowie seemed to attract people on lots of different levels. You didn't have to particularly "get it" with Bowie. "It" could be either his music or his look. There were a lot of straight, bricklayer types who liked Bowie, partly because he was so huge at that point. Roxy Music, who were stylish and camp, also served as common ground. As everything got going, these soul boy clubs sprouted up in London.

The soul boys would go down and shop at Sex on the King's Road and pick up vinyl T-shirts and do their hair up. Sometimes the music didn't particularly mean anything special to them, except that it was a great way to meet girls. That's how the scene sprung. Soul boys were usually tough, while the Teds might be considered more like a fifties/seventies equivalent to, say, the Hell's Angels. Soul boys could be considered the equivalent to the current Rave scene. Soul boys were only interested in music that wasn't generally available—lots of import and obscure dance and soul records. Oddly enough, they used to congregate in places like Essex. They were a kind of tribe. You might describe them as inherently intolerant, bigoted, and possibly racist. It was an edgy alliance between "the punks," as we were later called, and the soul boys. Meanwhile, the Teds were the enemy of everyone who looked different. It was all kind of strange when you stop to realize that the original reason the Teds and the soul boys dressed differently was because they didn't want to fit in, either. They only wanted to look sharp and smart. They should have understood what it meant to look different. However, they were a bit older, probably second-generation Teddys, and by then their look had become a uniform, far removed from their movement's original motivation, which was breaking away in the spirit of being different.

No doubt we represented the Pistols' first organized following, and Malcolm encouraged the whole idea of a following, a movement as such. He didn't give it a name. Nobody gave it a name. We just tried to be as irritating as possible to anybody who got in the way. Not in a violent way, but more in a clever, sarcastic way. The violence escalated a bit later.

Another thing I remember during the rise of all this was the heat of the summer of 1976. It was unbelievably hot! We've since had summers that have been hot, maybe hotter, but this seemed like the first one. Temper and temperatures were boiling to the point where you knew something, maybe something particularly unpleasant, was about to take place. The heat had a lot to do with what went on during the summer of 1976 although it never deterred anyone. Maybe that's why people mixed their clothes with a lot of see-through stuff. Also, a lot of the imagery that Malcolm was creating in the shop came from two movies, *The Rocky Horror Picture Show* and *Cabaret*.

The parents of one of our Bromley friends disappeared for a couple of weeks, so we planned a series of parties at his house. The first one was called the First Annual Bromley [Anti-]Nazi Party Rally. We all dressed up in a homemade, twenties, Berlin, cabaret, decadent style. The Pistols must have been playing out of town that night. They came to that party afterward, which marked the first social event between us. For some odd reason, you could buy these little pins down on the King's Road, little eagle badges with swastikas on them. So the whole thing was a bit of fun designed to provoke. And it did provoke a lot of people.

Although it may have seemed unusual for a band to be close to their fans, we became more like friends since things hadn't really gotten to the stage where the notoriety had set in. The Pistols had only done maybe half a dozen gigs. You didn't meet in bars. As it is with the blacks in America, you could let your hair down by taking over somebody's house and having a house party. A house party was part of everybody's youth.

As for the Pistols, for me, the whole group was John. He looked amazing—so skinny. He had a real style about everything he did. Each night he reinvented the band's sartorial side. A lot has been said about the Pistols stealing Richard Hell's look. I don't agree; John invented his look himself. While the shop was still called Sex, I don't believe it dominated the way the band looked per se. Once Malcolm and Vivienne's shop became Seditionaries, and they started showing all the bondage gear, they'd give it to John first so afterward his fans would buy it. It was manipulative from that angle, but before that, John was always mixing up styles, inventing as he went along. One of the strongest things about seeing the Pistols' live show was John's sense of humor—his wisecracks. There was also the lyrical content, even in a live situation, where lines that would pop out would really make you think, "Pretty Vacant." Oh, yes, I feel like this.

BILLY IDOL: They were what we wanted to happen. If we could visualize the rock band of the mid-seventies, there it was in front of us. The Sex Pistols. We all wanted to do music, and here was the prototype. In a way, it was like being in heaven. All our lives we read about other scenes. We wanted one of our own. We had gone away from rock as something to be believed in. Iggy, Lou Reed, and the Velvet Underground took me away from people like the Mahavishnu Orchestra. That's beautiful music, but, fuck, I can't play guitar like that! Going all that way for somebody else's religion was something I didn't want to do.

JULIEN TEMPLE: When I saw them play . . . and the kind of audience they attracted at their early gigs, it was clear to me that I should stop what I was doing and find a way of working with the Pistols. It was an earthquake in the first stages.

Here was a band talking about the very things I was feeling, and it all came back to Bromley. I desperately wanted to find what I wanted to do in life and break out of this suburban boredom. As far as we were concerned, here was a soft, hedonistic approach. We didn't know what we wanted to do. We especially didn't know where all of this was going, but for the first time in our lives we were having a brilliant time as it was happening. We were making waves, but they were ripples at first. It was also an adolescent search for identity, though we didn't think of it that way at the time. It's only with hindsight that I can see that.

At the time, John was the focus. He seemed the perfect front man, while Steve and Paul were more the lads. Although I'm not really an expert on other musical eras, I do know that the precursor of the hippie era in England came out of a rich upper-class set of Chelsea people. When the Pistols began, these people were still hanging over; hence they were the first wave that was going to be usurped. As far as we were concerned, the Chelsea hippie art crowd was going to be destroyed. They were too effete and ineffectual, they were safe in their own little world. Their artiness annoyed us. Ultimately they didn't really care about music, much less seeing it as a force for delivering anything meaningful. So they had to go. And they did. They were pushed aside—to the back of the hall, starting when the Pistols played at Andrew Logan's party, which actually seemed boring for the band. They played the same set twice. Nothing really happened until Jordan from the shop jumped up on stage. By the end of the evening I think the art crowd got the message that they were being pissed on from a great height. Ironically, Malcolm was part of that crowd, even though he wasn't the type to take a side about anything.

This was about the time that Siouxsie, Billy, and I were starting to experiment musically, in a Velvet Underground sort of way. Our influences were the Stooges, the Velvets, Roxy, and Bowie. Also the first Ramones album, which had come out around that time. All of this served as an Identikit for the next group of bands that would evolve after the Pistols. The three of us had this idea that we wanted to form a band for just one gig, a one-off happening. I was a nonmusician. Billy was working up his new band, Chelsea, with guitarist Tony James. Siouxsie had gone to a few auditions a few years earlier, through *Melody Maker* ads and the like. Those bands always turned out to be hopeless pub rock groups, so she'd never sung in public. In fact, what she was trying to audition for probably hadn't been invented until the Pistols came along. We'd just seen the Pistols at the Screen on the Green, a landmark gig in their growth and development. It was at that point that the music papers started taking them seriously, while at the same time the band hadn't yet propelled themselves to a national level. At the end of the show, we cornered Malcolm. We knew he was putting together a two-day festival at the 100 Club that was scheduled in about a month's time. We told him we were going to form a band and play there. He agreed. That was the way it was then; it was that easy.

We were set to play on a Monday or Tuesday. The Friday before, Billy rang me up.

"Tony James doesn't want me to play with you," he said. "He thinks my playing with you would be too much of a distraction and take away from Chelsea."

Even though we were going to do just this one gig for the one night, we had to find a guitarist quickly. We put everything together on the Saturday night at this bar called Louise's. We knew Marco Pirroni, who could play guitar. We asked Sid, "Do you want to play drums?"

"I'll play drums. I don't care."

The next day, Sunday, Bernie Rhodes decided to let us rehearse at the Clash's studio and to let us use their equipment. We practiced for

Malcolm, where's the beer? (John Gray)

about twenty minutes. Me on bass, Marco on guitar, Siouxsie on vocals, Sid on drums. After the twenty minutes, Sid jumped off the drums and said, "That'll do. We don't want to actually learn anything, do we?"

Then came the actual gig. There was a bit of a problem because Siouxsie was wearing a swastika. Bernie, who had supplied the equipment, took offense to that, so instead of using the Clash's gear, we ended up using somebody else's equipment instead. The thing I remember most about the performance was that John came right to the front of the stage and started leaping around. John was big pals with Sid. He, with Wobble and John Gray, intent on being the audience, went straight to the front of the crowd. He made no bones about it. Maybe they were returning the favor—a role reversal of all the times we were the audience. After the set, we walked back and melted into the crowd. We were interviewed for the *Evening Standard*. I told them, "We're splitting up. We just wanted to play for twenty minutes."

Two people cornered us. One was Nils Stevenson, who had worked with the Pistols. He wanted to manage us. The other was Kenny Morris, who became our drummer. They both said it was the best thing they'd ever seen.

Everything was so focused. As the music evolved, there were huge spreads in the papers about the events before they happened and after they happened. There were no other diversions, nor was there any diversity. The Pistols, and the few bands who evolved along with them, were the only thing going on in English music at that time. That was it. If there were other bands, the spotlight wasn't on them. It was on us. And the more music we tried, the more ways we could go.

I don't want to sound like this musical era represented a crusade. It was more like you're given this opportunity, which was not necessarily our only opportunity, but it was such a good time that we felt the need to do something special. It was a time that manifested itself. You couldn't even dream of the same opportunity coming along again.

In hindsight, I can see that the Pistols era cleaned the rock 'n' roll slate. As more time passes, it may not be looked back on so fondly, since the outcome of it all was fairly depressing. Some may have found the whole period too nihilistic, but I disagree with them. I think of it as an honest time. It appears now that if you bracket it next to the decade that followed—the positive, opportunistic, money-grabbing eighties—the Pistols era may seem to be lacking in terms of money-making attributes. But we were trying to throw away a lot of the false positivism of the hippies, whom we viewed as ostriches with their heads in the sand. Neither of the usual descriptions—asexuality or nihilism—fit the times. There was a lot of humor and a lot of provocation. A lot of people were making fun at the expense of a lot of other people. It certainly wasn't as calculated as other musical periods.

I can never understand why people perceive the period as asexual because there were lots of shenanigans going on. Asexual is the wrong word. Trisexual may be a better word, even though sex wasn't really that high on the agenda. It didn't really have too much importance in the structure of this little society that was building. That was one of the ways we were rebelling—by not getting into the usual stifling situations. It wasn't particularly promiscuous, but it certainly wasn't asexual. Wasn't it John who called sex "two minutes of squeaking noises"? That was on a par with Boy George saying he'd rather have a cup of tea.

HOWARD THOMPSON: There weren't hundreds of beautiful women hanging around the Sex Pistols. There was the occasional good-looking girl. The idea was not to dress up or down, but out. Provocative. Shocking. Apart from everything else, this whole movement brought fetish wear—leather, vinyl, and latex—out from the sex clubs right onto the street. I'll tell you, a lot of it was extremely sexy. As for how it changed the relationships between young men and women, I don't know if it changed anything at all. I'm sure everyone went home afterward, peeled their clothes off, and did what they did normally.

If the government sensed trouble, they had no idea what form it would take. As usual, they chose to come in with the iron fist first and ask questions afterward. Certainly, during the beginning, the scene was so underground they hardly knew it existed. All the police and the councils saw were a few strange—looking people walking about in the streets. But it was slowly building from the inside of nightclubs and small gigs that the Pistols were playing to the outside, the streets. Originally there was nothing the government or the police could put a handle on. Much later, John was systematically raided, which had more to do with the media grabbing hold after the Grundy show.

I didn't see Malcolm as a manipulating Svengali. My favorite incident came after we'd all been on "The Bill Grundy Show." In the heat of the moment, as the whole thing had began to snowball, Malcolm was convinced the incident marked the end of the group. He'd thought they'd blown it. Instead the band landed on the front page of the papers. Once we'd actually finished the Grundy interview, after Steve and John had taken it over, we went back into the hospitality room. There was the band, me, and Siouxsie. All the phones started ringing. Siouxsie and I were picking up the phones, telling people to fuck off. We also posed as the complaint department, bantering with the indignant callers:

"Well, actually, I thought they were rather articulate."

Malcolm was freaking out. "Don't you dare answer those phones," he shouted.

· The Grundy show was absolutely the hinge. Before, the Pistols were just a group of annoying musical hacks. There were a few little TV specials tracing the evolution of this strange youth culture. Art programs were very keen to find out what this stuff was all about. Mainly, though, there was lots of shooting in the dark, with everybody getting off on the energy of it. The Grundy show debacle gave the movement its shape. With or without the Grundy show, however, an explosion was inevitable. After all, the Pistols were so good. There's no other way of describing them. No matter what people say, the Pistols were a fantastic band. Something else would have happened that would have thrown them into the public eye.

The force with which they were thrown into the media's eye was the turning point. The Pistols scared people. People didn't know what it all was because it appeared to be so malevolent. It was misunderstood in the same way people misinterpreted Malcolm's role as a Svengali. It wasn't like that. On the inside, we were confused and sometimes unfocused. Maybe that's what made the Pistols so frightening to outsiders. You couldn't pin it down nor understand it, so the police, the Teds, and the government chose to smash it down as hard as they could.

Although I wasn't on the boat, the clamp-down seemed to have occurred during the jubilee celebration. That was the first indication that the band was a bit out of their league. The fact that the police had a semi-riot on their hands scared people like Malcolm. I think he liked to feel as if he were in control most of the time, even though by that point he clearly wasn't. He became outnumbered around the time things got out of control—when John started to get personally harassed on the street. The police now knew who he was and where he lived, leaving him open and vulnerable, and he took the hits. Malcolm could have cared more about what happened to the band, but I don't think he could have done much. What could he have done apart from hiring bodyguards?

By that time, if it wasn't the authorities, it was the Teds who were waging war. It was pretty scary to try to do anything. Ironically, whenever the Pistols played in the heart of London there was hardly any violence. However, there was a whole network of towns to the north that were notoriously violent. The Pistols did well up there because there was such a large number of disenchanted youths to play to. They got off on it. A lot of the crowd was soul boys.

I think the music also attracted Rasta people into the fold because initially it was more tolerant. There was always dub reggae around, and it was the most experimental music going. Before, there was mainly blue beat and ska, which was the province of the mods—which was bizarre in that the white followers of this early Jamaican music were, in essence, budding Nazis. From the mods came the skinheads who were the precursors of the National Front. We found it weird that their chosen musical form was created by black people. That's the way it still is to a degree.

Even when you consider all the trappings, the swastikas, leather bondage, and chains, we never felt much intolerance. To us these weren't badges of intolerance, but symbols of provocation to an older generation that had to get out of the way to make room for the younger voices. To do so, we made use of any form possible. However, the swastikas were dropped fairly quickly because we realized it wasn't the most clever way to get our point across. When it was still a small movement you could use symbols like that, but once the following got too big, you couldn't use symbols like swastikas and images of German decadence. On a broader scope, it would communicate the wrong meaning.

A lot of people associate Sid with his heroin days. Actually, before he got deeply into drugs, he was one of the funniest guys. He had a brilliant sense of humor, goofy, very sweet, and really cute. In a lot of ways he was like a cartoon character. We first met him at one of the concerts. He began bouncing around the dance floor, the so-called legend of the pogo dance. It was merely Sid jumping up and down, trying to see the group, leaping up and down because he was stuck in the back somewhere. Up until the time we rehearsed together for the 100 Club, I didn't know him very well. He was always around and, ironically, very quiet until he began to get involved with Nancy. She was this horrible whining woman who appeared as a spin-off of the Heartbreakers' scene when they arrived from New York. Up until that time, drugs consisted mainly of sulfate. However, it was Thunders and Nolan who wreaked heroin and havoc.

A mutual friend, Linda, had a flat in Victoria at the St. James Hotel, a place where we'd all go to stay over because none of us had flats in London. Most of us were still living with our parents, so we'd stay at

Linda's, waiting for things to happen, making things happen. Linda was . . . kind of a dominatrix . . . . She'd tell stories about TV celebrities that she was hired to beat every now and again. They were people into children's programming and stuff. I remember thinking, Really? Him?

Also, Simon Barker was renting one of the rooms, so we'd stay there quite a lot. Jordan would stay there. That's where I met Nancy—she was hanging out with Sid. None of us could understand why Sid was involved with her. They seemed completely different from one another. I never really saw Sid much after he got together with Nancy. Siouxsie and I did go to see him after he'd been arrested for throwing a glass at the 100 Club. He was sent down to a detention center in Ashwood in Kent, and he was beaten up; he had a black eye and was down in the dumps.

Sid did throw the glass. Siouxsie and I were standing right next to him. He was aiming at the Damned, so he had my full support. The three of us were saying, "What is this band? Nonsense, nothing to do with anything. Pantomime seaside—special stuff."

So Sid drank his glass empty and threw it in the direction of the stage. Instead of landing on the stage, it hit a pillar, and I think it shattered and hit some girl. It was one of those irresponsible Sid things that have been chronicled ever since, even though I had never seen him act like that before.

CAROLINE COON: My instinct at the time was that Sid didn't do it. However, if he was at the bar sneering around, he could have. Whether he did or didn't, I would have been there to defend him. So the next day after he got out, I took Sid to one of the Bond Street Release lawyers. It was very funny. I also took him to Fortnum & Mason's tea room and soda fountain for an ice cream. You couldn't get more posh. They still sell the most fantastic Knickerbocker Glories! It was just around the corner from the lawyer's office. Sid and I walked in. At the time, the more high-classed the places were, the more likely you could wear anything you liked. That's why I thought I could easily take Sid there.

His jacket was absolutely unbelievable. We're sitting at the soda fountain bar, and it's even beyond their tolerance level. The waitress said to Sid, "Will you please take off your leather jacket?"

Sid took off his leather jacket, and underneath he had on this ripped, filthy T-shirt, with burns up and down his arms. At that point the waitress couldn't say anything since it was far worse than if she had let him keep the jacket on. So we sat and ate ice cream together.

Later we went to court together as well. I was quite content to bail these rock 'n' rollers out when they got busted. I didn't think it was a good lesson for any young person to be taken into prison.

The Ashwood detention center visit is the last vivid memory I have of Sid. I was shocked when he died. I heard about it on the radio. Certainly by this point, any closeness between the Pistols and what was called the Bromley contingent had totally vanished. We were more concerned with our own careers as the Banshees. Although we were still friends, we never saw the Pistols much. They'd be off on the Anarchy Tour or they were doing gigs under pseudonyms. Things had seemed to be going pretty badly for them, and our paths no longer seemed to cross. The split between Nils Stevenson—his working for us and leaving Malcolm—was probably looked at by the Pistols as a bit of a betrayal. Nils certainly felt betrayed by Malcolm if only because he paid him three hundred pounds for a year's work. Nils took us over when we had only a few hundred pounds in the bank. Since then we've managed to make everything last. Our estrangement with the Pistols wasn't as if anything went sour; our relationship just sort of dispersed. We also couldn't handle the fact that the media had gotten hold of things and there were so many new people turning up-the bridge and tunnel crowd. It was on to the next thing—on to our music.

I saw Sid's first show with the Pistols. It was at Notre Dame. By that point, the band had gotten too big for me. It wasn't quite the same anymore, but I thought they played well. It wasn't their fault that things were escalating out of control. In our own way, we English people view music as our own personal, closely guarded secret. By that time there were too many people, so eventually I got shoved to the back of the hall as well. I never resented the band for getting that popular. I never felt they'd changed. They were as vibrant as ever. Yet this seething mob in front wasn't for me. That was never my scene. I just liked to stand and watch the band and dig what they were doing. I remember thinking, the monster took over and ate itself.

It was weird hearing of the Pistols' decay secondhand and from afar. It all happened in America. Sid had been accused of killing Nancy, and that was so terribly depressing. Yet I don't think Sid deserved that fate at all. He was a victim of circumstance. Sid may have been self-destructive, but he wasn't mean. But then I didn't see the effect that heroin had on him; that can totally change anybody. That may have brought out things in him that I'd never seen before.

The person I was reacting to, the Sid that I knew before Nancy, had died. I couldn't believe it. It was such a waste. At the same time, I was really pissed off. I've never really understood the band's reaction to his death. I don't know if it was true, but the reaction seemed to be, "Sid asked for it. It was long overdue."

Whether or not that was their true reaction, there was never ever any public display of remorse. Sid deserved better than that from all of us. Yet by the time he died I was well on the outside, so it was hard to tell what was going on. After the American tour, everything crumbled.

I look at the early Pistols period as an apprenticeship of sorts. Not in a musical way. The music of the Banshees, even the music we do now, evolved from a time before the Pistols. But as far as attitude, how to do the music, how to approach the business, how to approach life in general, it all comes from that explosion of my adolescence, and the farther it recedes into the distance, the more important it seems. I keep waiting to see if something as powerful, as equally meaningful, will happen again, and I haven't seen it. There have been movements since, but none of them have had such an awesome ideology or attitude behind them. Nothing has had the kind of single-mindedness or focus that the Pistols had. And there hasn't been anything as crafty since. Hip Hop is too sexist and intolerant, detracting from the fact that it is a very interesting and experimental type of music.

Though not in a Protestant type of way, there was a kind of paradoxical punk ideology at work. There were the unspoken rules. Anything was possible, a rule in itself. There were the unspoken perimeters, like not having to be Phil Collins or Paul McCartney to be a musician.

CHRISSIE HYNDE: The thing about the punk period was that to be a musician went against the whole idea. The minute anyone got serious about their musicality, they lost what was interesting about the punk scene. Not having a fucking clue and getting on stage and just doing it was what made it so exciting. I was down at the Roxy Club every night for the first six months. I used to just stand there and laugh. Don Letts was the disc jockey in the box. We'd smoke a spliff, and then he'd be in the box and I'd be out front. We'd be looking at each other, and some nights I would be crying. It wasn't a matter of being so bad as it was being so "out there." I can remember one band coming off and asking the guitarist, "Is that some special tuning you were playing in?"

Turns out they just didn't know how to tune their guitars. It wasn't a matter of being judgmental, it was purity and innocence.

All the second-generation bands of that era have since invented nonsensical rules, like not living like a rock star or not dealing with Americans. Originally, with the Pistols anyway, there were never any of those "us and them"-type barriers. We were more pissed off at the people we had liked in the past who had gone sour. We weren't pissed off that these people played in huge places so much as it was the type of music they played in those huge places. The Genesises, the Yeses—it was all redundant garbage. The Pistols had nothing to do with the fact that you shouldn't play in a big place or you shouldn't be on "Top of the Pops." That was nonsense. The idea was to do as much as you can, get in there, shake things up, the fly-in-the-ointment approach.

As far as the music being academic, at the time very little of it seemed so. The references to the Situationists—I've only read about that in the last three years! Everybody knew about the Surrealists and Dadaists, but who the hell were the Situationists? I don't know if Malcolm or Bernie ever talked to the Pistols about all of that, but I don't think it would have stuck. They would have gone down to the pub—certainly Steve would have. Steve wouldn't have grasped it for a second, he wouldn't have wanted to know. Rather, everything was much more intuitive and exciting; it was never preconceived or manipulated to cause any kind of intellectual outrage. It was clever and smart, while it certainly didn't have a political philosophy behind it.

CAROLINE COON: Malcolm and Bernie were anti-intellectual. . . . That's why they went into Situationist politics. Situationist politics is merely sloganeering—second-rate sloganeering at that—all pulled out of the sixties dustbin. However, there was a positive side, it being graphically quite interesting. Yet it was also incoherent.

PAUL COOK: Situationism had nothing to do with us. The Jamie Reids and the Malcolms were excited because we were the real thing. I suppose we were what they were dreaming of. We didn't spend any time philosophizing, nothing was contrived, and everything just happened quickly and naturally—which is how things should happen. We were out there doing it.

As for "God Save the Queen," there's always going to be this aristocratic segment of English society who are untouchable and unflappable. They wouldn't know what you were talking about should you attempt to even comment on their atrocious behavior. They just don't see it. It's all a part of their bunkered upbringing. The whole British class structure is alive and well today to the point that one of the fundamentals of pop music is that it's still a great escape for working-class people. Either it's music, football hooliganism, or boxing.

RAMBO: There were a lot of punks over at Arsenal. We actually adopted a Pistols football song:

> We're so pretty,
> We hate Man-City,
> We're violent,
> And we go spare!

Perhaps it's crime. Obviously that was Steve Jones's background. Or there was the reason people would move from the inner city out to a suburb like Bromley—to slowly rise up and become some deputy executive assistant in an insurance company. That's a black-collar job that's dead end forever. Those were your choices in England. That's why these suburban towns breed so many pop bands. You don't get many opportunities to do something with your life.

Apart from happening in the middle of one of the hottest summers in 1976, the Pistols rose to prominence right in the midst of one of our worst recessions. I remember nobody having any money. If the Pistols were being paid thirty pounds a week, that was a lot. Obviously it wasn't a lot for what they were generating in terms of revenue and importance, but it was enough to live on. That was a lot more than we had at the time. But you made do. You survived. It was a reality that you had no money, but you were young and you didn't care. That's where John and I are similar. We both come from London Irish families. John was brought up in Finsbury Park. I was born about three miles west, in Archway. While my Irish connection isn't as strong as his, it still touches me. What we call "London Irish" is a particular emotional base that's peculiar to our generation.

Whether he likes it or not, John was the icon for that period, and through that one person you have the identity that epitomizes the chaos that was going on. I don't think John invented the chaos of the Pistols era, it just happened. Things sometimes need a figurehead. Maybe that's where it all went wrong. Maybe Malcolm was jealous that he wasn't it. Come to think of it, I can't think of any other reason why Malcolm would want to go out and make his own records afterward.

Johnny "harping" on a hankie. (John Gray)

CAROLINE COON: To see Malcolm wanting to become like Johnny was very interesting. Malcolm copying Johnny was bizarre. I have this scenario about Malcolm. He had to fight hard. He could not intellectually face the dire circumstances of his childhood. He had horrendous, tough shit to deal with but didn't. There he was, floating around . . . .

SHOOTING IN THE DARK

The press reported a ruckus at London's Heathrow Airport before our flight to Amsterdam. Tales of vomit and drunkenness. Now what are ashtrays for but to spit in? You do that, some old woman gets offended and there's forty journalists there to blow it out of all proportion. Suddenly you've vomited all over the airport. Okay, Steve did vomit in Heathrow Airport. What was he supposed to do? Why was it news?

I never liked playing in Amsterdam or Holland. The Dutch were too hippie and laid back for us—the audience tended to be a hell of a lot older than us, too. They looked like a bunch of Grateful Dead rejects. The young kids weren't allowed into the halls because the shows would start very late. The smell of incense, the joss sticks, and the hash-burning counters pissed me off. The whole scene struck me as retarded or stuck in a time warp. Every time I've ever been back there, I still have that same vision.

I preferred Scandinavia because they were much more hard and brutal. Playing there was like going to a Viking beer monster's tea party. The Scandinavian tours were wild and crazy events. The crowds would be well sozzled, very much younger, and way more aggressive than British audiences—but not violent, at least not to us. They weren't out there to kill us, but to be *with* us. Big difference. A long time before the British, Scandinavian audiences were the first ones who clocked on to what the Sex Pistols were about. Absolutely. We were still having trouble with London audiences. They were fashionably overdressed. Up north, English kids were still into long pudding bowl hairdos and booing and hissing. But Norway, Sweden, Finland, and Denmark were so bang on the money. They all had the attitude right from the start and understood the energy. They were sick of the long hair too: "Look how badly I've hacked my hair off!"

Londoners would call them disasters and suggest, "Why don't you just dab a little pink here or quiff it to one side?"

Scandinavians were already punked out without the clichés and trying to follow a set image. They were completely on their own, and I loved going back there. The music media's opinions meant nothing to them. The girls were phenomenal. You could get raped and have a sauna at the same time. Buxom beauties, every single one. They destroyed that ridiculous, thin model look. Malcolm only came out once with us. Scandinavia wasn't for him because it was too far away from the fashion world of London and he couldn't pull any strokes out there. Nordic people are more interested in the guts of the music while Malcolm would be completely absorbed with the trimmings.

A lord provost in Scotland spoke out against the Sex Pistols in one of his speeches, saying Scotland had enough hooligans without importing them from south of the border. That was odd. I'd always seen these people as the powers that be, people we'd never have direct contact with at all. But when they started screaming and shouting about the Sex Pistols, the titillation level rose.

After the release of "God Save the Queen," we got beat up on the street. That's another reason I tended to hang around with large amounts of friends, particularly hooligan elements. They would stop that. It was physically impossible for me to walk around the streets on my own. I would be attacked. High visibility and all this daily nonsense in the newspapers. If I farted, it was an affront to society and I had to be chastised.

You always get this in England—gangs of drunks roaming the streets who think that they're there to protect society. Lo and behold, that's what happened. Some of the attacks were quite severe. I was stabbed right near the studio, while we were recording the *Bollocks* album. This is before the record was even fucking released. The singles were out, but the album wasn't. We went to a pub around the corner—not far from the same old Arsenal area in Highbury where I was brought up. This bunch of bastards just tore into us with gurkha knives, blades, razors, the lot. I was with the producer Chris Thomas and Bill Price, the engineer. We managed to run into the car park and lock ourselves in Chris's car. This mob smashed the car and windscreen to shit while we were inside it. They broke one of the windows and stuck a blade in. I had on a pair of very thick leather trousers at the time. It went straight down them. If I'd had on anything less, it would have probably ripped my leg out. The blade stuck in my knee. I got a stiletto blade pushed straight into my hand, next to my thumb. It came out the other side by my little finger. That affected the tendons in my left hand. I'll never play guitar again because of that. Boo. Hiss. I can't close a proper left fist. That's a bit hard because I'm left-handed. I thought I was going to die. Pretty damned close to it. Yet the police didn't want to know.

"Look at the state of ya!"

Thanks very much. I'm not a fighter. I'll defend myself, but there's not a lot I can do against that kind of artillery. There was at least twelve of them. They taunted us.

"We love our queen."

That struck me as very odd. It was such a stupid thing to say. I'm sure they made her proud that night.

BOB GRUEN: In America, whether you liked the president or not, you could at least say whatever the fuck you wanted. I can't imagine somebody at CBGB's saying they hated a band because they'd insulted the president. But in England, other musicians were genuinely incensed by the Pistols' attitude. It was interesting to see kids so volatile and emotional over something political like the queen. In America, it was sex, not politics, that created controversy.

Later on it was very hard for any of the Pistols to go out socially anywhere or sit in any of the pubs around Fulham, King's Road, Ladbroke Grove, or any of those music areas. We would get criticism from these so-called long-haired, rebellious rock bands. They all stood behind the Union Jack and the queen. There they were standing up for the very things that kept them down all their lives. The Pistols made clear that we didn't need to be kicked in the teeth and accept it any longer. We wanted to stand up and see it for the rubbish it was. Physical violence, like what the Pistols experienced, is very rare. I don't think that's ever happened to a band before or since. There hasn't been a band on this planet that enticed that kind of response and attitude. Quite frankly, I wasn't happy with it, either. Knives hurt.

BOB GRUEN: Once I was in a bar called the Speakeasy with Steve Jones and Johnny Rotten. Steve and I went into the bathroom, into the stall to smoke something. We could hear two people washing their hands and talking. Since this was a rock star bar full of musicians, I assumed the artists at least got along with each other and had a sense of free thought. But these guys were talking about how angry they were and how much they hated the Sex Pistols because they'd insulted the queen. I couldn't believe it. Steve and I were listening to all this anger. I didn't get it at all. That's when I felt like a tourist. Musicians angry at a band because they sang a song against the queen? I guess Steve had a better idea of what was going on. Afterward we went back out into the bar and were drinking beer out of these big, heavy beer mugs. To me, it was still just a bar full of musicians, but Steve was aware of the undercurrent. Johnny Rotten was a couple of feet away from us talking to somebody. All of a sudden Steve said, "Get down, there's gonna be a fight."

Just as we ducked under the edge of the bar, every glass in the place went flying in the air. It was the most amazing thing I've ever seen. From every direction, heavy beer glasses came crashing down on us, smashing against the walls and pillars of the bar. Within seconds the place was ankle deep in broken glass. I asked, "What the fuck was that for?"

Steve answered, "Some people don't like us."

My father saw Malcolm unable to maintain control. The violence was really severe, particularly when I got slashed outside the recording studio. Sid and I were living in Chelsea Cloisters. We weren't like Paul and Steve. We didn't have any permanent place to stay, so we were more open to being victimized. When I was slashed there was a problem at the hospital and they wouldn't treat me. Malcolm wouldn't even organize a cab to take us anywhere.

One photo session originally done for the *Daily Mirror* had me tied to a crucifix. It seems hard to believe that in 1977 it offended so many people. Again, it made any kind of public social activity almost impossible. I don't know what it is with the English. They're so easily outraged. Ironically, this is the kind of stuff Madonna does now, and it's all considered very chi-chi. Now it's called market planning and self-promotion, and she's given more than a nod and a wink. When we shot the photo in 1977, the photographer had a cross set up on the corner.

"Would you like to stand in front of it?"

"Oh, why not."

It wasn't a setup, but it didn't occur to me or the photographer that this would be a total catastrophe. If it annoys people that much, then you know you're doing something right. No great planning or no Malcolm involvement there.

My mum thought the Pistols were amusing, but she felt sorry for Sid. Both she and my old man always thought he was a bit thick. When I got Sid into the Pistols, my mum sighed. "What kind of wicked reasons have you got behind that?" I didn't have any wicked reasons at the time, but I think my parents spotted it as a bad move. I was too young to know at the time. At that age, you can't hold yourself responsible for other people's behavior.

My parents didn't turn up at any Pistols gigs, while my brothers did. Perhaps Mum might have seen us once. I really didn't want my parents there. It was too chaotic. To be frank, I don't think they would have got it. They certainly couldn't have coped with the audience and the sheer abandon of it all. It was no tea party. Maybe I should have invited my parents. But it was something I didn't want to happen. Deep down inside, it would be something to be ashamed of. Isn't that odd? Exposing yourself to the public is one thing, but to your own parents, you just can't do it. It's not the same. They would have been like your most severe critics—they'd see right through me—and I could not have that happening at eighteen or nineteen years old. No fucking way! I had an arrogance of being a self-made man, but when I look back on it, it's so stupid.

But you have to go through that stage. It's so relevant. If you can't get through it, then there's nothing for you in the future. That was Sid's problem. He just couldn't get through the concept of self-identity. He hadn't formed enough of his own personality to have enough self-esteem in himself to go forward. That's why he was so easily led.

CHRISSIE HYNDE: I knew how close John was to his mother. I remember embarrassing him one night—or impressing him—early on in the Roxy Club. He had a new watch on, a digital one with a red face that would light up when you pressed a button. He was standing there and I asked, "Is that what your mum gave you for Christmas?"

I knew by the look on his face that, indeed, that's what his mum had given him for Christmas. After that I knew he was close to her.

My parents did see the Pistols on the telly. My father would yell, "Oh, Jesus!" while my mummy would be knitting a cardigan, look up, and say: "Oh, that's nice."

She had the "why do you have to scream so much?" approach, but whatever extremes I was up to, she just let me get on with it. That's what my mum always did. She didn't ignore me. She would never be so trite as to tell me I was just going through a phase. There would be some very subtle hints, however imperceptible it was to someone outside the family unit, but I definitely knew, I could just feel it. Sometimes when people say nothing, it says more than reams of sentences. She thought the swearing was terrible. Mum never liked swearing. The Grundy TV incident would have been unforgivable, yet she convinced herself that it wasn't me.

"That was Steve Jones who did that."

I would nod in agreement. "Yes, you're right there, Mum!"

JOHN GRAY: Eileen Lydon was proud of her John; she was proud of all her children, whatever they'd done. For friends of the Lydons, part of the fun of the household was that we could go over there for drinks and beers and play records 'til midnight. I could crash on the sofa in the front room. In the morning someone would come down and make you a cup of tea. That was unheard of in my house. There, people were all over. Jimmy might have a mate or a girlfriend. Sometimes they'd have breakfast and would be careful not to wake us up. In a tiny flat! Not a word would be said. If it was my house, my mum would be downstairs blasting your head off.

I know my dad was proud of all of it. I was in the newspaper. Well, that was something good. If he didn't understand the rest, fine. He could sweep that away into a corner and just deal with "That's my son there!" His friends would never say anything bad to him. He's rather on the tough side, definitely not one to shirk away from a fight. If there would be any insults thrown, it would be greeted with fists on face. He's shorter than me, but like a lot of small people, he's always been quick-tempered. He's quieted down a lot over the last couple of years.

My mother used to egg me on. She was an absolute fun-loving person. Mum loved Alice Cooper and saw him as a wonderful joke and silly theater. She liked modern music of any kind—all dance music. She was very open. I took her to see Gary Glitter, and she thought that was fabulous. I bought the tickets and took her to the concert, but I couldn't get my old man to go. Gary was really nice; someone in his management spotted us sitting in the audience. They took us backstage, then to Tramps, a posh disco. We drank wine until four in the morning. My old man was furious when we both got home pissed.

"You bringing that dirty drunk shit on my wife, you fucking hooligan. Get out of my house!"

He was jealous because he'd missed out, but at the same time his pride wouldn't let him go because it was something he couldn't fit into. He's shy about big crowds.

You'd see newscasters and TV stars at our gigs trying to punk it up, man. "Gee whiz, you kids!" I saw lots of old rock stars—and lots of jealous rock stars, too. One of the most verbal instances was Mick Jagger. "The Sex Pistols are awful, and they can't play!" Shame on you, Mick. The Stones were one of the most notoriously inept bands in music, and here was this old coke hag pointing fingers and calling us disgusting. The Stones were into patting themselves on the backs and being self-congratulatory, like many of those old-timers. The Pistols were an absolute threat to that nice little world they had all built for themselves. They came out of the ever-so-generous-and-love-everyone sixties and soon turned into fucking greedy, shifty little businessmen doing their utmost to stifle the opposition. The lot of them deserved the name *dinosaurs*—too big, too pompous, elaborate, enormous amounts of equipment, only playing very large auditoriums or open-air festivals. Music became as remote from the general public as you could possibly get. They became like little royal families unto themselves. They carted themselves around the country, waving to us occasionally. They bought immense houses, joined the stockbrokers' belt, and sent their kids to—*public schools*! See? The system! They became it.

CAROLINE COON: By the mid-seventies, we were disappointed with what the rock 'n' roll cultural leaders were doing. They were shaking hands with the fucking royalty! They had turned into English gentlemen! Street-fighting, man? Huh! The tragedy was seeing Jagger at an aristocrat's table having nothing to do with Jagger joining the aristocracy. The aristocracy has always had clowns at the dinner table, and there was rock 'n' roll, emasculated, shaking hands with royalty.

For some weird reason, Elton seems to be all right. He's more like Coco the Clown, so utterly harmless I'd put him in the Barry Manilow category. Elton is not pretending to be something he's not. He's a fat buffoon who plays piano—adequately.

Cliff Richard is a joke. He's bad-mouthed me over the years. During the Pistols he supported what was known as the Festival of Light, a Christian light movement held on Trafalgar Square, to save the world from the likes of punk and Johnny Rotten. I remember seeing it on the news. I was thrilled at hearing Cliff bad-mouth me in front of thousands of Christian hypocrites. It was lovely. They were burning candles in the middle of the hot sun on a Sunday afternoon. For God and humanity!

Oh, God. David Bowie mentions the Sex Pistols in a lyric on his *Tin Machine* album. Well, how strange for him! This is the man who had me thrown out backstage. I was at an Iggy Pop gig at Camden Palace in London, and I went backstage to say hello because I had met Iggy a year before. Mr. Bowie wanted me removed—thrown out, in fact. He wasn't touring with Iggy, he was just backstage. I thought it was odd. It was Iggy's gig, and Mr. Bowie got his personal bouncers to have me removed.

I've had an utter loathing for Bowie since then. What a pompous prat! A couple of years later, PiL were playing a nice nightclub in Switzerland. In trots Mr. Bowie. He made his way backstage. It's two minutes before we go on. "Hi, I'm Dave Bowie, and this is my son. He'd like to meet you." I don't know anyone who could deal with that shit two minutes before going on. We're just going up the stairs, and I had to cope with this. I wasn't rude to his son. His son had never done me any harm. But to him—blank. "Now if this was your gig and I came back, would you have me thrown out?" I walked away and left it at that. And I'll bet he would have. Again and again.

ZANDRA RHODES: Whereas some people might question how something like colored hair could be considered beautiful, I think some
of the extreme punk with the points and the safety pins was so
heavily designed, it was beautiful.

I made no point of condemning fashion designer Zandra Rhodes for her high-priced punk fashions. I thought the safety pin trend was hysterical. If someone was going to pay two thousand pounds for a torn dress with a safety pin on it, well, it serves them right. They don't deserve the money. I enjoyed the absurdity. There were fools going around in clothes like that because the fashion houses had moved down to street wear. The joke was a joke was a joke, as Zandra would do chat shows while her clothes would raise great titillations from the audiences.

ZANDRA RHODES: The concept of what is rebellious and what is ugly can be turned into beauty and new thought. Its rebellion has a huge influence on how the youth culture looks and how it wears things.

The Pistols used to gig under assumed names, more based on humor than anything else. The undercover SPOTS—Sex Pistols on Tour Secretly—was a way of keeping things alive while not having to deal with the mass hysteria of the press. We did the gigs to stay fresh and fully rehearsed for better days. It was agreed by all that a low profile was sensible. We went out under several different names: Tax Exiles, Acne Rabble, and the Spots. We thought of the names as we arrived or the day before—the silliest thing we could think of.

We once played a gig in Hounslow at a Teddy boy convention. We booked ourselves under some cowboy name. Then we trotted onstage as the Sex Pistols. My God, was that a hoot! They thought it was the cheekiest, most sarcastic thing done to them, yet there was no violence at the gig, even though there was all this so-called, high-profile press animosity between Teds and punks. We weren't supposed to get on together, but there we were on stage playing our songs and there they were in the audience dancing. Then you'd read in the *Daily Mirror* and the *Sun* about all this punks versus Teds nonsense.

There was so much sex around in the seventies, it got very boring. It made you feel kind of grubby because somehow it wasn't right. When I met my wife, Nora, we had such a row, but I knew there was something about that woman that I wanted. It wasn't just the sex. I wanted that person in my life, and I never got that before. It was always just little trysts and these situations—like grabbing a bag of speed, then thinking, That was all right, but now I've got a headache.

The first time I met Nora, we absolutely hated each other on sight, but I loved her image because she wears forties clothing. Nora doesn't follow fashion. She has her own thing. She was warned that I was the most awful person on earth, so she behaved accordingly. There were a few bitter words. It turned around because the warnings came so thick and fast that Nora's curiosity was piqued. "He can't be all that bad, can he?" She invited me over to her place, and from there on in, we got on really well. This was through the Pistols days. The way she puts it, she had escaped from her native Germany. I was living around when we first met. We were together occasionally at that time. It fluctuated; I was young, I needed my freedom, and I hadn't been naughty enough in the real world for anything permanent.

With Nora, my life is total commitment. I couldn't go home night after night to a brain-dead zombie. Being a two-career family eliminates boredom. Boredom is the killer of any relationship. That will get you every time. The one-income family structure is wrong to me. Both should have an outside life, because without it, things won't work. I'm the kid in this family. So is Nora. We can play any role we like.

I don't think my old man liked any of my girlfriends at all. If I'd bring them to the house, he'd say, "That one's on drugs, I'm telling you!" "That one looks like she's got fleas!" Probably has. But he loved Nora the first time she walked in. It was so funny when he said, "God! She's more my kind of woman. Wha' are you doin' with a good woman like dat? Leave her here!" Nora was saying, "Mr. Lydon, get your hands off me!" I suppose our age difference—Nora being older—meant something to him, but not to any great offense. He was just trying to think of himself as younger. My mum was gone by then, so he was just lonely. After the Sex Pistols there were many punk girls who went through his bedroom. One was affiliated with bananas. A lot of the punk girls at the time were intrigued. What's Rotten's father like? Is he anything like him? Some probably went from me to him. I didn't bother to think about it too much at the time. I just thought it was good that he was having fun.

I was a bit bored making the Sex Pistols album. There was something like twenty-one guitars laid down and only two tracks for vocals—one for the verses and one for the choruses. I did most of the songs all the way through, one or two takes, and that's it. There was very little bouncing of tracks, and I got annoyed about it. We did some different versions of songs, I did a different version of "Submission" with Sid, which wasn't put on the album when it was first released in Britain. It was a lot different from the Glen Matlock version because it was a hell of a lot less musical and I thought more chaotic and important.

STEVE JONES: I loved recording the *Bollocks* album. I remember when I was doing some guitar overdubs late at night, I heard on the radio that Elvis Presley had died. I remember it clearly because I wasn't sad. I just thought I'd better get back and do those guitar overdubs. No one gave a fuck about Elvis Presley, especially us lot.

Chris Thomas did a hilariously good job as producer of *Never Mind the*

Bollocks. I liked the idea of using him because I liked Roxy Music, although I knew we would never sound anything like them. I didn't realize until we got in the studio that Chris was hearing impaired in one ear. He has engineers like Bill Price to tell him what's in and out of tune. "Chris, the guitar's out of tune." "Is it? Where is it?" Can you imagine that at a recording session? Bozo yobs! A producer with one good ear. Sid was so bad in the studio that even Chris Thomas knew. The whole thing went way over his head so Sid drowned himself in vodka. He could not hold a tune, and I think it was a fear of the whole situation. It was all too much, which is understandable. Sid was thrown into the deep end just like me—from a member of the audience to suddenly being in the group. Outside of Glen, there were no hired musicians. Any talk otherwise is all bullshit. By that point we were playing very well. Steve was very good and certainly didn't need session musicians to come in and back him up. If they were used, they were used without my seeing them—unless they sneaked them in when I left.

STEVE JONES: Sid wanted to come down and play on the album, and we tried as hard as possible not to let him anywhere near the studio. Luckily he had hepatitis at the time. He had to stay at the hospital, and that was really good. He actually came down a couple of times and played on "God Save the Queen" and "Bodies." He played this farty old bass part, and we just let him do it. When he left I dubbed another part on, leaving Sid's down low. I think it might be barely audible on the track.

The Pistols album compromised too much. It was most definitely too traditional. The music was traditional sixties, but my approach wasn't. The tunes can almost be found on old Who or Small Faces records. It used the mod, Kinks approach of quirky little melodies and three chord progressions. If the sessions had gone the way I wanted, it would have been unlistenable for most people because they wouldn't have had a point of reference. "This doesn't remind me of anything! I can't relate to it!" You know the attitude; the general public are exceptionally lazy. They like what fits in neatly with everything else. I have had to learn to deal with this, I'm afraid. I've found ways of using that and twisting it into other things. The approach is more subtle these days than initially. While there's no compromise as far as what the vocals do, I guess it's the very nature of music; if you want people to listen, you're going to have to compromise. You can't go totally out into space. Nobody will follow and a voice in the wilderness is rather pointless.

CHRISSIE HYNDE: The Pistols were a true band. Although they hated Glen Mattock so much for his musicality, songs like "You're So Pretty Vacant" were very musical, and I reckon he had something to do with that. Then Sid was brought in, and he wasn't musical, which, spiritually, could have been a good thing. Ultimately, though, a band has to be musical, and John will admit to that now. If you go through John Rotten's record collection, you will find some very musical albums. He likes music and is a music fan. That must have been a bit of a dilemma for him.

The only way I could make waves in the Sex Pistols' music was lyrically and vocally. The music was right in one respect, that it reflected back to a more working-class, ground-roots way of approaching music. My ideas at the time might have been too heady for most people. If you want to change things, you have to do it slower, you have to learn to have patience.

CHRISSIE HYNDE: There was nothing musically unique about the Sex Pistols, it was their spirit that was unique. By 1977 nothing could be unique. After all, there are only twelve notes to the scale, and these were twelve-bar songs they were writing, in a four-piece band-bass, drums, guitar, and vocals-rhythm guitar is the basic ingredient. With four pieces in a band, you can evoke almost any kind of music you want. Everything had been done before, and that's what was so great about the Sex Pistols. They actually came out with an original voice and look that said something.

The Pistols' ultimate mark wasn't left by recording. We were a threat—for what reason is anyone's guess. Our record wasn't done according to how the industry felt it should be done. That stumped a lot of people, particularly the major record companies. They had their set formats, and if you break out of that mold, then they have no space for you. I only wish Malcolm was a bit more humble about it and didn't try to pretend that it was all his work of art and genius. It certainly wasn't. He was shooting in the dark like the rest of us, but he would never accept that anyone else but him could have any thoughts about it at all. You can't do that to people like the Pistols.

BILLY IDOL: Lydon always said exactly what he thought, and he never kowtowed to anybody. Once he and Malcolm were on this TV program together, and he argued as much with Malcolm as the host did. He had a larger-than-life charisma. The Pistols said and did what they wanted to do, and it wasn't just Malcolm thinking it up.

What is the point in arguing and trying to take credit for a title like *Never Mind the Bollocks*? Steve Jones said it when we were debating over what to call the fucking thing. Steve said, "Oh, fuck it, never mind the bollocks of it all." That will do.

I was in Nottingham with Richard Branson when they banned the cover in some record stores. It was declared illegal and offensive. They were offended by the word *bollocks*. We fought it in court and showed them that the word was in the dictionary. How could it be illegal? It was a valid Anglo-Saxon term for testicles. Branson enjoyed the jolly good fun of it. Heaven forbid if politicians like Mary Whitehouse ever liked anything we did—that would be slash-your-wrists time for me. I didn't give a damn who didn't like what.

The cover concept comes from a blackmail letter. A ransom note. If the cover had been left totally to me, I'm sure I would have come up with something vile, so it was best to keep it simple. We already had the reputation, there was no point in compounding it. We just wanted to put the album out, plain and simple. There it is. A really horrible, ugly, cheesy cover with absolutely no consideration about it. There was no great master plan, it was just the simplest and ugliest thing we could come up with on a bored afternoon. No genius. However, now, of course, it's become the punk Venus de Milo, and everyone is claiming credit for it.

BOB GRUEN: The first time I got the Pistols record, I couldn't believe it. It was so pink, yellow, and green, with boxes, shapes, and angles. Nothing was even. It was truly chaotic—nothing like I expected. I brought the record to Sheila Rock's house. She was into the avant garde movement and very open-minded. We played the record and looked at each other in horror.

What the fuck is this? we thought.

We didn't sit around and wax Situationist philosophy. Never. I understood who the Situationists were. Jamie Reid was very into it, but I always thought it was foolishness—art students just being art students. The Situationists had no situation—no rules, no regulations. That's their apparent philosophy. But the trouble was that they thought about "organized" chaos. They were too structured for my liking, word games and no work. Plus they were French, so fuck them. I don't know what the big palaver was about the Situationists, anyway. Mind games for the muddled classes.

Artwork for the "God Save the Queen" single was just a picture stuck on to a tattered flag and photographed. Safety pin in the nose. Big deal. They were apparently trying to ban that, too, yet there was no law to stop us. The controversial "Holidays in the Sun" sleeve cover was done by a kid who just turned up at the office one day. Some travel agents, like Thomas Cook, thought we were having a serious dig at them. That wasn't the idea, but we didn't deny anything. Why? It's much better than promoting yourself. The press don't realize how much publicity they're giving you.

Managers are supposed to get together an efficient team and elevate you into situations you normally wouldn't be in. Our gigs were chaotic enough. It wasn't because we couldn't play or were too lazy, the equipment was so goddamned third-rate awful. We had a very important concert at Brunel University in December of 1977. It was presumed that if we broke that one, we could be one of the biggest bands. Four and a half thousand people turned up, and we had the cheapest, shittiest PA with a spray-can piece of canvas hung behind the stage. The PA wasn't good enough for a small nightclub, let alone an aircraft hangar with four thousand screaming people. You couldn't hear anything except fuzzy noise. The backdrop was a piece of black plastic hanging on the wall. Paul Simonon of the Clash spray-painted something on it, and that was it. The Clash were very into their slogans at the time. No monitors and no lights. No music playing in the hall beforehand, so the audience grew very angry and impatient. Everything ran late. There was no consideration for the crowd having to get home afterward, since transport in London is not good in certain areas after hours. Backstage I knew it was making the Pistols look bad. I said so at the time, but Malcolm wouldn't have it. He's well and fine with his hindsight of wanting to create that sense of chaos. But this was rubbish. He wouldn't put the money into a marvelous show. Instead it backfired on the Pistols rather pitifully. We could have turned that one pivotal gig into an important movement. In hindsight, Malcolm might say he did it deliberately. Yet Malcolm is full of big schemes, although he has never done anything minimally, except spend.

Malcolm had no qualms about spending on that movie, *The Great Rock 'n' Roll Swindle*. Hundreds of thousands of our pounds went into that. He thought doing a movie was the most novel thing we could have done. I liked the idea of our own movie—think of what we could have been up to! But no. It turned into a Russ Meyer script, tits and God knows what. After I met Russ Meyer, this dirty old man, I felt really shabby about the whole thing. I didn't want to know from there on. I knew fuck-all about scripts, but I had ideas. When we got there it became, "Shut up and listen!"

That kind of attitude never appeals to me. I hated Russ Meyer from the first second I saw him—an overbearing, senile old git. Malcolm was in love with the idea because it was his idea, if not quite his money.

BILLY IDOL: The best thing about Malcolm—he said things to you that were volatile and helped put you into a position where you had to come up with something.

I was asking too many questions. "What's happening here? Where's the money?"

PAUL COOK, DRUMMER

PAUL COOK
GLEDHOW GARDENS, LONDON

Before the Sex Pistols, I was working in a brewery as an electrician fixing plugs and electronics. One time I got caught stealing nine hundred pounds' worth of gear. As usual, Steve got away and I was using a van, and we got caught very early on. Steve was great. I'd known him since we were little; we went to school together. We used to go and see bands like the Faces and the Stones and thought, They're not that fucking great. They can't play that well. We also felt they were losing touch; they had nothing to say.

We wanted to create our own thing, so when we initially decided to get a band together Steve was learning the drums, then he went on to play guitar and sing, so I took over. He already had the drum kit, the equipment, and the rehearsal space, so he and I would practice every night.

Steve and I used to hang out in the Sex shop while Glen worked there, especially on weekends. We'd see John come in with his two mates, Sid and John Gray. We'd also see the three of them on the

King's Road. I noticed John because he was quite striking with his green cropped hair. When we began looking for a singer, Glen talked about the guy with the cropped green hair. John seemed mad enough, and we wanted to know what he was like. We met him and set up the famous meeting at the Roebuck pub.

We talked about music, and John had a lot to say for himself. It must have been nerve-racking for him to come back to the shop and sing in front of a jukebox while we watched. He broke into this spasmodic routine-arms and legs flailing to Alice Cooper's "Eighteen"—and it was then I had the earliest inkling that we could work together. At first I thought he was really funny, then I said to myself, We've got it! I knew it straight away, but Steve wasn't too sure. Glen and Malcolm thought John was okay, but I knew right then we were going to give it a go.

John is a stickler for being on time. He was a very uptight, angry young man, and it didn't take much to make him fly off the handle. We were all over the place that time and were late to meet him for the first rehearsal. I remember he got very upset at us.

JOHN LYDON: But I'm my own worst critic. It had to be that way, even as a little kid. I think it's very constructive. I just can't let things slide and say, "Oh, well, it doesn't matter." It matters to me. Most people find it annoying when I throw those same standards on others. I can make such a big deal out of someone not turning up for a recording or a rehearsal. I'll take that so personally. There you go. I still have to go through my little ceremony. Isn't it odd that for someone who hates the German mentality of time, that I can be so rigid about the fucking clock myself?

From the start, John and Malcolm didn't get along. John was a very difficult person to get on with, but I got along with him fine. I hung out with him the most. We used to stay over at his mum's house and go out drinking together. John's mum would do anything for you. She was a very nice lady. She'd have dinner ready like mums who look after their boys do. She had four boys—four Lydons—to deal with. She ran an open house and was very supportive of John. Among the other band members, I was the one who made the biggest effort to get along with him.

STEVE JONES: I remember once Paul beat John up on Denmark Street. We'd been out drinking, and John had been going off on Paul. John, Paul, and I were drunk, and we went upstairs. John just wouldn't shut up, and Paul couldn't take it anymore, so he started pounding him. John was helpless, and I had to get Paul off him because he was beating him up pretty bad. Still, there wasn't much physical violence; it was mainly all talk.

Malcolm couldn't handle John's observations. John has a habit of putting people on the defensive straight away. He tests you out. So he started ridiculing Malcolm, and Malcolm couldn't handle it. Malcolm could take it if it came from Steve and/or me, but he couldn't handle John rubbing him up the wrong way. John couldn't handle some of the things Malcolm would be doing. They both took it all personally.

John always had this thing about his not being invited anywhere. Malcolm never said to me, "Let's go. We don't want John coming." Since we were all so highly strung, what usually happened was that sometimes after we had a big row we'd all go off on our own and wouldn't bother to speak to each other. I wouldn't want to speak with John if we just had a row. The rest of us would go off and do our own thing, and he would go off and do his.

John loves verbal rapport, plays on words, the odd put-down. He thrives on those things because he's so good with words. He's a semanticist, and he would push Malcolm, who would try not to take the bait. While Malcolm always said he didn't want to be a baby-sitter and mollycoddle everyone, John would always ask Malcolm to do certain things.

BILLY IDOL: They played the strip club, El Paradise, with the big mirror behind them on stage. They looked really fantastic. Apart from the lighted stage, it was all black. They were getting better and better, and just the fact that the club was so small and the audience was made up of people like us who knew them made it possible for them to relax, get on with it, and be themselves. Week by week we saw them get better, take out the sixties numbers, and add new songs. Yes! Here we go! Throwing off the shackles of the past. It was exciting, and that antagonism between them and Malcolm made it happen. The first time I saw the Sex Pistols must have been when they played the 100 Club. Johnny kept haranguing Malcolm. He would say, "Get me a beer, Malcolm, you cunt." Nobody was in the audience, and Malcolm was standing off stage saying, "Fuck it, get it yourself." There was only us lot in the audience. The Pistols would play a song, then stand around.

Up until the time we signed our first record deal with EMI in 1976, I was still working at the brewery. John was on the dole, and Steve wasn't working, either. Forty pounds a week spending money for each band member seemed like enough at the time. I had somewhere to live, sharing our rehearsal hall with Steve on Denmark Street.

JOHN GRAY: Steve was a burglar. Steve was a bit older than us. He had big, brutish, thuggish mates. When Glen goes on about John bringing his own mates with him, he forgets to mention that for every Wobble, Sid, and me, there were three brutish Steve mates, three dumbo Paul mates, three wanky, middle-class, Beatles-fan Glen mates. A lot of times, after we left the pub, we'd crash out at the studio. Nobody wanted to go home. You'd have Glen in one corner on the floor in a sleeping bag, and in another corner would be one of his wanky mates. Steve and Paul over here; John over there. It was mad. There was a whole gang of us that crossed class barriers, and the friction between the different elements was funny and made for a great social grouping at a gig or a party—all these different people thrown together who normally wouldn't spend five minutes with each
other.

Like the band, it was a microcosm of what a typical Pistols audience would later become.

In the early days things happened very quickly, and we played a lot of gigs. We got so popular right after the Bill Grundy television thing that we had to be careful where we played. We had to deal with the crowds and trouble. A week after the show, I was attacked on the street by some Teds. There was violence going on between Teds and punks at the time. We always have rival gangs fighting in London—skinheads and rockers, mods and rockers. When the punks came along, the Teds, who were English reactionaries, seemed to take to warfare. One day my girlfriend and I were walking to my home in west London when I got jumped by three Teds. I don't know if they knew I was in the Pistols. They did know I was a punk. We reacted mostly in self-defense against the Teds. Punks sparked something in people, so they were ready for anything. We started fighting back; it turned into a pitched battle down on the King's Road on Saturdays. People were so bored. Things happened more out of excitement than aggression. There was a lot of violence in 1976, but if anything happened it was blown up by the press. If someone got injured at a concert, it would be big news.

HOWARD THOMPSON: I remember going to the 100 Club to see the Sex Pistols with Nick Kent of the *NME* and Michael Beale, who was the graphic art designer for Eddie and the Hot Rods. The three of us showed up early, standing against the back wall in a line toward the right-hand side of the stage. While I knew Nick Kent a little bit—not very well—I remember pointing out to Michael this guy toward the stage. About twenty yards to the edge of the stage was this kid leaning against the front of the stage, looking directly at Nick Kent. He was giving Nick "the eye," staring, looking as tough, as mean and aggressive, as he possibly could. I don't know whether Nick had noticed it, but I had already sensed that this guy was looking for a little trouble. Who was this person? I'd never seen him before. It was uncomfortable. While Michael had noticed it, he thought nothing of it. As the band ambled onto the stage, this guy walked straight toward us and then turned around, so his back was to us, right in front of us as the band started to play.

By this time two chairs had come up, and Nick and Michael sat down. I was still leaning against the wall. Suddenly this guy who had stood in front of us, turned around and pulled out a small knife and held it under Nick Kent's nose. Then he put it away. Michael was a bit freaked out and stood up. The kid then began kicking Nick's foot, irritating him and winding him up a bit. I asked Nick and Mike if they wanted a drink. I went to the bar and ordered three lagers. I come back to find Nick holding his head, bleeding, while Sid Vicious was being beaten to a pulp on the floor by bouncers. Amid the chaos, the Pistols were playing. Malcolm McLaren was running around, trying to calm everybody down. Michael was in pain, holding his arm after, apparently, Sid had pulled out a bicycle chain and swung it across Nick's head and Michael's, too.

And that was the first time I ever saw Sid. He was a nasty piece of work. Two or three months later he joined the band.

CHRISSIE HYNDE: Why all the fighting? I don't know. It's an English thing. London can be very violent. There's a sadism and an element of intrigue involved. Everything here has to have a twist. There's no such thing as an out-and-out murder. There's got to be a riddle, always a mystery.

With regard to other bands, I suppose our attitude was a bit snobbish. We were full of ourselves—maybe rightly so. The Sex Pistols started the whole thing, and the rest of the bands came later. We were the forerunners, and we were by ourselves on the front line. There was no big rivalry. At the time we did slag a lot of bands, but we used to slag everyone. There was no big punk movement, no camaraderie between the bands, like in bebop or jazz. We knew each other, but we were seldom friendly. Everybody was just starting out in music, and many of us had never picked up an instrument before. We weren't a collection of musos, and we were skeptical of the other bands' motives. Fits of insecurity entered into it early on, but eventually we all got on better as we grew up a bit more and felt more comfortable with ourselves and our bands.

CAROLINE COON: Punk was said to be very alcoholic because of the drinking, but I think they used it to calm down, to get on stage. You don't have that amount of drink in other performing professions—theater, ballet—because the performers have fifteen years of technique to fall back on. It was very interesting to see where the terror was in rock 'n' roll. But how do you replace that?

At the time we were naive about Sid and the drugs. We didn't realize how serious his problem was until we did the gigs in Sweden, then went to America. When he first joined the band, Sid was fine. That was one of the best times for the Sex Pistols. Sid was learning and was really into it. He had to prove that he could do it.

I never dealt directly with Nancy Spungen. I used to see her out and about, but she wasn't allowed anywhere near our rehearsals, so Sid would go to meet her after. I had nothing against her because I didn't know her that well. But John couldn't take her, so we kept her at arm's length. That was Malcolm's main problem; he should have taken control of that situation. With the band falling apart, he should have done his job as a manager, but he just let it go.

We got lazier and lazier. Although some people said we couldn't, we wrote some of our best songs after Glen left—"Bodies," "EMI," and "Holidays in the Sun." We could have carried on writing songs, but there was a breakdown between Steve, John, and myself that affected the songwriting. It's difficult to explain what was going on at the time. It all happened so fast that time seemed to flash. We were short of songs by then and were concentrating on getting the album out in 1977. There were the musical differences, but early on that's what made the band work.

S E G M E N T

1 4 :

"HOW BRILLIANT! THEY HATE THE BEATLES!" PAUL
STAHL, MARCO PIRRONI & DAVE RUFFY

PAUL STAHL

We had a very strong soul tradition in the U.K. since the mods. Before the Pistols' era, I came from the soul circuit background. I was in college at the time. Just prior to that time in 1973, the standard look of the day was flares, long pointed-collar shirts, and suits with epaulets. Then we started cutting our hair short, which was radical. People would come up to me and ask which battalion I belonged to. They figured I got out of the navy or the army or just got out of prison. They couldn't believe that you had your hair cut around the ears. I don't know where the idea came from, but we also used to dress in forties' fashion zoot suits. I think it came from a Bryan Ferry style. We weren't into rock music at all; we were listening to stuff like Ronnie Laws. The mods adopted that kind of music, and it never left certain sectors.

The soul boys, an offshoot of the mods, were essentially working-class kids from rural areas and suburban parts of London. Now these soul boys clubs, although very much underground, carried on right through 1976 and beyond. The kids from the soul background never got into the band scene. They didn't form bands because they didn't come from that guitar-playing background. But they were the fashion icons to early punks. It was a real crazy situation. A quiet guy like Marco Pirroni with an art school background listening to Roxy Music was suddenly mixing in the same company as . . . maniacs who just lived for a fight in the tradition of football hooligans. But they looked fantastic. All their clothes were from Sex—the earliest things they ever wore. This was from 1974 onward because Sex was around a long time before the Sex Pistols. The national newspapers once did a piece on this scene in Canvey Island, Essex—real soul boys country. Everybody in Essex was implanted there from the East End of London. An American equivalent would be an overspill of the Bronx to Connecticut. All these kids were dressed in zoot suits with big quiffs. Girls had Veronica Lake-type hairdos.

The real turning point for me in the mid-seventies was short hair and tapered trousers. Before that, old men of eighty and young guys all wore flares. It was that ingrained. Then, because of the tapered trousers thing, people started looking fifties again as a reaction against the long-haired hippie thing. Soon the soul boys actually changed their fashion and mixed in a lot of Bowie influences and effeminacy. You started to get a crossover with the arty kids and the tougher soul boys. Some of the early punk look was built on the fringes of that soul boys era. Because there were so few people who dressed like that, they all went to the same clubs and you had this incredible intermingling. I think it was Bowie more than anybody that made punk acceptable to the soul element, much more than Roxy Music. Bowie was the soul boys' rock act. Everybody liked Bowie, and it was through him that punk became acceptable to the soul boys element. Mod, rockabilly—everything—had all been absorbed by punk. In terms of fashion, there has never been a more creative period—even if a lot of it was retrospect. It still had the mark of the day on it.

There weren't many bands in the early days. The Sex Pistols had only played a few gigs. There was already an audience when the groups got there. The bands that came along were quite in earnest. A lot of them were serious about making good music, but the audiences were just pigs. When a band would come on stage at the Vortex, it was like a momentary inconvenience. People would get pissed off because you couldn't hear anything. Bands would be up there for a half hour, and people would take the piss at them. After a while it was like saturation bombing. Every group was called "the" something. The Gnats, the Crabs, the Dicks, the Ants, the Mosquitoes. It became a comic situation. The Vortex used to book five or six bands a night, and they did-n't use the same two bands, apart from the headliners. It was crazy after

Paddies' night out in Finsbury park. That's Finsbury park pal John Stevens on the right. (John Stevens)

a while. They never ran out of bands. They had four a night, every Monday and Tuesday. Where these fucking bands came from, I don't know. It got so chronic that the bands that stuck out in your mind were the really dreadful ones. We used to make lists of them.

One band that had credibility was the Heartbreakers. I guess I was one of the few people who didn't like the Heartbreakers because they represented everything that was ten years before punk—especially [Thunders'] drugs and heroin. When Thunders came over to the U.K. and started playing, he was literally falling on his face by the second song. All the other groups would groupie around the Heartbreakers, hanging in their dressing room. Lydon was well above all that. He was cleverer than they were. I remember once when Lydon said he liked reggae, and that was it—everybody liked reggae. There was a picture of the Sex Pistols on the cover of the *Record Mirror* with Lydon dressed as a Ted. Then every-fucking-body at that lesbian club Louise's was dressed exactly like a Ted with their hair up. He really had that much clout. It was unbelievable. Ultimately, what the Sex Pistols added was the slovenly. Before the Pistols, everyone was quite fastidious. Before the Pistols, even if you wanted to look like shit—with ripped jeans, T-shirts, or whatever—you would try to look smart. Johnny Rotten always looked like he'd just crawled out of bed wearing what he had on. Whatever he said, that was it.

RAMBO: John was slovenly then. That was his sort of style. I remember once before John had a concert, he would be lying in his bed, and when it was time to go, off would come the blanket. He'd be fully dressed and that was it. Shoes and everything. He'd kick right up and leave for the concert.

I used to visit Marco in Harrow, and going there was like fucking *Blade Runner*. Harrow was the Ted's emporium of the Western world. There's a barber shop there that specializes in Ted haircuts, but Marco was all right because they all knew him. He used to get his clothes in the same shops as them. But oh, God, the times I had to leg it from his house to that station! Working-class types wanted to kick your fucking teeth down your throat, and the intellectuals wanted to slag you off on an intellectual level. You just couldn't win. But it was exciting. I remember once I fell asleep on the fucking train, then I woke up and there were literally Teds everywhere. They were sitting on the seats opposite me. I got off at South Harrow. I was so frightened, I was green when I got round to Marco's house.

In the end I think McLaren fucked it all up. The Sex Pistols play-ing Texas, for Christ's sake! It was totally absurd making them play to those isolated rednecks in Rattlesnake, Arizona, or wherever they went. I can't believe they didn't get killed. They should have been playing New York to people who would have appreciated them. New York would have opened its legs to them. But it was fashionable to slag New York.

In the end, what really ended it for me and my mate Marco was when those Sham 69 fans called him a poser for wearing Sex clothes. I was standing at the bar in the Vortex, and Marco came up to me really out-raged, totally indignant about the whole punk thing. He said, "That is it! That's the end." I don't think Marco was the same. There was abso-lutely fuck-all to do after that. Once punk was obviously gone, the other bands were faced with the same choice as the Sex Pistols. They need-ed to develop the music or fuck about forever.

MARCO PIRRONI

There was a mate of ours who ran with a whole gang of these soul boys and they all came from Aylesbury. Their big look was to wear mohair jumpers and see-through T-shirts. They usually wore jeans, and all of them wore those pointed brothel creepers, colored hair, and multiple pierced earrings. You had a lot of the early seventies glam bands like Roxy Music, a bit of David Bowie—and especially Wizzard and Mud—all dressed as Teds. That was a popular look, a Teddy Boy draped jacket and waistcoat. Some of the band members in Wizzard looked just like Teds. That alternative English fifties look was the strong undercurrent theme just before punk. That was the whole basis for Sex. I don't know if Malcolm started it originally. It was one of those things that people picked up.

When I first started playing guitar at home, I didn't fit in anywhere musically. All I wanted to play was "Rebel, Rebel" and Velvet Underground songs. I got into the Velvet Underground in early 1973 through Lou Reed's *Transformer* album, which I bought because David Bowie and Mick Ronson were on it. I did the same with Iggy Pop's *Raw Power*. I used to read the music press every week, but all they covered were bands like Yes, Emerson, Lake and Palmer, and Genesis. In early 1974 the New York Dolls were also interesting because of their trashi-ness. Their sound was an influence, but they made the unforgivable mistake of having long hair and wearing platforms. So people in Britain wrote them off a little bit. You had to figure they were American because they had long hair and platforms. When I was thirteen and first wanted to be a musician, bands were judged primarily on musical talent. The big thing that made the early seventies so exciting was David Bowie and Roxy Music. Those were the people I emulated. But even they were still very slick musicians, and at the time I could never hope to play with them.

There I was trooping down on my own, all the fucking way down to 430 King's Road. I bought my first pair of brothel creepers. That was me making what now would be called "my fashion statement." I actually wanted to look like Andy Mackay, the sax player from Roxy Music. He had this whole fifties look down perfect. It wasn't a "Girl Can't Help It" fifties look, it was glitter, leopard skin, green quiffs, and eye shadow. It happened in stages for me. I didn't go down to Sex with thirty bob and buy my whole punk outfit. I picked up bits and pieces every week. The 1976 punk look was a mixture of absolutely everything. A lot of Ted, a lot of rocker, a lot of fetish stuff, transvestite sort of stuff, a bit of mod, and a lot of glam. That's what it was. People didn't wear leather motorcycle jackets in 1976. Mohawks didn't exist then, either. Even though it was a relatively short period of time, it was started by maybe a hundred and fifty people, all bringing a little bit to the whole. It wasn't individuals, it was more like small gangs of people that used to hang out. The real impact of John Lydon's look was, "Fuck, he's ripped everything up!" They were far more punk than what I came from. But it was all still linked. There were a lot of people who came from all these offshoots of Roxy Music, the Sex shop, whatever.

Then the Pistols started. They happened to be first, and a lot of people gravitated toward them, and suddenly a scene evolved around them. These people had already existed, but they didn't have anyone to connect with. I remember going down to the Sex shop one day and hanging about and being pretty shy, but desperately trying to get in with everybody. I guess they liked me, because I was tolerated and I wasn't asked to leave. There was a jukebox in Sex. Somebody put on a Beatles record, "I'm Down," and someone yelled, "Awwww! My God! The Beatles," and then grabbed it. They started kicking this Beatles record around the shop. "We hate the fucking Beatles!" I thought: How brilliant! They hate the Beatles. What a fucking brilliant thing to say. I'm going to go back to college and say, "The Beatles are shit!" It was like saying "Jesus is queer" or having a shit in church. You just didn't say it!

BOB GRUEN: When John Lennon was a househusband, I talked to him about the Pistols and what was happening in England. Sean was born in 1975, and that's when John withdrew from the whole scene. Still, John was mildly curious. It seemed to him that what the bands like the Pistols were doing was somewhat derivative of what the Beatles had already done, so he generally adopted a "been there, done that, glad they're doing it, more power to them" attitude. In 1980 just before he returned to the studio, I gave Lennon some of Don Letts's videos and film footage of the punk era, so John could catch up and know who the Sex Pistols, the Clash, and the Slits were. He watched those films one weekend, but I didn't get to discuss it with him. He had the tape for a week and returned it to me. In fact, the tape was at the front desk of the Dakota, waiting for me the day Lennon was shot.

It was like the Nazi gear. I don't think anyone knew what all the Nazi clothing really meant, and if they did know, it was perceived as a reaction to a right-wing thing. It was a reaction against Mum and Dad talking about World War II. It was just a look. Vivienne's Anarchy shirts even looked like concentration camp shirts with their badly painted stripes. They had a round collar with two holes in it, like the college boy shirts in America where they stuck the gold bar through it. It also had the double cuffs like a proper dress shirt, and there were pictures of Lenin and Chairman Mao together with some sort of slogan. Mine said, "Only Anarchists Are Pretty." Then she stuck an upside-down swastika armband on it and festooned it with every political slogan you could have. Mine cost thirty-five quid. That was ludicrous, big money then, so I used to ponce off my mom and dad. They ran a restaurant, and I had to work in there. One time I nicked a couple of T-shirts and a pair of leather trousers from Vivienne. Sid was working at the Sex shop for two weeks and said, "I'll turn a blind eye. You can have them." He let me steal them. Unfortunately I wore them the next night at the Roundhouse and Vivienne was there. It was the only pair they had. She sussed me out, and I had to give her the money. She said she knew what Sid had done and didn't really mind. Vivienne was actually all right about it.

Malcolm McLaren really was a real menswear obsessive. He actually knows a lot about the history of menswear. He knows all the looks, the youth cults, and stuff like that. That's where many of his ideas came from. He once told me about some French aristocrats after the French Revolution who were really dandies and wore a red lipstick line around their neck. Punk fashion came from ideas like that.

BOB GRUEN: Malcolm tried to politicize the Dolls but failed to realize that they had already created a sensation just by wearing lipstick. People assumed they were being openly homosexual, which at
the time was still very much an underground lifestyle in America.
No one used the word *gay*, homosexuality was illegal and you seldom
talked about it. Everyone assumed the Dolls were a bunch of
queens because they walked around wearing women's clothes and
lipstick. In fact, the Dolls weren't queens at all.

By 1976 I suppose I was as good a guitarist as Steve Jones. Actually,
going on stage in 1976 wasn't like being on stage at all. It was like getting into a pit. Every band that walked onto a stage was just gobbed at.
As soon as you walked up—one, two, three—everything they had just
came at you. When they ran out of the glasses they were holding, all
they had to throw was to gob at you.

JULIEN TEMPLE: When the Pistols finally played at Leeds, all the kids
in the audience felt that they had to wear safety pins, tear their
clothes and spit at the stand. I still remember that amazing image.
When Rotten finally came out on the stage, it was like Agincourt.
There were these massed volleys of gob flying through the air that
just hung on John like a Medusa. It was like green hair or snakes.

It was the punk idea of What's the furthest thing you could do to
show adoration to your heroes? We won't say "We love you" . . .
we'll gob at them! That was it. I think the worst place for spitting of
all was the Croydon Greyhound. It was a big place. It was a big ballroom upstairs that used to hold about a thousand. For some reason
that was the worst place, and it was unbelievable. I played there
with a band called the Models. As soon as we started it was un-fuck-
ing-real. I had never seen anything like it in my life. There was no
way to dodge it because it was like standing under a shower. I
remember this big greenie landed on my guitar and it stopped working. It was a big splat and it landed right on the pickup. I shook my
guitar. It was horrible—all these big phlegmy gobs would land on
the strings. You had to shake it off somehow and keep on playing.
They were still spitting even when I played with Adam and the Ants.
The only reason I stopped being spat on in 1981 was because we
were playing theaters. There was a pit between the band and the
audience, and they couldn't reach us. Then they finally gave up.
There was actually a bit of a movement, the nonspitting movement.

It was written up in *Sniffin' Glue*. "Bands are getting fucking pissed off with being spat at. So don't do it, you cunt!" It did absolutely no good. Adam Ant got conjunctivitis from getting spat in the eye on one of our tours in 1980. That's why he had to wear his eye patch. Everybody thought it was part of his pirate scene, his big look.

Once I was supposed to be in a band that John named the Flowers of Romance. They never got together on any one occasion, ever. There were originally fifteen people in this band, and I never actually met the others until years later. We never rehearsed. The idea of it became famous. I think I only knew two of the other members—Sid and Viv Albertine. Sid had some song ideas, "Belsen Was a Gas" and "Postcard from Auschwitz." Then he got arrested after the 100 Club bottling incident. It was definitely Sid who threw the glass, but I don't remember any girl who actually had her eye put out. Those were the two great casualties: the mysterious girl who had her eye out at the 100 Club Festival and the bloke who had his ear bitten off at the Clash gig.

I met Shane [MacGowan] one night on the train. He said, "I've seen you before. You go see the Pistols, don't you?" I was a big Pistols fan, so I had all this Seditionaries stuff on. He still had a jacket with big lapels. There were a lot of people trying to get into punk, and they would cut their hair and get themselves some drainpipe trousers. But they still had these jackets with big lapels, and Shane was one of them. One time I saw Shane, and I couldn't believe it. He was dressed from head to foot as "The Prisoner," the Patrick McGoohan TV serial. He had the slacks, boating shoes with the white soles, a black turtleneck, a scarf, and the black jacket. It was strange with him. Shane was one of those Irish guys you would see on the building site wearing a suit. He'd work all day in his suit with mud all over it. He was one of the ugliest guys on the scene.

There was a time when Teds popped up from wherever they had been hiding and decided they didn't like us punks. It was Teds versus punks. The Harrow Road station was the worst, especially when you went down to the platform. My most vivid memories about the Teds and punks wars was getting on the train. You always had to suss out which carriage was okay. Are there any skins in this carriage? Any football hooligans, Teds, in this one? If you walked in dressed like a punk, you were dead meat. Practically everybody fucking hated you.

These were the bands I always went to see: the Pistols. The Clash were really good when they started off. At the time there were five geezers playing guitar at the front. There was about a week when I couldn't decide if the Clash were better than the Pistols. Then I came to my senses and thought the Pistols were much better. I also really liked the Buzzcocks, Subway Sect, and the Banshees. The Heartbreakers turned up in the middle of 1976 to play the Roxy. They brought two things with them—colored leather jackets—which everyone started wearing—and [Thunders's] drugs.

Rotten realized what he was—a figurehead of everything. John could keep himself apart from things. From the beginning, Lydon was the one—anything he said went until people would then catch themselves and say, "Hang on, we might be getting a bit fan-struck. He's a cunt!" If you were to be a punk, then everything that somebody said, you had to do the opposite. If John brought out the best record in the world, he'd be a cunt. Suppose Lydon would say to the press, "Mick Jagger is a cunt." I'd guarantee there would be two hundred people with that written all over their leather jacket the following week. Plus there would be fifty more that would have "Mick Jagger isn't a cunt" written on their jackets. I still think the lyrics to "God Save the Queen" are even more relevant now. Especially that bit about "tourists are money." Or in "Holidays in the Sun," where you investigate the conditions of other people's miseries. Let's go take a drive through Compton and investigate the conditions of the poor American black man.

Sid was desperate to get into anything that would kill him. He got into a fight at the Speakeasy with Bob Harris, the deejay who hosted "The Old Grey Whistle Test." Now Harris was the complete antithesis of punk. He was a real hippie with long hair and a beard, and he would talk in whispers. He liked a lot of shit music like Keith Christmas and String Driven Thing. He hated Roxy Music and the New York Dolls, but he liked Little Feat and Rory Gallagher. If John Lydon was the outspoken figurehead of punk, Bob Harris was the timid figurehead of the ones who intellectually attacked punk. That made us hate him even more. Sid came up to Harris at the Speakeasy once and gave him a kicking. I went to a party on Neal Street near the Roxy when Sid first joined the Sex Pistols. It was an opening for Andy Czezowski's clothing shop. Sid bottled four people that night. He bottled Nils Stevenson, the manager of the Banshees. When I went to see the Clash at the Royal College of Art, there was a big fight there that Sid actually started. He threw bottles at the Tyla Gang, some horrible support band.

The Pistols era proved to me that ideas were far more important than how well or how badly you could play. That was the most vital thing. Without punk there certainly couldn't have been anything like Prince. His first couple of albums were really raw—the same sort of drum pattern all the way through. Until the Sex Pistols, nobody ever talked about this expression, "overproduced." You never thought about it. You never knew the difference between an overproduced band and a raw band because, before punk, there were no raw bands. All the bands had a little drum kit, a combo bass amp, one bass, and one guitar. You used to recognize bands by their back line. I always had a Marshall and a Gibson Les Paul. Nobody minded, you could do whatever you wanted on stage. You could be as shitty as you wanted to. No one would like you if you were brilliant anyway. It didn't make any difference.

NORA: Hippies were supposed to be friends with everyone. Punk meant you could be frank with everyone. You could tell someone to get out of your way or drop dead. Before, we were always diplomatic. Since I've known John I've become much more open. I don't give a damn. I tell people when I don't like them. *Ich sag's ihnen in's gesicht.* Don't beat around the bush.

Punk challenged the class concept. The whole class system in England is Know Your Place. You keep the place that you were born to. That's the old idea of it. I've actually met members of the royal family, and they are the most unpleasant, disgusting, vile people you could ever meet anywhere. It's like that point of racism where you hate everybody just because they are not born in your family. Everybody is below them. The queen is not this happy, smiling lady. She's not that at all. She's a fucking hard bitch.

CAROLINE COON: During the punk movement, the atmosphere for women was glorious! For the first time in the working art environment, apart from ballet, where there was a good percentage of women. Apart from Siouxsie, there were the fans like Jordan, musicians, and poets like Patti Smith. It was such fun. I loved it. You could feel the power. The balance was coming. It was still tough, and we were all fighting in different ways, but I loved it. The playing field was leveling in the sense that the theater of rock 'n' roll art had always been an arena that was slightly looser than straight culture. Although the misogyny in the rock 'n' roll culture was bad, it sure wasn't as bad as the orthodox corporate world, the overground.

NORA: The gays didn't come out of the closet in the sixties. They came out when punk came out. So the women came out, too. If they fancied someone, they didn't wait around. Now the gay movement has turned into an organized thing. It's like joining the army.

I don't think anybody actually looked down on women. They were equal, and everybody was as stupid as each other. You would sort of hit women the same way you would a guy if she was taking the piss at you or spilled your drink. But it wasn't an antisex attitude or a matter of acting puritanical. People just didn't give it the same importance as it had before.

"I think I might fuck that girl."

"How boring."

It was a rebellion against the lad ethic—get drunk, pull a bird, and get around the back, wherever. The punks believed they had some kind of intellectual capacity—each and every one of them—and didn't want to slip back into that rock thing. There were millions of people doing that. That was just one part of it. Most of these kids lived with their parents, so the opportunity wasn't there anyway. People didn't go out of their way so much. It was just a rebellion against what you saw college kids doing. Anything that came before was naff—falling in love and all that. People did pair off, and there was lots of sex going on in the toilets. That's where it happened the most. You could get it out of the way. You remember the famous Lydon quote when he describes sex as "two minutes of squelchy noises"? That was a good summary for a lot of people. This thing was building its own sort of rules as it went along. There were days when I would ask myself, "What do I think about girls? What is the hip way to get on with them? Am I queer or something?"

JOHN LYDON: All these punk girls started turning up at our gigs. It was like learning how to have sex properly, rather than having someone know all the right moves. It was clumsy and deeply confusing. Always in toilets. And quick. And messy. There would be stains left all over the place. But that was excellent. I know it's far more calculated in "the world of rock 'n' roll," but we were young kids guessing as to what to do next, enjoying it for that amateurishness. The girls were new to this, not old-timers who ran through the scene before. They didn't come around with an attitude from the past, not a repeat of history.

I went through the cheap sex period. We really did attract a definite kind of harlot. They were new, and that's what was so exciting. Nothing like that had ever happened to me before. When we started, the old-style groupie couldn't take us at all. Hence there was a whole new breed of groupie that came along. That was interesting to me. Fascinating. I liked that very much. But then it got boring because it got as predictable as the old ways.

When Sid joined the Pistols, it all seemed to change. It got much more serious. You didn't see them around anymore. The Sex Pistols started to think about what they really were. Before that they were just a bunch of blokes in a band, I think the Pistols stopped being a real band when Sid joined, and I couldn't really be into them anymore. I saw one gig at Screen on the Green when Sid was playing, just before "God Save the Queen." He was really crap. I could see the rot setting in because the Pistols were getting heckled. They had never been heckled before! Then after the Grundy thing, the secret was out. I kinda lost interest, but I didn't hold any malice. I still thought the Pistols were good. When Sid joined I figured they would make him learn proper. But they never did. Sid just fucked about. That Screen on the Green appearance was when I thought they lost it. They only had one new song, "Holidays in the Sun." Sid joining contributed to their lack of productivity. I know what it's like to have to keep the group going with one hopeless member, and he was one hopeless member they couldn't really get rid of. They couldn't dump him.

Malcolm must have decided he had two choices: they could become a real band, make real music, and really fucking do it. The Pistols could have gotten a proper bass player and risked losing some credibility. They would have been good, but it would have been a different market. They would have cleaned up and conquered the world. Personally, I would have thought, Great. That's brilliant, but I wouldn't have been as interested, to be honest. They chose the second option and just brought Sid in. After that, it was nothing to do with music anymore. It would just be for the sensationalism and scandal of it all. Then it became the Malcolm McLaren story and going with silly ideas like using Ronnie Biggs. Nobody was going to buy a fucking Ronnie Biggs record. They just couldn't carry on without Johnny Rotten.

When the Pistols broke up, that was the real end of punk. I remember sitting in Watford bus depot. The Sex Pistols breakup was the front headline of every newspaper. It was all over, and there wasn't anything to replace it. We stuck with it for a bit, although I remember being aware of trying not to wear leather jackets and not wanting to be a punk anymore. Then when Sham 69 came in and the Pistols broke up, that really was the end. You couldn't possibly be interested in any part of it after the Pistols broke up. Once I had actually been that involved, it was hard to just became a Clash fan. I had lost my innocence, I wasn't impressed anymore. I listened to the first track of the Clash's *Give 'Em Enough Rope* and that was it. I didn't buy any more of their records or go to any more of their gigs. Then to really ram it home, Sid died.

Every other band, except for the Pistols, had the choice to carry on as a band and sell records. Malcolm had the big idea that you didn't have to know how to play to be a band. But the Pistols could play. If they had made shit records, there's no way anybody would have been interested in them. They would have been a joke. Believe me, they had it.

DAVE RUFFY

The summer of 1977 was a funny old time because there was some political fervor, but very few people had a clue about what they were talking about. There was Rock Against Racism, and they were canvassing and getting lots of youth on their side. They took advantage of the skinhead thing. We had skinheads back in the sixties as well. They would go Paki bashing. When I used to live in the East End, you'd see black guys in gangs with the skinheads and they'd all go Paki bashing together in Leyton and Forest Gate. With the skinhead thing there was suddenly all this Rock Against Racism outrage. But punks were outcasts. Even your liberal music fans who loved music were saying, "Hey, I love jazz, rock 'n' roll, I love Detroit, the MC5." Yet they were really, really annoyed with punk. Personally, I always liked a lot of black music, and reggae was a good soundtrack. It was a music you could actually listen and chill out to.

The Pistols made really good records that had edge. I was reborn during the Pistols era. I had a really weird life as a kid. I had gotten married really young and had a baby. My first wife and I got on quite well, but we didn't know what we wanted to do, so we both went on the dole. Then I went to work in a record shop for a while. After, I decided to go for it. If it weren't for punk, I probably wouldn't have become a musician. During the Pistols era, it was, "Yeah, yeah, you can do it!" The whole thing about English society is that if you're a poor boy, you've got nobody to tell you that you can do anything. Everyone thinks you're just crap. No one is there to encourage you. The important thing about the Sex Pistols is that they were years ahead of today's realities. "No future" is much more of a reality for more people now than it was then.

BILLY IDOL: The Sex Pistols operated on many different levels. They weren't just a little band—they had a world view for being so young, and somehow that made them seem revolutionary. Politics was walking hand in hand with rock 'n' roll. Because it was oriented around artwork, T-shirts, and clothes, a lot of it had shock appeal. That was the point of wearing a picture of Karl Marx—it was the politics of outrage.

When I was in the Ruts, the punk thing took off big our second year in. We went everywhere and met thousands of punk rockers. It was quite good for a while because you met a lot of genuine kids who could be part of the movement without having the money to buy a uniform. They could use their imagination. Normally it's the music that brings everyone together. In a sense it did during punk, but it wasn't directly acknowledged as important. That was the whole turnaround. I could already play the drums when we formed the Ruts in 1976. We were quite successful, but the whole vibe was that although you were accepted and you were in a way exonerated by your fans, instead of saying they thought you were great and your music moved people, the ultimate sin was to be a pop star. You couldn't be seen enjoying it. They'd say, "Fuck off!" You'd say, "Fuck off!" back.

I remember during the punk days when it was considered uncool to go on about sex. When you used to play and girls used to come and see you, it wasn't the scenario that everyone imagined. It was the complete opposite of "You're in the band, we think you're groovy, so let's fuck each other." It was more like "We think you're groovy, so we're going to slag you off." It was a reaction of the sexual chase thing with groupies in the sixties and the early seventies. Plus a lot of these guys were young blokes. They didn't really have it sussed out on how to treat women. It wasn't going on like high school, "Hey, can we go steady tonight or go on a date?"

BOB GRUEN: Johnny Rotten was aloof. You rarely saw him hustling up the girls like most musicians do. His attitude was that nothing was right. He was alone, cynical, and angry. He seemed to be in it for the reaction he was getting from being nasty—something he did quite well.

Looking back, I knew it was near the end when the Pistols went to America. I don't think anybody really ever expected them to do anything after that. The whole idea of them going to America seemed a bit ridiculous. But the Pistols would have been massive if they'd played New York. Everybody there would have loved them. I remember watching *The Great Rock 'n' Roll Swindle* at the Danceteria on my first visit to New York. They billed it as *Hurrah*. It was this crap film, and everybody was trying to analyze it. I thought it was just pretentious bollocks—everybody looking for the mystery of the great god punk.

SEX PISTOLS TRACK BY TRACK
FIRST PHASE: EARLY SONGS AND OTHER PEOPLE'S MATERIAL

"DID YOU NO WRONG"

PAUL COOK: "Did You No Wrong" was one of the only songs that came along before John joined. We were just learning still. We finally recorded it properly at Wessex for the B side of "God Save the Queen."

JOHN LYDON: I changed the lyrics because I didn't like the niceties of the song. It's a *News of the World* epic, which is a fairly good indication of where I was heading, completely antisocial.

"SEVENTEEN"

COOK: John rewrote the song because he couldn't read Steve's writing.

LYDON: AKA "Lazy Sod." This was around the time Steve Jones was learning to read and write. It was originally called "Lazy Sod." There's some Glen Matlock input in there—but I'm not quite sure how much. The song was already set up by the others before I came along. I remember laughing at Steve's original words. I could not read the original set of lyrics, and Steve couldn't remember them. Everything was misspelled. *"I'm all alone, Give a dog a bone."* That was one of the original lines.

It was about being young, having nothing to do, and going through the typical emotions that every seventeen-year-old goes through. You're lazy, you don't see any future, and you really don't care. You give up before you even begin. Everybody goes through that period. Unfortunately, most English people stay there.

"LIAR"

LYDON: Self-explanatory, really—considering. . .

COOK: We never used to believe anybody then. "Liar" was another song with Glen. It was one of the earliest songs that John and Glen worked on together. It was the friction in the band that made it work well.

LYDON: I never got on with Glen, but we'd somehow work together all right. We'd put the animosity aside, and good things would come out of that. I think it was the animosities between us that made the songs what they were. Nice guys come in second.

"I WANNA BE ME"

COOK: We used to work on these songs together in our rehearsal studio on Denmark Street, a famous musical area in London. It was just an old shack out the back of Tin Pan Alley. We'd be there every night rehearsing and writing songs. The rehearsal room was downstairs, and there was a living dump upstairs. Steve used to stay there a lot because he didn't have anywhere to live. Glen, John, and I used to stay there on and off.

LYDON: By the beginning of June 1976 we had "Did You No Wrong," "No Lip," "Seventeen," "Stepping Stone," "New York," "Whatcha Gonna Do About It?," "Submission," "Satellite," "No Feelings," "No Fun," "Substitute," "Pretty Vacant," and "Problems." Even though we look back on ourselves at the time and think what a load of lazy sods we were, we really were quite proficient. That's also considering that money was so damn hard to come by. Just raising two shillings to get on the subway and travel to rehearsals was a major effort. Most of the band's money went toward maintaining the rehearsal space.

"NO FUN"

LYDON: "No Fun" is a song I love. We made up our version on the spot. I always wanted to do it. I asked Steve to learn the riff, which he did very quickly. Paul filled in, and it went on from there. I hummed and hawed around the words because I didn't quite know them. That's fairly typical of me. While I love the feel of "No Fun," I don't like the actual lyrics. I think they're flippant in some places while they can be very astute in others. No fun was definitely what we were having at that particular time.

"SATELLITE"

COOK: It's about us running around London doing our earliest gigs in the satellite towns.

LYDON: We used to play in the satellite towns around London—St. Albans. We'd get twenty pounds to play Middlesborough. We had to hire a van, and there was no chance of any hotels. It was just trundle off up there, then trundle back the same night. There wouldn't be a lot of change left over. It's the story of the traveling nonsense and picking up enough money to survive for a day or two. We had to do it. But in a way, that's what built the Sex Pistols' crowd. They came from all those godforsaken new towns—Milton Keynes, St. Albans. As bad as it was in London for young people, they had nothing at all in the satellite towns. No social scene, nothing.

COOK: We played those gigs outside London—Northeast London Polytechnic, St. Albans Art and Design College, Welwyn Garden City—because we thought we'd be so awful, we didn't want that many people to see us. We were still learning to play and just be comfortable in a band. It was a chance for us to get away from the bullshit of London.

LYDON: The only other gigs available would have been pubs or art colleges. Art colleges at that time were not the place. You would get snotty attitudes thrown at you. There was a semifashionable scene in London, which focused on Dr Feelgood and the pub rock thing—something I personally never wanted to be a part of at all. It tended to be older people who were much more proficient with their instruments playing retro R&B.

COOK: There was another reason we liked playing a bit farther out. There was a bit of a buzz about the band before we even played a gig. It was ridiculous. We were this band that had something to do with

Malcolm, the Sex boutique, and Seditionaries. We wanted to do some gigs for ourselves, get together as a band, and beat each other up on a transport van away from the motorway.

LYDON: We didn't have Malcolm McLaren's friends turning up. At that time it was just a clothes horse display by that lot. None of the band wanted to be a part of that.

"NO LIP"

COOK: "No Lip" is a Dave Berry cover version that was totally changed. It's a jumpy uptight pop ditty. Berry was a crooner who fancied himself as a sex symbol. It was Glen's idea to do it.

LYDON: I made it offensive, that's what I did. The people who write these songs don't realize how easy it is to do. It's so nice that you just grab it by the fucking bollocks and squeeze. You give it an edge. Instead of being the victim in these songs, you turn yourself into the protagonist.

COOK: That's what we tried to do with all the cover versions.

"STEPPING STONE"

LYDON: We were actually plumbing the depths here. There wasn't a lot of songs out there that you could connect yourself with. We just wanted straight rock songs. A lot of these records would be picked up from a couple of little stalls on the Soho market that sold old mod records and stuff. The mods were the last people—before they turned into soul boys and skinheads—to do anything musically in the U.K. After that it was all about pomposity and glitter rock. I was interested in the mod energy. We had to begin somewhere, and that was as good a place as any to start. We just took that as a launching pad and went on to something else. It showed the Pistols were a hell of a lot better than the rest. You must bear in mind that at the time, any real music going around was from the likes of Yes and Emerson, Lake and Palmer. It took about fifteen trucks to carry their equipment and elaborate keyboard nonsense around. It was brain-dead and had no energy. It was art college stuff, certainly nothing for young people.

SECOND PHASE: LET RIP, VOLATILE, FULL-FLEDGED
SONGWRITING ON OUR OWN

"NO FEELINGS"

LYDON: This originally came from a Steve Jones riff. It would work this way: one night someone would have an idea, and then everyone else would just build around it until it was done.

COOK: Steve would come in with the riff, and John would be writing the lyrics. We'd be playing away and come up with other ideas. It evolved as simply as that.

LYDON: I had very little to do at all with the Pistols' music. I knew nothing about music. While they'd be fiddling about, I'd be in the corner writing. I'd just shout out if I liked certain bits and I had lyrics to fit in. It's a haphazard way, but that's the way it was. You don't need to be technically proficient at your so-called art to write songs. If you are musically proficient, usually you won't be any good at writing songs because you won't be able to express your feelings. You'll be bogged down in the technology of note perfections, set patterns, and set ideas.

"ANARCHY IN THE U.K."

COOK: It was Glen's riff originally, and Steve beefed it up.

LYDON: I kept really quiet that evening until about an hour before we left. I had written the words down while the band were in the corner arguing. I used to have terrible trouble rehearsing because I was so fucking shy about it. I always wanted to be brilliant, excellent, loved, and adored right from the start. When I finally finished the words, Glen was absolutely furious. He thought it was appalling and a silly idea for a song. I proved him right.

COOK: Glen felt a little precious about it being his song. He was upset about John's terrain being thrown over the top. But the tension was working. John and Glen had such different ideals, and Steve and I were in the middle. "Anarchy" was the classic example of everything working perfectly.

LYDON: When I left the room during writing and rehearsal, I used to leave the door open just a little. I'd wonder, What the fuck is Glen on about?

"SUBMISSION"

LYDON: We were in Camden Town rehearsing at the Roundhouse for a small period. The arguments between Glen and me became severe by this time. Malcolm finally insisted we go to a small pub upstairs and sit down and work it all out. We did. We were given twenty quid to sit down and get drunk and put our differences aside. The result was we both got along on the Doors. The Doors was the common ground—we found a band that we, shockingly, both liked.

COOK: "Submission" had a classic riff that's been done millions of times before. We slowed it down. It was similar to that Doors' riff in "Hello I Love You," the Who's "I Can't Explain," and the early Kinks. We made it more subversive.

LYDON: Malcolm gave us his list of words and ideas. It was so funny. One of the words was "submissive." We turned it into "Submission"—a submarine mission. Glen and I enjoyed the humor of it all. I don't think Malcolm did.

"PROBLEMS"

LYDON: We had run out of ideas for songs—a major problem. The idea was put to Steve—the guitar hero of the band, who couldn't come up with any riffs at all that particular evening—to put something together using an A, B, C, and D chord sequence. As the song progressed it got better. The cynicism of the title and the chords being A, B, C, D is still there. We didn't add any bridges. We were very good at burning them, though.

"NEW YORK"

COOK: Malcolm had this big thing about the New York Dolls. He was fascinated with them. He loved New York and thought it was all so great. He had been there once. "New York" was originally Steve's riff, and John came up with the lyrics to wind up Malcolm. There's still a lot of talk that New York started the punk scene and we ripped them off or such bullshit. People think we were influenced by it. We weren't. The track was ultimately a put-down of that scene.

LYDON: The only thing anybody knew about this so-called New York scene was what Malcolm would tell us. It was hard to listen to the same old stories night after night, slightly changed each time. It got blown out of all proportion, and the mythology of it became unbearable. The song is a reaction to that. It used to be spectacular fun to play the song live, particularly down south in America. The folks at the Longhorn Ballroom in Texas had the same opinion as us about New York. Everything that came out of New York was poetry-based and too artsy. These people were much older than us and had more old-fashioned attitudes.

"PRETTY VACANT"

COOK: Glen reckons the original riff was influenced by Abba's "SOS." I can't see how he worked that out. John changed the lyrics again here. It's about being young and hanging around being vacant.

LYDON: Glen was a closet Abba fan, and funny enough, so was Sid. We got rid of one Abba fan and got another one in its place. Once Sid ran up to the girls from Abba in the Stockholm airport to ask for their autograph. Sid was completely drunk and stuck his hand out. They screamed and ran away. They thought they were being attacked—or maybe they thought he wanted money or something. Steve toughened it up because the original guitar line was very sissy. Glen wanted it to be very nice. My accent would have been on "Vacant" while Glen's would have been on "Pretty." "Va-cunt" is me all over. I love to play with words and throw them into different arenas. They didn't mind it on the radio because they didn't notice,

THIRD PHASE: FINAL GROUP OF SONGS WRITTEN CLOSE
TOGETHER, MORE MUSICAL; NO LONGER CONFUSED ABOUT
WHERE WE STOOD

"GOD SAVE THE QUEEN"

COOK: It started with Glen's bass riff. Then Steve got hold of it, then I started playing. Suddenly John came up with "God Save the Queen." We thought, What's this? We hadn't worked on songs for ages. They came about quickly. I would slow the band down. Relax, let's not go too mad. Most people think about punk songs being three-minute thrashers. Our songs aren't fast. Our songs were slow in tempo compared to those sorts of songs. I would hold everyone back a bit, especially Steve. He liked to go full steam ahead without thinking too much about it. It was hard sometimes because everyone was so pumped up. The songs could get much faster live than the way we recorded them in the studio.

Jean junction, you won't catch me in denim

LYDON: The whole thing was written in one go. I had the lyrics ready. I wrote them a while back but never used them. The words didn't fit in with any of the other tunes. I didn't think they would ever fit in with the pattern that Glen had. Steve fell into it very quickly. Paul aided and abetted it very quickly with the drums.

COOK: It wasn't written specifically for the queen's anniversary jubilee. We weren't aware of it at the time. It wasn't a contrived effort to go out and shock everyone. No way. It didn't even click that there was a jubilee coming up. Eventually it did come out on the anniversary.

LYDON: I had so many arguments with Glen and Steve. Where's the chorus? You can't write a song like that. It's not musical. My flippant answer was: What is musical? The "No Future" part was an end refrain, an outro.

"EMI"

LYDON: I recommend a lousy record company every time you run out of songs. The material is glorious. It's one of my faves of the lot. Again, it's not done in the way a song technically should be. These songs break so many traditions of songwriting. Isn't it funny? After sacking the Pistols, EMI ends up with them again fifteen years later.

COOK: We weren't trying to be clever. Just blatant. EMI. You know what this is about. Direct.

"HOLIDAYS IN THE SUN"

COOK: We had to get out of London. Malcolm wanted us to leave for a while because we were causing too much trouble at the time. We were fed up with not having any money and the pressure of London. All the publicity and the fights were going on. Malcolm was trying to put a deal together and we didn't want to be around. We went down to Jersey, then had quite a good time in Berlin for a couple of weeks holiday. Some people used to compare the song musically to a Jam song called "In the City." It's about everyone's paranoia.

LYDON: We tried our "Holidays in the Sun" on the isle of Jersey, and that didn't work. They threw us out. Being in London at the time made us feel like we were trapped in a prison camp environment. We didn't have enough money to escape from the infamy of it all. There was hatred and a constant threat of violence. The best thing we could do was to go set up in a prison camp somewhere else. Berlin and its decadence was a good idea. The song came about from that. I loved

Berlin. I loved that wall and the insanity of the place. Twenty-four hours of chaotic fun. It was geared up to annoy the Russians. West Berlin at the time was inside the communist state of East Germany. It was a fairground with only one airport and one motorway leading into it—surrounded by downtrodden, dull, gray, military-minded bastards who live thoroughly miserable lives. They looked in on this circus atmosphere of West Berlin—which never went to sleep—and that would be their impression of the West. I loved it. I had this feeling of Berlin being this wall all around me. It was a ridiculously small wall, and the whole thing seemed absolutely absurd. You'd get that marching vibe when you'd look over the wall at them. All you'd see would be soldiers. I'd be up on one of those stands at the wall giving two fingers up to the soldiers. The West Germans told me that they would shoot me and maybe cause an international incident. I would say, "That's what I'm here for! To me, that's a holiday!"

"BODIES"

COOK: Pauline was a mad fan who used to turn up everywhere. She turned up at my door, too. She was dangerous and very crazy—someone you really had to worry about. She was a pretty girl, but she had these really mad eyes. You had to keep your distance from Pauline.

LYDON: Pauline was a girl who used to send these letters to me from some nuthouse up north in Birmingham. She was in a mental asylum. She turned up at my door once wearing a see-through plastic bag. She did the rounds in London and ended up at everybody's door. She had a very curious way of finding out where everybody lived. Like most insane people, she was very promiscuous. The fetus thing is what got me. She'd tell me about getting pregnant by the male nurses at the asylum or whatever. There's a line in the song about Pauline living in a tree. She actually had a treehouse on the estate of this nuthouse. The nurses couldn't get her down, and she'd be up there for days. Apparently, punk rock pulled her out of her cocoon. She might have had wealthy parents who buggered up her life—probably a bit like Nancy Spungen, really. She was one of many lunatics who used to attach themselves to us.

"MY WAY"

COOK: Sid doing "My Way" was for *The Great Rock 'n' Roll Swindle* film. Eventually they recorded it in Paris. I wasn't on the song. Steve came over and played guitar on the track. John had left the band by this time, and I was sort of out of it by that time, too. I didn't have much to do with Malcolm. He was off on his own trip making the film. Steve was involved in the film much more than me. Sid was in the band when we wrote "Bodies" and "Holidays in the Sun," but he wasn't really involved in the songwriting during the Pistols.

LYDON: Didn't Sid have hepatitis in the hospital at the time? We still credited the band with songwriting. We weren't mean about that shit. Once you start separating people when it comes to copyright on publishing, you're not a band anymore. It becomes egos and you get nothing but trouble. We'd see that with a lot of the other bands around at the time. Falling apart over nothing. I was beginning litigation against Malcolm. The name *Sex Pistols* continued without me for the film. I'm not going to be prissy here and insist that "My Way" not be included. It should be included because the name just went on. If you notice a drop in quality, that's neither here nor there.

COOK: A lot of stuff came out under the Sex Pistols name after John left because Malcolm was trying to get the film together. He was desperate, and Virgin was giving him money to finish it. Using the name Sex Pistols was the only way to raise cash.

"SILLY THING"

COOK: "Silly Thing" was a thing Steve and I put together for the film. It was originally called "Silly Cunt." It was about Sid or it could have been about Malcolm. Everyone. It dealt with the stupidity of the whole Pistols fracas after we had all broken up. Steve's singing on this track.

LYDON: I liked it when I first heard it because it was really funny. It was deeply cynical and showed that the boys had learned something over the years. It was an affectionate dig. When it all fell apart we really were stupid with each other. "Silly Thing" was an ominous note to end with. It's absolutely right. The fanatics out there take things far too seriously. They'd probably be appalled at the way we view our own material because they see it quite differently. They want us to have their visions and represent their attitudes about our work. Audiences are far too fucking demanding on the people they like and dislike. The truth always lets them down because it destroys their fantasies. One thing I always wanted with the Sex Pistols was that it wasn't about fantasy. That was clear right from the start. We never hid anything.

JOHN WAYNE LOOK-ALIKES IN DRESSES

UNITED STATES TOUR,
JANUARY 1978

We were paid a pittance of ten dollars a day on the road. The food was not exactly high quality, and it was all pretty shabby. Going to America was all about imagining this wonderful spectacle, and in a way that's exactly what we got, though not according to the rules of the day.

It wasn't a question of throwing the band to the wolves when we chose to just play the South during the American tour. San Francisco was as far north as we played, and there was great debate about playing there. I didn't want to because I thought it was too far north. We felt that if we were ever going to be taken seriously in America, it would be from a base we built down south. The northern territories already thought they knew it all, so it was closed doors to the Pistols. I thought it would have been silly to go play New York. It was pointless. They had already decided that they hated us and their bands were so much better. New Yorkers believed that nonsense about Richard Hell inventing punk.

There was hostility toward us in the South and everywhere we played. But it had to be, because through that, people started to think. Things were working in their own mad little way. What we wanted as a band was not mass acceptance, but understanding. Yee hah. At that time, rock music in America was becoming too much of a northern thing. The South was left to country and western and ignored. Not many bands toured down there. If the South were treated as badly as we were, they were the very people we should be playing to.

I found southerners to be extremely open. All that bullshit fed to us about them wanting to shoot us was nonsense. They partied much heavier, they drank more and did everything else to excess in a wonderful way and without the violence. Yes, I think they are violent people, but they don't need to resort to it quite as much. Southerners had a restraint I admired. They don't need to prove how tough they are. They build them big down there. A fifteen-year-old southern kid is like a thirty-five-year-old New York trucker.

The whole idea of us touring down south was horrible to Warner Brothers, our new American label. They had their own set routine—New York, Los Angeles, and a few big towns up north. Nobody took a rock 'n' roll band down south like we did and particularly avoided New York like it had a disease. I loved the idea. I was very chuffed about that, just the sheer naughtiness of it. It was marvelous-one of Malcolm's greatest contributions. "You'll get killed!" Fine. Proved them wrong. Some of us got killed, though none of the ones that counted.

"They're all Bible maniacs with guns going off."

Well, there were Bible maniacs and there was gunfire, but none aimed at us. It was all a bang in the air.

"Meet my wife! Hey, honey, go rustle up some beans for the boys."

We had a black coach driver and he said, "You can't go here, you can't go there." Why the hell not? Our driver was absolutely terrified of the South. He hated being down there and thought we were pushing our luck all the time.

In a way he was right. Look who we were playing to, for God's sake, real cowboys! These weren't, by any stretch of the imagination, rock 'n' roll venues. If you're going to put yourself in that environment, you'd better go the whole hog, hadn't you? You have to really play up to it and enjoy it for the fiasco it really is. The British press, however, looked at it as war.

"There will be death tonight."

But there never was. These cowboys seemed to take it for the joke it was meant to be. We weren't there to destroy their way of life or anything like that. Quite the opposite. We sought to bring a little freshness into their boring, daily routines. The people we'd meet in America were mostly exceptional. Friendly and open. I've not met people like that since. Down south, for all its bad points, the people are genuine, they have less need for pretension, and they're actually very individualistic, not a uniformed lump.

Sid landed in America in bad shape. There was a kind of cleaning-up process going on until we got to San Francisco. Honestly, the Sex Pistols tour bus was like a mobile hospital. It helped to just keep him occupied. He was very impressed with the bikers on board. Sid buying a pair of biker's boots was better than his buying drugs.

BOB GRUEN: It was a funny situation. The bodyguards were obnoxious Vietnam vets with beards, knives, and boots. Also, the tour manager, Noel Monk, tore the band apart. He was really afraid of them. Monk was working for Warner Brothers and had to get this tour across the country in one piece. Malcolm was dying for confrontation. He wanted nothing more than to have journalists screaming at the band and writing some outrageous story, whereas Noel Monk and Warner Brothers had this traditional idea of bands being polite to the press.

Malcolm didn't turn up at the first American gig in Atlanta. I didn't see him for a long time, even though he booked us on this fiasco tour. This is why I let Sid's anger run loose on Malcolm. I could have stopped it, but I thought it was justified. We never knew what the hell Malcolm was up to, where he was and what he was doing. He was usually off pontificating in his usual way and telling the world how great he was and all the things he'd done. Meanwhile the band had to take the front-line flak.

When we checked into our motel in Atlanta, the cops stopped Sid and me in the parking lot to keep us from going into town. Both the Warners people and the police didn't want us to go out since they thought it would incite all kinds of trouble and there were people out there trying to lynch us. We found that not to be true. Things were weirder out on the streets of Atlanta than anything going on on stage at the gigs.

We were foiled briefly, but we still went out. There was this cheesy disco in Atlanta that had all these straight people in jeans and plaid shirts dancing to insipid disco. We only stayed there for three minutes at the most.

JOHN GRAY: When the Pistols started, we'd go into gay clubs in London like the Sombrero on High Street Kensington, hardly realizing they were gay. They were the best clubs, and we'd descend en masse.

We were looking for entertainment and to see how far entertainment would take us, so we went to a weird, funny club in a shopping mall on the outskirts of town. This club had a load of transvestites with their "Y'all come on down, now" southern accents. Tough cowboys dressed up as women. It was bizarre—literal John Wayne look-alikes in dresses. It was good fun. They had these cubicles in the back where they showed porno loops. The films were way severe, triple-X hard-core flicks. Little transvestites were back there offering you blow jobs for nothing. I was thrown out because I pissed in someone's mouth. Others took it more seriously. It was so mad.

Those booths were hilarious, and the queues for them were astoundingly long. You had to keep pushing quarters into this little coin box to keep the movies going while there would be some transvestite sucking away.

Oh, come on, is there any such thing as a pretty transvestite? You look close and there's whisker bristles sticking out of their faces. There's no way I could be turned on by this. It was the sheer hell of it all. You couldn't keep a hard-on.

Sid went off with a black transvestite and I went off with a cowgirl I found. She had a cowboy hat, and she had just got out of prison. She told me her sob story. I was fascinated. We never saw any place in the whole of America that could ever compare to that place. They had the worst laser show I had ever seen, but the music was insane! The deejays couldn't give a shit and mixed everything up—country music followed by some deep black funk groove. The whole thing was a contradiction, and I loved it for that. It's not what you'd think the South was all about. It's funny how the city fathers could allow that stuff to go on, then condemn the Sex Pistols on stage.

The London clubs could never compare to this place. There's something very weak in the English. They like the clothes and the imagery of it all, but when it comes to delivering the goods, they tend to back down.

One of the biker bodyguards on the American tour took us up to his place outside Atlanta. He was a giant of a man with a big ginger beard who owned a nightclub as well. His house was fantastic and strange. He lived in one of those frontier-style houses with a big wagon wheel out front. I loved it because it was so normal in an abnormal way, like visiting the set of "Bonanza." We stayed up all night drinking, partying, and playing funny country and western songs. I'd also been speeding all fucking night. On the way back to the bus the next morning at about five or six A.M. he took us to a doughnut shop as a joke. It was supposed to be where all of the cops hung out. Lo and behold, they were there. American cops are the same all over. Doughnuts and coffee. Despite our paranoid state, it was great fun just to sit in among all that. It was the first I'd seen of it, especially after a night of being crazy in the hills listening to all this country and western noise. That's what I wanted from America. I didn't want to go to a rock 'n' roll club and find the same-old, same-old shit. Sid and I were very intrigued by truck stops and doughnut shops. We had the greatest time on the bus because of all the truck stops. That's when Sid wasn't doing any bad gear or heroin, mainly because there was none about. The adventure of places like truck stops would keep him level. You'd go in and see these truckers with their Dolly Parton women and experience the whole down-south thing, the romance of it all.

I wanted to know everything about America. I'm not a social snob; I can move inside any group and feel comfortable, I don't care if it's old women talking about knitting quilts. It's all about human beings. I can find that as fascinating as anything else. Sid, Paul, and Steve had a very hard time understanding that. "It's not rock 'n' roll." Of course it is! Rock 'n' roll is supposed to relate to everybody! If everybody isn't involved, then it's sectarianism. The people who condemn and slag you off do so because they have little knowledge of you. If you confront them and give them that knowledge, things will change. That's the whole point of living! You can learn off each other and enjoy.

That might be an Irish way of thinking on my part. For instance, there's no such thing as a generation gap in Irish social clubs. You're listening to whatever is being played; kids are running around. The whole gamut of life as it should be is there. I could never understand why the Sex Pistols audience should be a bunch of clones wearing torn shirts and leather jackets. You should never have to look at your audience and say, "Ugh! Look at what they're all wearing." It was such a militaristic and foolish approach.

We bought tons of American souvenirs. Look at the photos at the time. Leather waistcoats, cowboy hats, and belts. Puff-sleeved shirts. Cowboy boots. We found out there was a whole hierarchy of hat wear down there. Sid would never wear a hat because it would spoil his hairdo. With Sid, above all else, looks were what mattered. Even during his most messed-up period, he still was thinking about the right look. He was always vainglorious about his image. It's a shame that it later became a leather-jacketed cliché through no fault of his own. But on the American tour, we had the lot, it was a menagerie of clothing that we dumped after three wears. That's when the joke wore thin. But I remember loving those loud cowboy shirts, dressing up in cowboy gear and going into those places.

"Yee-ha! We're the Sex Pistols!"

(I still do a very bad impersonation of a southern accent with the cockney creeping through.)

The Sex Pistols did a few American in-store appearances. It was mad fun. Invariably, Sid and I would run in and grab everything we could. It was Freebeeville. Sign a few autographs and walk out with hundreds of dollars' worth of product, which we'd then throw out the window halfway down the road. It was our way of getting one over on someone; childish, but necessary for the fun of it all. The stores didn't mind. It brought in loads of people. We'd sign autographs and talk. That's where we met the most people. One in-store was in Atlanta. We got there and thought that no one was there. It was a huge store in the middle of nowhere. The car park was underground. When we got inside, it was mobbed with more people than at the gigs. It was the first time I'd ever seen a record store as big as an airplane hangar, and it left an absolutely vivid impression of America. In England all we had were small corner shops. Mile after mile of music—and Muzak—all of it, to record collectors like Sid and me, absolute heaven. We were after anything that looked interesting, especially bizarre country and western things. The whole country and western look was far more severe than anything the Sex Pistols could come up with. Particularly the women; they seemed overdone and freaky. Loved it.

That's where I met Granny Rotten. She decided that she was going to adopt me because I was gorgeous. Really old, she brought a huge cake. To this day whenever I go down south she comes to the gigs with cakes and home-baked cookies. She brings her family, her sons.

We'd meet Hasidic Jews. Sid thought they were great because he loved their clothes. They were so stylish with their beaver hats, the locks, and their long black coats. There was a time when Sid actually wanted to start wearing that stuff. They wouldn't sell him the clothes because they thought he was going to be disrespectful to their religion.

It seemed like everything in America—especially food—was too much and too big. I couldn't finish anything. That's America to this day. You greedy bastards, was the impression that left on me. You have to have too much. Such waste. Triple-decker hamburgers. God almighty! Feed an army.

I knew nothing about America. I also didn't know what to expect. I knew there were problems in the band. I thought we could keep things together by the skin of our teeth. I never spoke to them the entire tour except for one night toward the end. Steve rang me up and I went to his room. We sat down and he had this shoebox full of marijuana. We smoked ourselves silly. We were supposed to discuss the problems at hand, but the gear was so good, it just didn't matter. The next morning Paul rang Steve, wondering why we hadn't sorted things out. All we'd sorted were the seeds and stems.

I hardly ever slept because, well, it was America. I kept my eyes open, glaring out the coach window all day, all night. I was fascinated by any flashing lights that went by. The sheer expanse of America never failed to impress. When you come from a tiny little place like Britain, you always feel the shore isn't too far away.

BOB GRUEN: The trip was calm as we listened to Don Letts's reggae tapes. Don was a black Rasta guy back in London who knew all the white punk rockers and was their reggae connection. He made the greatest tapes because he had access to all the latest dub sounds. It was music I had absolutely no knowledge of. I was surprised that these guys who were known for loud, crashing music were listening to such spiritual dub sounds. There we were, driving down the road to a soundtrack.

There was one concert in America where the Bible lot turned up. They had one of their banners up, quoting some verse about when the world turns to rottenness or whatever. That thrilled me. "Ahh, they care. They've noticed, at last." I invited them to come into the gig, but nobody came in. It was one of those censorship scenes where the parents and the grandads of the town were out front. Anybody who wanted to see us had to go through this gauntlet of abuse, exactly what they do in front of the abortion clinics in America. Just like in Caerphilly in Wales, the religious fanatics threatened the audience in their locale. "I'll tell your mum!" "Please do! I'll buy two tickets just for that." The emptiness of the American gigs could be startling. But others would be absolutely jam-packed, really overcrowded, and that frightened me, even with all the security, in the heart of country music with rednecks abound, the breeding place, the hornet's nest. There was loads of horses tied up outside. In Texas, people rode in on horseback. "We have some good ol' boys from England now . . ." There was a lot of Mexicans in the audience. They looked like wild Indians to me. This very large Mexican contingency decided that they liked us, so that shut the cowboys up and the bottles stopped being slung. It was two huge mobs of people facing each other off with the Pistols screaming blue murder in the middle. In the middle of all that were the English journalists. Noel Monk, our tour manager, told me that the first person who started throwing stuff was a British newspaper journalist. They had all their cameras ready, while this same person tried to incite something. Malcolm would be constantly arguing with Noel about publicity. Malcolm would have the British journalists there, and Noel would say no. They would just cause trouble and deliberately create chaos. I'll accept all publicity, good or bad—but not false publicity. I can deal with it if it's real. If it's all just show bizzy, it makes you feel rather pointless. The British press loved to make things up. They were spotted starting incidents throughout the tour. That's unforgivable. I'm the star. That's my job, you bastard.

BOB GRUEN: I spent a few weeks riding across America with them, smoking, drinking beer, nobody getting too loaded, kicking back, watching the American horizon go by, listening to very spiritual reggae music. We'd pull up for the gig in Oklahoma, Dallas, or wherever, and when they opened the door, there would be three or four television cameras pointed at us. Someone would clear his throat and spit, and the newspeople would all freak out. That turned into a news break. I never understood why spitting was news.

Sid was a naughty boy on the road, half because he was well cut and half for the sheer hell of it. He finally had an audience of people who would behave with shock and horror. Hands in hair. It was too much good fun. Sid was easily led by the nose. The American record executives kept their distance from the band. They were told, right or wrong, that we would try to tear their heads off. That titillated them no end. "Oh, wow! We got a monster."

BOB GRUEN: In Dallas, one of the girls in the audience who had been following the tour kept punching Sid in the face. In retaliation, he'd spit blood back at her. This went on, back and forth, through the first couple of songs. A few days before, Sid had carved "Give Me a Fix" on his chest. It was a desperate message. He wanted anybody to give him some dope. He hoped some fan would see it and come backstage before he was whisked away by Noel, who was keeping him removed. I honestly thought Sid had popped one of those stage blood capsules. It turned out he was really bleeding, and he had this big smile on his face. While he was spitting the blood at this girl, the bloody nose she gave him dried up, so he went over to his amp, shattered a bottle of whiskey, and began cutting his chest to get more blood. That's when Noel grabbed him by the wrist, after which Sid looked down at the floor like a little kid who had been caught being stupid. Meanwhile the band was yelling at him. While he was messing with the bottle, he'd accidentally turned off his amp, which meant that while he was playing away for a song and a half, nobody heard him. I could see Johnny getting pissed off, especially as Sid got more and more attention.

Eventually I sewed up Sid's cut myself. Two days had gone by and the wound was dirty and started to fester. That's when I realized that nobody was going to take care of him. I was an ex-Boy Scout, so I washed and dressed the wound with butterfly stitches, I pulled the skin back together and taped him up. I did that mainly because I was tired of looking at it.

I got on all right with some of the Warners people. The late Bob Regehr was splendid, I really liked him. He was a bundle of fun. He got it right from the start. He knew there was a sense of fun in all of this. He absolutely hated Malcolm, as indeed most good people did. It was Bob Regehr's idea to sign us to Warners in America. He had the perception and was the only one with the real rock 'n' roll sense. He was always laughing. You could tell that this man had an NFL physique in his younger days, with an enormous belly to go with it. You know instantly when people "get it." It's a terrible thing, but it's also a good thing, when you're caught out. When I was being moody, a typical Johnny Rotten stance—he'd just burst out laughing. Oh, I'll have to change the rules of this game. Here was the only one who understood.

An all-black heavy-metal band opened up for us in Memphis. That struck me at the time as highly curious. They were very good, but because of color prejudices down south, they were doomed. The audience didn't get it at all. I thought it was unfair. They were very good—better than us. American bands always seem older and tend to spend a lot more time learning their craft. Maybe that's why American music is so confined.

I absolutely did not visit Elvis's Graceland. I think Paul and Steve might have gone. I know I didn't, even though we drove past it on the way to the gig. I deliberately turned my head away. I didn't even want to see it. Some books have said that I loved Elvis! God! I've always hated Elvis Presley from an early age, and there's a specific reason. A really boring Irish cousin of mine used to be in the Irish army military brass band. He was an Elvis fan, and he came over to my family's house and brought all these awful, godforsaken Elvis records and sat down in my room because I had the record player. He played them for eight solid hours, over and over. I've never forgotten that nonstop crap. It left a solid hateful impression for that Elvis Presley. If anyone who plays in a brass band digs Elvis, then it's clearly not for me!

Compared to Britain, playing in America was like starting all over again. There was a lot of animosity from the crowd, too. They were force fed all of the usual press garbage drivel. It was "You ain't so hot!" before we even started. Those were very difficult audiences. In most places we won them over, but it's hard to know what singing a song like "God Save the Queen" means to an American. They probably thought we're talking about the fags in Atlanta.

During the American tour, Tom Forcade from *High Times* was definitely after Sid, trying to interview him. While I didn't know anything about the magazine at the time, Forcade wanted a drug scandal, which is what this magazine dealt with, the recreational use of drugs. It was difficult to keep him away from Sid because he followed us from hotel to hotel. I found it curious that he always knew where we were. He would always turn up. He tried to bribe Noel in order to get him to cooperate, but he did keep him away. There was one instance when we found him in Sid's room. Sid had let him in. You couldn't turn your back on Sidney. Sometimes he was so stupid. "It's press. You're ruining my career!" Oh, Sid! There were fisticuffs and some camera bashing before he was physically ejected from Sid's room.

Sid had become like a wild animal unleashed for the first time. He believed that's what it was all about—to be a rock 'n' roll hero. He had an inflated ego, and all of that was cultivated by Nancy before he left Britain. "You're the star, Sid! You don't need these guys. That fuckin' Johnny Rotten. Man, he's bad!"

Nancy was excess baggage—definitely not wanted on this tour. That annoyed Sid no end, but that was just too bad. It was quite simple: if he was going to bring Nancy, then I was going to bring a couple of my mates. Sid wouldn't want that because these were people who were cruel to Nancy. Big guys, fighters these people. They love their physical stuff. Nancy was a horror freak show, just crying out for a slap in the kisser. Many of us, at one time or another, actually physically hit her because she was that pushy. I know I did.

"Oh, don't hit her!" quoth Sid. "You mustn't!"

Do you think I was going to put up with that garbage heap?

I can't have people flitting around when I write songs. There has to be absolute silence. Sid would get very angry—more like jealousy—on the bus.

"What you writing there?"

When I showed Sid, Paul, and Steve the lyrics to "Religion" on the bus, their only response was "Whoa!" It was now time for the serious stuff. The Sex Pistols had never dealt with those topics before. I tried to get Steve and Paul involved. We had a very long wait at the San Antonio gig when we got there very early. I wanted them to listen to what I was doing, but they wouldn't have it under any circumstances. I knew it was over with Steve and Paul from that point onward. We never spoke much after because the next day they started to fly everywhere. They went off with Malcolm and I was left with Sid, the Hell's Angels on the bus and a couple of journalists.

I always get sick on tour, but the Pistols' American bus tour was largely due to a total lack of discipline. I would drink too much the night before and not eat enough because of the late night performances. There was rarely any food around during the gigs, never any money and the booze was always supplied free by the local promoter. I ran myself down. With the Pistols, it was pointless to moan to anyone about it because nobody gave a fuck. I got more and more ill.

I began coughing up blood at one point and thought, Fuck, is this cancer? Then I started getting nosebleeds. Turned out it was the constant air-conditioning. Since it was the first time I had ever been to America, I didn't realize I was straining myself night after night with a totally dehydrated throat—a severe case of Vegas throat. I was ripping the back of my tonsils out. To this day I can't have air-conditioning anywhere when I travel. I can't stand it, even on short flights. It fucks me up in thirty minutes. I gag up huge snotty lumps.

Quite frankly, whatever illness I had on the road in America didn't compare to Sid's. The dear boy was coming down cold turkey, and it was tough as all hell. I could hardly sit there and moan, "Ooooo look, Johnny's got a sore throat." I couldn't be doing that, even at my cruelest.

But it did get to the point where I finally said, "Look, I'm actually starving to death here and now. Could somebody get me some food?" I never had more than ten dollars in my pocket on the road in America. Any money I had was what I took out with me from Britain. Money wasn't exactly floating around in large amounts within this organization. We weren't being well paid for these concerts. We should have been receiving rather large amounts for the size of the crowds we were pulling in. The sheer campaign of it all seemed bigger than the Stones by that point. I shared the cover of *Rolling Stone* with Willie Nelson, and here I am broke, hungry, stuck on a bus, dehydrated—with a junkie. Seriously, Sid had come off by that time and he was settling down. A few beers would be enough for him to pass out. We had a lot of fun at the truck stops, and we would talk. Even the Angels' security would be horrified at our behavior in these places. It was mostly Sid. He loved to approach these Dolly Parton look-alikes and their trucker boyfriends with the big cowboy hats. Remember, fifteen years ago and today are two different cultures—it was way redneck back then. Sid and I would sit among these people, and they were appalled because they didn't know where we came from and couldn't understand the image or the look of us. There was nothing like us in America at the time—much less in the truck stops.

There would be some fights in the redneck truck stops. They would stand up and say, "I think you insulted my wife!" Sid, of course, didn't have the common sense to back down and say, "No, I didn't, and sorry if you think so." He'd say something daft like "I think her wig's an insult enough." To Sid, it was all just fashion statements. He didn't realize that these people lived and died by their hairdos. Just like Sid himself.

BOB GRUEN: Half the time we were riding on the bus; Noel wouldn't let the band get off. If we pulled into, say, a truck stop, Noel would go in and come out with a menu, as if we needed one. What else do you order at a truck stop besides hamburgers? He'd bring the greasy burgers back to the bus and we'd eat on the highway. One time early in the morning Noel was sleeping as we pulled up to a restaurant. I got off the bus with Sid and we sat down at the counter and ordered hamburgers and a steak. There was a cowboy sitting nearby with his wife and kid. He recognized Sid and invited us to come over and sit down. The guy said something about Sid being vicious and then put his cigarette out on his own leathery hand. Sid, who was eating his steak and eggs, casually took his knife, sliced his own hand open, and kept eating while the blood dripped into his food. The cowboy took his wife and kid and left the place.

I was well into reggae a long time before the Pistols, but Don Letts just carried it ten stages farther with the road tapes he gave us for the American tour. Deep grooves on the southern highways. That's all I played on the bus during that tour. If Steve and Paul didn't like it at the time, they should have said so. I would have played it regardless. All they had was bloody Iggy Pop and the Stooges and the New York Dolls. I had heard that a thousand times before. Now Paul is totally into reggae—fifteen years later. Sid loved the reggae bass lines. It was much easier for him to get a reggae groove going.

Noel Monk was just doing his job when it came to protecting the band. He had to cope with extreme chaos. He didn't understand us, and we didn't understand the American way. He was very uptight and thought we would all be murdered at any one point. It was his job to make sure we weren't. He decided to misdirect our routes and stay in out-of-the-way motels because of the amount of press following us, mostly British. All of them were looking for a scandal, and if they didn't get one, they would invent one. That kind of exaggeration could put us all in jail, and none of us wanted that to happen. I didn't fancy meeting Mr. Big in a Texas penitentiary. It wasn't my idea of heaven. It was common sense, the way it had to be. Otherwise we were unprotected.

BOB GRUEN: Noel switched things around a lot. We had a complete itinerary of where the bus was supposed to stop, where they had reserved rooms for the night. But Monk would pull into town, check out the venue, and then divert us to these dumpy motels. He'd hide the bus behind the motel and book the band into it, the result being that nobody knew where the band was. That way he was doing his job. It got to be very boring because we were alone a lot of the time.

Our coach driver was quite worried about driving through some of the places we were going through. He would say so.

"I don't like my black ass down here."

Sid thought it was hilarious. He offered to sit up front with him. Sid didn't have a clue about the racism in the South. He saw all these John Wayne films and that was it for him. I don't think Sid met real hatred in his entire life, and if he did, he wouldn't notice it. He could be quite dense about things like that. He could judge individuals, except when they were en masse or in groups. He never ran with mobs of people or went to football matches. He didn't have that kind of street education, where you move on so you don't get your head whacked.

BOB GRUEN: Johnny had a more serious side, whereas Sid didn't have much of a clue. Everything was coming at him so fast. He didn't know what to do except to get high with Nancy. She was the only real feeling he had in his life, but she was back in England. They would talk on the phone once in a while. The band wouldn't let her on the tour, nor would they allow any dope. Hence Sid spent a lot of the tour crashing the dope, ultimately getting sick for a few days, after which he would drink peppermint schnapps, which was like sucking on a candy cane full of alcohol. It's disgusting stuff. You might put half a jigger in a holiday mixed drink, but here was Sid drinking this sticky, sweet liquor straight out of the bottle.

Sid was naive but full of wit about things. Excellent person, but drugs did him in and turned him into a deeply unpleasant Mr. Hyde—one who would make us "hyde" from him at times. It's not nice to be with someone talking ga-ga and gibberish and being belligerent about his own hangovers and hang-ups. There's a terrible incoherence that comes in with drugs. Any kind of addiction is self-torture and slow suicide.

Before drugs, Sid was such a funny chap when he was on a roll. He could take the piss out of anyone and anything and totally have them down. Again, he had great perception with people. He knew their weaknesses straight away. Steve Jones can be like that, too. If Steve gets on a roll, he can really murder someone verbally. In that respect, the Pistols were quite a literate band. We were very good at being sarcastic, and I think my qualities in this area can speak for themselves. Paul would stay quiet and not understand why we would rag on people that way. It's a "dissing thing," isn't it? You notice it a lot in black culture in America these days, this thing of putting each other down all the time, and whoever comes out with the best one-liner—that's it—and you burst out laughing. "You can't top that!"

That's the game that used to go on with the Pistols. Used to. It all went sour some time before we left for America. The lack of playing in England did it in. It ended up backfiring and destroyed the band. It broke our spirit because the very thing that we were always good at was being on stage. That was the unification, and if you take that away from a band, then they will start to separate and be suspicious of each other because there's nothing else to do. Our minds wandered because we were bored.

We could hardly go out and socialize with other people at that time because the animosity from the British public was so intense. It became impossible. How do you lock four people up in a room and tell them they can't do anything? What are they going to do but turn sour? A good manager would have occupied our minds, got us working on a new album, or got us thinking long term. Malcolm wouldn't tell us anything he was up to, so we all felt manipulated and fed up. There's no point in rehearsing if you don't see any long-term prospects on the horizon.

Sid and I never had the chance to speak with Malcolm on the road. He wouldn't look at me, and I wouldn't look at him. Paul and Steve had a different situation, and that used to piss Sid and me off a lot. We felt we were alienated, and I couldn't quite see Malcolm's percentage in allowing that to happen. He found that out to his detriment when he took Steve and Paul to Rio. It was a horrendously bad flop. There wasn't anyone with enough intelligence to carry it off.

STEVE JONES: John was more worried because he didn't trust McLaren. I didn't mind him. I didn't give a fuck. Anything I got was better than where I came from. I really didn't ask any questions, even though we got screwed. The real musicians always get the short end of the stick. It's been happening for years to folks like Little Richard and all those guys in the fifties. Like most musicians into their thing, I'll just fucking sign anywhere like a moron. I don't think sincere rock 'n' rollers are business oriented.

During the beginning of the American tour, somebody from Warner Brothers came out to one of the gigs, and I distinctly remember one of them saying, "Well, you're not so special. All you've done is imitate Rod Stewart." That's when Malcolm picked up on the Rod Stewart put-down. They said my hairstyle was an imitation of Rod Stewart. Malcolm took it farther and decided that I had become Rod Stewart. It's beyond me how he concluded that. When people want to be nasty they'll see just what they want to see.

If at any point he'd just sat down with all of us and discussed things, everything could have been cleared. If we did decide to go our separate ways, we could have done it properly instead of through the noncommunication courtroom bullshit. It was cowardly of him to have run away when it got too hot. To this day, I don't understand it. Maybe he couldn't confront us. He could tell Paul and Steve anything he liked. As long as Sid was being pumped up with drugs, he would go with the flow. Sid at the same time violently hated Malcolm all through the American tour. Sid would want to attack him on site.

Another stupid idea Malcolm had on the American tour that caused friction was that he was going to ring up Charles Manson. What a great idea! Somehow he was going to take part in the film or, worse, produce the next record from prison. This was Malcolm's silliness. Nonsense, fantasy, none of it reality based.

Malcolm flew everywhere with Paul and Steve. I stayed on the bus with Sid and the Hell's Angels road crew. Sid loved the jive these people used to feed him. "Oh, us bikers are so tough. We don't dare wear our colors in this town." Sid was wide-eyed. By the next stop, of course, Sid had to buy a pair of biker boots because that's what they were wearing. He already wore the proper leather jacket. This was the impressionable Sid at work.

I'm watching all this. Where's the fucking money? Why don't we have a hotel room? Why don't we get to fly? I had to take the bus because Sid would never travel anywhere with Malcolm, which put Sid's problems on my back. That was fine because he was my mate. Malcolm didn't have the knack to deal with people. He was only good when he had a receptive audience. Otherwise it was a tantrum and running off screaming like a spoiled, vindictive little schoolgirl.

PAUL COOK: In retrospect, breaking up was a hasty decision. Our final band meeting was really awful. John finally made his way over to the hotel. Malcolm was totally pissed off at him, and Steve and I were totally pissed off, too. When John turned up at the Miyako, Steve and I had been up in Malcolm's room telling him how pissed off we were. I don't know what happened between John and Malcolm regarding the trip to Rio. But John didn't want to go, and Steve and I wanted to go just to get a break because we were all supposed to fly back to Sweden for another tour. There was no way we could have done that with Sid being the way he was. Still, we thought that by going to Rio, we could get away from everyone, have a break, and relax. I would rather have gone there than go back to England, tour Sweden, or stay in America.

Malcolm, Steve, and I went downstairs to the hotel lobby, and John was there. Steve said to John, "It's getting too much. We can't see it going on much longer. It's falling apart." I said I agreed. To give John his due, he tried to hold it together. He told us we were stupid and we should get rid of Malcolm and carry on. Steve and I told him we didn't think that was the answer. In the end, John turned out to be right.

When I got to the Miyako Hotel in San Francisco, nobody said anything to me about Rio other than Joe Stevens. Malcolm wouldn't come out of his room to speak to me. I had no idea where Sid was when he OD'd. None of Malcolm's people would speak to me, so I didn't know. I had no hotel room in the Miyako, and nobody who knew anything was speaking to me. I had no plane ticket in my possession. When I rang up Warner Brothers in Los Angeles, they told me over the phone I wasn't me. They knew for a fact that I had gone back to London. Record companies will mostly deal with the manager. They never like talking to the act themselves. If you look at it sensibly, it makes sense. The secretary on the other end was laughing: "Oh, yeah, sure. Johnny Rotten's on the phone. Ha, ha, ha. As if he can use a phone."

When I got back to London after the American tour, Vivienne Westwood had sprayed on her shopfront: "John Fucks the Pope." That was supposed to offend me. Silly cow. She couldn't have got it more wrong. It amused me no end, silly bitch.

After the sixties, some took the attitude that nothing could surprise them any longer. They were very wrong. But the current crop of bands, particularly from England, have no bollocks. No guts. They're all young, bored, and fed up with their lives. But they don't sing about it! Modern music is terrible. They don't do anything to change it. They just go along with the system in a happy-go-lucky disco-beat way. It's very sad. As much as I hate heavy metal, I prefer it anytime over that. Isn't heavy metal a joke? Long hair, flappy flares—but at least it's a vicious joke and there's a nastiness to it.

After the Pistols that term *New Wave* was the kiss of death! Elvis Costello into Joe Jackson into Tom Robinson. Poncey journalists who read all the right mags came up with that term. The first time I heard the term it sickened me and turned my stomach. If you settle for something so flimsy and vacuous as New Wave, you certainly don't deserve to buy anything I put out. I'd be appalled if that was my audience. I don't want them, they can go to hell quick. Modern New Romantics. New Wave turned disco. That was another farcical wimp-out. It's all so limp-wristed, there's no energy in it.

The Sex Pistols weren't New Wave at all, and they didn't have anything in common with the bands that became New Wave, just as we had nothing to do with the bands that became punk; I always wanted to be completely separate from them. These were all just imitators jumping up on our bandwagon and trying to mellow it out so they could go for the big bucks and the easy life. All of them, to a man, wanted stardom.

I wanted to work with Sid in London after the Pistols broke up because Sid had told me that he had cleaned up his act. He was sick of Malcolm and didn't have any liking for Paul and Steve anymore. I was working with Branson over at Virgin during that time, helping him sign some reggae bands, which annoyed Sid no end. I thought about it and decided it might work out, so I presented Sid with the opportunity of us working together again. I told him to meet me at my house on Gunter Grove so we could talk, provided he didn't bring Nancy, which he did. Nancy was getting at Sid and wanted to be his manager. The ego games were so appalling, it resembled something out of that rock 'n' roll satire movie, *Spinal Tap*.

Nancy started whining, "Sid's the star, and any band you guys get together, Sid's gotta be the front man. Playing bass isn't for him. He's a lead singer!"

"That's very nice," I asked, "but where am I in this scheme of things?"

"You can play drums."

"Don't think so, dearie." I had to point out to Nancy who actually wrote all these fucking songs.

"Those songs are shit," Nancy said. "Sid can write better ones than those."

"Well, he hasn't so far," I shot back.

It went on like that until it became insane. That was it. I couldn't cope with it any longer. I didn't want anything to do with the two of them. Then Sid and Nancy wanted to borrow money. That was the crux of it for me. I told them to get the fuck out of my house. I told Sid, "I don't want to ever see you again when you're with her!"

They wanted money for drugs, so I sent them off. About three days later they came back to the house at some ungodly hour at night, shouting and banging on the door. They wanted to borrow money. Again. Urgently. I opened the window from the top floor and told them they were not coming in and I wasn't giving them any money. "Go away. You got the same amount as me. Equal rights and all that."

One of my mates staying in my house at the time ran down with a hatchet because they tried to kick the door in. Sid and Nancy ran off, but they came back twenty minutes later with the same old bollocks. Then I went out with a sword, and it went on like that all bloody night. They were so desperate for money, but I didn't carry amounts like that and I certainly didn't want to keep people in their bad habits. The very thing destroying Sid was certainly not going to be the thing I'd be paying for. Soon after, Sid left for New York with Nancy.

Yes, Sid was my mate and I thought about putting a band together with him after the Pistols. I even got Sid to work on several ideas because I was writing all the way through the American tour during the bus rides. In my own mind, I'd already formed the first Public Image album. I had already written three of the songs, "Religion" and a couple of others. I asked Sid if he wanted to be a part of that. I told him it was a completely different direction, which Sid thought was excellent. It was anything to get away from the trap that we were both in. That's when Sid was away from Nancy. He was a different person, like Jekyll and Hyde. But when we both returned to London after the breakup, in came Nancy, his new manager. It didn't work, and as soon as she turned up, Nancy had something bad to say about everybody. I believe Sid went on to do the "My Way" song for the money. According to Julien Temple, Sid would be at Malcolm's throat at every opportunity possible.

JULIEN TEMPLE: In terms of Sid's relationship with Malcolm, when we did "My Way" in Paris, Boogie and I would go to the studio every night and come back to report to Malcolm that the guy didn't want to do the song. Sid would spend all the time in the studio trying to learn the bass. We would have to come back and tell Malcolm we had wasted another night's money.

When we came back the next morning with the same news, Malcolm was still in bed. Finally Malcolm grew tired of it. He picked up the phone and started screaming at Sid about what a useless junkie he was and so on. Meanwhile, Sid had given the phone over to Nancy and while that was going on, suddenly the eighteenth-century door of Malcolm's hotel room flew off its hinges. Sid crashed into the room wearing his swastika underpants and motorbike boots. He dragged Malcolm out of bed and started hitting him. Then Sid chased a naked Malcolm down the corridor intent on beating the shit out of him. The ancient floorboards went up and down like a ship as the chambermaids started screaming.

"*Monsieur, monsieur.* Stop! Stop! Stop!"

Jerry Nolan, the late drummer for the New York Dolls, lied about having given me heroin. He was a junkie, for God's sake. It's their nature to lie about everything. I tried heroin just once, and it was years later than the Pistols. I got sick as all hell, and it was horrible. Heroin is just not fun, and I cannot understand why these fools say, "It's only like that the first time." Why would you want to go for it a second or third time? Who wants an instant hangover? The London scene in the seventies was definitely not drug free. The punk drug of choice was amphetamine sulfate. Marijuana or any kind of downer drug didn't go well together with the early punks. It's oversimplification to say Johnny Thunders brought heroin over to London. It was always there. Eric Clapton was doing his stuff a long time before. But New Yorkers like Thunders definitely brought it into the punk thing, which was supposedly very anti-heroin in its early days. It intrigued a lot of very foolish people because of the romance of New York. Sid was one of the major gullibles. Gullible's travels.

Sid couldn't see that it was just a sham and an image. To Sid, that was the way New York rock stars lived their lives—morning, noon, and night. He thought they all went to bed with their high heels on. I don't think so, Sid. "They have their breakfast in a pink negligee." Don't think so Sid. It's just an image. Give it up.

"You have to spoil everything." That would be his attitude with me.

BOB GRUEN: Malcolm gave Sid and Nancy ten thousand pounds to come to New York. I saw them at Max's the night they arrived. Sid was in a stupor with a glass in his hand, a straw in his mouth. Nancy would occasionally take the empty glass and replace it with a full one, all the while talking a mile a minute. "Can you lend us ten bucks? We need a cab back to the hotel."

She pulled out this huge roll of money, ten thousand pounds sterling, all in ten-pound notes. Unfortunately they didn't take pound notes in New York, so I lent them the ten bucks.

Nancy Spungen, twenty, was stabbed to death in New York with a hunting knife in October of 1978. It was a disgusting period, and I was furious with Sid—but not so much when I found out he was up for her murder inside. Riker's Island. I felt, Oh, dear, no! I still think he was incapable of such a thing, particularly seeing that he was so deeply fascinated by Nancy. Even a squabble over heroin wouldn't make him kill her. I did go to the press at the time to say I wanted to help him. I thought the whole thing was being turned into a circus, and that's when I wanted to get involved and help sort it out.

BOB GRUEN: I still don't believe Sid did it. I don't think he had it in him. First, he was a wimp. He wasn't vicious—it may have been his name, but it wasn't his nature. Because of all of the things he told me about Nancy, I don't think he could ever hurt her. I think somebody might have come in and killed her. Face it, this is New York City, where there are lots of bad people, particularly inside the Chelsea Hotel. On the other hand, if Nancy was whining about some suicide pact, maybe he did it to shut her up. Something like "Here, take the knife."

But he couldn't have knowingly or violently killed her.

CHRISSIE HYNDE: To tell you the truth, at the time it wouldn't have surprised me if he or anyone killed her, she was that obnoxious. When she started up with that incessant whining she was more than the human mind could bear.

Sid did send a message to me through Joe Stevens when he was in jail. He wanted to speak to me, and I wanted to get a lawyer for him. There was no way I could speak with him. That was canceled very quickly by Malcolm and Sid's mother. I couldn't get through to him without going through one of them. I was in London and they were in New York, so there was no point flying over because I would never get in to see him. Sid asked for me in a roundabout way. No letter, just a phone call from Stevens in New York. I asked for Sid to ring me or send a letter. Nothing came. So I tried to get in touch with Sid through Joe again, but he said that Malcolm was putting the mockers on that. It was a no-no.

Sid died on a minor American holiday called Groundhog Day, February 2, 1979, a year and a month after the Pistols' demise, three and a half months after Nancy's. According to folklore, the ground-hog emerges from hibernation. If he sees his shadow, six more weeks of wintry weather follows. Neither Sid the hamster nor Sid the groundhog saw his shadow that morning. They found his nude body

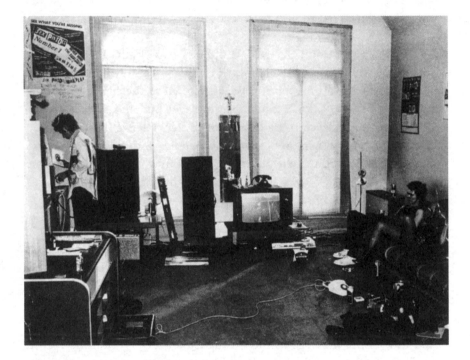

Life on Gunter Grove. Can you find the following? Arsenal cup game on box. John playing Reggae. Sid & Nancy drinking my booze. Gunners poster on wall. Guinness in abundance. Monopoly game on floor. Empty lager crate. Blessed crucifix on wall. Ancient Sex Pistols poster inscribed by fan, "I wish the fuck they would jurry, I'm getting impatient." (Paul Young)

just past noon in the Greenwich Village apartment of a twenty-two-year-old unemployed actress.

I was sitting in my front room when I heard about Sid's death. I got a phone call from Joe Stevens. It didn't seem to mean anything to me. It's funny, that. I kept thinking, Should I feel something here? I didn't. Not for years, actually. It was much later that it struck me as sad. I shoved it to the back of my mind. I knew it would happen, so . . . Quite frankly, the wrong person died. I was happy when Nancy went. I thought that was great, but I knew in my heart that Sid didn't kill her. I think he got set up. Sid would have probably gone to jail for a sizable amount of time, although now you get less time for murder than you do robbery. There is a lingering rumor that Sid was murdered. He was detoxified when he was in Riker's Island, but the night he came out, he was suddenly on drugs again. One night, a matter of hours, really. It's very curious. Was Sid set up to fall?

JULIEN TEMPLE: The most wonderful memory I have of Sid was as a member of the audience—before he joined the band. He was an extraordinary model of punk. I remember seeing him at a Clash gig. These drunk guys in the audience were hurling big beer glasses at the band and chiming for Led Zeppelin. Out from behind the stage came this figure, Sid. Suddenly, he ran as fast as he could from behind the drums, jumped from the stage, flew through the air and landed in the audience, on top of these guys, flailing away. It was like a kamikaze run because there was about ten of these big fat beer drinkers. You knew Sid was going to get beaten to shit. But he didn't care. That was his strength. He was fearless with this total belief that gave him a strange power.

I still think of Sid. The whole thing was awful for him. There's no point. He died, and that's the end of it. I wish he was around, but only the way he was originally. All that self-destruction was just too much. You watch someone deteriorate before your eyes in the space of a year, and that's it. They erase any good memories you have of them. Time after time, they get worse and worse and more offensive. Self-pity gets people into drugs. Sid was a lost little boy utterly beyond help, and like all arrogant teenagers, he knew it all, and that's all there was to it.

CHRISSIE HYNDE: The first time the Pretenders played in London I was nervous because everyone I knew was at the gig. I was dying. I was in the bar around the back of the club in a little place called

the Railway Pub having a drink. The place we were playing at was
up in West Hampstead and it was called the Moonlight Club, when
someone came up to me and said, "Wow, what about Sid?" I
looked at him and said, "What about Sid?" Then I realized no one
had told me Sid had died that day because they were afraid it
would bum me out before the gig. Instead, I found out right before
I went on! We used to do a punky version of an old Troggs song
called "I Can't Control Myself." I distinctly remember the night he
died because we played that song especially for Sid.

Nobody will ever conclusively solve the mystery of Sid's death
because it's all just Fantasy Island. No one will tell the truth about it,
and the tragedy is that it's all buried in drugs and the drug culture.
Death becomes those situations.

CHRISSIE HYNDE: I loved Sid. Where John liked colorful things, Sid
was into black leather jackets. He also didn't have the creativity
John had. It seemed like the punk thing was his last stand. His style
was unique. Before punk, only reggae was unique; everything else
had been recycled. Punk cleared the slate, but it was only temporary. It did some good for a few years; it brought things back to a
decent, honest level.

I was utterly appalled when I heard the damned urn with Sid's ashen
remains was dropped and smashed to the floor at Heathrow Airport. It
was common gossip at the time of Sid's death. Classic Sid mythology.
Sid was such a hopeless failure at everything, it was so typical. Such a
horrible way to end—just blowing around the air-conditioning at
Heathrow is kind of funny. At least he's occupied. What a marvelously
ironic way to end; it's so extreme, it's deeply hilarious. Poor sod. No
peace even for the dead.

What I knew the Pistols could be and what they sickeningly
became were two different things. The band thought they could
trundle on like the Rolling Stones ad infinitum pumping out the
same kind of sound, appeasing the same kinds of people. That's just
not the way I am. If there's no challenge in it, then I'm not interested. I formed PiL because I got bored with the extremist point of
view that I'd had in the Sex Pistols. PiL has had its successes and
its failures, but you've got to keep doing it. PiL is much more of a
democracy than the Sex Pistols, which was just a war, constant
arguing about the stupidest of things.

The glorification of Sidney at first was nice because when we took Sid in, what we had to do was make him instantly appreciated as a valid member of the band. The trouble was that he actually believed that to be the case, which of course it wasn't at first because he could neither play, record, nor contribute to songwriting. Technically he contributed zero, apart from the image of it all. That became too show bizzy for me. That was much more Malcolm's field than mine.

When we went our separate merry ways, I knew Malcolm would continue his own way. It was sad to see what they'd done to the Sex Pistols because I thought that toward the end, they trivialized us. They'd taken away the real importance. On the American tour I was writing PiL songs even though I didn't know they'd be PiL songs at the time. "Religion" and "Public Image" were being put together during the tour. "Low Life" was in my mind. Steve and Paul, during the sound checks, didn't want to know about any new songs. It was an impossible situation. When that happens, you've just got to call it a day and move on.

Sid showed a lot of interest in what I was doing and wanted to be a part and work with me. It would have been his first real contribution. When we hit San Francisco and he hit the drugs, that ended that right there and then. He went back into Nancy mode and didn't understand why I would not tolerate that. By that time, Sid was just into chaos for the sheer hell of it. Destroy everything. That's well and fine, but you don't destroy things offhand and flippantly. You've got to offer something in its place. Since I always have to have a point and purpose to everything I do, that's why people accuse me of being calculated. But it's the way I am. I always know my next move. I could never conjure up a death wish. This is all I have, life. I don't know what comes next, and frankly, I'm in no rush to find out. I didn't believe in playing the martyr just for the sheer hell of it, either. And to die over something as vaguely childish as rock 'n' roll is not on. Even though there's a lot of popularity in Sid's character, the people who buy the Sid myths, they don't buy records. They're wasters. That's the drug culture thing for losers and junkies, people who bemoan their sorry lot. I'm not part of that. I never was. I'll always go out and make sure it gets better. That's the difference between the Sid fanatic and the Johnny Lydon Appreciation Society. Life and death! There's nothing glorious in dying. Anyone can do it.

I managed to put together PiL—Public Image Limited—and package it in a credible way. I got the name *Public Image* from a book by that Scottish woman, Muriel Spark, who wrote *Prime of Miss Jean Brodie*. When I was in Italy, somebody introduced her writings to me. I checked out some of her other books when I went home. One of them was called *The Public Image*. It was all about this actress who was unbearably egotistical. I thought, Ha! The Public Image. Limited. Not as a company, but to be limited—not being as "out there" as I was with the Sex Pistols. I didn't have the enigma of the Sex Pistols dragging me down, but it was difficult at the start because many people wanted the Sex Pistols Part Two—particularly Virgin Records. They would recommend that I work with Paul and Steve on various projects. The answer would always be no.

HOWARD THOMPSON: The first time I saw the video of John and Public Image Limited doing "Public Image," I flipped. That song took exactly what the Pistols stood for and put it in a musical and very original context. It was a real step forward for John. As seriously as one could take him previously, now you knew he was coming through as an artist. He didn't need the safety pins and all the outrageous shock paraphernalia that surrounded the Sex Pistols. John has a lot to say, not only musically, but in sociological terms. He's a bright man. He's got a great opinion on many important issues. Unfortunately he's looked at by too many people as somebody who isn't serious, whereas he's as serious as a heart attack. John's done a lot with PiL. He's got a great repertoire behind him, and boy, hasn't it been colorful and interesting all along the way?

There was one really awful situation when Branson called me to his boat one day. This happened right after we released the second PiL album, *Metal Box*. "Come over. We'll have a few drinks. Ha ha ha ha." Lovely. I didn't know that it was a total trap. He had a tape there that Paul and Steve had sent him, and the idea was for me to sing over these Ramones rip-offs. They wanted to call themselves the Professionals. No. It was very bad music with shitloads of money as an incentive. I'd rather die. The implication was, "Look, you and PiL are going bankrupt fast. If you do this, it will only take a year out of your career. Then you can always go back to PiL later." They had forgotten who they were talking to.

RAMBO: I remember when Public Image first played the Rainbow in 1978 on Christmas Day and Boxing Day. He had all the Arsenal mob doing the security. We had Public Image T-shirts on. We done it well. Some West Ham people turned up to give us grief, but we didn't steam into people when it wasn't necessary.

People were changing and moving on. Why couldn't I?

For instance, I was never what you would call friends with Siouxsie, but I knew a lot of that crowd, the Bromley contingent. A few years after when I was with PiL, she moved across the street from Jeanette Lee, who worked with us at that time. Siouxsie came over, bragging about her new washing machine and spin dryer. She said we were all welcome to come over and wash our clothes. A washing machine party. You can imagine what I let rip. I couldn't sit there and take that from her. Housewife superstar. I took the piss at her for about twenty minutes, and she has never spoken to me since—all because of a washing machine. I thought it was so funny that this punked-out girl was coming across the street and telling me about her washing machine. The picture I can conjure up still is of her in her rubber-and-leather bondage wear. "Oh, it's a really good one! Why are you laughing?" Now she's acting like a dreadful housewife. After, she used to walk down the street and I'd open the window and shout out, "How's the washer?"

The Slits were one of the few punk bands I really liked. They were so shambolic. The idea of girls dressing so badly and not bothering to look pretty—without being ugly—and going on with the dolly bird image was great. If somebody forgot the song, well, too bad. Bang, crash, wallop their way through it. It was great anarchic stuff. A lot of the punk audience would just stand there with their bottom jaw dropped to the floor, appalled.

The Pistols had just broken up, and brother Jimmy had just formed his own group, the 4 be 2's. They asked me to come over to Ireland with them for a laugh. Within about forty-five minutes of getting off the plane, I was in deep shit. I had gone to the pub around the corner from the hotel. Two yobs copped an attitude with me, and unfortunately one of them was an off-duty policeman. I got done for GBH (grievous bodily harm) because I attacked two policemen's fists with my face several times.

I was charged with assaulting two police officers—no small thing. I got out on bail that Friday afternoon. At first it was no big deal, just a silly fine. But they wanted to make an example out of me. These two cops decided to push it, so they came back to the hotel that night and dragged me to the cop shop where I had just been released earlier that day. I was let out again and told to turn up in court on Saturday morning for an initial hearing.

Richard Branson paid for some English lawyers to come over. One of them had this upper-class, twitty English voice. "Ohhh Yawwww. Yourrr Honourrrr."

To say this irritated the judge is putting it mildly.

They canceled my bail and sentenced me automatically to six months. Then they transferred me and put me in Mountjoy Prison. From there on in it was hell on earth, and it looked like it was going to go on forever. A friend of mine offered to put up a brand-new BMW as collateral toward my release, but they wouldn't accept it. Then they said I needed an Irish address, so I gave them my uncle's in Cork. They wouldn't accept that, either, and went on a tirade about "damned kulchies," which is what Dubliners call people from the country whom they consider thick, ignorant louts.

Mountjoy was filled with IRA, UDA, psychopathic murderers, and the lot. I was lucky in this respect that the warders decided to make an example of me. They stripped me naked and threw me out in the exercise yard and hosed me down. The rest of the prisoners watched and figured I must be all right. If the warders hated me that much, I must have been doing something good. There I was on a Saturday night, we had one hour of TV a week, and what do the warders decide to put on to show the prisoners? Don Letts's *Punk Rock Movie*! I figured I was doomed. The Pistols opened the movie singing "God Save the Queen."

"It's him."

I squirmed. "Ouch . . ."

They put me in a cell with this so-called big-time jewel thief. I asked him, "What did you do?"

"I was walking home drunk one night," he answered, "and I threw a brick through this window. It had an iron grill on it, and the brick bounced back and knocked me out!" He got caught unconscious on the street. What a cruel world! He was my prison mate. Welcome to Ireland.

In the middle of the night two warders decided to come in and beat me with truncheons. You know the way they do: "Your blanket isn't straight!" The other prisoners started screaming, and I was all right from there on in. But there were so many lunatics, it might have gone any way at that point. I would get IRA chaps coming up and saying, "You're with us," but then they copped my accent, and suddenly I wasn't. Then the UDA came over and they said, "But your name's Lydon." I'd lost both ways because of my Irish name and my English accent. I was a doomed gang of one.

I learned to be vicious pretty quick in that environment. I was locked up for four days—felt like four years—before I was released on bail pending my appeal. My father flew into Ireland from London the day I was released from prison. We met with my new Irish lawyer in the hotel that evening. Later that night my father's hotel room was searched by the police for IRA weapons and fugitives.

The next morning he was sitting next to me in the courtroom, and I was shaking. We hired a local lawyer to help with the case. I was told if I lost my appeal, they would double the previous six-month sentence. The years were going by in front of me. Five. Ten. Fifteen. I was scared. I figured I could do six months, but a year wasn't too feasible. Mountjoy was a mad place.

I was convinced I was going to do time. There was this Gypsy woman before me being sentenced. She was done for nicking a watch. The judge said to the Gypsy woman, "Well, you bought this watch, and the watch was stolen. You gave seventy pounds for it. Now if I asked you to go back to the camp and find your seventy pounds, could you find the money for me?"

The woman said, "No, I can't find seventy pounds."

Then the judge said, "How come you found it for the watch?"

The woman answered, "I haven't got any more money."

So the judge said, "All right, I'll give you three months."

The Gypsy woman said to the judge, "Excuse me, Your Honor. I get a radio if I get three months, don't I?" The judge said yes. "Could you give me six?" she asked. "And I'll have two radios, then I can trade them in for a TV."

Up next, I was squirming on my seat—*Midnight Express* running through my brain. What's going to happen? People trying to bargain with the judge for radios and TVs.

Then my Irish lawyer came in. He said to the judge, "Hello, sir! How are you doing? I'll see you later on. We'll have a game of golf." Those were the first words out of the guy's mouth.

The whole case was eventually reduced to a hundred-pound fine.

I said, "That's fine!"

Then the two English lawyers came up to us, confused. "What happened? We missed something here. Did they give him a year?" My father told them it was over and dismissed, but I wasn't happy until I was on that damned plane. As far as I was concerned, anything could have happened.

LADBROKE GROVE, LONDON

DON LETTS: We used to frequent the Roebuck Pub because Jeanette
Lee and I managed a shop on the King's Road called Acme
Attractions. There were two happening shops on the King's Road at
the time—Acme Attractions and Sex. Prior to Sex, Vivienne used to
sell clothes to Teddy boys, and I used to go there before Acme
Attractions. Before the Pistols and Acme, I worked in some naff
high-fashion shops on the King's Road when I first found out about
Sex. Wow! I couldn't believe the designs. I was fooled by their stuff,
whereas John realized they were just copying old fifties stuff. One day
I remember looking at an old fifties magazine in the back of the shop,
and sure enough, I saw the things Sex basically ripped off. Vivienne
promised me a job in the shop when Malcolm was in America working with the New York Dolls. I used to go out with Vivienne occasionally, once to see Lou Reed. She gave me a crash course on a
white culture I hadn't been tuned into before—the Velvet
Underground and the New York Dolls. I ended up having a fight

with Westwood outside her shop when I went to work for Acme Attractions, which she saw as a rival. But she wouldn't give me a fucking job. Eventually Jeanette and I were banned from the shop.

JOHN LYDON: If Vivienne bothered to open the shop, because sometimes she wouldn't turn up—the final punch line was the price tag. That's why Acme Attractions really pissed her off. Acme sold original secondhand clothing, and that's what she was styling her clothes after at the time. I liked Acme more than Viv's shop. Sid and the rest of us would buy our gear there and then we'd go to Viv's to look at the prices. I got a job at Sex eventually because that was the only way I could afford the rubber and see-through T-shirts.

LETTS: Black people didn't wear earrings or rubber clothes, and I was the first person in Brixton to do all this shit. Once, on my own, I put on one of those gold rubber T-shirts upstairs in this house. I couldn't get it off, but I was too embarrassed to tell anybody. So I'm in this bedroom with this rubber T-shirt and it's up around my neck. I was dying and I couldn't breathe, so I ended up having to hook myself onto a bedpost and rip the fucking T-shirt off.

JEANETTE LEE: The first time I met Sid, he and Don did not hit it off. Sid was very soft and easy to push around, and Don was never easy on soft people. Sid would come into Acme and hang around the shop and just be a bit gormless, really. Don was awful to him and would try to throw him out and be rude to him. The first time Sid ever spoke to me, he came up and said, "Excuse me! Do you know how I can make my hair stay in a quiff like Bryan Ferry?" Then he showed me this picture of Roxy Music in *Nineteen* or *Honey*. "I love Roxy Music and Bryan Ferry and I don't know how to get my hair like that."

LYDON: This is how we know Sid—as this soft guy. He was very effeminate because that was the scene then. He came from his Dave Bowie, Roxy Music angle. Is my nail varnish right? It was the only viable thing happening at the time. There was nothing to do except dress up, be ludicrous, take some sulfate, have a few tins of beer and, if you were lucky, a joint.

LETTS: We sold Sid Keith Moon's jacket and told him it was Elvis Presley's jacket. The people who sold it to us told us it was Elvis's, but it was used in the movie *Stardust* and Keith Moon wore it. I wore the jacket first, then we sold it to Sid, then John wore it, then Viv Albertine wore it, then Palmolive wore it. All these kids used to come into the shop, and we used to like them and give them the clothes and feed them. It wasn't my money anyway. We were redistributing the wealth. In 1977 I became the deejay at the Roxy because the accountant at Acme, Andy Czezowski, started the club. I took the job at first for the money. I thought the punks were just a bunch of crazy white people. I didn't really tune into it. When I became the deejay and started meeting them, I picked up on what they were doing. I got the job first, and then got all my black mates to work there. Everybody who worked there, besides Andy, was black. We used to make joints before we went to work to sell to the punks over the counter. The people would come up and say, "Give me two beers and a spliff. No, make that two spliffs and a beer." They couldn't roll Jamaican cones.

LEE: The Roxy was only open for a hundred days, by the way, but it seemed like forever. One night when Don and I were there—we were only about nineteen—we had taken real purple haze acid. Don was deejaying on acid, and he had this cyst on his eye. Then Don disappeared from the club for about an hour when the band was on. When he came back, he had been to the eye hospital and had the cyst removed from his eye while he was on acid. He had his head in a clamp, and they took this thing off his eye, then he came back and continued deejaying.

LETTS: There is this myth about how reggae and punk came together. There were literally no punk records to play when the Roxy started, so I had to play something I liked, which was reggae. I guess I did turn a few people on to it. The crowd wanted to hear more reggae. John was already into reggae before the Roxy anyway. There was a famous reggae artist called Dr. Alimantado whom John promoted by playing his record on Capital Radio one day.

LYDON: Reggae was the only other radical music that was completely underground and not played on the radio. It wasn't played on the air until I did that appearance on "The Tommy Vance Show" on Capital. Then suddenly you'd get Joe Strummer and the Clash say, "We always loved reggae." But those fucks never did. They were not brought up with it the same way I was.

LETTS: We turned each other on through our different cultures. They liked me because I gave them access to Jamaican culture, and they turned me on to a white culture that didn't fucking exist before they came along. Punk was a focal point because there were a lot of people walking around dissatisfied, disinterested, with no hope and no future. I didn't speak to John for a while at first because there was something there. It was a threat-to-my-space kind of thing. He was captivating a lot of people's attention at that time, and I was a bit standoffish—just a bit of jealousy, really. Any of the guys who were

"I want you to know that I hate you, baby." (John Gray)

happening—like John and a few others—I respected from a distance. My way to do that was to not speak to him. I somehow got around to talking to John. It was some kind of respect, and we literally picked up on each other's vibes. I could see that John was a serious dude because there were very few people around during those times who gave off that aura. It took time for us to get to know each other, whereas people like Sid, I was messing around straight away. John had that older look, and I had my dark glasses and dreadlocks. I started taking him to reggae clubs. We went to a place called the Four Aces in Dalston, which is the heaviest reggae club in London. No white people went in there. The only white person there was John, because I took him. Everybody left John alone. We black people had a respect for him because he came across as a real dude. He wasn't created by the media. He seemed real to us. Wherever we went, people left him alone. He could walk into places white people could never go with total immunity. It was amazing that Johnny Rotten was so acceptable to the Rastas in London. They might not have liked his music, but it was like outlaws banding together. We all felt like society's outlaws.

LYDON: Don and I first said hello and hung out after a Pistols' gig at the Nashville. We went back to Forest Hill and spent the whole night rapping on about reggae or anything. Don didn't know, but it was the night I was frustrated and getting ready to quit the Pistols. Going to those reggae clubs gave me a lift.

LETTS: John used to come visit me in Forest Hill quite a bit. I was a deejay, and I had a car and money. We'd have Jeanette, John, the Slits, some of the Banshees, the Adverts, Neurotic Steve, and Keith Levene sitting around the apartment listening to reggae and burning spliffs. I would be driving around in the car with John, and my friends would see me with a punk in my car. They would take the piss out of me, then realize it was John. "Nuff respect, Rasta."

LYDON: Don used to drive this Zodiac—a great old English car from the fifties. It was great when Yah Mon Rasta was driving with fifty punks in the backseat. Sometimes we'd see some Teds on the street and drive by slowly.

LETTS: After Acme, Jeanette and I opened this fucking Boy shop in 1977. We didn't really like it because it was a total rip from Sex. By that time Saturdays became this meeting point for all the punks on the King's Road. They would pass by our shop on the way to Sex. Then the Teds got wind of this, and they used to go down there as well. Every single Saturday there were running battles. I used to get personally involved with the fights when I would see six Teds beating up one punk. I ran down the street and chased these Teds off with a mallet. Punks used to come and hide in the shop because the Teds were after them. Then next week you'd see six punks chasing one Ted. I even remember helping a Ted because I was impartial. Each gang would always pick on the most pathetic punk or the most pathetic Ted.

LYDON: Worse, when the Chelsea football club was at home, you'd get the Chelsea boot boys running down there after the away supporters. You'd get punks, Teds, away supporters, and football hooligans all together. You would see trouble, and because of the chaos, it was a very interesting place to be.

BILLY IDOL: It got really fucking heavy on the London streets. I'd stay off the King's Road when they had all that trouble with the punks and the Teds. All the punks would meet at one end, all the Teds would meet at the other, and then they would converge. The Teds were totally right wing, but people in England are always looking for a fight.

Before Thatcher was elected the police became even more heavy-handed. A few times we got hassled by the police on our way to Louise's in my van. The cops used to stand there laughing at us when they saw all of us piling out of the van. It got scary because we were the first people who looked like that. To them we looked like we were from some weird horror show. They just couldn't believe all the gear we used to wear.

LETTS: I remember when John bought the house on Gunter Grove, he lived like the Addams Family. He had a cat named Satan that he trained to fetch things. I'd never seen that before. One time we were there in the house bored on sulfate. I used to be so skinny from using sulfate. It was big in those days and so bloody cheap, cheaper than booze. One night I took a canister of gas and sucked in a whole load of it. But I took in a mixture of air and gas, and when I lit it, the flame shook the room. Boom! All the hair on my face—including my eyebrows—was gone.

LEE: Some fading pop stars would call the house, and they could never gain access. I remember Nico used to come around and bang on the door and yell, "John, John. You must let me in." I remember when Iggy Pop used to phone up. I'd answer the phone, a total stranger, and he'd say, "Is John there? I'm thinking of getting a new guitarist.

What do you think of Brian James of the Damned?" There were always people begging to come in. John could say one word and diminish people, and we'd have to sit and watch them. It was horrible. There were these lunatics who used to bring these T-shirts around that they had painstakingly hand-drawn and leave them for John. John would just give them away. There was always this guy who phoned up all the time named Victor Vomit. "Hello, Victor Vomit here. You don't know me. I'm really a punk. I could be good for you."

LYDON: A not sane girl came over. She had escaped from the hospital in Durham, then she took a train to London. She told me to destroy all plastic in the house because that's what they were attracted to. She also said she would kill herself if I didn't marry her.

LETTS: That was the best period of my life. People would come around Gunter Grove and would be dying to get in. I remember John abusing these people and me feeling really embarrassed. He sure knocked hero worship out the window. He owned the whole house, but there was this flat below and these people lived there. Imagine all those years not knowing who lived in the basement flat. They must have been terrified of John. He has these massive speakers playing reggae, Peter Hammill, Captain Beefheart, and Can ridiculously loud. They never came up to speak to him.

The Pistols were doing something, instead of the hero worship, I thought, Hey, I can do it, too. That was the message. It demystified the existing music movement. It was about using what you had to get what you needed. Personally, I saw that the band scene seemed to be covered. I couldn't play anything anyway, so I picked up a super-eight camera—inspired by John Lydon. I didn't know what the hell I was doing, but somebody from the media saw me and wrote, "Don Letts is making a film." Hey, that's not a bad idea. Jeanette used to help with the lights, and I'd run the camera. My only talent was I knew what to point it at. We'd go out and film these bands, then go back to Forest Hill and chop up the film with cello tape, and we made this movie. Basically, I reinvented myself through my punk experience. Think about it. I was this guy in dark glasses managing a shop. Then punk came along and I thought, Fuck me, I'm going to have some of that! I had to feel like I was contributing. I picked up the camera, made *The Punk Rock Movie*, and documented all the events I thought were interesting and ridiculous. My movie was an example of the whole movement. I was inspired to do it. It became *The Punk Rock Movie* through the media . . . . I went on from there to make videos. But from punk, my experience came from John's culture. At that time there wasn't many black examples of alternative lifestyles. It was magnetic; I felt an affiliation. The Pistols' era made people realize the creative potential within themselves. The shit I learned then still works for me now. I make videos for lots of people, but the thing that turns me on lately is I have this high-eight camera and I've gone out and started doing this punk stuff again. That's the stuff that's really turned me on. I'm telling you this so this book doesn't become some sort of nostalgic bullshit. What worked then is still really relevant now. It's obvious in hip hop today, punk's equivalent today. Until hip hop came along, none of the other movements since punk had that content and weight beyond the music. Again, it's coming from people who have nothing and use the least to make the most.

LYDON: The whole point was to get off your ass and do it yourself. If you weren't doing it, then you weren't no good only because you're damned lazy. The whole rock 'n' roll trip of the previous generation was a cliché. Subconsciously everything was shaken off that happened before. I was a young chap who thought I was severely ugly and nobody would ever speak to me. There was this movement full of people feeling exactly the same way. It was a social way of meeting equally ugly people, the Equally Ugly Club. There wasn't those prejudices. Sitting in Louise's, lesbians didn't have to act butch and beat us up. Gays didn't have to overreact around us. There was no need to define gay or lesbian, with previous generations trying desperately to be weird just for the sake of it. That was immediately redundant. It didn't make any difference after that. That was the most enjoyable aspect of it. I used to like that. You weren't threatened by sexuality from people. You could just be yourself. That was a very important part of the Sex Pistols era. It wasn't an antisex thing or a consciously premeditated attitude. We weren't going to play the games according to the previous shitheads.

LETTS: The English press painted articles on how to dress like a punk. It was amazing how ugly people could make themselves. It amazed me how the ones who picked up the *Daily Mirror* newspaper secondhand would get the wrong end of the stick. The secondhand punks looked fucking ridiculous. The inner circle was very stylish. Nobody we knew had staples in their noses or mothball earrings. It was based on good common sense because those things bloody hurt. But you'd see the later punks come into the shops and they would have a safety pin in their cheek or their nose. It was all sore and infected. The more they spoke, the more it hurt, and they would suffer.

LYDON: After the Pistols broke up, Branson wanted to sign up a load of reggae bands, and the only white person he knew in the world who knew about reggae was me. I told him I couldn't go there alone, so I roped in two associates—Don Letts and Dennis Morris.

LETTS: I was home one night doing what I normally do—playing reggae—and I get this phone call from John at one o'clock in the morning. "Do you want to come to Jamaica?" I figured his logic was to take black men—dreadlocks are real cool. But I had never been to Jamaica before! I said, "Yes, of course I'll go." Luckily I had a passport, and in a matter of hours, I went to the airport with a plastic carrier bag with an extra pair of underpants and my super-eight camera.

LYDON: We had no visas. We didn't know the flight stopped in Miami, and the security asked for our visas. We were escorted by armed guards to the transfer flight, and both Don and Dennis are looking at me and saying, "Where are they marching us off to? What have you brought us into?"

LETTS: I ended up in Jamaica for the first time through John, and it was a major trip! I was going home to my so-called roots because when I landed there it was almost as alien to me as it was to John. I was thinking, Wow! Where the fuck am I? John's thinkin', Yah, mon, everyt'ing's cool. In Jamaica, I met all these people I heard about for years. Branson wanted us to sign up reggae artists, so the word got around: White man on island with lots of money. Every single artist except Bob Marley who was anybody made an exodus to the Sheraton Hotel in Kingston. Branson had taken a whole floor and given John and me each a room. We met Big Youth, U Roy, I Roy, Burning Spear, Abyssinians, Prince Far I. These were all mythical names to me.

LYDON: We just sat at the pool and ate lobster all day. When it cost two dollars and you're not even paying for it, we would have two, three, four in the boiler. The staff would look at Don in shock and say, "Rasta eat shellfish? Rasta eat lobster?"

Don said, "Come and check my accent. I'm an English Rasta. That's a different culture."

They'd ask again, "Really? Rasta in England eat lobster?"

It was illegal to flash your dreadlocks, so Don had to keep them in a big hat. Rastas weren't allowed in the hotel, but because Branson was bankrolling it, the whole place was covered with people in queues trying to get a record deal or some bucks. The hotel hated it. You'd see dreadlocks floating around the swimming pool.

LETTS: Since we were in Jamaica, I really wanted to visit my grandparents, whom I had never seen in my entire life. Who do I go with? Mr. Motherfucker Lydon. What do we go in? A white Cadillac stretch limo with chauffeur in Jamaica in 1978 during the worst political violence on the island. You could literally hear gunshots at night, and we're cruising to this weird address in the back of a white limo. The address was like "left at the mountain, right at the bird's nest," etc. We were driving up to see the grandparents I've never seen in my life. We pull up in front of this hut in this white Cadillac. I met my grandparents, but they freaked. We just stood there facing each other and froze. There was this standoff, and they looked at this limo in the middle of this poor shanty town. The driver was loading mangos into the boot of the limo. It was the most unreal, surreal situation I've ever had in my life. I managed to say, "I'm Donovan, your grandson from England." They looked at me like I was an alien. They looked over at John and back at my dreadlocks—which were anti-Establishment over there. I said, "Look, I'll come back in a minute," walked back to the limo, and we drove off. I've never seen my grandparents since. I was upset! I couldn't speak to them and they couldn't speak to me.

John and I met U Roy, granddaddy of deejay reggae music. You get up with the sun over there, so we'd go round to U Roy's and get high with him at eight in the morning. U Roy would make up a big pipe of weed in his backyard. Each cup held a quarter of an ounce of weed and a half an inch of tobacco in it. John asked them why they did that. "Blend, mon. Blend, mon." I tried to smoke this huge pipe and immediately coughed my guts out. My man John picks up the pipe and somehow draws up the biggest load of smoke. I'm ashamed! The guy upstaged me in my roots backyard. U Roy was saying, "Yes, Rotten, cool Rasta."

LYDON: I couldn't walk, talk, or think for two hours, a major, major puff. I did it because I'd seen the album covers. Big draw, then hand on face.

LETTS: U Roy ran the sound system, this huge outdoor disco he takes out. We drive about twenty miles with U Roy, fucked out of our heads. While they're setting up the sound system, John and I sat down underneath a tree and nodded off. We woke up after it was over. The dance lasted for six hours with the loudest reggae music in the world, and we missed the whole thing. U Roy woke us up and said it was time to go. "Good gig, ya." Embarrassing shit. Everybody fell over themselves to meet us, take us to the most beautiful places, and give us the strongest herb. I got a crash course on my whole reggae culture in four weeks.

That's when Malcolm sent Boogie Tiberi to Jamaica. We saw Boogie hiding in the bushes by the pool of the Sheraton with his camera. He'd be filming John up on the balcony.

LYDON: He never asked my permission to film me.

LETTS: At night, we'd say, "Where's the Boogie bunch? Which bush were they in now?"

The local kids would come up and say, "Ya, mon, some white dudes in da bush over dere."

We'd be on the beach and you'd see this skinny white guy in shorts trying to film John. Big Youth rang up to say, "Some white guys are talkin' about ya. Been sayin' you give dem permission to talk about you."

I said, "No, wrong." He had them off the island in about an hour and a half.

See, John fucks up a lot of people, and he got me in trouble, too. John and I got invited to Joni Mitchell's villa through a mutual Jamaican friend. We were at the house, and there was this music playing. We must have been smoking as usual, and we're listening to this music and I said, "What is this shit? Why don't you take it off?"

Joni says, "Well, it's my new album, actually." I didn't recognize her music because I was so stoned. It was so embarrassing.

LYDON: We ended up there because we foolishly said at this hotel bar that we liked Joni Mitchell. We got there and both giggled at just how awful the music was we were listening to. We didn't know it was her new album, but we offended her, so it was time to leave the house immediately. I laughed hysterically.

LETTS: Punk was weird enough in London, so imagine the ultimate punk being in Jamaica. Some people knew he was Johnny Rotten. Number one. Gold discs. John walked around in a long black coat and a big hat because he didn't want to get a suntan. Jamaicans have vivid imaginations and are very into westerns, and John looked like the baddest motherfucker around. He looked like Lee Van Cleef.

LYDON: Walking through the marketplaces in downtown Kingston was always pure hell. They'd seen too many movies.

LETTS: You wonder what you must have looked like to them! When I go to funny parts of Ireland, they react to me just like that. They like to pull on my hair when I travel outside of Dublin. I think that's why John and I get on so well. In the development of England's history, there was a time when John's mob—the Irish—and blacks and dogs were thrown together. There used to be signs in the hotels and places for rent that said . . .

LYDON and LETTS: *No Irish, no blacks, no dogs!*

LETTS: I'm not sure who got top billing. Knowing the English, the dogs got the top billing. Irish and Jamaican people are definitely alike in spirit. No two ways about it.

LYDON: This is why they mate. In all the best areas like Brixton and Kilburn, they get on bloody well with each other in a pub. It gets fucked when people talk English shit. But Irish and Jamaicans definitely have a common bond. Irish moss is a seaweed drink, and when the English used to starve the fucking daylights out of them and steal their potatoes, the Irish ended up eating seaweed. When Don and I were in Jamaica, we would go into town and buy records in a place called Irish Town. We thought it was so ironic; all they had was Jim Reeves records and that was it. The older folks enjoy country and western, Perry Como, and Jim Reeves, and it was outrageous to see the same titles the older Irish people liked.

LETTS: What about this "shit sandwich" story? Was that ever true?

LYDON: It was at Nora's house. I arrived there and she said, "Of course I'm faithful," and there was Vic Godard of Subway Sect hiding under the table. That was it. That was your starter for ten. There were all these horrible Hell's Angels chaps there, and everyone decided an hour later that they were hungry. I was with a couple of mates, and Nora was foolish enough to let us cook the food. Now Nora would never eat anything we cooked in the kitchen, so we served it to Nora's friends. It was literally a shit in the frying pan cooked in olive oil. Then we all wanked into this fucking omelet—one egg and at least four good doses. They all thought it was the best food they ever ate. The shit sandwich was the killer. It was deep fried and put between two toasted slices of bread. They ate it and thought it was corned beef.

LEE: I remember us all being in a pub one night on Tottenham Court Road quite far down near Warren Street. We had been to the Scala and we just walked into this pub. I have this memory that John was wearing a white jacket and Sid came into the pub with Nancy. Sid left Nancy alone and came up to our table. I remember John said, "Leave it alone, Sidney. Get rid of it. It's bad news. Get rid of it." Nobody liked Nancy. She was such a low-life.

LETTS: I saw both Sid and Nancy just before they went to America. I had them come to this office to sign a release for *The Punk Rock Movie*. Sid came up with Nancy, and they both were really out of it. Sid had this knife with a blade six inches long. I was trying to get him to sign something, and he was sticking Nancy with this knife, but not really deep. She was saying to Sid, "Stop it. Stop." Not long after, all that shit happened. All the things we heard were just headlines in the papers. It was all getting distorted like *Valley of the Dolls* or something. I remember seeing a screening of *The Great Rock 'n' Roll Swindle* and of John playing in America. My heart really went out to John when I saw the images of him playing to the American crowds. I saw newspaper headlines, and the *Swindle* was my only way to see what happened there. I felt strong emotions seeing my mate in front of all those people—this thing coming to a massive halt in such a devastating way, leaving people dead and all that kind of shit. Here was John, the guy we hung out with in the Roebuck pub.

JULIEN TEMPLE: The film (*The Great Rock 'n' Roll Swindle*) was an interesting document of contradiction—to make the things the band really did seem like lies and make things they didn't do seem true. We tried to look at different sides of the story as gloriously unstable. The idea was to tell lies and play with the myths and cause them to explode. The Sex Pistols were about placing a charge inside your head and questioning what you thought about the world. By blowing it up, you were forced to think about the fragments and what it meant.

LEE: Just as the movie *The Great Rock 'n' Roll Swindle* started, they were dragging an effigy of John through the street. Then they burned it! I was horrified.

LYDON: The opening sequence was a quality act—the burning of the effigy of Johnny Rotten was excellent. It was also the best thing. It was filmed so brilliantly, I thought, Out, I want to die. It's the end of my life. Malcolm's come up with a stroke of real class here. But luckily it didn't last. From there on in the movie was just rubbish.

JULIEN TEMPLE: It was a major problem working around John's nonparticipation in the sense that there were two primal energies, John and Malcolm. At the time I believed in both aspects. When we made the film John had already broken with Malcolm and would have nothing to do with the film, so I tried to represent John in terms of him performing the songs and keep him as an important element.

LETTS: All this Pistols stuff—hanging out in the Roebuck to playing to the American audiences—only took place within two years. Living it felt like over five years. I'm only realizing now what to tell my kids. I'll just show them *The Punk Rock Movie.*

LEE: What about that fantastic police raid? This was during the early PiL period, probably one of the only times where we had gone to bed that night. Any other day at six in the morning, we would all still be sitting up. I was downstairs, and suddenly I woke up and heard all these feet on the ceiling. I lay there and immediately thought it was a police raid. I jumped up and ran around the house, saying to everyone, "We're being raided! Get rid of everything." Dave Crowe had a motorcycle in his room he had started dismantling.

LYDON: I had a package of weed upstairs, which the police didn't see.

LEE: Someone had given John this big sword for his birthday, so when John came down the stairs, not knowing who it was, he pointed this big sword at the police.

LYDON: They searched the whole of the upstairs flat and tore everything apart. They ripped my mattress and ripped up the floorboards in the bedroom upstairs. Their police dog chased the cat around the house. Eventually the police were disappointed and were ready to leave. I had a big bag of marijuana hidden in the teapot, but because the cat decided to stand on the speaker near the teapot, the police thought the dog was barking at the cat. Thank God for Satan! They took me down to the cop shop anyway after smashing down my front door. I didn't know if anybody was left in the house. Then they made me walk all the way home down the Fulham Road in my bare feet, pajamas, and red dressing gown. That was it for me. I had to get out of Britain. There was no point in being in London any longer. Very quickly after that, I fled to New York.

WHERE'S THE MONEY?

Malcolm was already putting together *The Great Rock 'n' Roll Swindle*, which had already started and stopped several times before with wanker film directors like Russ Meyer. Malcolm took Paul and Steve to Rio, and they did that farce down there with Ronnie Biggs. Then they went back to London, and from what I was told, Malcolm carried on auditioning for other Johnny Rottens. They even conducted the auditions at the Astoria in London's Finsbury Park—a real insult because this place is directly opposite where I lived all my life. I know this because friends of mine went down there and tried out for the part, along with various Johnny Rotten imitators. Even my little brother Martin went over. This all happened a long time after Rio. They were trying to get the Sex Pistols going again, but with a replacement for me. Malcolm desperately wanted to continue the Pistols, but he really couldn't. Joe Public wouldn't have been too interested. There was obviously going to be no Sid. Sid was still around because they used him in the movie, but they didn't have any intention of keeping him in the band. They were just using him. I know who won the audition—a wanker called Ten Pole Tudor.

PAUL COOK: We never figured on carrying on with another singer. There was never a serious audition to find another Johnny Rotten. That was done pretty much for the film. We couldn't have replaced Rotten and gone on calling ourselves the Sex Pistols, so we concentrated on cutting a few tracks for the film soundtrack and that was it. Steve was a lot more involved with the film than I was. I knew it was all over. I started to drift off, but Malcolm was obsessed with the film. We didn't know at the time, but he was finishing it off with our money. I hung around waiting for Steve to finish the film so we could start something else.

JULIEN TEMPLE: I eventually became disillusioned by the hypocrisy and the lying that went on. Malcolm wanted to take over the film and felt he should have all the credit. It wasn't going according to any plan. By the end stages of the film, it was imploding. It was like an atomic chain reaction going on inside the camp. Malcolm had the feeling that the band was kind of irrelevant and conventional, and it was him that was responsible for the brouhaha and the importance. He was seduced by that vision of himself in the film even though he was always aware that we were creating this provocative distortion, a preposterous tale.

That's the kind of underhandedness that was going on. Malcolm still wanted to use me to prop up his crap idea of a movie, but he didn't pay me. He claimed that I had nothing to do with it and I could just fuck off and die. That's when I decided to take legal action. It took me eight years to beat the bastard at his own game. Persistence does win through.

The way I fought the case was not me versus them, but rather for equal shares among me, Paul, Steve, and Sid's estate. I'm sorry, I can't play dirty. I only play fair. I don't like to cheat people. Even when they are trying to cheat me, that's not really the point. Paul and Steve were trapped in a kind of no-man's-land because Malcolm held the lease where they lived. It took them a long time to turn around. When the case *finally* went to court, they switched dramatically. They saw that it wasn't me versus the world and there was something in it for them. They saw the dollar bills and the pound notes, of course.

STEVE JONES: Cook and I got caught in the middle of the court battle between John and McLaren, and we didn't know which way to go. I was on McLaren's side from day one because I knew him and trusted him. Then I realized we were going to get screwed if I stayed on his side. So it wasn't a case of going over to John's side, it was a case of getting my share.

I didn't really have a dialogue with Steve and Paul until six months before the court case. We didn't speak at all for a long time, eight years. It wasn't that we were enemies or anything like that. It just never occurred to me or to them, either. We get along fine now, although it's still a bit strained—as indeed it has to be. I think they must feel slightly embarrassed about their original positions. It was rather a shitty thing to do. They didn't believe in me at the time, and Malcolm was pulling strings. They were just going with the flow. That's all Paul and Steve ever did. If you were to ask them what any of this was about, I don't think they'd be able to tell you at all. They didn't realize any of the implications or the long-range value of it all. It was always just rock 'n' roll to them—sex and birds, and that's it.

BILLY IDOL: Steve Jones came up to me after the Pistols broke up. We were in the Speakeasy, and he asked me, "What am I going to do, Bill? My band's gone."

The later works with the post-Rotten Pistols lacked humor, the very things the Pistols were all about. We might have frightened the living daylights out of people, but there was a deep humor in it. We worked on several levels, and going to meet Ronnie Biggs, a failed train robber, in Rio is hardly covering new territory. Deterioration set in. It all became very mean-spirited.

STEVE JONES: After all the excitement of the Pistols was over, I was left with a massive hole inside me. I had to fill it one way or another. I just happened to run into heroin, and it helped me survive a few years until even that stopped working.

British pop culture is now much more into the public mainstream forefront. They don't care about war in the Middle East. That's nothing to do with them. Samantha Fox wins every time over the Middle East. This is the nature of the British. They are very trivia-orientated, gossipy villagers. The English press are like those horrible old women peeping behind the lace curtains, watching the neighbors going in and out. Dot Cotton from "EastEnders"—that's Britain. All of this is very well manipulated by the public school boy system. They own the newspapers and run the show, keeping things down to that trivial level of permanent bitchiness. Real truths never come out because people aren't very interested. They've been denied access to the truth for so long that it really wouldn't matter since the working class tend to read the *Sun* and the *Daily Mirror*—two scabby papers that are nothing but tits on page three and gossip about dirty vicars. A few pop stars are thrown in with their drug overdoses or late night parties. That's about it. People don't know or bother to find out. There's access to all kinds of information, but the English are so lazy. If it doesn't come through the door every morning, then they just don't bother with it. It's the isolation of being British. Papers like the *Manchester Guardian* are looked upon as snobbish. A working-class person wouldn't even dream of buying it. There's too many words, and it's an awkward size, a lot like the guy in the New York subway reading *The New York Times*. It's odd when I hear some Americans clamoring for more isolationist political policies. They don't realize what that leads to. You'll just be narrow-minded and stupid like the British. You can't go through life with blinkered vision. That's why chaps like me are a real nuisance. They certainly don't want to see the likes of me smashing the shit out of some public school bastard in court. I'm attacking the very system they love—lies, cheating, fraud. If you attack that, you attack being British.

If the same stuff they put into the American supermarket tabloids were put in the *Sun* or the *Daily Mirror,* people in Britain would seriously believe it. The class system keeps it that way; it suits them fine. When it came to the Pistols, the press jumped on all the wrong things. The idea right from the start was to just let the press say whatever they wanted. We knew they'd do that anyway, so there was no point in denying anything. They had a field day. So did we. We were using them, but they dropped us when it came to court case time. My other band, Public Image, was working well by then, and I'd earned myself a lot of respect for the work I was doing. They couldn't call me a foul-mouthed yob anymore. I must have been a complete enigma.

"What is he up to?" That is the constant English press thing about me. They always put a question mark after my name. "Is this a joke, is he taking the piss out of us?" It's a pretty long joke, isn't it? They don't trust me. They think I'm some big elaborate hoax. Maybe I am. It's good not to be trusted. It certainly keeps people alert, and that's far better. I'd rather be hated or loved, rather than just thought of as all right or nice. "Nice" is the worst insult you could pay anybody. It means you are utterly without threat, without values. Nice is a cup of tea.

My values have hardly changed from day one as a boy in Finsbury Park. I don't like cheating, fraud, or lying. I can't do those things. I've tried, and it doesn't work, a bloody hard line to live by, particularly being in the music business with its many compromises. That in itself can be conceived as a lie. The length of time it takes trying to get the money out of the record company, you have to make all kinds of promises. That's the only time I enjoy fibbing and lying.

It became necessary to surround myself with lawyers and accountants for the case. There are some things you cannot do on your own; anything to do with the law is one of them, and finance is another.

When I got back to London after the end of the Pistols, I got in touch with a lawyer named Brian Carr through Gloria Knight, who worked at the *Sunday Mirror*—ironically, the wife of the editor! She figured I needed a lawyer, but I didn't know any. She suggested Brian, and I went and checked him out. I don't think he had anything to do with the music industry until he met me. But he loves a good legal fight, so he took on the case.

He was very good at keeping the hounds off and pursuing contracts. Since then, he's worked with many people in the music industry. Others followed me in, like the Clash and Spandau Ballet. It worked out fine. We got a barrister through Brian, and it took an awful long time for my case against Malcolm to reach court because British law is extremely slow. That's the whole idea of it. The system wants to grind you down so you'll give up. Brian Carr helped me out with business and helped me form PiL. He was useful, and I've learned a lot from him.

The court case against Malcolm was always touch and go because so much evidence was difficult to assemble. Funds weren't confirmed, and little was documented. Taxes weren't paid for a long time. Tax bills for the Pistols were sent to me personally. It didn't matter to Inland Revenue. For instance, if a husband runs away and leaves the wife, doesn't she have to accept the financial burden? Income tax people don't care. "You're one of them. We can't find the others. You'll do." That's one of the very last few things that Malcolm's office managed to handle well. They gave the tax people my address, and it scared the shit out of me, but it also dug my heels in a lot firmer. Creditors came crashing through my door. It toughened me up; I was determined not to back down. Again, another sink-or-swim situation. You have to get through it; you can't run away.

I remember how it started. Malcolm had presented us with a management agreement. It was late that evening when we went to Malcolm's lawyer's office; it was dark, and there was no one in the building. We were definitely pressured into signing. Nobody was given separate legal representation. I do remember being annoyed that it was sign quickly or else. It was that stressful. The whole thing stank to me. The office was tiny and smelly. The whole thing was too Dickensian. It reminded me of a Charles Dickens setup, only I didn't feel like Oliver Twist. There was no porridge.

As for our management contract with Malcolm, it was very crummy when I look back on it, and I know that Malcolm didn't understand it, either. He couldn't have. Where would be the benefit in a crap deal? As a manager, if you want to continue—and Malcolm did definitely want to continue—you can't formulate a reputation on crap deals. He is a great thinker and a waffler, but he's not very good at executing. So I fought him on the band's behalf. All on my own. Eventually we went to court—*Lydon vs. Glitterbest*. Malcolm thought he could turn it into another jamboree. He didn't quite realize just how purposeful I can be. I put together what I thought could be quite a case, which was actually quite frail. I was worried, and my lawyer was definitely worried, too, because we had no idea what the other side was going to come up with as a defense. If Malcolm had bothered to get off his stupid egomaniac arse, he could have done some serious damage to me. I had a telegram from my lawyer three days before the court date, advising me not to pursue my case. That's how tight it was. Malcolm could possibly have won it. In fact, I know he could have, but he was too busy playing the circus ringmaster. He missed the point and had to settle out of court, which made him give us everything. It was like a poker game. We both had empty hands.

Although I had rights and all those wonderful things on my side, they don't mean shit in a courtroom. Didn't mean crap. That just means it will go on for ten fucking years with everything frozen. Malcolm tried to take the name *Rotten* from me. I was legally obliged not to use it for one or two years. I had to get that out of the way first. By then the press got used to calling me Lydon, anyway.

All this is very odd. The British financial press were not interested in the court case at all. They never, ever reported on the details. The music press was not interested in my case. They would only write minor pieces about it without bothering to be accurate. They were very flippant about it because that's the system. It was an interesting situation, but they didn't want to pursue the subject of musicians' rights. I can't think of any other reason. Again, the music papers work for the Establishment, not the other way around. They don't like it when a musician threatens the Establishment, and Malcolm as the manager was part of that Establishment. Malcolm was part of the system. The press is the system. They're all connected. They don't like to see bands in any position of power. Particularly when the *artiste* wins! It turns it all on its head, then it's not in their control anymore. The whole lot of them work hand and foot together. If the musicians were in control, it really wouldn't leave much place for them since they're all part of the same old school-tie network. I know it sounds like paranoia, but it's deeply connected; the management system, the business world, the editorials. There was no value to them in me winning the court case. I thought it would have made marvelous press, certainly worth splattering over the worst tabloids. But no. Very odd.

I loved being in court. It went on for three days, just reading these silly affidavits. We made a motion to get it all into the witness box. That would have been the crunch. It would have been great seeing Vivienne in the witness box.

"I think it should have been Sid."

"Where's the money?"

Still, it should never have come to a court case. It dragged on for fucking years. Figures from accountants. Not getting replies. The tax bill was increasing dramatically. Eventually my accountants had to settle the tax bill out of Glitterbest's assets. My case should have been settled as soon as we separated, eight years prior. But that wasn't the way Malcolm wanted it. As far as he was concerned, I wasn't owed a penny by anybody.

I was on the edge of bankruptcy many times during the years after the Sex Pistols. That made it extremely difficult to form PiL. There was no money, so I had to do everything on a shoestring. I would go to Richard Branson, but that would only be for very small amounts. I would cut recording costs with PiL down to the minimum.

Being paid back all that money owed to me for such a long time barely covered all the debts I'd incurred over the years. Whatever there is now is split between us equally—myself, Steve, Paul, and Sid's estate. During the recording sessions, we paid Glen Matlock as a hired musician—not a songwriter. Whatever he gets in royalties goes through Sid's mother. It's because they both played bass, the one instrument most people don't listen to in rock music. There it is, a bone of contention. How typically Pistols that is!

Since the breakup I hadn't received a penny from the Pistols until the court case was settled. Then all of the bills came streaming in. I never thought there would be any money at the end of the Sex Pistols court battle. There wasn't much to speak of in the end result, but taking it out of Malcolm's hands was good enough for me.

NEVER MIND THE LOLLING ON THE SAND, HERE'S THE
AFFIDAVITS/A LEGAL PIE FIGHT

On September 20, 1976, the Sex Pistols entered into a management agreement with Malcolm McLaren, AKA Glitterbest Limited. The management agreement was drawn up by Steven Fisher, Malcolm's solicitor, who was appointed a director of Glitterbest. By January 15, 1978, the band was for all intents and purposes dissolved after the final performance in San Francisco. On November 9, 1978, I initiated legal proceedings to freeze Glitterbest's Sex Pistols assets and holdings, shouldering all the legal costs. The original cast read as follows:

John Lydon—Plaintiff
Versus
Malcolm Robert Andrew McLaren/Glitterbest Ltd—First Defendant
Stephen Jones—Second Defendant
Paul Cook—Third Defendant
Sid Vicious AKA John Beverly—Fourth Defendant

My claims were that the management agreement was so one-sided as to be legally unenforceable, that Glitterbest had not properly accounted to us for money it had collected on the group's behalf and that

Glitterbest had not paid the four of us what we were entitled to under the agreement. Malcolm and Glitterbest, of course, denied that the agreement was unenforceable, that they had failed to account or that they owed us any money. Malcolm and Glitterbest also countersued, claiming that I breached the agreement by failing to comply with management's directions, not participating in Malcolm's film, authorizing Don Letts's film, and leaving the group to set up PiL.

To show the chaos, truth, self-interests, deceptions, intentions, and perceptions of the Sex Pistols story, here are actual excerpts of sworn affidavits taken from May of 1978 to January 1979. What you get is a behind-the-scenes account of what happened in San Francisco.

JOE STEVENS

I was commissioned by the *New Musical Express* to cover the Sex Pistols' American tour. I missed the first concert but joined the band in Memphis and remained with them until after the final concert of the tour in San Francisco.

When I met up with the band in Memphis I had not seen them for fifteen months. It was obvious immediately that John and Malcolm were not getting along. For example when I met John in Memphis he introduced me to someone and said, "This is Joe, he's my friend, but he's also Malcolm's friend." It was less a situation of open hostility between them than of silence and lack of communication. Another thing I noticed straight away when I met Malcolm that same evening was that Malcolm seemed to have very little control over what was going on, and this was very much contrary to the situation in London when I had last seen them. I found that Noel Monk was not particularly pleasant toward me as a member of the press, and I complained to Malcolm, and he seemed to have no power to do anything about it. Malcolm missed the first gig in Atlanta and seemed a bit disoriented. The three Warner Brothers men seemed to be more in charge. Malcolm certainly said that he had nothing to do with the tour at one time and referred all complaints to Warners.

When the flying party, including Steve Jones and Paul Cook, arrived at the hotel in Dallas, people were doubling up, and I arranged to room with Malcolm. We began talking about the fifteen months that had gone by since I had last seen him and John. Malcolm also talked about what it was like being a manager of a labeled act and said it was quite boring, that every day you had to do the same things. He was talking about tedious everyday managerial problems. I remember being present when Malcolm made a statement to the press when they asked who really ran the Pistols. He said, "When I first met these wankers they couldn't get themselves organized to order four cups of tea."

One thing I would like to stress about the plans for Rio was that the band would be playing the gig in San Francisco and only a few days later had a further gig lined up for a Friday night in Stockholm. As far as I was aware, and I was present at most of the discussions, nobody ever worked out the details of time differences between the various countries or whether it would be physically possible to manage the trip to Brazil.

In San Francisco there was some discussion, during which Steve and Paul were brought over to the Rio idea, as they looked upon it as an opportunity for some sunbathing and liked the idea of meeting Ronald Biggs.

The first time I saw John in San Francisco was [at the gig] in the dressing room. I didn't say anything to him about Rio, as I thought he probably knew. After the San Francisco show Sid asked Malcolm for some money to buy the drug Mandrax, but Malcolm would not give him any. Sid called him a thief, and there was a definite row.

The next I heard from John was he wanted to speak to Malcolm, who was out, and asked what was happening. I did not give a clear reply to begin with, as I was aware of the fact that Malcolm had not told John about the Rio trip, and John did not appear to know about it. I told him about it in apologetic terms. He sounded surprised and asked if Stockholm was still on and wondered how we would be able to get there in time. I explained how we intended to do it, and he replied, "I am spitting blood, and they expect me to sit on a plane for a couple of days?"

Malcolm later told me that he fetched Sid and then en route to John's motel [in San Jose] he decided to turn right around and forget the whole trip. Malcolm was agitated and said that Sid had quit the band, and he said that he was not interested in managing the band or any band that didn't want to do productive ideas and couldn't get themselves together. I think that Malcolm told me that Sid had [later] taken an overdose and was in the hospital. Malcolm had said that Sid was having a fit in the car.

At about lunchtime that day, I met John in the bar. We were with two ladies. Steve and Paul came in and sat at another table but said nothing about the band breaking up. Malcolm was upstairs sleeping, ill with a cold. He rarely went out of the hotel. John was trying to check into the Miyako at the time because I understood that the motel had told him to leave that morning as there was no further booking. John said that he had tried to speak to Malcolm but had not been able to do so.

Malcolm said to me, "It's finished, I won't manage a band that plays games like this." He accused John of turning into a "Rod Stewart figure" and not making himself available for projects which Malcolm thought would be to the good of the band. He said, "Sid is bleeding crazy and is probably dead." I offered to go downstairs and produce John, and Malcolm said he didn't want to talk to the cunt.

The next morning I went down to the restaurant, and there was John eating. As far as I knew, he still had not been told what had happened, and he had no idea at that time that the band had walked out on him. Steve and Paul came down and asked to speak to John. I went to my room and told Malcolm. When I saw John emerge from the meeting with Steve and Paul, he asked me where Malcolm was. John said, "The band's walked out on me." I unlocked the door to my room and let John in. I left and didn't hear anything that was said [between Malcolm]. John was not there long; he left the room and went to his own room. Malcolm got up and packed and was out of the hotel with Steve and Paul in about an hour and a half. I said to Malcolm while he was packing that he was crazy. He replied, "I am not your usual run-of-the-mill manager who just makes money. If I can't do Rio, I can't do anything." I asked him why he had not been to see Rotten that morning to try and persuade him to go to Rio. "It wasn't worth the trouble going to see Rotten." In fact, in my opinion, he had proved himself lazy. He simply couldn't face seeing Rotten.

I would not blame John in any way for the breakup of the band and think that the main causes are Malcolm's lack of interest and, possibly, something that happened between Sid and Malcolm on the morning when they were to go to Rio.

JOHN "BOOGIE" TIBERI

I accompanied the group as their road manager on the American tour, which started in Atlanta, Georgia. Upon our arrival, organizational matters were taken out of my hands by the Warner Bros. road crew, who virtually took over the managment of the group. Warner Bros. had specially arranged the permits for the group to tour America and they were very concerned about security. The Warner Bros. crew were paranoid, in my opinion. They repeatedly threatened the members of the group with physical violence if they "misbehaved," as they put it. This menacing behavior bewildered the group to such an extent that it made them very nervous and only added to the tension and friction within the group.

Mr. McLaren and I had the idea of the South American trip. We felt it would be a publicity coup. All members of the group were consulted about the proposed trip and meeting with Mr. Biggs as a possible substitute for the U.S. tour. John Lydon had full knowledge and was consulted as well. Lydon was not told that the Brazilian trip was rescheduled until he showed up in San Francisco with the Warner Bros. road crew at the rehearsal [sound check] of Saturday afternoon, January 14, 1978. After I told Lydon of the [newly] scheduled flight on Monday, John did not say anything at the rehearsal about not going. He did, however, complain about the trip when I spoke to him on the telephone after the concert. He had failed to appear at the Miyako Hotel as arranged.

I was unable to reach Lydon by phone during the day on Sunday, so that night I drove out to the motel in San Jose, where we believed John was staying along with the Warner Bros. road crew. I was prevented from speaking to Lydon by Noel Monk, who tried to talk us out of going to Brazil. We decided to leave and come back to pick up Lydon early the next morning and then go straight to the airport. On Monday morning we did start to drive to San Jose but turned back after McLaren decided that Sid was so frustrated and annoyed at Lydon's behavior that it would be better to postpone the trip until John and Sid met to iron out their problems.

We therefore returned to San Francisco. During our time spent in San Francisco, it was becoming clear to me that the Warner Bros. people in America wanted to keep the Sex Pistols in the United States. Representatives of Warner Bros. promised the group money and a "good time." At the same time they warned them of the dangers for them in going to South America. In the final analysis, only John Lydon was affected by this talk. In my view his allegation that he was not told about the trip to South America is merely a cover-up for the fact that he was swayed by people in America. Moreover, he felt alienated from the rest of the group. Possibly a further reason for his not wanting to join them in South America was that he did not want to spend that much time with them.

Maybe John Lydon was not completely serious about leaving the Sex Pistols. It may be he was using it as a threat to the rest of the group in order to try to force his will on them. It may be that once he had announced his departure to the press, pride prevented him from going back.

I flew to Jamaica at Mr. McLaren's request to try to continue John Lydon's role in the film project. I told Branson on behalf of McLaren that the best way to reunite the group was for Lydon to go to Brazil. Branson said he thought John did not want to and that working with Ronald Biggs was a bad idea for the Sex Pistols.

NOEL MONK

After the first show in Atlanta I found McLaren in his hotel. He did not go to the show. My feeling was that he was afraid of violence.

Malcolm put his employee Boogie in charge of looking after the boys, particularly Sid. Boogie was, however, totally useless at this task. There was a fight the first night between Boogie and Sid in the car park in Atlanta. But Boogie could not control Sid, and eventually Sid went off on his own and later that night deliberately cut open his arm. Just before the second gig in Memphis, Boogie got totally drunk. I asked him where Sid was, and he said he didn't know but that he hoped he was in the lobby of the hotel. I found that he was not, but the other members of the band were. The other three members were excited and looking forward to the gig. I put them into a bus to wait, and forty minutes later I found Sid in a screaming fight with Boogie. John was very annoyed and said to Sid, "You are ruining everything we are doing here." Sid said that he was sorry. I then took it upon myself to room with Sid for the rest of the tour in order that he should not get lost again.

McLaren stayed mainly out of the way. I thought he was unhelpful and a useless person on the tour. Many times group managers are helpful on a tour, but not in this case. In Memphis I went to McLaren to get him to help in finding Sid before the gig, but he seemed immobilized and afraid to face Sid.

The tour's final show was in San Francisco, and the following day I went with John to the Chinatown district of San Francisco. We just had a day off, and we bought presents. John seemed happy except that he said he wondered why nobody got in touch with him. John tried to call McLaren three or four times during the day and left messages, unable to get through.

Joe Stevens eventually told me about the plan devised by McLaren for the whole group to go to Rio. I said to John that the whole idea of going to Rio was suicidal. They would be going with no security, and with Sid in the condition he was, I thought they would all end up in prison.

The following morning I went to the Miyako Hotel in San Francisco, where McLaren and Joe Stevens were. I handed over the passports, including John's, to McLaren. One of them told me that they were looking for Sid. At the time, as far as I knew, nobody had told John anything about the proposed Brazilian trip from the management side. John was still suffering from bronchitis at this time.

JOHN LYDON

We were performing on tour in the north of England when McLaren met us and informed us that EMI wanted to offer us a recording contract but would only do so if we had a regular manager and office. Malcolm had a draft agreement with him which he [said) would satisfy EMI, and he left a copy of it with me. A few days later, when we got back to London, I went with McLaren to have the draft agreement read over. I did not understand much of the draft agreement, but I thought it gave McLaren too much control over the group and I said so. I believe that some changes were made, but I still felt that I did not understand it properly and that I disliked it. McLaren told me that Cook, Jones, and Matlock had all signed it and that if I did not sign it quickly, EMI would lose interest in us. I remember wishing I could get advice about the situation, but I had no money of my own and there was no one I could ask for help.

My association with Cook, Jones, and McLaren came to an end on January 16, 1978, or thereabouts. I had become seriously discontented with McLaren for two reasons in particular, both of them stemming from the fact that he had no interest in our music and was only interested in the publicity.

In the first place, in the middle of 1977 he conceived the idea of a film about the Sex Pistols and brought over a director called Russ Meyer from Los Angeles. I found Meyer's script and ideas objectionable and refused to take part in his film for that reason; and the idea of a film by Meyer seemed to be dropped.

The second area of discontent was over live appearances, or gigs. I felt very strongly that for the sake of its music the group need the stimulus of regular appearances before live audiences; but through almost the whole of 1977 McLaren constantly told us that he was unable to arrange any, despite the success of our records. We had acquired some notoriety . . . and McLaren fostered this notoriety to the extent (I believe) of denying us live performances in the hope that record sales would be enhanced if our public were under the impression that we had been banned from concert halls. That was certainly untrue; some halls were unwilling to have us, but others applied to Glitterbest for engagements during 1977 and were either refused or simply received no replies. In the end, Jones, Cook, Beverly [Sid], and I secretly did three live performances under assumed names.

What happened in San Francisco was this. Beverly and I were staying in a motel in San Jose with the tour manager from Warner Brothers (Noel Monk) and his road crew; McLaren, Cook, and Jones were staying at a hotel in San Francisco itself. Our concert was on Saturday, January 14. Warner Brothers were not responsible for our arrangements after San Francisco. We were due in Stockholm for a live appearance on Friday, January 20. When I rang McLaren's hotel again, I spoke to Joe Stevens, an American journalist who was staying with the party there, and he told me that McLaren had arranged for the group to fly to Rio de Janeiro early the next morning; I complained to him that I was exhausted and ill with bronchitis and did not see how we could fit in a trip to Brazil before our engagement in Stockholm. I said that I would not go. I then went to bed at the motel.

At five A.M. [the next day] Beverly rang my room and said that McLaren had just been to visit him and complained about me and that he (Beverly) had had enough of the group. He sounded incoherent, and I have since heard that he took an overdose of heroin shortly after McLaren's visit. At nine A.M. on Monday morning I got through to McLaren on the telephone and asked him what was going on; he was noncommittal, and I said that I was coming to see him at his hotel. On Monday morning I talked first to Cook and Jones and then separately to McLaren. Cook and Jones told me then that on the preceding morning McLaren had sent them to the airport for a nine o'clock flight. It was then that I realized that McLaren had not contacted me regarding Rio de Janeiro. Cook and Jones made it clear to me that they did not wish to go on working with me or Beverly; McLaren at first seemed to be trying to persuade me to go to Brazil for a publicity appearance with Ronald Biggs, but I said that I did not like the idea of getting publicity out of a man who had left a train driver like a vegetable. McLaren said that he did not wish to go on with the group and it was all over and finished. Shortly after those meetings McLaren, Cook, and Jones left the hotel together, and since then I have had hardly any contact with them. I had one meeting with McLaren in about March 1978, when he asked me to appear in the Matrixbest film. I said that I would only appear if I could choose my own material, but he was unwilling to agree to that.

STEVE JONES

Both Paul Cook and I have known Malcolm for a long time, and I believe he has been an excellent manager and a friend. After all, he has got us famous very quickly. John says in his affidavit that Malcolm actually deliberately prevented the group from performing gigs. I do not believe that this occurred. Malcolm has always accounted to us with what I believe is due under the management agreement and taken care of all our tax and other liabilities. Through him we have been able to buy flats.

Malcolm had said that there was an opportunity to go to Rio de Janeiro, where we could do some filming and promote our record and have a bit of a holiday. We thought that this was a great idea, as by that time we really wished to avoid further touring commitments. When we went to the airport early the next morning after the concert, John did not turn up. We told John that we wanted to go to Brazil, but he said he did not. We were fed up with John's attitude. He was treating us as completely unimportant, and in fact, he said, "The main problem is Malcolm. Let's get rid of Malcolm." We wished to avoid a confrontation. It is quite wrong to say that we sacked him from the group.

PAUL COOK

The film was Malcolm's idea. Initially the group were keen, but as it dragged on we became progressively less keen. John was keen at the beginning, but then after a while he decided he did not want to have anything to do with the film. John was a moaner.

I do not think Malcolm ever stopped the group performing. It was a problem finding suitable venues to play because we were pretty famous and the group was banned at a number of places.

I think Malcolm was an excellent manager. He has arranged all our contracts. He has always paid us what is due, and if he cannot always tell us what we were owed, we ask the accountants, who show us all the records and books of account.

JAMIE REID

I believe the group was happy in their own way about Mr. McLaren and the way he managed them. The Plaintiff often criticized people and said that he hated everybody, but he did have an enormous respect for Mr. McLaren. After the Plaintiff was assaulted outside a pub near the recording studio in Highbury, he became really paranoiac and tended to cut himself off from people generally. In my view basically he was a normal, unemployed East End youth and could not cope with or handle the whole success thing.

VIVIENNE WESTWOOD

In late summer 1975, I was in favour of John Beverly joining the group; he used to come into the shop with John Lydon and John Gray. I always had a great feeling for John Beverly, who had a musical, deep speaking voice, and I felt that he could make a contribution to the group. Also that he had the right attitude.

JEREMY THOMAS

In August 1977 I was approached by 20th Century-Fox Productions Ltd. to meet Malcolm McLaren with a view to co-producing a film starring the Sex Pistols to be directed by Russ Meyer entitled *Anarchy in the U.K.* The idea appealed to me because I thought the film could break new ground in the cinema. The combination of Russ Meyer, known for his bombastic sex thrillers and the Sex Pistols, who at the time were England's number one enemy, was obviously a fascinating proposition . . . [One] reason why the project had to be aborted was the inability of Russ Meyer and myself to have any communication with John Lydon and John Beverly, who eventually became extremely aggressive.

JULIEN TEMPLE

The Plaintiff was initially enthusiastic about the idea of the film in the broad sense and was also keen to make a film about the group. But you have to know what the Plaintiff is like. He has a strange way of expressing enthusiasm for a project. He was never really openly keen on anything, or if he was, an outsider would not be able to appreciate it from his behavior. For example, he might be extremely abusive about something, yet this was his own way of being enthusiastic. His attitude to the film changed a bit later. The reasons for this are basically twofold:

1. From the beginning the Plaintiff clashed with Mr. Meyer. He seemed to think that Mr. Meyer was an "American fascist" who did not understand the whole "punk scene."*

2. The Plaintiff felt that Mr. McLaren was spending too much time on the film, which he considered to be to the detriment of the group's interests in the broad sense. The Plaintiff also apparently mistrusted films. He felt that music made for immediate communication and the Sex Pistols related to people best on a musical level. He seemed to feel that films were hypothetical in terms of saying things.

---

*As far as *The Great Rock 'n' Roll Swindle* was concerned, the whole thing from the hiring of Russ Meyer on was a joke and a waste of time and money. My original choice as director was Graham Chapman from Monty Python, but he behaved gloriously badly to Malcolm. That put the mockers on that. Then Malcolm brought in Russ Meyer, with whom I didn't see eye to eye. He was just going to turn this film into a tits-and-ass movie. I've never liked any of his films, one man and his childish fantasies. I didn't want to be a part of his regime because I felt we'd be second fiddle to his big tit phobia.

STEVEN FISHER

On August 17, 1976, I was appointed a director of the First Defendant Company [Glitterbest]. I have been involved in more negotiations over a two-year period with third-party record companies, music publishers, merchandisers, and booking agents on behalf of the the First Defendants and the Sex Pistols than on behalf of any other manager or artist . . . . It is my view that it was mainly due to the expertise and ability of Mr. McLaren that he was able to resurrect the group on each occasion when it appeared that their careers had come to an end.

MALCOLM McLAREN

The Sex Pistols are and have been probably the leading group and certainly pioneers in "punk" music, the new kind of music which is based on often violent self expression and disregard of convention.

By the beginning of 1977 I was experiencing substantial difficulties in obtaining booking for live performances. The well-known incident in December 1976 when the members of the group uttered obscenities on the television programme "Today" during an interview with Bill Grundy gave them added notoriety but increased the difficulties of obtaining venues. Their reputation was such that as the year went on many places refused to allow them to perform. As will be seen this did not inhibit but indeed increased their popularity so far as recordings were concerned but nevertheless I continued to make every effort to obtain live bookings and retained the services of Cowbell Agency, 153 George Street, London W1, who are well known specialists in arranging bookings. Most of the local councils banned the group from performing in public halls or theatres. There is now produced and shown to me marked "M.R.A.M. 2" a bundle of correspondence evidencing the almost impossible task it was to obtain bookings. Nevertheless I arranged tours in Scandinavia in August 1977 and Holland in December 1977, and a world tour was being arranged of which a tour of America was to be the first leg. As for the United Kingdom, the Plaintiff's allegation in the last sentence of paragraph 14 of his Affidavit that he arranged secret gigs is to the best of my knowledge untrue. I organised three gigs at the Screen on the Green cinema in Islington at my own expense, if this is what he is referring to. In addition I arranged in conjunction with Cowbell in the United Kingdom a tour in which the group could play with assumed names through a variety of privately owned clubs enabling us to perform in towns where we had been banned. This was called the "Spots" tour ("Sex Pistols on Tour Secretly") and a "Never Mind the Bans" tour in December 1977. This was basically a follow up to the Spots tour. We turned up at the clubs and only announced our arrival an hour beforehand.

I have never regarded myself as in any way divorced from the group but have at all times identified myself with them, but I do feel that I have at all times done my best for the group and that there must be truth in what is stated in *Melody Maker* in their article, July 9, 1977, namely that "like Epstein with the Beatles, McLaren constructed today's Sex Pistols from the rawest of raw materials." I would respectfully suggest that the facts speak for themselves, and it is noteworthy that the *Investors Review* for December 1977 chose the Sex Pistols as young businessmen of the year. As for the suggestion also seemingly made or implied by the Plaintiff that he in some way was unhappy with or disassociated himself from the unruly, unconventional, and in many ways publicly objectionable image of the group, I can only say that at all times he was the leading party in the development of that image . . . . I further refer to the lyrics that the Plaintiff himself composed. It is quite untrue to say that I was not interested in the group's music.

In San Francisco I learned that the group had been banned from Finland, the first scheduled stop on the forthcoming European tour. This left a free one-week period before the engagement in Stockholm. A trip to South America had been discussed in front of all the members of the group prior to the United States tour as a possible alternative if we were denied United States visas, and it was mentioned again as a replacement for the canceled tour of Finland and then go on to Stockholm. A short promotional trip to Brazil was discussed, and Virgin, whose territory included South America, agreed to meet the expenses of such a promotional trip. The advantage in going to Brazil was that a great degree of publicity could be obtained, particularly because the trip was to include a meeting with Ronald Biggs.

On Friday, January 13, we made reservations to fly to Rio early on Monday morning, January 16. Since the Plaintiff did not appear at the Miyako or contact me on Friday, he was not informed of the details of the Brazilian trip until the rehearsal on Saturday afternoon. I then told Boogie to tell everyone that we had tickets and were to be at the airport first thing Monday morning. The statement in the Plaintiff's affidavit that he was not informed of the proposed trip is untrue.

On Sunday morning I discovered that the Plaintiff was not in the hotel, and we could not locate him. Early the next morning we all checked out of the Miyako and left in two cars, stopping to pick up the Fourth Defendant [Sid] before setting out to San Jose. During the trip out to San Jose, [Sid] began to complain bitterly about the Plaintiff, his failure to tell anyone where he was staying or even to speak to the other members of the group during rehearsals, and the performance on Saturday night, which he considered to be a disaster. I decided while we were still in the car that the friction between [Sid] and the Plaintiff was so great that it was pointless to go off to Brazil until these two could settle their differences. [Sid] agreed, so we turned back to San Francisco after telephoning the others at the airport to cancel the flight reservations.

Later on in the afternoon I received a telephone call from the Plaintiff, who told me that he had spoken to Sid, who had threatened to quit the group because he could not get along with the Plaintiff. I told the Plaintiff to come to the Miyako as soon as possible so that we could discuss the matter. The Plaintiff arrived at the Miyako in the afternoon. Unfortunately I was not there when the Plaintiff arrived because I had received an urgent telephone call from the people with whom Sid was staying, telling me that he had collapsed and was unconscious. I left immediately to take care of Sid, which involved taking him by ambulance to a doctor's office, and did not arrive back at the Miyako until that evening, by which time the Plaintiff had left.

The Plaintiff returned to the Miyako the following morning, Tuesday, January 17, and to my knowledge met with Steve and Paul in either the hotel bar or restaurant. The Plaintiff later came up to my room and told me that Steve and Paul had decided that they wanted to take a rest and have some time to think everything over. I complained to the Plaintiff that the group had reached a crisis due largely to his own uncooperative attitude and failure to communicate with me or the other members of the group. I explained I was finding it well nigh impossible to carry out my job as manager of the group and that a short break might be the best idea for all concerned. The Plaintiff did not agree, but I told him that I did not see how anything else would be possible as long as he didn't follow my instructions regarding the management of the group.

Later that day I decided to fly to Los Angeles to see Warner Bros. and explain that the Brazilian tour had to be canceled and the arrangements for the European tour had to be changed. Steve and Paul decided to accompany me, but the Plaintiff did not want to come, and I left him with a return ticket to London, as he said that he wanted to go home. I warned him that his visa would expire in a few days. My last words to him were to the effect that I would see him back in London and we would try to resolve the group's future.

While in Los Angeles I received a telephone call . . . that the press had been telephoning to inquire about a statement that the Plaintiff made to the press in New York that the Sex Pistols had broken up and he had quit.

I decided I would have to go back to Los Angeles to discuss the situation with Warner Bros. Before leaving London, I did try to contact the Plaintiff, but . . . he was on his way to Jamaica with Richard Branson.

My next step was to fly to Brazil to confer with Steve and Paul, while Boogie flew to Jamaica to see if he could speak to the Plaintiff and convince him to cooperate in completing the film project. . . . I received several calls from Boogie, who said the Plaintiff refused to cooperate in any way with the film and that members of the Virgin management were refusing to let Boogie see the Plaintiff.

I spent several days in Brazil . . . then flew to Los Angeles. I received a call from Bob Regehr telling me that they had spoken to the Plaintiff, who wished to come out to Los Angeles to discuss his future. Regehr told me that the Plaintiff . . . was not interested in working with any of the other members of the group or with me as his manager, that he considered himself to have been the most important member of the Sex Pistols, and that he wanted to know if Warner Bros. would back him with a new group he was forming. Warner Bros. paid for the Plaintiff and his mother to come to Los Angeles.

I telephoned the Plaintiff, who said to me something to the effect, "What is all this rubbish about you trying to get the group back together again?" and he repeated that he would not play with the others ever again.

I met him the next day at his hotel [in Los Angeles], the Continental Hyatt House, to talk about future plans. I told him that whatever he decided to do we needed his cooperation in order to complete the film. He refused and then said that he would only cooperate if he was paid fifty thousand pounds up front, not on the condition that he chose the material. . . . When I returned to London . . . Sid and I left for Paris, where we spent approximately three weeks at the end of March and the beginning of April filming and recording.

No one has to my knowledge ever suggested, nor would it be true to suggest, that I am other than a capable manager and businessman.

ROBERT REGEHR

My company, Warner Brothers Records, arranged a number of interviews with television and newspaper reporters. The first date of the tour
was in Atlanta. Warner Brothers attended to such matters as the sound
check, lighting, and stage. Malcolm was nowhere to be seen. I would
have expected a manager to be present when the checks were being carried out, particularly as this was the group's first trip to America.
Warner Brothers also dealt with travel and booking arrangements. John
Lydon was sick and did not like traveling by air, so it was arranged he
would travel by coach with members of the road crew. I do not know
why Lydon stayed in San Jose. It would not have been his choice, but
by the arrangements made for him. I cannot accept the statement that
Malcolm was unable to locate the Plaintiff. The main complaint
Malcolm made to me was that my company was overorganized. He did
not like organization and indeed said that the group played better when
there was a chaotic situation.

The first I heard of the trip to Rio de Janeiro was on Saturday morn-
ing, January 14. I was preparing to go to San Francisco for the engage-
ment that night . . . . On arriving at San Francisco, I booked at the
Miyako and immediately called Malcolm and arranged to go to his
room . . . . I asked Malcolm what was all this about a trip to South
America. He said they were going to play some engagements in South
America and film a meeting with Ronald Biggs. I asked him who
Ronald Biggs was, and he told me. I said it was very unwise to go to any
Latin American country because Latin American governments do not
like rock 'n' roll and being predominantly Catholic would abhor the
Sex Pistols' lyrics. He dismissed my warnings. I told him I regarded it
dangerous for the members of the group to go, meaning that they might
have difficulty in getting out as South America and Latin American
countries were inclined to be "trigger happy." He replied that everything would be all right and I was not to worry about that. I asked him
who was going to pay for the trip, and he said that since he was going
to promote the album, Warners should pay. I said that Warners' territory did not cover South America, and he retorted he would ask Virgin
Records to pay if I would assist him on the travel arrangements. I told
him I would offer the services of Warners' travel agency, but that
Warners would take no part, financially or otherwise, in a venture that
I regarded as foolhardy.

After the concert my party returned to the Miyako. While we were at
the bar, Malcolm, Paul, and Steve entered. I asked Malcolm to come

and have a talk with me, and we went to an adjoining foyer. I expressed my belief that the tour and especially the evening's concert had been quite successful. Malcolm said he thought the concert was the worst show he had ever seen and John Lydon was no better than a Mick Jagger or Rod Stewart. He added that the American tour had ruined the whole idea of the Sex Pistols because Lydon now thought he was a star, and the idea of the group was that the Sex Pistols were the stars and there was no individual as a star. He said all the attention of the press in America was centered upon John, but in England he, Malcolm, could control the situation and the members of the group could obtain equal coverage. I told him that John was and had always been the star of the group and there was no way to prevent it. He continued by saying that this was against the political nature of the group, which he regarded as an extension of the idea of anarchy, which the group symbolized . . . . Malcolm said he was tired of the way things were going, and he would just as soon walk away from everything if the group was going to sell out to commercialism. He suggested that this was the end of the group, but I could not believe this.

[A few weeks later,] I went to England for the express purpose of finding out what was the situation of the group. I saw Malcolm, who said that everything would be all right after they had time to rest and get a new perspective on what they were doing. He said he thought he could sit down with the members of the group and get them back together. I said there was no way that Sid could continue to be a member of the group in view of his health problem (at that time I did not positively know he had a drug problem), and he replied he wanted him to. I indicated that Sid would destroy the group. He replied that he thought all Sid wanted was a rest and a vacation. I strongly advised him to replace Sid.

My impressions from the conversation I had with Malcolm was that the breakup of the group was due to John Lydon leaving the group, whereas my impressions from the conversations I had with Lydon were that the breakup of the group were due to Steve Jones and Paul Cook conspiring with Malcolm to get rid of him.

RUDI VAN EGMOND

I was employed by Virgin Records Limited, for whom the Sex Pistols recorded from August 1977 to October 31, 1978. I was responsible for promoting the Sex Pistols records on the radio stations. I first became aware that there were problems between the members of the group at a concert they gave in Huddersfield in December 1977. It appeared that Sid was becoming a problem for John, and John appeared to disassociate himself as much as possible from the rehearsals. In fact, at the rehearsals Sid and Steve were doing the singing, and it looked to me at the time as if they could carry on the group without John if they so chose. John did not rehearse, and in fact, before the concert he asked me if I would drive him without the rest of the group home to London after the concert. When John returned from the United States after the American tour, I called him as a representative of Virgin, and I informed the managing director of Virgin, Richard Branson, that I was in touch with John. Branson was very concerned about the situation, and he and I decided to visit John in his house in Chelsea. When we arrived Branson was most concerned that he should keep in John's good books as he, Branson, was going to Jamaica and knew that John was very interested in Jamaican music. Branson flattered John by suggesting that John should go as "the adviser" to the record company on Jamaican music. John said he would be delighted to go. Over a meal Branson asked John whether he was prepared to rejoin Steve and Paul; Branson did not include Sid as he, Branson, thought Sid's drug problems so great that the group would be better off without him. John said, "There is no way that I will reconsider rejoining the Sex Pistols." At that point Branson became rather alarmed and began to flatter John by suggesting that he could perform a valuable role for Virgin in Jamaica.

JOHN VARNOM

Originally Virgin Records, my company, turned down the opportunity of signing the Sex Pistols on the grounds that they had no talent and a general distaste of the group's image. After the EMI and A&M contracts had been terminated, it was clear to Branson that prestige and cash would accrue to the company if they signed the Sex Pistols. In addition, [Branson] looked forward to the stimulation of working with the now famous figure of Malcolm McLaren, and he, Branson, being a great competitor, felt that if there was to be a contest between him and McLaren, he felt sure he would come out on top.

Everyone at Virgin initially worked very hard to promote and market the Sex Pistols' first recordings on the label, the singles "God Save the Queen," "Pretty Vacant," and "Holidays in the Sun," with great success.

This gave Virgin a new lease of life and was the shot in the arm required, as for the past years they had been relying on the success of only one artist, Mike Oldfield. By this time I could see that the relationship between Branson and McLaren was degenerating horribly. By the autumn of 1977 the view began to crystallize at Virgin that the only talent among the group was that of John Lydon. There was general competition for his favors. Lydon began to respond to flattery and to behave fairly obnoxiously. He told whoever would listen that he regarded Steve Jones and Paul Cook as oafs; on a record promotional trip to the north of England, he held court in the hotel bedrooms, requesting people to hand him food and drink even though the plate or glass concerned was only inches away from his hand.

After the American tour had ended I was telephoned by Jamie Reid, who told me that Lydon had ceased to be a Sex Pistol. There was a great scramble for Lydon. Branson courted Lydon and whisked him off secretly to Jamaica. If the body was dead, in Branson's view, then in mine, it was being buried with indecent haste. I understand that Branson was allowing Lydon in Jamaica to indulge in all his tastes, including that of Reggae music and marijuana. Branson later told me that Lydon had recorded Sex Pistols' songs with Jamaican artists, which hardly seemed to me to be conducive to reuniting John with Steve, Paul, and Sid. There were pictures of John in the papers, lolling on the sand.

By late January or February of 1978, I cannot remember exactly when, there was a meeting in Branson's office. Branson explained that it was quite clear that Glitterbest Limited would be unable to record further product and that Virgin ought to consider its position. It could not be seen to sue Glitterbest, as this would make Virgin a laughing stock insofar as it had signed the group who had antagonized the established record companies, to which Virgin did not wish to be likened. However, the possibility of Lydon suing Glitterbest was raised, and Branson thought that this was a satisfactory substitute. He thought that McLaren had so far got the better of him in the competition between them, as he saw it, and that this would be a clever way of getting his own back. At the same time it appeared to be a good way of supporting Lydon, who looked as if he were going to be the sole product producer for Virgin.

The notion that the Sex Pistols were going to Brazil to record with Ronnie Biggs was greeted with derision. "Ronnie Rotten" did not appeal at all. At the weekly promotion meeting the project was greeted with disgust on the grounds that it was not music. It was assumed again quite without discussion that Lydon was the talent. In addition, without McLaren it was obvious that Lydon would be easier to handle.

I myself thought the Biggs project a splendid idea and in keeping with the Sex Pistols exciting image: seditious, good fun, and humorous. On the other hand, I was distressed by Lydon's efforts; he needed the discipline of a McLaren.

I was criticized for spending the usual Sex Pistols single record promotion budget in promoting the Ronnie Biggs song "No One Is Innocent." Branson particularly was furious about my having spent so much money. He thought that if this record were successful, this would be inconsistent with his prognosis for the future. The number one priority was not to upset Lydon. The Biggs record attained the top ten but could have done better if the campaign I initiated had been allowed to go to its conclusion.

In my view Branson will have to continue to court Lydon as much as he has done. To me it looks as if Lydon's relationship with McLaren ended because of unrequited homosexual affection. I do not think, however, that Lydon has any such affection for Branson.

RICHARD BRANSON

I have read the affidavit of John Varnom. It is true that my company, Virgin Records, did not at first see the true potential of the Sex Pistols. It was not, however, after the termination of the EMI contract that I first made an approach. When I had heard certain tapes during the time the group was contracted to EMI, I telephoned Mr. Hills, the managing director of EMI, expressing an interest in acquiring the group. I have never viewed McLaren as a contestant or competition. There is no truth in the statement that I felt I was capable of taming the group.

After the San Francisco concert McLaren telephoned me from the United States. He said John Lydon had left the group and that Lydon had not wanted to go to Brazil. He also told me he had had enough of John Lydon, but he also suggested that the breakup was temporary.

My principal concern was to keep the group together, and all my actions were directed toward that end.

I was going to Jamaica in any case. I had lunch with John Lydon and Rudi Van Egmond. It was Rudi Van Egmond who suggested that John might like to go to Jamaica. There is no truth in the allegation that I whisked John off secretly to Jamaica. Indeed, my visit to Jamaica with Lydon was the subject of press comment. I never saw John Lydon smoking marijuana, but if he did or did not indulge in smoking marijuana, it was not my concern. While in Jamaica John spent the major part of his time with reggae musicians. He did not like going to the beach. He may have lolled on the sand, but I do not recall the event.

It is quite untrue that I believed Glitterbest Limited would be unable to produce another record. I was impressed by McLaren's talent and felt he had it in him to produce further work. There was no question of competition between McLaren and me.

There was no open checkbook at Virgin for John Lydon. It is correct that John Varnom was criticized for overspending on promotion, but this was because the budget was ten thousand pounds. He spent a sum far in excess of that. It is completely untrue that I wished the single in question to be anything but successful.

Until I read the affidavit of John Varnom I had never heard any suggestion of John Lydon having homosexual tendencies, and indeed I do not believe he has, nor do I see the relevance of this suggestion.

It was my primary wish that John Lydon should rejoin the group. If that was not possible, [then] my company would have the benefit of John's services and the services of the other musicians, who made up the group. In no way did I want to alienate McLaren or take over McLaren's management functions. It is not correct that I flattered John Lydon or sought in any way to encourage his independence from the Sex Pistols.

★ ★ ★

By January 16, 1986—after a full eight years of legal pie fighting, affidavits, and depositions—the band's settlement gave it custody of the Sex Pistols legacy, to be split equally among the surviving members and Anne Jeanette Beverly, Sid's mum and executor of his estate. Eventually Steve and Paul reversed their allegiance to my side when Malcolm's case began to crumble. To this day, all Sex Pistols revenues belong solely to the band and continue to be split evenly four ways. That includes the proceeds from all singles and albums.

As for the Pistols' film, I opened the library of *The Great Rock 'n' Roll Swindle.* There's over 250 hours of footage. As far as I know, there was something like eight directors used, and none of them bothered to catalog or keep any records. I'm going to have to hire some serious film editors to organize it.

SEGMENT

2 1 :

NO IRISH, NO BLACKS, NO DOGS

I'm claustrophobic. I can't ride in subways, and I don't like heights. I'm epileptic as well, but I'm not on any medication. Strobe lights really set me off, also afternoon sun between the trees as you drive along in the car. I can't take that constant flash. I cannot sit in a club with red lights. Red light bulbs are the most nauseating thing in the world to me. It's supposed to make people look very sexy, but it makes me feel horrible. I'm no lighting director's dream when I tour—there's this huge list of things that can't be done. You might see subtle pink lighting on my stage, but never red. It makes me go all funny. It was all right during the Sex Pistols days. We literally only had a couple of torches on stage or one overhead one-hundred-watt bulb, and that would be it. Sometimes certain kinds of lighting can make me forget where I am and trigger a memory seizure. I always keep my lyric book on stage on the floor if the lighting does weird things in the middle of the song. I have a poor sense of balance, so if I do spins, I can fuck myself up. My eyes stay open when I spin, so all the different images on the stage flash by and my brain just stops. I never had seizures as a kid, so I must only have a mild case of epilepsy. It might have something to do with the meningitis when I was young.

Very first Pistols gig, St Martin's College of Art (John Gray)

Am I a walking contradiction? A singer who never sings along with records at home? A touring performer who can't handle flashing lights? A shy kid who became one of the most notorious pop figures around? Oh, yes, I'm not!

Those are the learning years that you don't realize at the time. It's all this information bombarding you, making you feel more hopeless. The biggest nausea I felt when I was small was no prospects. You have no prospects, no way out of what you're in. You have no future. I didn't plan on a future.

I'm not a revolutionary, a socialist, or any of that. That's not what I'm about at all. An absolute sense of individuality is my politics. All political groups that I'm aware of on this planet seem to strive to suppress individuality. They need block voting numbers. They need units. It doesn't matter if it's left or right, sometimes the tactics are the same. The things these people strive for is mass uniformity. The feminist movement became oppressive very quickly. Gay liberation is not after equal rights at all. It's to be accepted as this one great lump. If a homosexual inside that movement dares stray away from what they term as the norm, then they victimize that person. It's replacing the same old system with a different clothing. I hate all these groupings, any kind of gathering like that. It destroys personality and individuality. Maybe a roomful of people having very different ideas is chaotic, but it's wonderfully chaotic, highly entertaining, and very educational. That's how you learn things—not by everybody following the same doctrine. I don't suppose my kind of world could really exist at all because there are so many sheep out there that need leaders. Let them bleat among the flock, that's not for me. I'd rather be the lone sheep out there fending off the wolves. It's much better. When you grow up in a working-class environment, you're supposed to stay inside and follow the rules and regulations of that little system. I won't have any of that. It's all wrong, equally bad.

CHRISSIE HYNDE: John's a bastard, but there's still something sweet and tender about him. He's not the kind of person who would, for instance, abuse animals. Even today, John tries to wind me up about the "meat is murder" issue, but I know he's just being an asshole. And he knows I know, so I don't know why he even bothers. It doesn't push my buttons. He's an asshole, and as I've told him many times, every intelligent person will eventually become vegetarian, so you might as well get on with it.

No Irish, No Blacks, No Dogs. It's exactly the truth. People invent new prejudices, and these days the prejudices we face are substantially different. Our modern-day prejudices are, like, "You're in Greenpeace or you don't exist." "You're a Democrat or you're dead." It's a whole new bunch of authoritarianisms, but the same rules apply. They must be rebelled against because they're not sensible. They're based on slog-aneering.

"The youth!"

The youth always love a good battle but will forever fight the wrong one. And why not? Who created this nonsense of rebelling against your elders? This is what I said in the Pistols. I've learned everything from people older than me . . . because I learned how not to do it. I learned by their mistakes, and that doesn't seem to be the case anymore. It's all back to the old farm—the Animal Farm! Is the tragedy of history that we're all supposed to perpetuate the same mistakes and fuck-ups with no progression? The shame of modern times is that we want it all now. We've lost patience. When you read old literature it's steeped in the present; they rarely had a forward thought or looked back, either—they lived in one particular current stream.

I don't feel like I belong to a certain chunk of any time anymore. But disenfranchisement is not a bad thing, it's more a sign of progress and hope. I complain and moan because it makes me work harder. It's a special gift to be disenfranchised at an early age.

The Irish came to the New World and became the police forces in America to escape discrimination. How clever for these so-called dumb potato farmers. By God, what a skillful maneuver. Who needs the Mafia when you can run the police?

We have to make some moves first toward affirmative action, then the rest will follow. It's a very slow process, and yes, it does work over several generations. There is progress, but unfortunately not in black culture in America. They still seem segregated from the American Dream. The closest they get to it is joining the military. It's impossible for them to own their own businesses because that requires capital and better schooling for a start, which they haven't been entitled to. When you're born in the ghetto, that's where you fucking stay. It's very diffi-cult to break out of it. Then you go back and try to pull others out with you, and they hate you for it. They resent you for it because they think you're patronizing them.

Believe me, I know. Generally speaking, the more you try to help the people you leave behind, the more they hate you for it. They want you completely distanced from them. Then they like you. If you try to mingle back in or keep those old roots, they despise you because you embarrass them. You make them feel bad about themselves that they never had those opportunities. They automatically perceive those opportunities as "just your good luck," and it's a way of justifying their own mediocrity, which is fully understandable. It's a defense mechanism that you cannot deny anyone. That's how people reserve self-respect. Spike Lee deals with that same subject when he compares poor folks to crabs in a barrel. Whenever one tries to get out, all the other ones pull him back in. If you put a claw back in, they'll try to snap it off. You don't have to be black to experience that.

The Irish sing the saddest songs in the universe and just get on with it. But they had a choice to emigrate to America and elsewhere when they were kicked out of Ireland centuries ago via potato famine, starvation, and cruelty from the British government. The Irish don't give a fuck. These are concepts that never occur to them, yet you can hardly call the Irish nonsuffering. They know they are completely downtrodden and have been since time began—humiliated, conquered, slaughtered, abused, and used. But they don't seem to let that be a problem, and it's not right to say that it's because their skin is white.

Nothing is ever done to guarantee equal rights—whatever those may be. I certainly don't benefit from equal rights. Nobody ever treated me equally in this business, not since I began and onward. It made me work harder.

It takes a repressed financial and political situation like the one we experienced in Britain seventeen years ago for a band like the Pistols to work. It's not something that can go on and on and on and perpetuate itself. Times might get better, so what the hell are you moaning about?

Around the time of the punks, socialism wasn't working in England. The Labour party were unimpressive and tedious. The Conservatives, the same. It fluctuated from one party to another, four years of this, four years of that, and you wouldn't notice any change. Young people—in fact, most people—just walked clean away from politics as if it were a waste of time. A cloud of apathy had truly set in. Of course, that's exactly the environment the Conservatives want. That's when they can strut their stuff using prejudice, hate, family values, all the nonissues of political life. Grim. In our own way, I suppose, the punks absolutely guaranteed that Margaret Thatcher would take over. When things swing so far to the left, it always seems to bounce back just as hard to the right. A lot of us were screaming at the wrong enemies. We were blaming the wrong people. We should have been warning the world of the horrors to come rather than the horrors that were there

John & Nora. Lovey doves. (Howard Thompson)

already. But that's a hindsight thing. Still, there's nothing more destructive in this world than a politician touting family values. It's such nonspecific nonsense. It's a form of entrapment. Have kids. It's normal. Is it? Fuck. So they grow up disgruntled, fucked-off, fed up, and illiterate as the rest of us? Wicked.

I think the Sex Pistols did drive the first chinks into the British royal armor. Everything we said then is now common language. I can't even have a weird hairdo anymore—it's bog standard. We were the first rock 'n' roll band to throw stones at the queen, but we threw stones at everything. Yes, the royal family is collapsing and becoming dysfunctional, and all their marriages are breaking up. The women are so unhappy. The Pistols exposed the whole royal family as a farce.

Why do you think we signed the A&M record deal outside Buckingham Palace? Even then they were a farce, a fiasco, and that's why we were there—to ridicule the whole thing. The Sex Pistols getting a record deal was as deeply ridiculous as those old fucks living in that bloody stately mansion in the middle of London. What do they do for anybody? They're like Vivienne Westwood, OBE—they "merely go with the flow."

The royal family makes Britain seem preposterous and prehistoric. Before the Pistols, it was unheard of to slag off the queen in popular music. That's the tragedy of the British; they're so apathetic that they don't question these things. Somebody had to take the first step, and as always with Britain, you're hated for making that first step even though they may agree with you eventually. Afterward they'll want you to go away because you remind them of how foolish they were originally.

It's extremely sad that, economically, "No Future" is even more relevant and timely today than it was when the Pistols first played it. I'm not very happy about that at all. Frankly, I would have liked for "Anarchy in the U.K." to be seen now as a joke.

"Ha, ha, ha, ha, ha! Look at the doom and gloom this fool Rotten predicted. And here we are happy."

That's not the case, is it? I get no pleasure or joy out of that! But most important, I'm not Nostradamus, I'm not predicting ahead. It was a downturned social condition I felt was running rampant at the time, and it's a shame that it's gone on and on toward a downward spiral—not of my making, I submit. Of course I was idealistic when I was young. That was the whole point. But, sadly, today things have just gotten worse. I'm using the same rusty old tools of my trade, but the problems seem ten times compounded. How can I take any joy in exposing how bad things are? It's not very enjoyable at all when what you're saying is actually saddening.

All my life I've been told that because of the class system I've been born into, that makes me a lesser human being-and supposedly therefore stupid. Corruption is less inherent among the working class. People just want to get by. Their problem is apathy. Families run away from self-education and self-respect.

As for me, I don't care. I don't like structures.

The royal family has been brought up to believe it's God's will for them to be where they are. That's what I find so disgraceful. That upper-class stuff is intolerable, going back to feudalism and the Norman conquests. They were nothing but invaders who stole all the land and declared themselves better than the rest of us. Their ancestors are thieves, murderers, bullies, and crooks—medieval Mafia by any other names. The original gentlemen were knights, psychopathic murderers, who went out and killed peasants for no good reason. They were a law unto themselves.

Think back. The only group of knights that did good were the Knights Hospitaller and the Knights Templar. They were all exterminated because they gave up money, power, and position. They were like early Franciscans, and that could not be tolerated by the British Establishment, and they were slaughtered to a man. What would you call them? Early communists? Their love of humanity above the love of selfishness attacked the Establishment by their very existence. They fought all their wars and were a pre-SAS, the top assassins of their day, but they gave up all worldly goods, too frightening for the powers-that-be to tolerate for too long. Now I'm certainly no Knights Templar, and I'm not out looking for the Holy Grail. All religion to me is deeply wrong, and I see any organized religion as fundamentally wrong. The word *fundamental* these days implies intolerance, protectionism, and selfishness.

Which brings us back to the royal family. The French got rid of theirs. I would like to see the end of British royalty. It's not what makes Britain interesting; it's what make us antiquated, quaint, and doomed. It doesn't work. This is the modern world; get rid of those old problems. Brave New World, please.

The middle class is a deep confusion to me.

American middle class is equivalent to our working class in Britain, but the middle class in Britain strike me as a strange bunch. They don't necessarily come from money; they can also be poor—with non-working-class occupations like schoolteachers and nurses. It's very peculiar, and it doesn't make sense. It's ill defined. Statistically you live not in London, just in the 'burbs. You go to a nice school, sire 2.4 children, and you're basically boring.

The British middle class look up to the upper class and down on the working class. The working class, unfortunately, have no one to look down on but immigrants—and the immigrants look down on who comes next. That's British society and the upper class keep it this way because the confusion in the lower ranks is what maintains their stability. In England, if you vote Conservative, you're generally conceived as middle class. That means you're all right and you have a job, so why should you care about anyone else? Labour is working class, and why can't we all have jobs, thank you? Royalties and the uppers don't give a damn about any of that.

John Major came into power because Britain was sick of Thatcher. He's faceless, which is a product of the middle-class thing. You rarely see these people and where they come from, but somehow they manage to put all their restraints on the social structure by the strength of their numbers. The middle class are the people who say that sex is awful and horrible. Everything is pornographic to them because they're basically sexless themselves. They'll ban something because they can't understand it. They have no lives, nothing but a silly little cabinet in the corner with a few crappy antiques inside. That's their universe, and they keep up with the Joneses; our lawn is manicured much better than yours. They're competitive in all the wrong ways. They're competitive in trivia, but nothing substantial. What would the neighbors think if they had an opinion? Many lead horrible, lonely lives—so utterly mediocre.

The middle class in Britain is a dead end. It's what a lot of working-class people aspire to, and once they get there, they cease to exist. They develop a lack of communication among their neighbors and lose a community spirit you don't find in Britain middle-class neighborhoods. You get that in working-class environments.

Which brings me to the point of all this social commentary.

In Britain, the Sex Pistols embraced *all* the classes—*all* ages, too. It hit right across the board. We really did. The punk thing absolutely wasn't related to any one class at all—a combination of everything thrown in a dustbin, shaken violently, then thrown back out.

A lot of the middle-class kids outside London, like Siouxsie, Idol, and the Banshee types, would embrace the Pistols because they could wear new clothes, look weird, and frighten Mummy and Daddy. At the other end of the social scale would be the working class saying, "Oh, great! An excuse to go and riot!" Then the spoiled upper class suddenly realized there was no joy in driving around in a Porsche anymore. It was much more fun to be with a group of people your own age who

Late night Gunter Grove. Paul Young (left) and PolyStyrene. Couch cover courtesy Harp Lager. (Paul Young)

made you think about yourself rather than just believing you're better than everyone else.

We appealed to all classes. The violent aspect from the working-class end was canceled out by the clotheshorsing from the uppers, who would all merge into one very strong alliance. An excellent time; but, like all good things, it had to come to an end. It had to move on. Tons of potential, but badly seen. The press moved in, and that was the end of it.

Again—and, please, I hate to have to keep repeating this—I have to put this erosion down to Malcolm as the Sex Pistols' manager. He should have perceived this a lot more clearly. Sadly, his attitude would be, "Fuck the working classes! Everything good comes from the middle classes." Who were the Pistols? He thought we became middle class because we were in a band. There you go—the old problem. The manager bracketed us, while my crusade was to *break it down!*

M a l c o l m.

J u s t.

Didn't.

Get.

It.

He lacked the instinctive compassion for all classes of people to understand the massive groundwork we could have laid.

JULIEN TEMPLE: I know that both Malcolm and John have firm ideas about what happened, and I see aspects of both elements being important. Of both subjective point of views, I think there was more honesty from John in the end. The bitterness John feels is based on the out of control manipulation of the four guys in the band.

Malcolm wanted everyone to believe he was the instigator behind the Pistols, but if anything is to be believed, he was the destroyer of it. It went very well on its own until he decided that he was going to run the show, and that's when everything went wrong. That's when it become ridiculous and mean-spirited. Santa Claus turned into Stalin overnight.

CAROLINE COON: An artist absolutely needs someone around them. Otherwise, how can they find the time to learn their skill and craft, write their poems, songs, and melodies? The role of management is to give the artist space. Not only was John part of the punk triumvirate, he rode the wave of the punk times' zeitgeist, and when he needed the space to be creative, he had the pressure of being hugely successful, an enormous star, and nobody was doing the shitwork

for him. In light of that, he was having to put out product that can
be soul destroying. I think that if you consider how self-critical and
ambitious John was, you realize he really would have liked to have
more time to sit down and put his intelligent thoughts on paper.
But he didn't seem to have the space to do it. Artists need time.
There is this grieving in my heart—since you can't change
history—that the Pistols didn't carry on. I sometimes wonder what
it would have been like if John had been guided by a real educated
man, one who had been around men who had a real sense of their
own sexuality, and who had been educated and trained by the theater rather than by a fucking shuttered barrow. If only John had
come into contact with someone like Diaghilev, who was the patron
of Nijinsky, a man who was older than him who had real understanding of art history, a sense of value of performance and theater,
and who wasn't hung up about sexuality. I think those young men
had a real tough time with the ideas that Bernie and Malcolm were
putting in their heads. Bernie and Malcolm were basically disappointed chauvinist pigs.

Caroline Coon is a little too romantic in this respect. We knew
the Pistols' time had come and gone, and that was it. You give it a
rest, approach it differently, and go on to something else. The last
sixteen years in between have been years of deep confusion, but I
think it's important, too. There's no answers because there's no real
questions. There's no center or focus. You can't pinpoint. There's
no one big baddie and one real goodie. These days we have a see-
saw effect on a completely level playing field. I prefer the yin and
the yang of a more rugged terrain. You have to have the choice and
the variety, otherwise you get blandness.

Musically, all this disco stuff we still hear has managed to stifle the
energy. Heavy metal has become as safe as safe can ever be. Get out of
the middle. Go left or right. Rave is today's disco dance fodder. It's
easy to escape into, and it draws a herding instinct. Everybody does it.
That's a reason? Maybe people like Johnny Rotten have had their day.
Maybe I'm a prehistoric monster by being an individual. It's highly
likely. All I offer to others is their own individuality. Grab it! The rave
crowd call it freedom. They pay a fortune for the drugs to maintain this
idiocy, and it's all manipulated by seriously bad promoters and
evil-minded deejays. It's hypnotic, trancelike. It's enjoyable, but not
the be-all, end-all. Unfortunately the kids will come out the other end
very frustrated and will not make a better world. Unlike the Pistols, it's

about running away from the issues. This does not get you employment or self-respect.

The Pistols were a band that actually sat down and worked out their message. Nobody works anything out on a rave dance floor. It's a pile of computers sampling, ripping off other people's work. Make your own culture and don't live off others. Rave cultures are parasites, they're fleas, an infestation. No wonder they all huddle together and rave. They cling.

Most missed the point on many levels. Journalists never came to grips with the fact that the Pistols, without deliberately sending out a manifesto, broke so many barriers by just doing things instinctively and naturally. We didn't have barriers between men and women, black and white, gay and straight. Women up until that point didn't have a say in anything.

During the Pistols era, women were out there playing with the men, taking us on in equal terms. Sexy became not the old cliché of long, blonde luxurious hair, mild-mannered and sitting in the corner. Quite the opposite. Punk women were hounds from hell. Excellent. It wasn't combative, but compatible. Loved it.

If I was a kid today, I probably wouldn't be into music at all. I'd be into something completely different. I don't think I'd want to be a part of the modern music that's currently fashionable among teenagers at all. Products are much more mass-produced today. What they wear in Texas, they wear in Paris practically the same day it hits the streets in Los Angeles. It's that organized and structured. They dance to the same records, and there's no cultural expanson in areas, just mass fodder all across the board.

Meningitis is still the highest killer of children in Britain, more than any other disease. I know what it does to you. Personally, I think it's a class disease that has a lot to do with with poverty and poor housing.

Rest assured, there will always be poverty in Britain because the excesses of the royal family will keep people poor. We pay tax for that shit. We substantiate and perpetuate it when we don't look after our own. Our own is everyone—including the queen, Charles, Di, Fergie, and the lot. But I fail to see how my tax pounds should give these fucks skiing holidays. Why the fuck do we support monarchy? Who on earth gave them the right to dictate terms to me about what is right or wrong other than the bastard murderers of their ancestors? They give a sense of etiquette to the world and have a nice way of dealing with things, which I do admire. I don't admire the monetary upkeep this tradition costs, and I certainly don't respect a system that dictates alienation by fault of birth. There should be an English way for all of us, whether you come from a council flat or Buckingham Palace. Why shouldn't we all go to the same schools and treat each other with equal respect? Why is there this nonsense of one education for them and a lesser one for the rest? It creates the multi-tier systems and keeps civil wars brewing. These are none of the things I want, and this is an unacceptable order to me. It is the humiliation of one mass of human beings dictated to by one tiny little amount. Greed of the highest order. Selfishness of the worst aspect.

I was raised in England, and I am English in this way. Romantically, I would like to believe I'm Irish. While I have some vague vision of pastoral eloquence, I know this isn't real. It's like a romance novel. I am British.

"We're the flowers in your dustbin."

They are good words, bitter words. Real words.

I never had much interest in keeping old mementos from the Sex Pistols era. I've given away all the old clothes to charity—usually for orphanages and things like that. I have a soft spot for small charities. Rather than throwing them in the bin, I tried to make them more useful. Somewhere dotted all over Britain are some of my sweaty T-shirts. If you stormed into my room and looked through my closets, you wouldn't find any of the old Pistols clothes. I don't even have photos. It's all somewhere in the jungle I call a brain. I couldn't be a sentimental Sex Pistol, now could I?

JOHN CHRISTOPHER LYDON

During the Sex Pistols Johnny lived with us here in Finsbury Park on and off. When he really got into the music heavy, I had problems with television and newspaper reporters. It wasn't once, it was every day, every evening. They never left us alone. The phone calls were nonstop, day and night. They all had different versions of the Sex Pistols story. One would say they were horrible. One said they were okay. Everybody had their own opinion. My opinion was that Johnny had done well. I didn't mind what he'd done so long as he was happy doing it. It made no difference to me. I never tried to hold him back.

Throughout the Pistols days, we had nothing but problems with the police. Once when Johnny was living on Gunter Grove, he rang me up and said, "Dad, come down and see the house."

I went down. He reckoned that ten police had come in. Instead of knocking at the door, they'd smashed all the jams with crow bars. They never apologized, they just broke the doors down and raided the place, looking for drugs. Johnny was always a target. They'd raid him regularly, about every two months. If he got two months of peace, he was lucky. And it was always in the middle of the night when they thought he was having a party. Johnny was a sitting target. That's mostly why he lives so much in America. So much of the time they hassled him in London, I know the main reason he left Gunter Grove was that the police had his phone number and address.

That's always been the Lydon way with the coppers.

Up to her death, Johnny would ring his mum almost every day. One day, not long before she died in 1979, he called to say, "Mom, I'm off to America."

And she said, jokingly, "Can I come?"

And he said yes. Just like that. I didn't mind her going, so off she went.

Johnny worked for Warner Brothers then, so he took her to New York and Los Angeles. They rang me every night from New York. Johnny's mum had a fabulous time. She enjoyed every moment in America for three months. Bob Regehr, one of the executives at Warner Brothers, used to ring her to see how she was. When she was in Los Angeles, he would send a chauffeur-driven car for her and took her wherever she wanted to go—Disneyland, anywhere. Then Johnny sent her up to Canada to see her sister in Toronto. She had never been anywhere but Ireland, the Isle of Wight, or places like that. It was like she went to heaven before she died.

Eventually she came back home to England and died. She had cancer. We didn't know until she went into the hospital for a check-up. They thought she had a bug in her tummy, gastroenteritis, but when she went in for tests, they said that they'd have to keep her there three days for observation. Then they wouldn't let her out because they opened her up and found a malignancy in her lower bowel. They gave her eight weeks to live. She lasted ten.

Johnny sat with his mum all through her illness. He sat by her side for ten weeks—never spoke to anybody—never left her day or night. He washed in the hospital, slept on the seat. He was that close to her. She was in Whittington Hospital—the same one Johnny was in when he was young with meningitis. I've never known anybody to be as close as them. Never. Throughout his musical career, Johnny would ring her to ask her opinion, and she'd always tell him to carry on with his music. They used to slag me off. They'd laugh at me and say, "Oh, you're a silly old man. You're only jealous because you can't sing."

When Johnny was really ill as a child, I thought that was the end of him. I think his illness made him realize how his mummy felt when she was diagnosed with cancer. When he brought her to America, he made a big fuss of her. He finally had money, and he lavished what he had on her. Then to find out that she would come back to die—well, it's sad, isn't it? But that was Johnny returning the favor. As for where that put me, I was quite happy so long as I saw my wife happy with Johnny. I had no worries in life. The only one was when I lost my wife; I lost everything when I lost her.

JOHN LYDON: I missed my mother dying. It was not something to look forward to, but I would have liked to have been at the hospital. I wrote "Death Disco" for her. There was a tune running around in my head at the time, so I crossed it with *Swan Lake*—a brilliant goodbye, Mummy. I don't like doing that song live because tears do well.

After my wife died, Johnny and I became even closer—he would make such a fuss of me. I never show my boys that much affection. I let them work things out for themselves. I never pampered Johnny; he realizes that now. I'm proud of all my sons. I don't go telling Johnny that I'm proud of him. I don't show them how I feel. I let them work that out by themselves. It's like Johnny Cash's "A Boy Named Sue." I should have christened Johnny "Sue." I don't interfere with Johnny's life because I know he's not going to do anything silly. Johnny thinks before he does anything.

Johnny used to get the wrong impression: "You don't like me."

That's the way it goes in this family. I couldn't smack my children when they were young. My wife wouldn't have it. She was a very religious woman, a great Catholic. She wouldn't abuse her children or smack them around. Now we've gotten closer. It never used to be, but now it's always Dad, Dad this, Dad that. Before my wife died, it was Mum; now all of a sudden, it's Dad.

As far as girls were concerned, I never laid down the law with Johnny. I was the worst, so how could I? You have to practice what you preach. I'm not one of those do-as-I-say-not-what-I-do. I let my boys lead their own lives. I never spoiled them mainly because I grew up with the lads. I'm not that much older than Johnny, just twenty years, and that's not a lot. That's the way I wanted the family to be. Some people's daddies are sixty years of age when they're born.

As far as the girls, you'd want a bulldozer at the door to keep them away, but it wasn't like that so much for Johnny. He was always steady with Nora, and even now he never looks about. He's known Nora for over eighteen years. Jimmy, years ago, he'd take anybody's girl.

Johnny's not like that. He's very steady with Nora. I think they're very happy together. They always seem content; they suit each other. It's good to see my boys grown. They get on well together. Johnny and Martin are very close. Having four boys wasn't really a handful. It would have been more of a handful having one girl. I did want a daughter, but I don't think I could cope having a girl in this country. Boys can look after themselves, but how can you protect a little girl in these council flats, with all the attacks? How can a girl walk out there today, on the streets of London?

This district of Finsbury Park used to be all Irish; when I first got here, you'da t'ought you were in Ireland. We used to go to the community center with the children on a Saturday night. The babies would play around while we'd all have a drink with our friends. It was so nice. As the years went by, I don't know where the Irish have gone. There are no Irish at all in Finsbury Park anymore. There are lots of Greeks in Finsbury Park now. There are Turks and a lot of blacks—Africans, who can be really violent. My Bobby even had his throat cut with a Stanley knife one night just outside the door. It's terrible, but you cope and grow with it. Like everything else, it's all a part of life. That's why I travel. It takes my mind off my work and the world. That's why I think my Johnny should get a nice hobby like playing golf, or fishing or something. He should relax and get away. Then he'd go back to his music and be twice as good. But Johnny's hyperactive. He has to keep thinking something different all the time.

When the load of them from the press first came around, I left photographs out and they pinched everything I had, including pictures of my wife. Then they wrote lies about Johnny and his mum, when she wasn't even here to defend herself. Johnny got really annoyed over it, so that's why I barred the lot of them for years. I've never bothered. When people used to want to interview me, I wouldn't talk to them. I saw what they were doing—just setting me up. All they wanted was for me to say something notorious about my sons. But I never needed money so badly that I would run my sons down. I would never slag my sons, because no matter what they do, I'm proud of them. One time one of the newspapers wanted me to write an article, but they only wanted me to say exactly what they had in mind—that Johnny was outrageous and notorious—a villain. Johnny's notorious on stage. Off stage, it's a switch, on and off, and he can be quite different. There *was* an article not long ago in the paper where they wrote about Johnny—that he was one in a million who changed the world. By God, I think he did. My Johnny changed the world.

Before meningitis.

That last moment on stage in San Francisco was the truth. I had felt cheated. I felt that my life had been stolen from me by lesser beings. Our inabilities ruined something truly excellent. I'm sure history will bear me out on that. Right now it's still too close to the bone for people to judge it accurately because there are still too many vested interests floating about.

And I'm no saint. I'm as wrong as everyone else and as right as most.

Wrong in that I was young, stupid, and rash. I didn't have the perceptions I should have had. I ran away from problems rather than hitting them head on: the very thing I accuse other people of doing all of the time. Yet I know there's a certain aspect in my character where I actually enjoy things falling apart, where the chaos becomes far more enjoyable than the commitment. It will always be there, my impetuosity.

So I am not without guilt.

I could have helped Sid more. If only I hadn't been lazy and washed my hands of him like Pontius Pilate. That's something I'll have to carry to the grave with me. I don't know what I could have done, but I know

I should have done something. There are always ways. You must never be lazy when it comes to your friends.

Believe it or not, I have no animosity toward Malcolm. The last time we talked was when Bernie Rhodes was trying to set up a nightclub in New York in 1985. He wanted Malcolm and me to talk it out. He said we were two great minds who needed to get together and stop all this. Okay. I sat there, and Malcolm had attitude all fucking night. He just couldn't get off it. After a couple of double brandies, he was spouting and talking like a politician. I got up and said I was leaving. Bernie stopped me and asked me to stay. It was nice of Bernie to try to do that. But was it really? Then Bernie left the table.

I leaned over to Malcolm and said, "Look, Malcolm, Bernie's gone to the toilet now. You know you're going to talk rubbish all night, and you know I ain't listening. Why don't we just go home?"

We shook hands, and he went one way and I went the other. We left Bernie in the toilet with the bill.

Ever get the feeling you've been cheated?

CAST OF CONTRIBUTORS

Paul Cook plays in the reformed Sex Pistols and works on various other musical projects.

Caroline Coon is the author of many articles and books on music, and is also a painter. She lives and works as an artist in London.

John Gray is a primary school teacher in London.

Bob Gruen lives in Greenwich Village, New York, and continues to work as a rock photographer.

Chrissie Hynde fronts the Pretenders, now in their fourth decade, and is also a prominent activist for animal rights.

Billy Idol went on to form Generation X before becoming a successful solo artist. He continues to tour.

Steve Jones plays in the reformed Sex Pistols and works on various other musical projects.

Jeannette Lee took a break from the music industry after working with PiL, to become a mother. She returned to become co-director of Rough Trade Management.

Donn Letts is a respected filmmaker who has directed films, documentaries and videos. He was also in Big Audio Dynamite. He continues to make films and music and to DJ.

John Christopher Lydon still lives in London.

Nora and John Lydon married shortly after John formed PiL. They live in California.

Marco Pirroni is a guitarist who co-founded Adam and the Ants. He has played, written and toured with artists such as Sinead O'Connor, and also works on his own musical projects.

Rambo is a jewellery designer, plus being John Lydon's bodyguard and travelling companion. He is closely involved in many of Lydon's creative projects.

Zandra Rhodes is one of the UK's most respected fashion designers, with an international cult following. She is based in London where she opened her own museum in 2003.

Dave Ruffy co-founded the Ruts and is a drummer and songwriter who has worked with bands including Aztec Camera, Kirsty MacColl, Adam Ant and Zion Train.

Steve Severin is a founding member of the now disbanded Siouxsie and the Banshees. He works as a journalist, writer and primarily a musician, on projects including film soundtracks.

Paul Stahl is an advertising and PR executive in London.

Julien Temple is a filmmaker who has directed numerous videos as well as documentaries and feature films, most recently the Sex Pistols film *The Filth and the Fury*

Howard Thompson moved to America, and recently retired after working as an A&R executive in New York.